WORD LOVER'S
BOOK OF
Unfamiliar
Quotations

OVER 1500 UNIQUE QUOTATIONS
DRAWN FROM THE WISDOM OF THE AGES

WESLEY D. CAMP

PRENTICE HALL PRESS

Library of Congress Cataloging-in-Publication Data

Camp, Wesley Douglass, 1915–
    Camp's unfamiliar quotations from
2000 B.C. to the present / Wesley D. Camp.
        p.   cm.
    ISBN 0-13-619081-2
    1. Quotations.   2. Values—Quotations, maxims, etc.   3. Moral
conditions—Quotations, maxims, etc.   4. Human behavior—Quotations,
maxims, etc.   5. Responsibility—Quotations, maxims, etc.
    I. Title.
PN6081.C25   1990   89-37207
808.88′2—dc20   CIP

Printed in the United States of America

10 9 8 7 6 5 4 3

ISBN 0-7352-0098-X

Originally published as *What a Piece of Work Is Man: Camp's Unfamiliar Quotations from 2000 B.C. to the Present* ISBN 0-13-952102-X (paperback)

PRENTICE HALL PRESS
Paramus, NJ 07652

On the World Wide Web at http://www.phdirect.com

Prentice-Hall International (UK) Limited, *London*
Prentice-Hall of Australia Pty. Limited, *Sydney*
Prentice-Hall Canada Inc., *Toronto*
Prentice-Hall Hispanoamaricana, S.A., *Mexico*
Prentice-Hall of India Private Limited, *New Delhi*
Prentice-Hall of Japan, Inc., *Tokyo*
Pearson Education Asia Pte. Ltd., *Singapore*
Editora Prentice-Hall do Brazil, Ltda., *Rio de Janeiro*

Acknowledgments

The author and publisher are grateful for permission to quote excerpts from these works:

"Happiness" and "The Last Quarter of the Moon" excerpts from "Sword Blades," from *The Complete Poetical Works of Amy Lowell.* Copyright © 1955 by Houghton Mifflin Company. Copyright © 1983 renewed by Houghton Mifflin Company. Brinton P. Roberts, Esquire and G. D'Andelot Belin, Esquire. Reprinted by permission of Houghton Mifflin Company. Archibald MacLeish, Selection from *J.B.: A Play in Verse,* Copyright © 1956, 1957, 1958 by Archibald MacLeish. Copyright © renewed 1986 by William H. MacLeish and Mary H. Grimm. Reprinted by permission of Houghton Mifflin Company. Archibald MacLeish, "A poem should not mean . . . " from *New and Collected Poems, 1917–1982.* Copyright © 1985 by the Estate of Archibald MacLeish. Reprinted by permission of Houghton Mifflin Company. Sylvia Plath, excerpts from "Lady Lazarus" from *The Collected Poems of Sylvia Plath.* Copyright © 1963 by Ted Hughes. Reprinted by permission of Harper & Row, Publishers, Inc. Marianne Moore, from "O to Be a Dragon," *The Complete Poems* by Marianne Moore. Copyright © 1957 by Marianne Moore. Copyright renewed © 1985 by Clive Driver, Executor of the Estate of Marianne Moore. All rights reserved. Reprinted by permission of Viking Penguin, a division of Penguin Books USA, Inc. Excerpt from *W.H. Auden: Collected Poems,* edited by Edward Mendelson. Copyright © 1976 by Edward Mendelson, William Meredith and Monroe K. Spears, Executors of the Estate of W.H. Auden. Reprinted by permission of Random House, Inc. Excerpts from "But Will It Sell?" by Marya Mannes, from *Subverse,* copyright © 1959 by Marya Mannes, reprinted by permission of George Braziller, Inc. Excerpts from Rupert Brooke, "The Soldier," in *Collected Poems,* © 1915, Dodd, Mead & Co., Inc. E.B. White, "Commuter," © 1929, Harper & Row Publishers, Inc. James Thurber, excerpts from "The Patient Bloodhound" and "The Owl Who Was God," copyright © 1940 James Thurber, Copyright © 1968 Helen Thurber. From *Fables for Our Time,* published by Harper & Row. James Thurber, "The Magpie's Treasure, from *Further Fables for Our Time,* © 1956. James Thurber. Copyright © 1984 Helen Thurber. Published by Simon & Schuster. Robert Frost, excerpts from "Dust of Snow," "The Span of Life," "Reluctance," "The Road Not Taken," "The Lesson for Today," and "Birches," from *The Poetry of Robert Frost* edited by Edward Connery Lathem. Copyright © 1969 by Holt, Rinehart and Winston, Inc. Copyright © 1962 by Robert Frost. Copyright © 1975 by Lesley Frost Ballantine. Reprinted by permission of Henry Holt and Company, Inc. Excerpts from #57 and #149 from *The Dream Songs* by John Berryman. Copyright © 1969 by John Berryman. Reprinted by permission of Farrar, Straus and Giroux, Inc. "Grown-up," "First Fig," "Second Fig," "Midnight Oil" and excerpts from "Epitaph," "Poem and Prayer for an Invading Army," "Fatal Interview," "Theme and Variation, V," "Dirge Without Music," "Feast," and "What My Lips Have Kissed" by Edna St. Vincent Millay. From *Collected Poems,* Harper & Row. Copyright © 1921, 1922, 1923, 1928, 1931, 1939, 1944, 1948, 1950, 1951, 1858, 1967 by Edna St. Vincent Millay and Norma Millay Ellis. Reprinted by permission. Excerpt from "Renascence" by Edna St. Vincent Millay, © 1912, 1940, by Edna St. Vincent Millay. Theodore Roethke: "Open House," copyright 1941 by Theodore Roethke. From *The Collected Poems of Theodore Roethke* by Theodore Roethke. Used by permission of Doubleday, a division of Bantam, Doubleday, Dell Publishing Group, Inc. "The Minimal," copyright 1942 by Theodore Roethke. From *The Collected Poems of Theodore Roethke* by Theodore Roethke. Used by permission of Doubleday, a division of Bantam, Doubleday, Dell Publishing Group, Inc. Excerpt(s) from *Collected Verse* by Theodore Roethke, copyright © 1961 by Theodore Roethke. From *The Collected Poems of Theodore Roethke* by Theodore Roethke. Used by permission of Doubleday, a division of Bantam, Doubleday, Dell Publishing Group, Inc. Excerpt from *Marat/Sade* by Peter Weiss. Copyright © 1965 by John Calder, Ltd.; copyright © 1981 by Atheneum. Reprinted with permission of Atheneum Publishers, an imprint of Macmillan Publishing Company. Excerpts from "Outwitted" by Edwin Markham, © 1930, Doubleday. Excerpts from Emily Dickinson reprinted by permission of the publishers and Trustees of Amherst College from *The Poems of Emily Dickinson,* Thomas H. Johnson, ed., Cambridge, Mass.: The Belknap Press of Harvard University Press, Copyright 1951, © 1955, 1979, 1983 by the President and Fellows of Harvard College. "Sonnet to a Sister in Error" from *The Collected Poems of Dilys Laing,* copyright © 1967 by David Bennett Laing.

Excerpt from "The Hollow Men" in *Collected Poems, 1909–1962* by T. S. Eliot, copyright 1936 by Harcourt Brace Jovanovich, Inc., copyright © 1964, 1963 by T. S. Eliot, reprinted by permission of the publisher. Excerpt from "The Flight of Apollo" from *The Testing-Tree* by Stanley Kunitz, copyright © 1969 by Stanley Kunitz. Excerpt from "Route Six" from *The Poems of Stanley Kunitz, 1928–1978*, copyright © 1976 by Stanley Kunitz. Excerpts from "Reflection on Ingenuity," "Reflections on Ice-Breaking," "Inter-Office Memorandum," "I Have It on Good Authority," "Compliments of a Friend," "A Dog's Best Friend is His Illiteracy," and "The Perfect Husband" from *Verses from 1929 On* by Ogden Nash, copyright © 1930, 1935, 1948, 1949 by Ogden Nash. Excerpt from "A Word to Husbands" from *Everyone but Me and Thee* by Ogden Nash, copyright © 1962 by Ogden Nash. All reprinted by permission of Little, Brown and Company. Dorothy Parker, "Four Be the Things," "You Might as Well Live," and "Death and Taxes," from *Enough Rope*, copyright © 1927, 1971, Viking-Penguin. Phyllis McGinley, "Lament for a Wavering Viewpoint," "A Ballad of Anthologies," "Ballad of Lost Objects," "The Adversary," published by Viking-Penguin and Secker and Warburg, London. Excerpt from "The Fog" in *Chicago Poems* by Carl Sandburg, copyright © 1916 by Holt, Rinehart and Winston and renewed 1944 by Carl Sandburg, reprinted by permission of Harcourt Brace and Jovanovich, Inc. Excerpt from "Two Quatrains for First Frost" in *Advice to a Prophet and Other Poems*, copyright © 1959 by Richard Wilbur, reprinted by permission of Harcourt Brace Jovanovich, Inc. Dylan Thomas, "Do Not Go Gentle Into That Good Night," from *Poems of Dylan Thomas*, © 1952 by Dylan Thomas. Reprinted by permission of New Directions Publishing Corporation. Ezra Pound, "Ancient Music," from *Personae*, © 1926 by Ezra Pound. Reprinted by permission of New Directions Publishing Corporation. Excerpt, "God seeks comrades . . . and claims obedience" reprinted with permission of Macmillan Publishing Company from *Fireflies* by Rabindranath Tagore. Copyright © 1928 by Macmillan Publishing Company, renewed 1955 by Rathindranath Tagore. Excerpt from *Stray Birds* reprinted with permission of Macmillan Publishing Company from *Collected Poems and Plays* by Rabindranath Tagore. Copyright © 1916 by Macmillan Publishing Company, renewed 1944 by Rathindranath Tagore. Excerpt from "The Second Coming" reprinted with permission of Macmillan Publishing Company from *The Powers of W.B. Yeats: A New Edition*, edited by Richard J. Finneran. Copyright © 1924 by Macmillan Publishing Company, renewed 1952 by Bertha Georgie Yeats. Excerpt from "In the Seven Woods" from *The Poems of W.B. Yeats: A New Edition*, edited by Richard J. Finneran (New York: Macmillan, 1983). Excerpt from "A Grave" reprinted with permission of Macmillan Publishing Company from *Collected Poems* by Marianne Moore. Copyright © 1935 by Marianne Moore, renewed 1963 by Marianne Moore and T.S. Eliot. Langston Hughes, "A Raisin in the Sun," *Harlem* © 1951, Alfred A. Knopf, Inc. Kahlil Gibran, *The Prophet*, © 1923, Alfred A. Knopf, Inc. Robinson Jeffers, "Clouds of Evening," © 1930, Donan Jeffers and Garth Jeffers. Piet Hein, "The Noble Art of Saving Face," "The Road to Wisdom," "The Eternal Twins," from *Grooks*, © 1966, MIT Press.

(Note: these acknowledgments are in no particular order)

Preface

What a piece of work is man! How noble in reason! how infinite in faculty!
in form, in moving, how express and admirable! in action how like an
angel! in apprehension how like a god! . . . And yet to me, what is this
quintessence of dust?

—Shakespeare, *Hamlet*

Ay, there's the rub! Capable of sublimest thought, world-shaking action, man
is still dust. The weakest reed in nature, perhaps, but a thinking reed—one
who communicates not only his thoughts but his feelings, hopes, fears, and
dreams—all with humor, wit, and—sometimes—defiance, thumbing his
nose at the world. Because of language, man has access to the past and the
future. He can express the true and the untrue. Language helps him
understand both what is and what could be.

Collected in this book are mankind's thoughts and feelings from
earliest times to the most recent past, showing the depth and originality of
his mind on subjects as varied as atomic physics and the human soul.
Sources range from the social sciences to the natural sciences, from poetry
to philosophy, from theism to agnosticism, and from rationalism to
mysticism.

In making this collection, I have looked for contrasting as well as
complementary ideas: the popular: "Anything is possible," versus: "You
can't get blood from a stone." Generally, though, I have avoided clichés,
even Shakespeare's: "To thine own self be true," "All the world's a stage,"
"To be or not to be"—all good, all shopworn.

Judging by the way it has stimulated my own thinking, this may be a
thinking person's book. It's exciting to find comments that refute shib-
boleths. Take Montesquieu's:

If I knew something that would serve my country but would harm
mankind, I would never reveal it; for I am a citizen of humanity first and
by necessity, and a citizen of France second, and only by accident.

That would certainly raise the hackles of many right-thinking Congressmen. Or: "The noble art of losing face / may one day save the human race / and turn into eternal merit / what weaker souls would call disgrace" (Piet Hein).

If this is a thinking person's book, the juxtaposition of conflicting views should lead readers to some soul-searching of their own, rejecting one view or another, coming up with a new synthesis, or remaining in a state of suspense—which, according to F. Scott Fitzgerald, may not be so bad: "The test of a first-rate intelligence," he wrote, "is the ability to hold two opposed ideas in the mind at the same time and still retain the ability to function."

"If we are to achieve a culture rich in contrasting values," wrote Margaret Mead, "we must recognize the whole gamut of human potentialities." Thus, I include sources as varied as the Bible and the Koran, ancient Babylonian texts and French novels, sayings from Confucius to Mao Zedong, and from Homer's *Iliad* to the Columbia College *Jester*. Many of our global neighbors share aspects of our civilization—electricity, cars, television—but their value systems diverge widely from ours. To live in the same world, we need to know more about their ways of thinking, doing, and feeling—things that quotations often reveal, along with their prejudices and preconceptions, which, when compared with ours, may help us better understand both them and us.

Compare Jean Jacques Rousseau's: "I may not always have done what was right, but at least I had good intentions," with the English proverb: "The road to hell is paved with good intentions." When I mentioned this to a young lady recently, she said, "No, it's the road to *heaven* that is paved with good intentions." Proving that, while this collection may not always be a source of inspiration, it is one of controversy, leading perhaps to the discovery of new truths—and old errors?

Covering 4000 years in one book requires a high degree of (painful) selectivity. Result: almost every quotation is apt to be emotionally charged, dealing not only with politics but: business and labor, alcohol and drugs, love and sex, bread and circuses. Some ideas are so explosive that they have no simple antitheses: despotism, genocide, suicide. But authors find ways of dealing with them nevertheless: "In spite of everything, I still believe that people are good at heart" (Anne Frank); "Because I could not stop for Death, / He kindly stopped for me" (Emily Dickinson); "This world is gradually becoming a place / Where I do not care to be any more" (John Berryman).

A very personal collection, this. Once upon a time, when I was about 13, my father wandered into my room, saw an Elbert Hubbard quotation on the wall, and read it aloud: "The biggest mistake you can make in life is to be constantly afraid of making one." His face clouded over "Harrumph!" he said, and left—never to enter my room again. Then, if not sooner, I realized that quotations may be dangerous to one's equanimity.

Anthologies of quotations appear regularly in every country. Recently, French publisher Robert issued a 1,600-page dictionary of French quotations, followed shortly by his dictionary of "Quotations from Around the World." Needless to say, I have drawn heavily on both of these. While Anglo-Saxon authors outnumber others, the French run a close second;

Gallic writers often dare to think the "unthinkable," regarding such issues as atheism, nihilism, pessimism, and socialism.

A type of quotation that cannot be traced, of course, is the graffiti. However, those works of popular wit and wisdom can usually be dated rather precisely: Those at Pompeii, of course, as well as those in Paris in 1968, or in the New York subways any time. Quotations are related both to their time—XVIII Egyptian Dynasty, Italian Renaissance, Reagan Presidency—and also to us today in the sense that certain ideas are sempiternal, like those of Shakespeare, Molière, & Co.

In his autobiography, Winston Churchill wrote: "Quotations when engraved upon the memory give you good thoughts. They also make you anxious to read the authors and look for more." In addition to "good" thoughts, I have included some quite hateful—from Nero, the Marquis de Sade, Hitler, and the like. Good and evil are not easily separable. Like it or not, Dachau, My Lai, Iran-Contra are all part of our mental baggage—as much as the plays of Shakespeare or the poetry of Marianne Moore.

In hopes that some people might want to "read the authors and look for more," I list titles and dates, along with authors' names, after each quotation. Some of the titles should pique anyone's curiosity: *How to Avoid Love and Marriage, My Ten Years in Quandry, Off the Wall Street Journal, Zen and the Art of Motorcycle Maintenance, The Snake Has All the lines, Where Did You go?—Out. What Did You Do?—Nothing.*

Reading the words of Hitler, Stalin, or the Marquis de Sade may be hard on the nervous system, but set against the thoughts of a Jefferson or a John Stuart Mill they help us to see the deeper meanings of democracy and demagoguery, individualism and collectivism, intellect and propaganda. The largest number of issues in this book, however, are personal and social: How to agree— or disagree— with parents, mates, friends; what it means to be a child, a Jew, a black; how victims of mental illness think; how to cope with freedom and responsibility, love and lust, living and dying; Third World ideas on the family, religion, old age. The list is extensive—and growing.

W.D.C.

Contents

Table of Heads

S

IN MEMORIAM

FRANCIS HARVEY GREEN
Headmaster
The Pennington School
1921–1943

The old order changeth, yielding place to new,
And God fulfills Himself in many ways
Lest one good custom should corrupt the world.

Alfred, Lord Tennyson

ABSURD

. . . A statement or belief manifestly inconsistent with one's own.
Ambrose Bierce, The Devil's Dictionary, *1911*

The absurd is clear reason recognizing its limits.
Albert Camus (d. 1960), Le Suicide philosophique

The absurd is born of the confrontation between the human call and the unreasonable silence of the world.
Camus, The Myth of Sisyphus, *1942*

Man is able to do what he is unable to imagine.
René Char, Hypnos Waking, *1956*

ACTION

The great end of life is not knowledge but action.
Thomas Henry Huxley, "Technical Education," 1877

Deliberation is a function of the many; action is the function of one.
Charles de Gaulle, War Memoirs, *1960*

Determine never to be idle. No person will have occasion to complain of the want of time who never loses any. It is wonderful how much may be done if we are always doing.

Thomas Jefferson to Martha Jefferson, May 5, 1787

(*See also* **DEEDS, INVOLVEMENT, THEORY**)

ACTORS

Good actors are good because of the things they can tell us without talking. When they are talking, they are the servants of the dramatist. It is what they can show the audience when they are not talking that reveals the fine actor.

Cedric Hardwicke, Theatre Arts, *February 1958*

Players, Sir! I look on them as no better than creatures set upon tables and joint stools to make faces and produce laughter, like dancing dogs.

Johnson, in Boswell's Life of Samuel Johnson, *1775*

[Marilyn Monroe] was good at playing abstract confusion in the same way that a midget is good at being short.

Clive James, PBS TV, January 18, 1979

(*See also* **AUDIENCE, THEATER/STAGE**)

ADJUSTMENT: *See* CHANGE, COMPROMISE, CONFORMITY.

ADOLESCENCE

. . . A stage between infancy and adultery.

Ambrose Bierce, The Devil's Dictionary, *1911*

Weird clothing is *de rigueur* for teenagers, but today's generation of teens is finding it difficult to be sufficiently weird. . . . because the previous generation, who went through adolescence in the sixties and seventies, used up practically all the available weirdness.

P.J. O'Rourke, Modern Manners, *1983*

There's the thing about girls. Every time they do something pretty, even if they're not much to look at, or even if they're sort of stupid, you fall in love with them and then you never know *where* the hell you are.

J.D. Salinger, The Catcher in the Rye, *1951*

(*See also* **BOYS, CHILDREN, YOUTH**)

ADULTERY

... The application of democracy to love.

H.L. Mencken, Sententiae, *1920*

The psychology of adultery has been falsified by conventional morals, which assume ... that attraction to one person cannot coexist with a serious affection for another.

Bertrand Russell, Marriage and Morals, *1929*

Those who are faithful know only the trivial side of love; it is the faithless who know love's tragedies.

Oscar Wilde, The Picture of Dorian Gray, *1891*

There are few who would not rather be taken in adultery than in provincialism.

Aldous Huxley, Antic Hay, *1923*

Stan Waltz has decided to take unto himself a wife but he hasn't decided yet whose.

Peter De Vries, Let Me Count the Ways, *1965*

Sara could commit adultery at one end and weep for her sins at the other, and enjoy both operations at once.

Joyce Cary, The Horse's Mouth, *1944*

(*See also* **INFIDELITY, SEXUAL RELATIONS**)

ADVENTURE: *See* CHANCE, DANGER.

ADVERSITY

There is in every true woman's heart a spark of heavenly fire, which lies dormant in the broad daylight of prosperity; but which kindles up, and beams and blazes in the dark hour of adversity.

Washington Irving, The Sketch Book, *1820*

If we had no winter, the spring would not be so pleasant; if we did not sometimes taste of adversity, prosperity would not be so welcome.

Anne Bradstreet, Meditations Divine and Moral, *1664*

Watch a man in times of ... adversity to discover what kind of man he is; for then at last words of truth are drawn from the depths of his heart, and the mask is torn off....

Lucretius (d. 55 B.C.), On the Nature of Things

It is a painful thing
To look at your own trouble and know
That you yourself and no one else has made it.

Sophocles, Ajax, *c. 450 B.C.*

(*See also* **DIFFICULTY, SUFFERING, TROUBLE**)

ADVERTISING

In the ad biz, sincerity is a commodity bought and paid for like everything else.

Newsweek, *1967*

The deeper problems connected with advertising come less from the unscrupulousness of our "deceivers" than from our pleasure in being deceived, less from the desire to seduce than from the desire to be seduced.

Daniel J. Boorstin, The Image, *1962*

On the boobs of a barmaid in Crail
Was writ the price of pale ale,
And on her behind,
For the sake of the blind,
It was also written in braille.

*George B., Scottish soldier, written while his unit was bogged down
at the Arno in World War II, 1944*

(*See also* **BUSINESS, BUYING/SELLING, PROPAGANDA**)

ADVICE

You will always find a few eskimos ready to tell the Congolese how to cope with the heat.

Stanislaw Lec, Unkempt Thoughts, *1962*

I always pass on good advice. It's the only thing to do with it. It is never any use to oneself.

Oscar Wilde, An Ideal Husband, *1895*

AGE: OLD AND YOUNG

Old age isn't so bad when you consider the alternative.

Maurice Chevalier, New York Times, *October 9, 1960*

The old believe everything; the middle-aged suspect everything; the young know everything.

> *Oscar Wilde, "Phrases and Philosophies for the Use of the Young,"*
> *1894*

It well becomes a man who is no longer young to forget that he ever was.

> *Seigneur de Saint-Evremond to Mlle. de Lenclos, 1696*

I love everything that is old: old friends, old times, old manners, old books, old wine.

> *Oliver Goldsmith,* She Stoops to Conquer, *1775*

It's all that the young can do for the old, to shock them and keep them up to date.

> *G.B. Shaw,* Fanny's First Play, *1912*

The young man who has not wept is a savage, and the older man who will not laugh is a fool.

> *George Santayana,* Dialogues in Limbo, *1925*

(*See also* **YOUTH**)

AGING

Education is the best provision for old age.

> *Aristotle (d. 322 B.C.), in Diogenes Laertius,* Lives

An inordinate passion for pleasure is the secret of remaining young.

> *Oscar Wilde,* Lord Arthur Savile's Crime, *1887*

Somebody asked me the other day, "What do you do?" "I amuse myself by growing old," I replied, "It's a full-time job."

> *Paul Léautaud,* Journal littéraire, *1907*

The person who has lived the most is not the one with the most years but the one with the richest experiences.

> *Jean Jacques Rousseau,* Emile, *1762*

(*See also* **MATURITY**)

AGGRESSION: *See* **FORCE, VIOLENCE, WAR.**

AGNOSTIC

I . . . invented what I conceived to be the appropriate title of "agnostic," . . . antithetic to the "Gnostic" of Church history who professed to know so much about the very things of which I was ignorant.

Thomas Henry Huxley, Science and Christian Tradition, *1889*

Some people . . . profess to be agnostics, but any examination of their patterns of action reveals that all agnostics *act as though* they accepted one or another of the competing systems of belief.

Gerhard Lenski, The Religious Factor, *1963*

(*See also* **ATHEIST, DOUBT, SKEPTICISM**)

ALIENATION: *See* **ABSURD, SELF, SOLITUDE.**

AMBITION

Ah, but a man's reach should exceed his grasp,
Or what's a heaven for?

Robert Browning, Andrea del Sarto, *1855*

Early to rise and early to bed
Makes a man healthy and wealthy and dead.

James Thurber, Fables for Our Times, *1940*

One often passes from love to ambition but rarely returns from ambition to love.

La Rochefoucauld, Reflections, *1665*

(*See also* **IDEALISM, MOTIVE, SUCCESS/FAILURE**)

AMERICA/AMERICANS

There can be no 50-50 Americanism in this country. There is room here for only 100 percent Americanism, only for those who are Americans and nothing else.

Theodore Roosevelt, Address, Republican National Convention, 1904

The American creed is a humanistic liberalism developing out of . . . the Enlightenment when America received its national consciousness and its political structure.

Gunnar Myrdal et al., An American Dilemma, *1944*

These lands are ours. No one has a right to remove us, because we were the first owners. The Great Spirit above has appointed this place for our use.

Tecumseh to Joseph Barron, 1810

The making of an American begins at that point where he himself rejects all other ties, any other history, and himself adopts the vesture of his adopted land.

James Baldwin, Notes of a Native Son, *1955*

Here in America we are descended in spirit from revolutionists and rebels—men and women who dare to dissent from accepted doctrine.

Dwight D. Eisenhower, Address, Columbia University, May 31, 1954

If I were asked . . . to what the singular prosperity and growing strength of [Americans] ought mainly to be attributed, I should reply: To the superiority of their women.

Alexis de Tocqueville, Democracy in America, *1835*

The Americans who are the most efficient people on earth . . . have invented so wide a range of pithy and hackneyed phrases that they can carry on a . . . conversation without giving a moment's reflection to what they are saying and so leave their minds free to consider the more important matters of big business and fornication.

Somerset Maugham (d. 1965), Cakes and Ale

The thing that impresses me most about America is the way parents obey their children.

The Duke of Windsor, Look, *March 5, 1957*

The Americans are a funny lot; they drink whiskey to keep them warm; then they put some ice in it to make it cool; then they put some sugar in it to make it sweet, and then they put a slice of lemon in it to make it sour. Then they say, "Here's to you," and drink it themselves.

B.N. Chakravarty, India Speaks to America, *1966*

America is a passionate idea or it is nothing. America is a human brotherhood or it is chaos.

Max Lerner, Actions and Passions, *1949*

An American who can make money, invoke God, and be no better than his neighbor, has nothing to fear but truth itself.

Marya Mannes, More in Anger, *1958*

(*See also* **BUSINESS, IDEALISM, PATRIOTISM**)

ANARCHY

Things fall apart; the center cannot hold;
Mere anarchy is loosed upon the world . . .
The best lack all conviction, while the worst
Are full of passionate intensity.

W.B. Yeats, The Second Coming, *1921*

It is not honest inquiry that makes anarchy; but it is error, insincerity, half-belief and untruth that make it.

Thomas Carlyle, On Heroes, Hero-Worship and the
Heroic in History, *1841*

Anarchy is the stepping stone to absolute power.

Napoleon I, Maxims, *1815*

(*See also* **GOVERNMENT, SOCIETY**)

ANGER

When angry, count four; when very angry, swear.

Mark Twain, Pudd'nhead Wilson, *1894*

Beware the fury of a patient man.

John Dryden, Absolam and Achitophel, *1680*

He who doesn't know anger doesn't know anything. He doesn't know the immediate.

Henri Michaux, Selected Writings, *1952*

(*See also* **INDIGNATION**)

ANIMALS: *See* PETS, HOUSE; WILD KINGDOM.

ANGUISH

The beauty of the world has two edges, one of laughter, one of anguish, cutting the heart asunder.

Virginia Woolf, A Room of One's Own, *1929*

I teach the art of turning anguish into delight.

Georges Bataille (d. 1962), Somme Athéologique

(*See also* **PAIN, SUFFERING, SAD/MELANCHOLY**)

ANTIQUITY

An archeologist is the best husband any woman can have: the older she gets, the more interested he is in her.

Agatha Christie, news summaries, March 9, 1954

There's a fascination frantic
In a ruin that's romantic.

W.S. Gilbert, The Mikado, *1855*

Had the Greeks held novelty in such disdain as we, what work of ancient date would now exist?

Horace (d. 8), Epistles

(*See also* **HISTORY, PAST, TRADITION**)

ANXIETY/WORRY

Tenterhooks are the upholstery of the anxious seat.

Robert Sherwood, news summaries, November 15, 1955

There is no such thing as pure pleasure; some anxiety always goes with it.

Ovid (d. A.D. 18), Metamorphoses

We are, perhaps, uniquely among the earth's creatures, the worrying animal. We worry away our lives.

Dr. Lewis Thomas, The Medusa and the Snail, *1979*

(*See also* **FEAR, SELF-DOUBT, TROUBLE**)

APHORISMS

An aphorism is never exactly true.
It is either a half-truth or a truth and a half.

Karl Kraus, Sprüche und Widersprüche, *1909*

What is all wisdom save a collection of platitudes? . . . [But] the man who orders his life according to their teachings cannot go far wrong.

Norman Douglas, South Wind, *1917*

I am not fond of aphorisms . . . they are one-size-fits-all; each has its opposite, and whatever line of conduct you follow, there is always one to back you up.

Alfred de Musset (d. 1857), Emmeline

(*See also* **QUOTATIONS, TRUTH**)

APPEARANCES

The human mind invents its "Puss'n Boots" and coaches changing-into-pumpkins-at-midnight because neither the theist nor the atheist is satisfied with appearances.

André Malraux, Anti-Memoirs, *1967*

They are not all saints who use holy water.

English proverb

(*See also* **DRESS/FASHION, HYPOCRICY**)

APPEASEMENT

Yield to all and you will soon have nothing to yield.

Aesop, "The Man and His Two Wives," Fables.

No man can tame a tiger into a kitten by stroking it. There can be no appeasement with ruthlessness. There can be no reasoning with an incendiary bomb.

Franklin D. Roosevelt, Fireside Chat, December 29, 1940

(*See also* **COMPROMISE**)

APPRECIATION

Hay is more acceptable to an ass than gold.

Latin proverb

Neither cast ye pearls before swine, lest they trample them under foot, and turn again and rend you.

Matthew 7:6

Ignorant men
Don't know what good they hold in their hands until
They've flung it away.

Sophocles, Ajax, *c. 450 B.C.*

ARCHITECTURE

. . . is inhabited sculpture.

Constantin Brancusi, in Igor Stravinsky, Themes and Episodes, *1966*

The Gothic style historically, more perhaps than any other, released architecture from its earthbound confines.

David W. Dunlap, An Act of Optimism, *1980*

Of all forms of visible otherworldliness, it seems to me, the Gothic is at once the most logical and the most beautiful. It reaches up magnificently—and a good half of it is palpably useless.

H.L. Mencken, The American Mercury, *February 1931*

Architecture begins where engineering ends.

Walter Gropius, in Heyer, ed., Architects on Architecture, *1978*

Space and light and order. Those are things men need just as much as they need bread or a place to sleep.

Le Corbusier (d. 1965), in conversation

(*See also* **ART, HOUSES**)

ARGUMENT

He who strikes the first blow admits he's lost the argument.

Chinese proverb

A disputant no more cares for the truth than the sportsman for the hare.

Alexander Pope, Thoughts on Various Subjects, *1727*

The aim of an argument or discussion should not be victory, but progress.

Joseph Joubert, Pensées, *1842*

(*See also* **DISSENT, OPINION, PERSUASION, REASON**)

ARISTOCRACY

In America everybody is of opinion that he has no social superiors, since all men are equal, but he does not admit that he has no social inferiors.

Bertrand Russell, Unpopular Essays, *1950*

A society without an aristocracy, without an elite minority, is not a society.

José Ortega y Gasset, Invertebrate Spain, *1922*

The nobles have been essential parties in the preservation of liberty . . . against kings and people. . . . By nobles, I mean . . . the natural and actual aristocracy among mankind.

John Adams to Thomas Jefferson, 1813

I agree with you that there is a natural aristocracy among men. The grounds of this are virtue and talent.

Jefferson to Adams, October 28, 1813

(*See also* **CLASSES, DEMOCRACY, EQUALITY**)

ARMS RACE

Will . . . the threat of common extermination continue? . . . Must children receive the arms race from us as a necessary inheritance?

Pope John Paul II, speech at the UN, 1979

Before we give you billions more, we want to know what you've done with the trillion you've got.

Representative Les Aspin, Armed Services Committee, to Defense Secretary Weinberger, New York Times, *February 5, 1985*

Move over, $7,000 coffeepots! Stand aside, $400 hammers! We now have the $792 doormat.

Senator William Proxmire, New York Times, *October 4, 1985*

Every gun that is made, every warship launched, every rocket fired, signifies in the final sense a theft from those who hunger and are not fed, those who are cold and are not clothed.

President Eisenhower, speech, American Society of Newspaper Editors, April 16, 1953

Let officers and directors of our armament factories, our gun builders, and munitions makers all be conscripted — to get $30 a month, the wage paid to the lads in the trenches . . . That will stop the racket, that and nothing else.

Smedley Butler, Commander, U.S. Marines, Forum, *September 1934*

(*See also* **DEFENSE, MILITARY, WAR**)

ART

. . . A human activity having for its purpose the transmission to others of the highest and best feelings to which men have risen.

Leo Tolstoy, What Is Art?, *1898*

Painting is poetry that is seen rather than felt, and poetry is painting that is felt rather than seen.

Leonardo da Vinci (d. 1519), Treatise on Painting

The more controlled, limited, and tormented art is, the freer it is.

Igor Stravinsky, Poetics of Music, *1948*

Art . . . does not take kindly to facts, is helpless to grapple with theories, and is killed outright by a sermon.

Agnes Repplier, Points of View, *1891*

The world of sight is still limitless. It is the artist who limits vision to the cramped dimensions of his own ego.

Marya Mannes, More in Anger, *1958*

(*See also* **CINEMA, CREATIVITY, MUSIC, THEATER, WRITING**)

ART AND MORALITY

The morality of art is in its very beauty.

Gustave Flaubert to Louis Bonenfant, 1856

The work of art may have a moral effect, but to demand moral purpose from the artist is to make him ruin his work.

Johann Wolfgang von Goethe (d. 1832), Maxims

The art of the isms [cubism, surrealism, dadaism], the weapon of the Russian Revolution, . . . threatens to overawe . . . and overpower the fine art of our tradition and inheritance. So-called modern or contemporary art in our own beloved country contains all the isms of depravity. . . .

Representative George Dondero, Congressional Record, *1949*

(*See also* **CENSORSHIP, MORALITY**)

ART AND NATURE

Paradox though it may seem, it is none the less true that life imitates art far more than art imitates life.

Oscar Wilde, The Decay of Lying, *1889*

Art hates nature. If art is always seeking nature, it is like a hunter waiting in ambush, or a rival, embracing it only in order to strangle it.

André Gide, Journal, *1911*

(*See also* **NATURE**)

ART AND REALITY

I do not evolve, I *am*. In art there is neither past nor future. Art that is not in the present will never be.

Pablo Picasso, The Art, *May 25, 1923*

What is most real for me are the illusions I create with my paintings. Everything else is quicksand.

Eugène Delacroix, Journal, *February 27, 1824*

(*See also* **REALITY**)

ART AND SCIENCE

Art disturbs, science reassures.

Georges Braque (d. 1963), Le Jour et la nuit

Art is science made clear.

Jean Cocteau, Le Coq et l'Arlequin

(*See also* **SCIENCE**)

ART: CUBIST, DADAIST, SURREALIST

Geometry is to the plastic arts what grammar is to the art of writing.

Guillaume Apollinaire, The Cubist Painters, *1913*

There wasn't any nude [in Duchamp's "Nude Descending a Staircase"], there wasn't even a staircase!

Theodore Roosevelt, to reporters, after visiting the Armory Exhibit,
New York, March 4, 1913

Freedom: DADA DADA DADA, the howl of clashing colors, the intertwining of all contradictions, grotesqueries, trivialities: LIFE.

Tristan Tzara, Dada Manifesto, *1918*

My art belongs to Dada . . .

Tom Stoppard, Travesties, *1975*

ART: MEANING

A work should convey its entire meaning by itself, imposing it on the spectator even before he knows what the subject is.

Marcel Proust, Within a Budding Grove, *1919*

If your [friend] says of some picture, "Yes, but what does it mean?" ask him . . . what his carpet means or the circular patterns on his shoes.

Stephen Potter, One-Upmanship, *1952*

(*See also* **CREATIVITY, CRITICISM**)

ARTIFICIALITY

The first duty in life is to be as artificial as possible. What the second duty is no one has yet discovered.

Oscar Wilde, "Phrases and Philosophies for the Use of the Young," The Chameleon, *1894*

A cynic might suggest as the motto of modern life this simple legend — "Just as good as the real."

Charles Dudley Warner, Backlog Studies, *1873*

(*See also* **APPEARANCES, HYPOCRICY, ILLUSION**)

ARTIST

The true artist will let his wife starve, his children go barefoot, his mother drudge for his living at seventy, sooner than work at anything but his art.

G.B. Shaw, Man and Superman, *1903*

The artist today, . . . besides lacking merit, . . . is simply a *spoiled child.* How many honors, how much money [are] lavished on people with no understanding and no training!

Charles Baudelaire, Salon de 1859

The great artists are those who impose their peculiar illusion on the rest of mankind.

Guy de Maupassant, Pierre et Jean, *1888*

Art-for-art's sake [and] art-for-people's sake are equally ridiculous. I suggest *art for God's sake.*

Jean Cocteau (d. 1963), Letter to Jacques Maritain

An artist cannot talk about his art any more than a plant can discuss horticulture.

Jean Cocteau, Newsweek, *May 16, 1955*

(*See also* **CREATIVITY, VISION**)

ASPIRATION

It is only the fools who keep straining at high C all their lives.

Charles Dudley Warner, Backlog Studies, *1873*

An aspiration is a joy forever, a possession as solid as a landed estate, a fortune which we can never exhaust and which gives us year by year a revenue of pleasurable activity.

Robert Louis Stevenson, "El Dorado," 1881

(*See also* **AMBITION, HOPE**)

ATHEIST

. . . A man who has no invisible means of support.

Bishop Fulton J. Sheen, Look, *December 14, 1955*

The three great apostles of practical atheism, that make converts without persecuting, and retain them without preaching, are wealth, health and power.

Charles Caleb Colton (d. 1832), Lacon

(*See also* **AGNOSTIC, GOD, ORTHODOX/UNORTHODOX**)

ATOMIC AGE

Gods are born and die, but the atom endures.

Alexander Chase, Perspectives, *1966*

A tremendous flash of light cut across the sky. Mr. Tanimoto has a distinct recollection that it traveled from east to west, from the city toward the hills. It seemed a sheet of sun. Both he and Mr. Matsuo reacted with terror.

John Hersey, Hiroshima, *1946*

The bomb that fell on Hiroshima fell on America too.
It fell on no city, no munition plants, no docks.
It erased no church, vaporized no public buildings, reduced no man
  to his atomic elements.
But it fell, it fell.

Hermann Hagedorn, "The Bomb That Fell on America," c. 1960

Man has wrested from nature the power to make the world a desert or to make the deserts bloom. There is no evil in the atom; only in men's souls.

Adlai Stevenson, speech, Hartford, Connecticut, September 1952

I do not believe civilization will be wiped out in a war fought with the atomic bomb. Perhaps two-thirds of the people of the earth might be killed, but enough men capable of thinking, and enough books, would be left to start again, and civilization could be restored.

Albert Einstein, Atlantic Monthly, *November 1945*

We must dare to think "unthinkable" thoughts. . . . We must learn to welcome and not to fear the voices of dissent. . . . Because when things become unthinkable, thinking stops and action becomes mindless.

J.W. Fulbright, speech, U.S. Senate, March 27, 1964

(*See also* **SCIENCE, TWENTIETH CENTURY, WAR**)

AUDACITY

I love the valiant; but it is not enough to wield a broadsword, one must also know against whom.

Nietzsche, Thus Spake Zarathustra, *1892*

Tact in audacity is knowing how far you can go without going too far.

Jean Cocteau, Le Rappel à l'ordre, *1926*

Audacity augments courage; hesitation, fear.

Nigerian proverb

(*See also* **COURAGE, HEROES**)

AUDIENCE

If one talks to more than four people, it is an audience; and one cannot really think or exchange thoughts with an audience.

Anne Morrow Lindberg, North to the Orient, *1935*

The audience is not the least important actor in the play and if it will not do its allotted share the play falls to pieces. The dramatist then is in the position of a tennis player who is left on the court with nobody to play with.

W. Somerset Maugham, The Summing Up, *1938*

To have great poets, there must be great audiences too.

Walt Whitman, Notes Left Over, *1881*

(*See also* **ACTORS, THEATER/STAGE**)

AUTHORITY

Most men, after a little freedom, have preferred authority with the consoling assurances and the economy of effort which it brings.

Walter Lippmann, A Preface to Morals, *1929*

Authority has every reason to fear the skeptic, for authority can rarely survive in the face of doubt.

Robert Lindner, Must You Conform?, *1956*

Every great advance in natural knowledge has involved the absolute rejection of authority.

T.H. Huxley, Lay Sermons, *1870*

(*See also* **GOVERNMENT, LEADERSHIP, POWER, RULER**)

AUTOBIOGRAPHY

Autobiography is now as common as adultery, and hardly less reprehensible.

John Grigg, London Sunday Times, *February 28, 1962*

When writing of oneself one should show no mercy. Yet why at the first attempt to discover one's own truth does all inner strength seem to melt away in floods of self-pity and tenderness and rising tears?

Georges Bernanos, The Diary of a Country Priest, *1936*

(*See also* **BIOGRAPHY, SELF-IMPORTANCE, WRITING**)

AUTOMOBILITY

Everything in life is somewhere else, and you get there in a car.

E.B. White, One Man's Meat, *1943*

Speed provides the one genuinely modern pleasure.

Aldous Huxley (d. 1963), Music at Night

The automobile changed our dress, manners, social customs, vacation habits, the shape of our cities, consumer-purchasing patterns, common tastes and positions in intercourse.

John Keats, The Insolent Chariots, *1958*

The car has become . . . an article of dress without which we feel uncertain, unclad, and incomplete.

Marshall McLuhan, Understanding Media, *1964*

The automobile has not merely taken over the street, it has dissolved the living tissue of the city. Its appetite for space is absolutely insatiable; moving and parked, it devours urban land, leaving the buildings as mere islands of habitable space in a sea of dangerous and ugly traffic.

James Marston Fitch, New York Times, *May 1, 1960*

(*See also* **SUBURBS**)

BABIES

Infancy conforms to nobody; all conform to it.

Ralph Waldo Emerson, "Self-Reliance," 1841

Adam and Eve had many advantages, but the principal one was that they escaped teething.

Mark Twain, Pudd'nhead Wilson, *1894*

(*See also* **CHILDREN, PARENTS**)

BARBARISM

. . . The absence of standards to which appeal can be made.

Ortega y Gasset, The Revolt of the Masses, *1930*

Barbarism is needed every four or five hundred years to bring the world back to life. Otherwise it would die of civilization.

Edmond and Jules de Goncourt, Journal, *September 3, 1855*

The real barbarism is Dachau; the real civilization is that part of the human being the [concentration] camps wanted to destroy.

André Malraux (d. 1976), La Condition humaine 2

The crimes of extreme civilization are certainly more atrocious than those of extreme barbarism.

> *Barbey d'Aurevilly (d. 1889),* La Vengeance d'une femme

(*See also* **CIVILIZATION, SAVAGES**)

BEAUTY

What no beautician would ever tell a woman is that the secret to being beautiful is thinking the right thoughts.

> *Panel discussion on women's issues, WNBC radio, 1979*

Remember that the most beautiful things in the world are the most useless; peacocks and lilies for instance.

> *John Ruskin,* The Stones of Venice, *1851*

It is because everything must come to an end that everything is so beautiful.

> *Charles Ramuz (d. 1947),* Adieu a beaucoup de personnages

Let us leave the beautiful women to men with no imagination.

> *Marcel Proust,* Albertine disparue, *1925*

Outward beauty is not enough; to be attractive a woman must . . . [use] words, wit, playfulness, sweet-talk, and laughter to transcend the gifts of Nature.

> *Petronius (d. 66),* Fragments

Rarely do great beauty and great virtue dwell together.

> *Petrarch (d. 1374),* De Remediis utriusque fortunae

(*See also* **CHARM**)

BED

A man's bed is his cradle, but a woman's is often her rack.

> *James Thurber,* Further Fables for Our Time, *1956*

The average, healthy, well-adjusted adult gets up at seven-thirty in the morning feeling just plain terrible.

> *Jean Kerr,* Please Don't Eat the Daisies, *1957*

Was it for this I uttered prayers,
And sobbed and cursed and kicked the stairs,
That now, domestic as a plate,
I should retire at half-past eight?

        Edna St. Vincent Millay, "Grown-up," *1920*

(*See also* **SLEEP**)

BEING

To be what we are, and to become what we are capable of becoming,
is the only end of life.

        Robert Louis Stevenson, Of Men and Books, *1882*

Man is the only animal for whom his own existence is a problem
which he has to solve.

        Erich Fromm, Man for Himself, *1947*

(*See also* **EXISTENTIAL MAN, LIFE**)

BELIEF

People readily believe what they want to believe.

        Julius Caesar, Gallic Wars, *49 B.C.*

It is not disbelief that is dangerous to our society; it is belief.

        G.B. Shaw, Androcles and the Lion, *1912*

I believe because it is impossible.

        Tertullian (d. A.D. 240), De Carne Christi

Believe nothing, O monk, merely because you have been told it.
. . . But believe what, after due examination and analysis, you find
conducive to the . . . welfare of all beings.

    Gautama Buddha (d. 483 B.C.) Sermon of the Turning of the Wheel
of the Law

Religion is a fashionable substitute for Belief.

        Oscar Wilde, The Picture of Dorian Gray, *1891*

To believe everything is to be an imbecile.
To deny everything is to be a fool.

        Charles Nodier (d. 1844), Inès de La Sierra

Be not afraid of life. Believe that life is worth living, and your belief will help create the fact.

William James, The Will to Believe, *1897*

(*See also* **CREDULITY, DOUBT, FAITH**)

BENEVOLENCE

The most melancholy of human reflections, perhaps, is . . . whether the benevolence of mankind does most good or harm.

Walter Bagehot, Physics and Politics, *1869*

We think that love and benevolence will cure anything. Whereas love and benevolence are our poison, poison to the giver, and still more poison to the receiver.

D.H. Lawrence, Fantasia of the Unconscious, *1922*

True generosity consists precisely in fighting to destroy the causes which nourish false charity.

Paulo Freire, Pedagogy of the Oppressed, *1970*

(*See also* **HUMANITARIANISM, KINDNESS**)

THE BIBLE

Thy word is a lamp unto my feet, and a light unto my path.

Psalms 119:105

Christian, n. One who believes that the New Testament is a divinely inspired book admirably suited to the spiritual needs of his neighbor.

Ambrose Bierce, The Devil's Dictionary, *1911*

We pick out a text here and there to make it serve our turn; whereas, if we took it all together, and considered what went before and what followed after, we should find it meant no such thing.

John Selden, Table Talk, *1689*

BIOGRAPHY

Biographies are but the clothes and buttons of the man — the biography of the man himself cannot be written.

Mark Twain, Autobiography, *1924*

Read no history: read nothing but biography, for that is life without theory.

> *Benjamin Disraeli*, Contarini Fleming, *1844*

(*See also* **AUTOBIOGRAPHY, WRITER**)

BIRTH, BIRTHING, BIRTH CONTROL

Living is being born slowly. It would be a little too easy if we could borrow ready-made souls.

> *Antoine de Saint-Exupéry*, Flight to Arras, *1942*

I should like to abolish funerals; the time to mourn a person is at his birth, not his death.

> *Montesquieu (Charles-Louis de Secondat)*, Persian Letters, *1721*

There is nothing like a start, and being born, however pessimistic one may become in later years, is undeniably a start.

> *William McFee*, Harbours of Memory, *1921*

The quality of the culture and farsightedness, rather than living standards, seem to govern the limitation of births.

> *Alfred Sauvy*, Population, *1960*

Among white-collar workers, as among artists, there are many more abortions than birthings.

> *Honoré de Balzac*, Les Employés, *1837*

The states are not free, under the guise of protecting maternal health or potential life, to intimidate women into continuing pregnancies.

> *Justice Harry A. Blackmun*, Roe v. Wade, *January 22, 1973*

I will not give to a woman an instrument to procure abortion.

> *Hippocratic oath, c. 400 B.C.*

(*See also* **POPULATION**)

BLACK

I am an invisible man. . . . I am a man of substance, of flesh and bone, fiber and liquids — and I might even be said to possess a mind. I am invisible, understand, simply because people refuse to see me.

> *Ralph Ellison*, The Invisible Man, *1952*

Just being a Negro doesn't qualify you to understand the race situation any more than being sick makes you an expert on medicine.

Dick Gregory, Nigger, *1964*

What happens to a dream deferred?
Does it dry up
Like a raisin in the sun? . . .
Or does it explode?

Langston Hughes, "Harlem," *1951*

I speak to the black experience, but I am always talking about the human condition — about what we can endure, dream, fail at, and still survive.

Maya Angelou, quoted in Current Biographies, 1974

(*See also* **PREJUDICE, RACE/RACISM**)

BLACK AFRICA

. . . is caught in the vicious circle of an unproductive agriculture carried on by undernourished people on unfertilized land.

René Dumont, L'Afrique noire est mal partie, *1962*

All at once, Africa has to learn the intricacies of writing, banking, farming, and governing, . . . while at the same time trying to cope with the Industrial Revolution.

Dumont, ibid.

The African race is a rubber ball. The harder you dash it to the ground, the higher it will rise.

African proverb

BLOOD

So, he was born of a king, and I of a simple shepherd,
Is the color of his blood any different from mine?

Cyrano de Bergerac, Death of Agrippina, *1654*

"Let there be light!" said God, "and there was light!"
"Let there be blood!" says man, and there's a sea!

Lord Byron, Don Juan, *1819*

The tree of liberty must be refreshed from time to time with the blood of patriots and tyrants.

Thomas Jefferson to William Stevens Smith, 1787

BOHEMIANS/HIPPIES

Bohemia, bordered on the North by hope, work and gaiety, on the South by necessity and courage, on the West and East by slander and the hospital.

Henry Murger, Bohemian Life, *1849*

Bohemia is nothing more than the little country in which you do not live. If you try to obtain citizenship in it, at once the court and retinue pack the royal archives and treasure and move away beyond the hills.

O Henry, The Trimmed Lamp, *1907*

Bohemia is the state of mind inhabited by those who, whether or not they are creative or particularly intellectual, like to stand on the margins and scoff at the babbitts.

Vance Packard, The Status Seekers, *1959*

The hippies have usurped the prerogatives of children — to dress up and be irresponsible.

Mark Harris, "The Flowering of the Hippies," Atlantic Monthly, *September 1967*

(*See also* **NONCONFORMITY**)

BOOK(S)

It is chiefly through books that we enjoy intercourse with superior minds.

William Ellery Channing, "Self-Culture," *1838*

Books are a world in themselves, it is true; but they are not the only world. The world itself is a volume larger than all the libraries in it.

Thomas Hardy, Tess of the D'Urbervilles, *1891*

Camerado, this is no book,
Who touches this touches a man.

Walt Whitman, Leaves of Grass, *1855*

There is no such thing as a moral or immoral book; books are well written or badly written.

Oscar Wilde, Picture of Dorian Gray, *1891*

Up! Up! my Friend, and quit your books,
Or surely you'll grow double. . . .

William Wordsworth (d. 1850), "The Tables Turned"

A good book should leave you . . . slightly exhausted at the end. You live several lives while reading it.

William Styron, interview, Writers at Work, *1958*

I've never known any trouble that an hour's reading didn't assuage.

Montesquieu (d. 1755), Pensées Diverses

Books are the curse of the human race. Nine-tenths of existing books are nonsense, and the clever books are the refutation of that nonsense. The greatest misfortune that ever befell man was the invention of printing.

Benjamin Disraeli, Lothair, *1870*

(*See also* **LITERATURE, NOVELS, READING, WRITING**)

BOREDOM

. . . The desire for desires.

Leo Tolstoy, Anna Karenina, *1873*

Boredom is a sickness the cure for which is work; pleasure is only a palliative.

Le Duc de Lévis (d. 1787), Mémoires

A scholar knows no boredom.

Jean Paul Richter, Hesperus, *1795*

Society is now one polished horde,
Formed of two mighty tribes, the *Bores* and *Bored.*

Byron, Don Juan, *1819*

(*See also* **TALKING**)

BOURGEOIS

What is a bourgeois? I propose this definition: It is a person who has something put by.

André Siegfried, Tableau des partis en France, *1930*

The bourgeoisie . . . is quite simply the contented portion of the population. A bourgeois is a person who now has time to sit down.

> *Victor Hugo*, Les Misérables, *1862*

I call bourgeois anyone who, in a fight or love affair, surrenders for safety's sake. I call bourgeois whoever puts anything ahead of feeling and sentiment.

> *Jean Paul Fargue (d. 1947)*, Sous la Lampe

(*See also* **MIDDLE CLASS**)

BOYS

A boy becomes an adult three years before his parents think he does, and about two years after he thinks he does.

> *General Lewis B. Hershey*, News summaries, *December 31, 1951*

Boys are capital fellows in their own way, among their mates; but they are unwholesome companions for grown people.

> *Charles Lamb*, Essays of Elia, *1823*

When I grow up I want to be a little boy.

> *Joseph Heller*, Something Happened, *1974*

(*See also* **ADOLESCENCE, CHILDREN, YOUTH**)

BREAD

Two things only the people anxiously desire — bread and circuses.

> *Juvenal (d. 117)*, Satires

I recalled the thoughtless saying of a great princess, who, when told that the country people had no bread, replied, "Let them eat cake."

> *J.J. Rousseau*, Confessions, *1781* (This comment was later attributed to Marie Antoinette during the French Revolution.)

BREEDING

Good breeding consists in concealing how much we think of ourselves and how little we think of the other person.

> *Mark Twain*, Notebooks, *1935*

The test of a man or woman's breeding is how they behave in a quarrel.

> *G.B. Shaw*, The Philanderer, *1893*

(*See also* **MANNERS**)

BREVITY

Least said is soon disavowed.

Ambrose Bierce, The Devil's Dictionary, *1911*

When I struggle to be terse, I end by being obscure.

Horace, Ars poetica, *13 B.C.*

Yes and No are soon said, but give much to think over.

Baltasar Gracian, The Art of Worldly Wisdom, *1647*

(*See also* **PUBLIC SPEAKING**)

BROTHERHOOD

A "fraternity" is the antithesis of *fraternity*. The first . . . is predicated on the idea of exclusion; the second (that is, the abstract thing) is based on a feeling of total equality.

E.B. White, One Man's Meat, *1944*

While there is a lower class I am in it, while there is a criminal element I am of it; while there is a soul in prison, I am not free.

Eugene V. Debs, Cleveland, *1917*

(*See also* **CLASSES, COMMUNITY, FRIENDSHIP**)

BUREAUCRACY

. . . A giant mechanism operated by pygmies.

Honoré de Balzac, attributed

The working of great institutions is mainly the result of . . . routine, petty malice, self-interest, carelessness, and sheer mistakes. Only a small fraction is thought.

George Santayana (d. 1952), The Crime of Galileo

The perfect bureaucrat everywhere is the man who manages to make no decisions and escapes all responsibility.

Brooks Atkinson, Once Around the Sun, *1951*

(*See also* **GOVERNMENT, INSTITUTIONS**)

BURIALS/FUNERALS

"Let the dead bury the dead." There is not a single word of Christ to which the . . . Christian religion has paid less attention.

André Gide, Journals, *July 13, 1930*

The purpose of a funeral service is to comfort the living. It is important at a funeral to display excessive grief. This will show others how kind-hearted and loving you are and their improved opinion of you will be very comforting.

P.J. O'Rourke, Modern Manners, *1983*

(*See also* **DEATH AND DYING**)

BUSINESS AND INDUSTRY

While the law [of competition] may be sometimes hard for the individual, it is best for the race, because it insures the survival of the fittest in every department.

Andrew Carnegie, The Gospel of Wealth, *1889*

Capitalism inevitably and by virtue of the very logic of its civilization creates, educates and subsidizes a vested interest in social unrest.

Joseph Schumpeter, Capitalism, Socialism, Democracy, *1942*

Corporations cannot commit treason, nor be outlawed nor excommunicated, for they have no souls.

Sir Edward Coke, Sutton's-Hospital Case, *1612*

Monopolists, by keeping the market constantly understocked, by never fully supplying the effectual demand, sell their commodities much above the natural price, and raise their . . . wages or profit . . . greatly above their natural rate.

Adam Smith, Wealth of Nations, *1776*

The individual serves the industrial system not by supplying it with savings and the resulting capital; he serves it by consuming its products.

John Kenneth Galbraith, The New Industrial State, *1967*

To turn $100 into $110 is work. To turn $100 million into $110 million is inevitable.

Edgar Bronfman, Newsweek, *December 2, 1985*

Junk bonds are the Holy Grail for hostile takeovers.

Roger Miller, New York Times, *April 14, 1985*

The trouble with the profit system has always been that it was highly unprofitable to most people.

E.B. White, "One Man's Meat," Harper's, *1942*

In 1909–1912 . . . I helped pacify Nicaragua for [an] international banking house. . . . I helped make Mexico safe for American oil interests. . . . I helped in the rape of half a dozen Latin American republics for the benefit of Wall Street.

> *Smedley Butler, Commander U.S. Marines,* New York Times,
> *August 21, 1931*

(*See also* **ADVERTISING, ECONOMY, PROPERTY**)

BUYING/SELLING

When a man is trying to sell you something, don't imagine he is that polite all the time.

> *Edgar Watson Howe,* Country Town Sayings, *1911*

Forgive us for frantic buying and selling; for advertising the unnecessary and coveting the extravagant, and calling it good business when it is not good for you.

> *United Presbyterian Church,* Litany for Holy Communion, *1968*

(*See also* **ADVERTISING, BUSINESS AND INDUSTRY**)

CAESAR, GOD, AND THE POPE

Render unto Caesar the things which are Caesar's; and unto God the things that are God's.

Matthew 22:21

I know that we should render unto God that which is God's, but the Pope is not God.

Napoleon to the Ecclesiastical Committee of Paris, 1811

CANT

The grand *primum mobile* [prime mover] of England is cant; cant political, cant poetical, cant religious, cant moral, but always cant, multiplied through all the varieties of life.

Lord Byron to John Murray, February 7, 1821

Politicians who cant about humanitarian principles find themselves sooner or later compelled to put those principles into practice — and far more thoroughly than they had ever originally intended. Without political cant there would be no democracy.

Aldous Huxley, Jesting Pilate, *1926*

(*See also* **HYPOCRISY**)

CAPITALISM: *See* BUSINESS, COMMUNISM, GOVERNMENT.

CAUSES

The mark of the immature man is that he wants to die nobly for a cause, while the mark of the mature man is that he wants to live humbly for one.

J.D. Salinger, The Catcher in the Rye, *1951*

Faith in a holy cause is to a considerable extent a substitute for the lost faith in ourselves.

Eric Hoffer, The Ordeal of Change, *1964*

CELEBRITY

. . . A person who is known for his well-knownness.

Daniel Boorstin, The Image, *1962*

We are too interested in becoming somebody.

Henri Michaux, Plume, *1937*

Popularity is a crime from the moment it is sought; it is only a virtue where men have it whether they will or no.

George Savile, Political, Moral, and Miscellaneous Reflections, *1750*

(*See also* **HEROES**)

CELIBACY

I say to the unmarried . . . that it is good for them if they remain [celibate] even as I. But if they do not have self-control, let them marry; for it is better to marry than to burn.

Paul to the Corinthians I, 7:8–9

Except for the rare good fortune of finding a congenial . . . partner, the least unhappy condition in life is . . . celibacy.

Bernardin de St.-Pierre, Paul et Virginie, *1788*

Full many a flower is born to blush unseen,
And waste its sweetness on the desert air.

Thomas Gray, "Elegy . . . ," *1750*

CENSORSHIP

Books won't stay banned. They won't burn. Ideas won't go to jail. In the long run of history, the censor and the inquisitor have always lost. The only weapon against bad ideas is better ideas.

A. Whitney Griswold, New York Times, *February 24, 1959*

Burn the libraries, for their value is all in this book [the Koran].
Omar I, Caliph, at the capture of Jerusalem, 637

Wherever they burn books they will also, in the end, burn human beings.
Heinrich Heine, Almansor, *1823*

(*See also* **PRESS/MEDIA, RIGHTS**)

CHANCE

We cannot bear to regard ourselves simply as playthings of blind chance; we cannot admit to feeling ourselves abandoned.
Ugo Betti, Struggle till Dawn, *1949*

History abhors determinism but cannot tolerate chance.
Bernard De Voto, The Course of Empire, *1952*

A wise man turns chance into good fortune.
Thomas Fuller, Gnomologia, *1723*

(*See also* **CIRCUMSTANCES, FATE, FORTUNE**)

CHANGE

When it comes to changes, people like only those they make themselves.
French proverb

"Yes," I answered you last night;
"No," this morning, sir, I say:
Colors seen by candlelight
Will not look the same by day.
Elizabeth Barrett Browning, "The Lady's 'Yes,'" *1844*

The absurd man is he who never changes.
Auguste Barthélémy, Ma Justification, *1831*

Change is one thing, progress is another. "Change" is scientific, "progress" is ethical; change is indisputable, whereas progress is a matter of controversy.
Bertrand Russell, Unpopular Essays, *1950*

(*See also* **CONSISTENCY, INNOVATIONS, PROGRESS**)

CHARACTER

Happiness is not the end of life: character is.
Henry Ward Beecher, Life Thoughts, *1858*

Genius is formed in quiet, character in the stream of life.
Goethe, Torquato Tasso, *1790*

People seem not to see that their opinion of the world is also a confession of character.
Emerson, The Conduct of Life, *1860*

(*See also* **IDENTITY, INDIVIDUALISM**)

CHARM

. . . A quality in others that makes us more satisfied with ourselves.
Henri Frédéric Amiel, Journal, *1883*

Charm is a sort of bloom on a woman. If you have it, you don't need to have anything else; and if you don't have it, it doesn't matter what else you have.
Sir James M. Barrie, What Every Woman Knows, *1908*

Charm is . . . a way of getting the answer yes without having asked any clear question.
Albert Camus, The Fall, *1956*

CHASTITY

. . . The most unnatural of the sexual perversions.
Aldous Huxley, Eyeless in Gaza, *1936*

Give me chastity and continence, but not right now.
Augustine, Confessions, A.D. *401*

The essence of chastity is not the suppression of lust, but the total orientation of one's life toward a goal.
Dietrich Bonhoeffer, Letters and Prayers from Prison, *1953*

(*See also* **CELIBACY, PURITY, SELF-DENIAL**)

CHILDREN

The more people have studied different methods of bringing up children the more they have come to the conclusion that what good mothers and fathers instinctively feel like doing for their babies is the best after all.

> *Benjamin Spock,* The Common Sense Book of Baby and Child Care, *1946*

Thou, straggler into loving arms,
Young climber up of knees,
When I forget thy thousand ways,
Then life and all shall cease.

> *Mary Lamb,* "Parental Recollections," *1809*

Grown-ups never understand anything for themselves, and it is tiresome for children to be always and forever explaining things to them.

> *Saint-Exupéry,* The Little Prince, *1943*

Children need models rather than critics.

> *Joseph Joubert,* Pensées, *1842*

A torn jacket is soon mended; but hard words bruise the heart of a child.

> *Henry Wadsworth Longfellow,* Driftwood, *1857*

Children are natural mythologists: they beg to be told tales, and love not only to invent but to enact falsehoods.

> *George Santayana,* Dialogues in Limbo, *1925*

You may give [children] your love but not your thoughts,
For they have their own thoughts.
You may house their bodies but not their souls,
For their souls dwell in the house of tomorrow.

> *Kahlil Gibran,* The Prophet, *1923*

You are worried about seeing him spend his early years in doing nothing. What! Is it nothing to be happy? Nothing to skip, play, and run around all day long? Never in his life will he be so busy again.

> *Rousseau,* Emile, *1762*

(*See also* **BOYS, DAUGHTERS, PARENTS**)

CHILDHOOD

... knows what it wants: it wants out of childhood.

Jean Cocteau, La Difficulté d'être, *1947*

Literature ... is the rediscovery of childhood.

Georges Bataille, La Littérature et le mal, *1957*

The barb in the arrow of childhood suffering is this: its intense loneliness, its intense ignorance.

Olive Schreiner, The Story of an African Farm, *1884*

Credulity is the man's weakness, but the child's strength.

Charles Lamb, Essays of Elia, *1823*

In all our efforts to provide "advantages" we have actually produced the busiest, most competitive, highly pressured, and over-organized generation of youngsters in our history—and possibly the unhappiest.

Eda J. LeShan, The Conspiracy against Childhood, *1967*

The United States in the 1980s may be the first society in history in which children are distinctly worse off than adults.

Sen. Daniel P. Moynihan, New York Times, *May 6, 1986*

(*See also* **PARENTHOOD**)

CHOSEN PEOPLE

Remember [the Lord's] marvelous works ... O ye seed of Abraham his servant, ye children of Jacob his chosen.

Psalms 105:5–6

Remember, the German people are the chosen of God. On me, the German Emperor, the spirit of God has descended. I am His sword, His weapon, and His vice-regent.

Wilhelm II, Germany, addressing the soldiers, 1914

Those who labor in the earth are the chosen people of God, if ever He had a chosen people, whose breast He has made His peculiar deposit for substantial and genuine virtue.

Jefferson, Notes on the State of Virginia, *1785*

CHRIST: *See* JESUS.

CHRISTIAN

One day a man was asked if there were any true atheists. Do you think, he replied, that there are any true Christians?

Denis Diderot, Pensées philosophiques, *1746*

The Christian ideal has not been tried and found wanting. It has been found difficult and left untried.

G.K. Chesterton, What's Wrong with the World? *1910*

If there is one part of the Christian message that people have rejected with incomparable obstinacy, it is faith in the equal worth of all souls and races before the Father who is in heaven.

François Mauriac, Life of Jesus, *1936*

(*See also* **CHRISTIAN LIFE**)

CHRISTIANITY

Christianity is an idea, and as such, indestructible and immortal, like every idea.

Heinrich Heine, Religion and Philosophy, *1834*

I wish [Christianity] were more productive of good works. I mean real good works . . . not holy-day keeping, sermon-hearing, or making long prayers filled with flatteries and compliments despised by wise men and much less capable of pleasing the Deity.

Benjamin Franklin, Works 7:75

No man is a Christian who cheats his fellows, perverts the truth, or speaks of a "clean bomb," yet he will be the first to make public his faith in God.

Marya Mannes, More in Anger, *1958*

The Christian religion is essentially a religion of sensual pleasures. Sin is the great attraction, . . . the more one feels oneself a sinner, the more Christian one is.

Novalis (d. 1801), Fragments

Christians have burnt each other, quite persuaded
That all the Apostles would have done as they did.

Lord Byron, Don Juan, *1824*

I reject Christianity because . . . it preaches Peace on Earth.

Erich Ludendorff (d. 1937), Belief in a German God

(*See also* **JESUS, RELIGION**)

CHRISTIAN LIFE

Here is what Christian living entails: wishing in all things whatever God wishes, desiring His glory, seeking nothing for oneself, either now or in the hereafter.

Martin Luther (d. 1546), On the Epistle to the Romans

If you love, you will suffer, and if you do not love, you do not know the meaning of a Christian life.

Agatha Christie, An Autobiography, *1977*

The root of the matter . . . is love, Christian love, or compassion. If you feel this, you have a motive for existence, a guide for action, a reason for courage [and] for intellectual honesty.

Bertrand Russell, Impact of Science on Society, *1952*

(*See also* **THE BIBLE, CHURCH**)

CHURCH

I have no objection to churches so long as they do not interfere with God's work.

Brooks Atkinson, Once around the Sun, *1951*

The real ecumenical crisis today is not between Catholics and Protestants but between traditional and experimental forms of church life.

Harvey Cox, The Secular City, *1966*

(*See also* **CHRISTIANITY**)

CHURCH VS. THE WORLD

The Church Militant wages eternal war with those implacable enemies, the world, the flesh, and the devil.

Council of Trent, Decrees, *1563*

Christianity, with its doctrines of humility, of forgiveness, of love, is incompatible with the State, with its haughtiness, its violence, its punishment, its wars.

Leo Tolstoy, The Kingdom of God Is within You, *1893*

The church must be reminded that it is not the master or the servant of the state, but rather [its] conscience.

Martin Luther King, Strength to Love, *1963*

Some political and social activities of the Catholic Church are detrimental and even dangerous for the community as a whole, . . . [e.g.] the fight against birth control at a time when overpopulation [is] a serious obstacle to peace.

Albert Einstein to the Brooklyn Tablet, *1954*

(*See also* **MATERIALISM**)

CINEMA

Through the magic of motion pictures, someone who's never left Peoria knows the softness of a Paris spring, the color of a Nile sunset, the sorts of vegetation one will find along the upper Amazon and that Big Ben has not yet gone digital.

Vincent Canby, New York Times, *May 18, 1980*

Thanks to the movies, gunfire has always sounded unreal to me, even when being fired upon.

Peter Ustinov, Dear Me, *1977*

The more marvelous is the progress of the motion picture industry, the more pernicious and deadly has it shown itself to morality, religion, and even the very decencies of human society.

Pope Pius XI, Vigilanti cura, *1936*

Hollywood is a dreary industrial town controlled by hoodlums of enormous wealth [with] the ethical sense of a pack of jackals.

S.J. Perlman, quoted in New York Times *December 18, 1988*

(*See also* **ACTORS, THEATER/STAGE**)

CIRCUMSTANCES

There is neither vice nor virtue, there are only circumstances.

Balzac, Le Père Goriot, *1834*

Man is not the creature of circumstances. Circumstances are the creatures of men.

Disraeli, Vivian Grey, *1826*

People are always blaming their circumstances for what they are. I don't believe in circumstances. The people who get on in this world are the people who get up and look for the circumstances they want, and, if they can't find them, make them.

G.B. Shaw, Mrs. Warren's Profession, *1893*

(*See also* **CHANCE, NECESSITY**)

CITIZENSHIP

That man's the best cosmopolite
Who loves his native country best.

Alfred, Lord Tennyson (d. 1892), "Hands All Round"

The voice of protest, of warning, of appeal is never more needed than when the clamor of fife and drum, echoed by the press and too often by the pulpit, is bidding all men fall in and keep step and obey in silence the tyrannous word of command. Then, more than ever, it is the duty of the good citizen not to be silent.

Charles Eliot Norton, True Patriotism, *1898*

Those self-important fathers of their country
Think they're above the people. Why they're nothing!
The citizen is infinitely wiser.

Euripides, Andromache, c. 426 B.C.

(*See also* **PATRIOTISM**)

CIVILIZATION

. . . A movement and not a condition, a voyage and not a harbor.

Arnold Toynbee (d. 1975), Civilization on Trial

When civilizations fail, it is almost always man who has failed — not in his body, not in his fundamental equipment and capacities, but in his will, spirit, and mental habits.

Philip Lee Ralph, The Story of Civilization, *1954*

Th' fav'rite pastime iv civilized man is croolty to other civilized man.

Finley Peter Dunne, Dissertations by Mr Dooley, *1906*

The civilized are those who get more out of life than the uncivilized, and for this the uncivilized have not forgiven them.

Cyril Connolly, The Unquiet Grave, *1945*

(*See also* **BARBARISM, CULTURE**)

CIVILIZATION, TEST OF

A decent provision for the poor is the true test of a civilization.

Samuel Johnson, in Boswell's Life, *1791*

Avarice and luxury, those evils which have been the ruin of every great state.

Livy (d. A.D. 17), History of Rome

The true test of civilization is . . . the kind of men the country turns out.

Emerson, Society and Solitude, *1870*

(*See also* **HUMANISM, HUMANITARIANISM**)

CLASSES

Society comprises two classes: those who have more food than appetite, and those who have more appetite than food.

Chamfort (d. 1794), Maximes

The struggle between age classes is a distinctive class struggle in its own right.

Gerhard Lenski, The Religious Factor, *1963*

In the view of the Constitution . . . there is in this country no superior, dominant, ruling class of citizens. There is no caste here. Our Constitution is color-blind, and neither knows nor tolerates classes among citizens.

Justice Harlan, dissent, Plessy vs. Ferguson, *1896*

The diminution of the reality of class, however socially desirable in many respects, seems to have the practical effect of diminishing our ability to see people in their differences and specialness.

Lionel Trilling, The Liberal Imagination, *1950*

(*See also* **ARISTOCRACY, DEMOCRACY, EQUALITY**)

CLEVERNESS

Here's a good rule of thumb:
Too clever is dumb.

Ogden Nash, "Reflection on Ingenuity,"
Verses from 1929 On, *1949*

Some people take more care to hide their wisdom than their folly.

Jonathan Swift, Thoughts on Various Subjects, *1711*

(*See also* **WIT**)

COLONIALISM: *See* **VIOLENCE, COLONIAL.**

COMEDY: *See* **TRAGEDY.**

COMMON SENSE

Logic is one thing and commonsense another.

Elbert Hubbard, The Note Book, *1927*

A man of great common sense and good taste — meaning thereby a man without originality or moral courage.

G.B. Shaw, Caesar and Cleopatra, *1906*

(*See also* **PRUDENCE, REASON**)

COMMUNICATION

There are . . . two kinds of people in this world, those who long to be understood and those who long to be misunderstood. It is the irony of life that neither is gratified.

Carl Van Vechten, The Blind Bow-Boy, *1923*

To think justly we must understand what others mean: to know the value of our thoughts, we must try their effect on other minds.

William Hazlitt, The Plain Speaker, *1826*

(*See also* **PROPAGANDA, SPEECH, WRITING**)

COMMUNISM

The history of all hitherto existing societies is the history of class struggles. . . . The modern bourgeois society . . . has but established new classes, new conditions of oppression, new forms of struggle in place of the old ones.

Marx and Engels, The Communist Manifesto, *1848*

Communism is based on the belief that man is so weak that he is unable to govern himself, and therefore requires the rule of strong masters. Democracy is based on the conviction that man has the . . . capacity to govern himself with reason and justice.

Harry S. Truman, Inaugural Address, 1949

I have spent all my life under a Communist regime, and I will tell you that a society without any legal scale is a terrible one indeed. But a society with no other scale than the legal one is not quite worthy of man either.

Alexander Solzhensitsyn, Address, Harvard, 1978

As soon as classes have been abolished and the dictatorship of the proletariat has been done away with, the Communist Party will have fulfilled its mission and can be allowed to disappear.

Joseph Stalin, Speech, *1924*

(*See also* **GOVERNMENT, SOCIALISM**)

COMMUNITY

Rain does not fall on one roof alone.

Cameroon proverb

When the head aches, all the members share the pain.

Cervantes, Don Quixote, *1605*

No individual is isolated. He who is sad, saddens others.

Saint-Exupéry, Flight to Arras, *1942*

A community whose life is not irrigated by art and science, by religion and philosophy, day upon day, is [only] half alive.

Lewis Mumford, Faith for Living, *1940*

(*See also* **BROTHERHOOD**)

COMPANY

In general, American social life constitutes an evasion of talking to people. Most Americans don't, in any vital sense, get together; they only do things together.

Louis Kronenberger, Company Manners, *1954*

To be social is to be forgiving.

Robert Frost, New Hampshire, *1923*

Good company and good discourse are the very sinews of virtue.

Izaak Walton, The Compleat Angler, *1653*

(*See also* **ASSOCIATION, FRIENDSHIP**)

COMPETITION

A horse never runs so fast as when he has other horses to catch up and outpace.

Ovid, The Art of Love, *c. A.D. 8*

Competitions are for horses, not artists.

> *Béla Bartók*, Saturday Review, *August 25, 1962*

(*See also* **AMBITION**)

COMPLAINTS

The wheel that squeaks the loudest
Is the one that gets the grease.

> *Josh Billings (d. 1885), "The Kicker"*

Learn to accept in silence the minor aggravations, cultivate the gift of taciturnity and consume your own smoke with an extra draught of hard work.

> *Sir William Osler, in H. Cushing,* Life, *1925*

COMPLIMENTS

A compliment is something like a kiss through a veil.

> *Victor Hugo,* Les Misérables, *1862*

There is nothing you can say in answer to a compliment. I have been complimented myself a great many times, and they always embarrass me — I always feel that they have not said enough.

> *Mark Twain, "Fulton Day, Jamestown," 1923*

(*See also* **FLATTERY**)

COMPROMISE

All government — indeed, every human benefit and enjoyment, every virtue and every prudent act — is founded on compromise and barter.

> *Edmund Burke, Second Speech on Conciliation with the American Colonies, 1775*

Compromise is but the sacrifice of one right or good in the hope of retaining another — too often ending in the loss of both.

> *Tryon Edwards (d. 1894), American theologian*

Compromise makes a good umbrella, but a poor roof; it is a temporary expedient, often wise in party politics, almost sure to be unwise in statesmanship.

> *James Russell Lowell,* Bigelow Papers, *1867*

(*See also* **APPEASEMENT**)

CONCEALMENT

Have an open face but conceal your thoughts.

Italian proverb

It is most absurdly said, in popular language, of any man, that he is disguised in liquor; for, on the contrary, most men are disguised by sobriety.

Thomas de Quincy, Confessions of an English Opium-Eater, *1856*

Our greatest pretenses are built up not to hide the evil and the ugly in us, but our emptiness. The hardest thing to hide is something that is not there.

Eric Hoffer, The Passionate State of Mind, *1954*

Talking about oneself can also be a means to conceal oneself.

Nietzsche, Beyond Good and Evil, *1886*

(*See also* **HYPOCRISY**)

CONCEIT

To say that a man is vain simply means that he is pleased with the effect he produces on other people. A conceited man is satisfied with the effect he produces on himself.

Max Beerbohm, And Even Now, *1920*

Talk about conceit as much as you like, it is to human character what salt is to the ocean; it keeps it sweet, and renders it endurable.

Oliver Wendell Holmes, The Autocrat of the Breakfast Table, *1858*

What is the first business of philosophy? To part with self-conceit. For it is impossible for anyone to begin to learn what he thinks that he already knows.

Epictetus, Discourses, *c. A.D. 100*

(*See also* **COMPLACENCY, PRIDE, SELF-LOVE**)

CONFESSION

It is not the criminal things that are the hardest to confess, but the ridiculous and the shameful.

Rousseau, Confessions, *1770*

Confession of our faults is the next thing to innocence.

Publius Syrus, Moral Sayings, *first century B.C.*

We confess to little faults only to persuade ourselves that we have no great ones.

La Rochefoucauld, Maxims, *1665*

(*See also* **SECRETS**)

CONFLICT

. . . The gadfly of thought. It stirs us to observation and memory. It instigates to invention. It shocks us out of sheep-like passivity, and sets us at noting and contriving . . . reflection and ingenuity.

John Dewey, Human Nature and Conduct, *1922*

Far from being necessarily dysfunctional, a certain degree of conflict is an essential element in group formation and the persistence of group life.

Lewis A. Coser, Functions of Social Conflict, *1956*

(*See also* **CONTROVERSY**)

CONFORMITY

Success, recognition, and conformity are the bywords of the modern world where everyone seems to crave the anesthetizing security of being identified with the majority.

Martin Luther King, Jr., Strength to Love, *1963*

"Queumania" is an ailment that afflicts people with a compulsive urge to line up behind someone or something, even a lamp-post.

Thomas P. Ronan, New York Times, *August 23, 1955*

Men are created different; they lose their social freedom and their individual autonomy in seeking to become like each other.

David Riesman, The Lonely Crowd, *1950*

Adjustment, that synonym for conformity that comes more easily to the modern tongue, is the theme of our swan song, the piper's tune to which we dance on the brink of the abyss, the siren's melody that destroys and paralyzes our wills.

Robert Lindner, Must You Conform?, *1956*

We are half ruined by conformity, but we should be wholly ruined without it.

Charles Dudley Warner, My Summer in a Garden, *1871*

(*See also* **INDIVIDUALISM, NONCONFORMITY**)

CONQUERING

The fate of unborn millions will now depend, under God, on the courage and conduct of this army. . . . We have, therefore, resolved to conquer or die.

> *George Washington, addressing the Continental Army, 1776*

When you have gained a victory, do not push it too far.

> *Eustace Budgell,* The Spectator, *1711*

Minds are conquered not by arms but by love and magnanimity.

> *Spinoza,* Ethics, *1677*

(*See also* **WAR**)

CONSCIENCE

. . . The inner voice that warns us somebody may be looking.

> *H.L. Mencken,* A Mencken Chrestomathy, *1948*

The fact that human conscience remains partially infantile throughout life is the core of human tragedy.

> *Erik Erikson,* Childhood and Society, *1950*

There is only one way to achieve happiness on this
terrestial ball.
And that is to have either a clear conscience or none at all.

> *Ogden Nash,* I'm a Stranger Here Myself, *1938*

Men never do evil so thoroughly and cheerfully as when they do it for conscience sake.

> *Pascal,* Pensées, *1670*

(*See also* **GUILTY/INNOCENT**)

CONSCIENCE, SOCIAL

Conscience is the guardian in the individual of the rules which the community has evolved for its own preservation.

> *W. Somerset Maugham,* The Moon and Sixpence, *1919*

The Negro was willing to risk martyrdom in order to move and stir the social conscience of . . . the nation. . . . He would force his oppressor to commit his brutality openly, with the rest of the world looking on.

> *Martin Luther King, Jr.,* Why We Can't Wait, *1964*

(*See also* **CITIZENSHIP**)

CONSEQUENCES

All systems of morality are based on the idea that an action has consequences that legitimize or cancel it. A mind imbued with the absurd thinks such consequences should be judged calmly.

> *Albert Camus,* The Myth of Sisyphus, *1942*

Logical consequences are the scarecrows of fools and the beacons of wise men.

> *Thomas Henry Huxley, "Animal Automatism," 1874*

(*See also* **INTENTIONS, IRREVOCABLE**)

CONSERVATION

We abuse land because we regard it as a commodity belonging to us. When we see land as a community to which we belong, we may begin to use it with love and respect.

> *Aldo Leopold, in Stewart Udall,* The Quiet Crisis, *1963*

The earth we abuse and the living things we kill will, in the end, take their revenge; for in exploiting their presence we are diminishing our future.

> *Marya Mannes,* More in Anger, *1958*

(*See also* **NATURE, NATURAL RESOURCES, POLLUTION**)

CONSERVATISM

I often think it's comical
How nature always does contrive
That every boy and every gal,
That's born into the world alive,
Is either a little Liberal,
Or else a little Conservative.

> *W.S. Gilbert,* Iolanthe, *1882*

Conservatism is . . . an instinctive belief that today's society is built on several thousand years and that in those years men have found things they should fasten to. . . . The instinct to conserve, we think, never left the American people.

Editorial, Wall Street Journal, *April 29, 1955*

When a nation's young men are conservative, its funeral bell is already rung.

Henry Ward Beecher, Proverbs, *1887*

In the matter of belief, we are all extreme conservatives.

William James, Pragmatism, *1907*

Conservative people are undoubtedly right in their distrust and hatred of science, for the scientific spirit is the very spirit of innovation and adventure — the most reckless kind of adventure into the unknown.

George Sarton (d. 1955), History of Science

(*See also* **LIBERALISM, EXTREMISM**)

CONSISTENCY

A foolish consistency is the hobgoblin of little minds, adored by little statesmen and divines.

Emerson, "Self-Reliance," 1841

The consistent thinker, the consistently moral man, is either a walking mummy or else, if he has not succeeded in stifling all his vitality, a fanatical monomaniac.

Aldous Huxley, Do What You Will, *1929*

Happiness is never as welcome as changelessness.

Grahame Greene, The Heart of the Matter, *1948*

The man who never alters his opinions is like standing water, and breeds reptiles of the mind.

William Blake, The Marriage of Heaven and Hell, *1790*

(*See also* **CHANGE**)

CONSTANCY/INCONSTANCY

To be capable of steady friendship or lasting love, are the two greatest proofs, not only of goodness of heart, but of strength of mind.

William Hazlitt, Characteristics, *1823*

Constancy in love is a perpetual inconstancy, in which the heart attaches itself successively to each of the lover's qualities, giving preference now to one, now to another.

La Rochefoucauld, Maxims, *1665*

Out upon it, I have loved
Three whole days together;
And am like to love three more,
If it prove fair weather.

Sir John Suckling, Fragmenta aurea, *1646*

Faithfulness is to the emotional life what consistency is to the life of the intellect — simply a confession of failure.

Oscar Wilde, The Picture of Dorian Gray, *1891*

(*See also* **INFIDELITY, INTEGRITY**)

CONTEMPORARIES

Men are more like the times they live in than they are like their fathers.

Ali ibn-abi-Talib, Sentences, *c. 650*

A man is wise with the wisdom of his time only, and ignorant with its ignorance. Observe how the greatest minds yield in some degree to the superstitions of their age.

Thoreau, Journal, *January 31, 1853*

(*See also* **GENERATION GAP**)

CONTEMPT

. . . The feeling of a prudent man for an enemy who is too formidable safely to be opposed.

Ambrose Bierce, The Devil's Dictionary, *1911*

Many can bear adversity, but few contempt.

Thomas Fuller, Gnomologia, *1732*

Moral contempt is a far greater indignity and insult than any kind of crime.

Nietzsche, The Will to Power, *1888*

There is no being so poor and so contemptible, who does not think there is somebody still poorer, and still more contemptible.

Samuel Johnson, in Boswell's Life, *February 15, 1766*

CONTENTMENT

I have learned, in whatever state I am, therewith to be content.
Paul to the Philippians 4:11

Who is content with nothing possesses all things.
Nicholas Boileau to M. Guilleragues, Epîtres, *1669*

I have not a word to say against contented people so long as they keep quiet. But do not, for goodness' sake, let them go strutting about, as they are so fond of doing, crying out that they are the true models for the whole species.
Jerome K. Jerome, The Idle Thoughts of an Idle Fellow, *1889*

Oh, don't the days seem lank and long,
When all goes right and nothing goes wrong
And isn't your life extremely flat
With nothing whatever to grumble at!
W.S. Gilbert, Princess Ida, *1884*

(*See also* **COMPLACENCY, SAD/MELANCHOLY**)

CONTROVERSY

Never in the world were any two opinions alike, any more than any two hairs or grains of sand. Their most universal quality is diversity.
Montaigne, Essays, *1580*

Even if the [prevailing] opinion be not only true, but the whole truth; unless it is . . . vigorously and earnestly contested, it will, by most of them who receive it, be held [merely as] a prejudice.
John Stuart Mill, On Liberty, *1859*

A civilization in which there is not a continuous controversy about important issues . . . is on the way to totalitarianism and death.
Robert M. Hutchins, The University of Utopia, *1953*

(*See also* **ARGUMENT, DISSENT**)

CONVERSATION

Would you like to be a brilliant conversationalist? Just give your natural enthusiasm free reign and say whatever comes into your head. Your rashness will be taken for extraordinary courage.
Alain René Lesage, Gil Blas, *1715*

Never speak of yourself to others; make them talk about themselves instead: therein lies the whole art of pleasing.

> *J. and E. de Goncourt,* Idées et sensations, *1866*

The reason why so few people are agreeable in conversation is that each is thinking more about what he intends to say than about what others are saying. . . .

> *La Rochefoucauld,* Maxims, *1665*

For parlor use, the vague generality is a life-saver.

> *George Ade,* Forty Modern Fables, *1901*

Good nature is more agreeable in conversation than wit, and gives a certain expression to the face which is more amiable than beauty.

> *Joseph Addison,* The Spectator, *September 13, 1711*

(*See also* **COMMUNICATION, TALKING**)

CONVICTIONS

Convictions are more dangerous enemies of truth than lies.

> *Nietzsche,* Human, All Too Human, *1878*

We know too much and are convinced of too little.

> *T.S. Eliot,* A Dialogue on Dramatic Poetry, *1928*

Human beings are perhaps never more frightening than when they are convinced beyond doubt that they are right.

> *Van der Post,* The Lost World of the Kalahari, *1958*

(*See also* **PREJUDICE, THOUGHT**)

CORRUPTION

Public money is like holy water; everybody helps himself to it.

> *Italian proverb*

Power corrupts the few, while weakness corrupts the many.

> *Eric Hoffer,* The Passionate State of Mind, *1954*

The first gold star a child gets in school for the mere performance of a needful task is its first lesson in graft.

> *Philip Wylie,* Generation of Vipers, *1942*

(*See also* **EVIL, SIN**)

COUNTRYSIDE

It is only in the country that we can get to know a person or a book.
Cyril Connolly, The Unquiet Grave, *1945*

God made the country, and man made the town.
William Cowper, The Task, *1785*

The lowest and vilest alleys of London do not present a more dreadful record of sin than does the smiling and beautiful countryside.
Arthur Conan Doyle, Sherlock Holmes, *1891*

I lived in solitude in the country and noticed how the monotony of a quiet life stimulates the creative mind.
Einstein, Out of My Later Years, *1950*

COURAGE

You gain strength, courage and confidence by every experience in which you really stop to look fear in the face. You are able to say to yourself, "I lived through this horror. I can take the next thing that comes along."
Eleanor Roosevelt, You Learn by Living, *1960*

Life shrinks or expands in proportion to one's courage.
Anaïs Nin, Diary, *1969*

The paradox of courage is that a man must be a little careless of his life even in order to keep it.
G.K. Chesterton, All Things Considered, *1908*

Until the day of his death, no man can be sure of his courage.
Jean Anouilh, Beckett, *1959*

Sometimes even to live is an act of courage.
Seneca (d. A.D. 65), Letters to Lucilius

(*See also* **COWARDS, FEAR, STRENGTH**)

COURTESY/POLITENESS

Politeness, n. The most acceptable hypocrisy.
Ambrose Bierce, The Devil's Dictionary, *1911*

It is wise to apply the refined oil of politeness to the mechanism of friendship.

> *Colette*, Earthly Paradise, *1966*

Everyone has to think to be polite; the first impulse is to be impolite.

> *Edgar Watson Howe*, Country Town Sayings, *1911*

The knowledge of courtesy and good manners is a very necessary study. Like grace and beauty, it begets liking and an inclination to love one another at first sight.

> *Montaigne*, Essays, *1588*

(*See also* **BREEDING, MANNERS**)

COURTSHIP

Courtship to marriage is as a very witty prologue to a very dull play.

> *William Congreve*, The Old Bachelor, *1693*

Better to be courted and jilted
Than never to be courted at all.

> *Thomas Campbell (d. 1844), "The Jilted Nymph"*

Men are always doomed to be duped, not so much by the arts of the [female] sex as by their own imaginations. They are always wooing goddesses and marrying mere mortals.

> *Washington Irving*, Bracebridge Hall, *1822*

(*See also* **LOVE, MARRIAGE, SEDUCTION**)

COWARDS

Cowards die many times before their deaths;
The valiant never taste of death but once.

> *Shakespeare*, Julius Caesar, *1600*

Cowardice, as distinguished from panic, is almost always simply a lack of ability to suspend the functioning of the imagination.

> *Ernest Hemingway*, Men at War, *1942*

The human race is a race of cowards; and I am not only marching in that procession but carrying a banner.

> *Mark Twain, "Reflections on Being the Delight of God."*

The weak in courage is strong in cunning.
>*William Blake*, The Marriage of Heaven and Hell, *1790*

(*See also* **COURAGE, HEROES**)

CREATIVITY

Neither intelligence nor judgment are creative. If a sculptor is nothing but science and intelligence, his hands will have no talent.
>*Antoine de Saint-Exupéry*, Flight to Arras, *1942*

The creative person is both more primitive and more cultivated, more destructive, a lot madder and a lot saner, than the average person.
>*Frank Barron*, Think, *November-December 1962*

The creative person is not well brought up, he is ill-mannered [and] thumbs his nose at respectability.
>*Elsa Triolet (d. 1970)*, Le Monument

Human salvation lies in the hands of the creatively maladjusted.
>*Martin Luther King, Jr.*, Strength to Love, *1963*

(*See also* **ARTIST, POETS, WRITING**)

CREDULITY

The most imaginative people are the most credulous, for to them everything is possible.
>*Alexander Chase*, Perspectives, *1966*

Our credulity is greatest concerning the things we know the least about. And since we know least about ourselves, we are ready to believe all that is said about us. Hence the mysterious power of both flattery and calumny.
>*Eric Hoffer*, The Passionate State of Mind, *1955*

Each one readily believes what he fears or what he desires.
>*La Fontaine*, "The Wolf and the Fox," Fables, *1694*

There is no crime in the cynical American calendar more humiliating than to be a sucker.
>*Max Lerner*, Actions and Passions, *1949*

(*See also* **BELIEF, FLATTERY**)

CRIME

The study of crime begins with the knowledge of oneself.
> *Henry Miller,* The Air-Conditioned Nightmare, *1945*

Most men commit great crimes only because of their scruples about little ones.
> *Cardinal de Retz,* Mémoires, *1718*

The greatest crimes are caused by surfeit, not by want.
> *Aristotle (fl. 300 B.C.),* Politics

His reason for committing the crime [the murder of a stranger] was precisely to do it for no reason at all.
> *André Gide,* Lafcadio's Adventures, *1914*

CRISES

When written in Chinese the word "crisis" is composed of two characters — one represents danger and the other represents opportunity.
> *John F. Kennedy, Address, April 12, 1959*

We learn geology the morning after the earthquake.
> *Emerson,* The Conduct of Life, *1860*

(*See also* **ADVERSITY, FATE**)

CRITICISM

If a given combination of trees, mountains, water, and houses, say a landscape, is beautiful, it is not so by itself, but because of me, of my favor, of the idea or feeling I attach to it.
> *Charles Baudelaire,* Salon de 1859

You may scold a carpenter who has made you a bad table, though you cannot make a table.
> *Samuel Johnson, in Boswell's* Life, *June 15, 1763*

The greater one's love for a person the less room for flattery. The proof of true love is to be unsparing in criticism.
> *Molière,* The Misanthrope, *1666*

When a work lifts your spirits and inspires bold and noble thoughts in you, do not look for any other standard to judge by: the work is good, the product of a master craftsman.
> *La Bruyère,* Les Caractres, *1688*

A good writer is not necessarily a good book critic. No more so than a good drunk is automatically a good bartender.

> *Jim Bishop*, New York Journal American, *November 26, 1957*

(*See also* **FAULTS, JUDGING**)

CRITICISM, ESTHETIC

The real connoisseurs in art are those who make people accept as beautiful something everybody used to consider ugly, by revealing and resuscitating the beauty in it.

> *Edmond and Jules de Goncourt*, Journal, *June 30, 1881*

A good critic . . . describes his adventures among masterpieces.

> *Anatole France*, La Vie littéraire, *1892*

(*See also* **ART, LITERATURE**)

CROWDS

Nothing is so uncertain or unpredictable as the feelings of a crowd.

> *Livy*, Ab Urbe condita, *c. 29 B.C.*

In the crowd, herd, or gang, it is a mass-mind that operates — which is to say, a mind without subtlety, a mind without compassion, a mind, finally, uncivilized.

> *Robert Lindner*, Must You Conform? *1956*

He who goes into a crowd must now go one way and then another, keep his elbows close, retire, or advance, and quit the straight way, according to what he encounters.

> *Montaigne*, Essays, *1588*

(*See also* **PEOPLE, POPULATION**)

CRUELTY: *See* SADISM.

CULTURE

When I hear the word "culture" . . . I reach for my revolver.

> *Hanns Johst*, Schlageter, *1933.* [Comment mistakenly attributed to Hermann Göring.]

Man is born a barbarian, and only raises himself above the beast by culture.

> *Baltasar Gracian*, The Art of Worldly Wisdom, *1647*

Knowledge of [another] culture should sharpen our ability to scrutinize more steadily, to appreciate more lovingly, our own.

Margaret Mead, Coming of Age in Samoa, *1928*

The most powerful obstacle to culture . . . is the tendency to aggression, [which is] an innate, independent, instinctual disposition in man.

Freud, Civilization and Its Discontents, *1930*

[Culture] is a product of man: he projects himself into it, he recognizes himself in it; that critical mirror alone offers him his image.

Jean Paul Sartre, The Words, *1964*

We have ignored cultural literacy in thinking about education. . . . We ignore the air we breathe until it is thin or foul. Cultural literacy is the oxygen of social intercourse.

E.D. Hirsch, Jr., Cultural Literacy, *1987*

(*See also* **CIVILIZATION; LITERACY, CULTURAL**)

CURIOSITY

One shouldn't be too inquisitive in life
Either about God's secrets or one's wife.

Chaucer, The Canterbury Tales, *c. 1400*

Curiosity is one of the permanent and certain characteristics of a vigorous mind.

Samuel Johnson, The Rambler, *1750*

Ambition and curiosity are the two scourges of the soul: the latter prompts us to poke our noses into everything; the former prevents our leaving anything in doubt or undecided.

Montaigne, Essays, *1580*

(*See also* **QUESTIONS**)

CUSTOMS

Laws are sand, customs are rock. Laws can be evaded and punishment escaped, but an openly transgressed custom brings sure punishment.

Mark Twain, letter, 1908

Custom, that unwritten law,
By which the people keep even kings in awe.

Charles Davenant (d. 1714), Circe.

The despotism of custom is everywhere the standing hindrance to human advancement.

John Stuart Mill, On Liberty, *1859*

Custom adapts itself to expediency.

Tacitus, Annals, *c. A.D. 115*

(*See also* **LAWS, TRADITION**)

DANCING

. . . The loftiest, the most moving, the most beautiful of the arts, because it is no mere translation or abstraction from life; it is life itself.

Havelock Ellis, The Dance of Life, *1923*

Dancing is discovery and recreation, especially . . . the dance of love. Besides, it's the best way to get acquainted.

Léopold S. Senghor, au Congrès de la Jeunesse de Mali, 1960

Dance is the only art of which we ourselves are the stuff of which it is made.

Ted Shawn, Time, *July 25, 1955*

In my ballets, woman is first. Men are consorts. God made men to sing the praises of women. They are not equal to men: They are better.

George Ballanchine, Time, *September 15, 1980*

A good education is usually harmful to a dancer. A good calf is better than a good head.

Agnes de Mille, News summaries, February 1, 1954

DANGER

... The spur of all great minds.

George Chapman, Bussy d'Ambois, *c. 1604*

The wise man in the storm prays God, not for safety from danger, but for deliverance from the fear.

Emerson, Journals, *1833*

Danger past, God is forgotten.

Thomas Fuller, Gnomologia, *1732*

(*See also* **COURAGE**)

DAUGHTERS

Daughter am I in my mother's house;
But mistress in my own.

Rudyard Kipling, "Our Lady of the Snows," *1898*

These are my daughters, I suppose.
But where in the world did the children vanish?

Phyllis McGinley, "Ballad of Lost Objects," *1954*

My daughter! O my ducats! O my daughter!
Fled with a Christian! O my Christian ducats!

Shakespeare, The Merchant of Venice, *1596*

(*See also* **PARENTS, CHILDREN**)

DEATH AND DYING

Death may be the greatest of all human blessings.

Socrates (d. 399 B.C.), in Plato's Apology.

It is as natural to die as to be born.

Francis Bacon, Essays, *1625*

Death is the only thing we have not completely succeeded in vulgarizing.

Aldous Huxley, Eyeless in Gaza, *1936*

Death be not proud, though some have called thee
Mighty and dreadful, for thou art not so,

For those whom thou think'st thou dost overthrow,
Die not, poor death, nor yet canst thou kill me.

> *John Donne*, Holy Sonnets, *c. 1610*

It is a modest creed, and yet
Pleasant if one considers it,
To own that death itself must be,
Like all the rest, a mockery.

> *Shelley, "The Sensitive Plant," 1820*

Do not go gentle into that good night,
Old age should burn and rave at close of day.

> *Dylan Thomas, "Do Not Go Gentle . . . ," 1952*

Death in itself is nothing; but we fear
To be we know not what, we know not where.

> *John Dryden*, Aurengzebe, *1676*

To die is poignantly bitter, but the idea of having to die without
having lived is unbearable.

> *Erich Fromm*, Man for Himself, *1947*

Dying
Is an art, like everything else.
I do it exceptionally well.

> *Sylvia Plath, "Lady Lazarus," 1966*

Most people die at the last minute; others twenty years beforehand,
some even earlier. They are the wretched of the earth.

> *Louis Céline*, Voyage au bout du monde, *1932*

Thou, divine Death, to which everything returns and disappears,
Receive thy children into thy star-studded bosom;
Free us from time, number, space;
Give us back the peace that life interrupted.

> *Leconte de Lisle*, Poèmes antiques, *1852*

(*See also* **BIRTH, LIFE, SURVIVAL**)

DEBT

. . . is the worst poverty.

> *Thomas Fuller*, Gnomologia, *1732*

Let the world slide by, let the world go;
A fig for care, and a fig for woe!
If I can't pay, why I can owe
And death makes equal high and low.

> *John Heywood, "Be Merry, Friends," c. 1550*

A small loan makes a debt; a great one an enemy.

> *Publius Syrus*, Moral Sayings, *c. 50 B.C.*

First payment is what made us think we were prosperous, and the other nineteen is what showed us we were broke.

> *Will Rogers*, Autobiography, *1949*

DECEPTION

The easiest person to deceive is one's self.

> *Edward Bulwer-Lytton*, The Disowned, *1828*

Without some dissimulation no business can be carried on at all.

> *Lord Chesterfield*, Letters to His Son, *May 22, 1749*

Those who corrupt the public mind are just as evil as those who steal from the public purse.

> *Adlai Stevenson, speech, Albuquerque, NM, 1952*

The art of pleasing is the art of deceiving.

> *Vauvenargues*, Réflexions et maximes, *1747*

There are some things about which the public always wants to be deceived.

> *Cardinal de Retz (d. 1679)*, Mémoires.

(*See also* **CONCEALMENT, HYPOCRISY**)

DEEDS

Great naiveté is needed to perform great deeds.

> *René Crevel (d. 1935)*, L'Esprit contre la raison.

A man makes no noise over a good deed, but passes on to another.

> *Marcus Aurelius (d. 180)*, Meditations.

What I must do is all that concerns me, not what the people think.

> *Emerson, "Self-Reliance," 1841*

Nothing great was ever achieved without enthusiasm.

Emerson (d. 1882), Circles

Saying is one thing, doing another. We must consider the sermon and the preacher distinctly and apart.

Montaigne, Essays, *1588*

Most men are more capable of great actions than of good ones.

Montesquieu (d. 1755), Variétés

Our deeds determine us, as much as we determine our deeds.

George Eliot, Adam Bede, *1859*

(*See also* **ACTION, CONSEQUENCES**)

DEFEAT/VICTORY

Some defeats [are] more triumphant than victories.

Montaigne, Essays, *1588*

All victories breed hatred and a victory over one's superior is foolish or fatal.

Baltasar Gracián, The Art of Worldly Wisdom, *1647*

Frequently a big advantage can be gained by knowing how to give in at the right moment.

Fénelon, On the Education of Young Women, *1687*

(*See also* **ADVERSITY, CONQUERING**)

DEFENSE

Diplomacy and defense are not substitutes for one another. Either alone would fail.

John F. Kennedy, campaign speech, September 6, 1960

To be prepared for war is one of the most effectual means of preserving peace.

George Washington, speech, Congress, Jan. 8, 1790

(*See also* **SURVIVAL, WAR**)

DEMAGOGUE

The demagogue is usually sly, a detractor of others, a professor of humility, who avoids open and manly expositions of his course, [appealing] to passions and prejudices rather than to reason.

James Fenimore Cooper, The American Democrat, *1838*

Among men who have overturned the liberties of republics, the greatest number have begun their career by paying obsequious court to the people; commencing demagogues, and ending tyrants.

Alexander Hamilton, The Federalist, *1787*

The demagogue, whether of the Right or Left is an undetected liar.

Walter Lippmann, Atlantic Monthly, *1939*

(*See also* **DEMOCRACY, LEADERSHIP, POLITICS**)

DEMOCRACY

The one pervading evil of democracy is the tyranny of the majority, or rather that of the party, . . . that succeeds, by force or fraud, in carrying elections.

Lord Acton, The History of Freedom, *1907*

One of the evils of democracy is, you have to put up with the man you elect whether you want him or not.

Will Rogers, Autobiography, *1949*

Democracy is unstable as a political system as long as it remains a political system and nothing more, instead of being . . . not only a form of government, but a type of society and a manner of life.

R.H. Tawney, Equality, *1965*

I am opposed to parliamentary government and the power of the press, because they are the means by which the herd become masters.

Nietzsche, Will to Power, *1888*

Universal suffrage is the most monstrous and iniquitous of tyrannies —because the force of numbers is most brutal, having neither courage nor talent.

Paul Bourget, Le Disciple, *1889*

The danger is not that a particular class is unfit to govern; every class is unfit to govern.

Lord Acton to Mary Gladstone, April 24, 1881

Democracy is the worst form of government there is, except every other that's been tried.

Winston Churchill, attributed

(*See also* **EQUALITY, GOVERNMENT, POLITICAL PARTIES**)

DEMOCRACY AND CIVIL RIGHTS

The Right to Safety and Security of Person.
The Right to Equality of Opportunity.
The Right to Citizenship and its Privileges.
The Right to Freedom of Communication and Expression.

The President's Commission on Civil Rights, 1947

The very purpose of a Bill of Rights was to withdraw certain subjects from the vicissitudes of political controversy. . . . One's right to life, liberty, and property, to free speech, a free press, freedom of worship and assembly . . . may not be submitted to vote; they depend on . . . no elections.

Justice Jackson, W.Va. Board of Education vs. Barnette, *1943*

We hear about Constitutional rights, free speech and the free press. Every time I hear those words I say to myself, "That man is a Red, that man is a Communist." You never hear a real American talk like that.

Frank Hague, New York World-Telegram, *April 2, 1938*

(*See also* **FREE COUNTRY**)

DEMOCRACY, DEMISE OF

The death of democracy is not likely to be an assassination from ambush. It will be a slow extinction from apathy, indifference, and undernourishment.

Robert M. Hutchins, Great Books, *1954*

There are but two parties, . . . founded in the radical question, whether *People* or *Property* shall govern? Democracy implies a government by the people . . . Aristocracy implies a government of the rich.

Thomas Hart Benton, speech, U.S. Senate, 1835

Democracy cannot flourish half rich and half poor, any more than it can flourish half free and half slave.

Felix G. Rohatyn, New York Times, *June 3, 1987*

(*See also* **GREED, INDIFFERENCE**)

DEMOCRATIC IDEAL

Democracy . . . is a society in which the unbeliever feels undisturbed and at home. If there were only half a dozen unbelievers in America, their well-being would be a test of our democracy.

Alfred North Whitehead, The New Yorker, *February 18, 1956*

The dream of democracy is to raise the proletariat up to the level of stupidity of the bourgeois, which it has partially already achieved.

Gustave Flaubert to George Sand, 1871

Democracy is itself a religious faith. For some it comes close to being the only formal religion they have.

E.B. White, The New Yorker, *Feb. 18, 1956*

(*See also* **EDUCATION, INDIVIDUALISM, RIGHTS**)

DESIRES: *See* WANTS.

DESPAIR: *See* FORLORN, WORLD-WEARY.

DESPOTISM

When the white man governs himself, that is self-government; but when he governs himself and also governs another man, that is more than self-government —that is despotism.

Abraham Lincoln, speech, Peoria, Ill., October 16, 1854

The strongest phases of our new American philosophy . . . are the desire for enormous business, more wealth and less liberty, more despotism and less freedom of education, which always accompanies the absolute rule of the few.

Theodore Dreiser, Tragic America, *1931*

Q. What are the duties of Christians toward their rulers?
A. Love, respect, obedience, military service, . . . taxes.
Q. Why do we owe these duties to our Emperor [Napoleon]?
A. . . . Because God has established him as our savior and made him the agent of His powers, and because Jesus Christ bade us render unto Caesar that which is Caesar's.

Napoleonic catechism (1806), Grand Dictionnaire universel du XIXe
siècle 3:567

The people always have some champion whom they set over themselves and nurse into greatness. . . . This is the root from which a tyrant springs; at first, he is a protector.

Plato, The Republic, *c. 400 B.C.*

When the tyrant has disposed of foreign enemies by conquests or treaties, . . . he then stirs up some kind of a war, so the people will need a leader.

Plato, ibid.

(*See also* **DEMAGOGUE, TYRANNY**)

DESTINY: *See* FATE.

DEVIL

God seeks comrades and claims love,
the Devil seeks slaves and claims obedience.

Rabindranath Tagore, Fireflies, *1928*

An apology for the Devil: It must be remembered that we have only heard one side of the case. God has written all the books.

Samuel Butler (d. 1902), Note-Books.

Theology by its very nature tends and under given circumstances always will tend to become demonology.

Thomas Mann, Dr. Faustus, *1947*

(*See also* **GOD, HELL**)

DIFFERENCES

This nation was conceived in liberty and dedicated to the principle — among others — that honest men may honestly disagree; that if they all say what they think, a majority of the people will be able to distinguish truth from error.

Elmer Davis, But We Were Born Free, *1954*

If a man does not keep pace with his companions, perhaps it is because he hears a different drummer. Let him step to the music he hears, however measured or far away.

Henry David Thoreau, Walden, *1854*

To be alone is to be different; to be different is to be alone.

Suzanne Gordon, Lonely in America, *1976*

(*See also* **NONCONFORMITY**)

DIFFICULTY

Our energy is in proportion to the resistance it meets. We can attempt nothing great, but from a sense of the difficulties we have to encounter.

William Hazlitt, Characteristics, *1823*

Have the courage to face a difficulty lest it kick you harder than you bargained for.

Stanislaus I (d. 1766), Poland, Maxims

There is nothing so easy but it becomes difficult when you do it reluctantly.

Terence, Heauton Timoroumenos, *c. 150 B.C.*

(*See also* **ADVERSITY, COMPLAINT**)

DIPLOMAT

. . . A man who thinks twice before saying nothing.

Frederick Sawyer

. . . A person who can tell you to go to hell in such a way that you actually look forward to the trip.

Caskie Stinett, Out of the Red, *1960*

An ambassador is an honest man sent to lie abroad for the commonwealth.

Henry Wotton, Reliquiae Wottonianae, *1651*

[Advice to statesmen:] Keep strong, if possible. In any case, keep cool. Have unlimited patience. Never corner an opponent, and always assist him to save face. Put yourself in his shoes. Avoid self-righteousness like the devil — nothing so self-blinding.

Sir Basil Liddell Hart, Deterrent or Defense, *1960*

DISCIPLINE: *See* EDUCATION, SELF-CONTROL.

DISCONTENT: *See* HAPPINESS/UNHAPPINESS.

DISOBEDIENCE

Human history begins with man's act of disobedience which is at the same time the beginning of his freedom and development of his reason.

Erich Fromm, Psychoanalysis and Religion, *1950*

Let no man deceive you with vain words: for because of these things cometh the wrath of God upon the children of disobedience.

Paul to the Ephesians 5:6

(*See also* **REBELLION; SIN, ORIGINAL**)

DISSENT

The dissenter is every human being at those moments of his life when he resigns momentarily from the herd and thinks for himself.

Archibald MacLeish, "In Praise of Dissent," New York Times Book Review, *December 16, 1956*

That community is already in the process of dissolution where each man begins to eye his neighbor as a possible enemy, where nonconformity with the accepted creed, political as well as religious, is a mark of disaffection, . . . [and] where orthodoxy chokes freedom of dissent. . . .

Judge Learned Hand, speech, October 24, 1952

(*See also* **ARGUMENT, OPPOSITION**)

DISTRUST

It is more shameful to mistrust one's friends than to be deceived by them.

La Rochefoucauld, Maxims, 1665

There is nothing makes a man suspect much, more than to know little.

Francis Bacon, "Of Suspicion," 1625

Suspicion on one side breeds suspicion on the other, and new weapons beget counterweapons.

John F. Kennedy, Address, American University, 1963

(*See also* **TRUST**)

DIVORCE

Divorce is the psychological equivalent of a triple coronary by-pass. After such a monumental assault on the heart, it takes years to amend all the habits and attitudes that led up to it.

Mary K. Blakely, Parade, July 12, 1987

When a couple decide to divorce, they should inform both sets of parents before having a party and telling all their friends. This is not only courteous but practical. Parents may be very willing to pitch in with comments, criticism and malicious gossip of their own to help the divorce along.

P.J. O'Rourke, Modern Manners, *1983*

My mother and father are both speaking to solicitors. I expect they are fighting over who gets custody of me. I will be a tug-of-love child, and my picture will be in the newspapers. I hope my spots clear up before then.

Sue Townsend, The Secret Diary of Adrian Mole Aged 13-3/4, *1982*

Interviewer: How did you feel when you learned your parents were getting a divorce?
Jessamyn (aged 5): I thought the sun would never shine again. But it did.

ABC TV segment on divorce, Nov. 7, 1988

(*See also* **CONFLICT, MARRIAGE**)

DOGMATISM

The modern world is filled with men who hold dogmas so strongly that they do not even know they are dogmas.

G.K. Chesterton, Heretics, *1905*

There are many who lust for the simple answers of doctrine or decree. They are on the left and right. They are not confined to a single part of society. They are the terrorists of the mind.

A. Bartlett Giamatti, Address, Yale, May 26, 1986

Jesus does not think dogmatically. He formulates no doctrine. He is far from judging any man's belief by reference to any standard of dogmatic correctness. Nowhere does he demand that his hearers sacrifice thinking to believing.

Albert Schweitzer, Out of My Life and Thought, *1949*

(*See also* **FANATICISM, TOLERANCE/INTOLERANCE**)

DOGS: *See* **PETS, HOUSE**

DOING

Great actions are not always true sons
Of great and mighty resolutions.

Samuel Butler, Hudibras, *1663*

Fais ce que voudras [Do as you please].
> *Motto of coeducational monastery in Rabelais's* Gargantua

Those who don't do anything never make mistakes.
> *Théodore de Banville,* Odes funambulesques, *1857*

Here lies our sovereign lord the King [Charles II]
Whose promise none relied on;
He never said a foolish thing,
Nor ever did a wise one.
> *John Wilmot, Earl of Rochester, 1685*

(*See also* **ACTION, DEEDS**)

DOUBT/CERTAINTY

There is one thing certain, namely, that we can have nothing certain; therefore it is not certain that we can have nothing certain.
> *Samuel Butler,* Note-Books, *1912*

Doubting everything or believing everything are two equally convenient solutions, both of which save us from thinking.
> *Henri Poincaré (d. 1912),* La Science et l'hypothèse

Doubt is part of all religions. All the religious thinkers were doubters.
> *Isaac Bashevis Singer,* New York Times, *December 3, 1978*

Freedom of speech and freedom of action are meaningless without freedom to think. And there is no freedom of thought without doubt.
> *Bergen Evans,* The Natural History of Nonsense, *1946*

It is easier to believe than to doubt.
> *E.D. Martin (d. 1941),* The Meaning of a Liberal Education

The first step towards philosophy is incredulity.
> *Diderot,* Entretiens sur le Fils naturel, *1757*

The certainties of one age are the problems of the next.
> *R.H. Tawney,* Religion and the Rise of Capitalism, *1926*

Doubt is not a pleasant state of mind, but certainty is absurd.
> *Voltaire to Frederick the Great, 1767*

(*See also* **DOGMATISM, SKEPTICISM**)

DRAMA: *See* THEATER/STAGE.

DRESS/FASHION

The first thing the first couple did after committing the first sin was to get dressed. Thus Adam and Eve started the world of fashion, and styles have been changing ever since.

"Gilding the Lily," Time, *November 8, 1963*

Contrary to popular . . . opinion, aerobics have absolutely nothing to do with squeezing our body into hideous shiny Spandex, grinning like a deranged orangutan, and doing cretinous dance steps to debauched disco music.

Cynthia Heimel, Sex Tips for Girls, *1983*

To call a fashion wearable is the kiss of death. No new fashion worth its salt is ever wearable.

Eugenia Sheppard, New York Herald Tribune, *January 13, 1960*

The miniskirt enables young ladies to run faster, and because of it, they may have to.

John V. Lindsay, New York Times, *February 2, 1967*

For the wife she used to ramble through me pooches
When I was fast asleep aneath the quilt;
In the morning when I woke
I was always stoney broke
That's the reason noo I wear a kilt.

Harry Lauder (Scottish singer), "That's the Reason Noo I Wear a Kilt," 1906

You don't have to be dowdy to be a Christian.

Tammy Faye Bakker, Newsweek, *June 8, 1987*

(*See also* APPEARANCES, NOVELTY)

DRINK

Debauchee, n. One who has so earnestly pursued pleasure that he has had the misfortune to overtake it.

Ambrose Bierce, Devil's Dictionary, *1911*

Alcoholism isn't a spectator sport. Eventually the whole family gets to play.

Joyce Roberta-Burditt, The Cracker Factory, *1977*

Miniver Cheevy, born too late,
Scratched his head and kept on thinking;
Miniver Cheevy coughed and called it fate,
And kept on drinking.

> *Edwin Arlington Robinson, "Miniver Cheevy," 1910*

Drunkenness is temporary suicide.

> *Bertrand Russell (d. 1970),* The Conquest of Happiness

Candy
Is dandy
But liquor
Is quicker.

> *Ogden Nash, "Reflections on Ice-Breaking,"*
> Hard Lines, *1931*

Good liquor, I stoutly maintain,
Gives genius a better discerning.

> *Oliver Goldsmith,* She Stoops to Conquer, *1775*

'Tis not the drinking that is to be blamed, but the excess.

> *John Selden,* Table Talk, *1689*

You may be sober without being tactful, but you can never be tactful
without being sober.

> *Charles de Saint-Evremond to the Count d'Olonne, 1674*

Those that merely talk and never think,
That live in the wild anarchy of drink. . . .

> *Ben Jonson,* Underwoods, *1640*

There is wan thing an' on'y wan thing to be said in favor iv dhrink,
an' that is that it has caused manny a lady to be loved that otherwise
might've died single.

> *Finley Peter Dunne,* Mr Dooley Says, *1910*

Drink! for you know not whence you came, nor why;
Drink! for you know not why you go, nor where.

> *Omar Khayyam,* Rubaiyat, *c. 1200*

Over the bottle many a friend is found.

> *Hanan J. Ayalti,* Yiddish Proverbs, *1949*

Then trust me, there's nothing like drinking
So pleasant on this side the grave;

It keeps the unhappy from thinking,
And makes e'en the valiant more brave.

> *Charles Dibdin (d. 1814), "Nothing Like Grog."*

(*See also* **EXCESS, MODERATION, WINE**)

DRUGS

Drugs are boring with their [promise of] paradise. Better they should offer us wisdom; our age doesn't go for paradise.

> *Henri Michaux,* Connaissance par les gouffres, *1961*

Cocaine isn't habit-forming; I should know, I've been using it for years.

> *Quoted in Lillian Hellman,* Pentimento, *1962*

Marijuana . . . makes you sensitive. Courtesy has a great deal to do with being sensitive. Unfortunately marijuana makes you the kind of sensitive where you insist on everyone listening to the drum solo in Iron Butterfly's "In-a-Gadda-Da-Vida" fifty or sixty times.

> *P.J. O'Rourke,* Modern Manners, *1983*

The country hears about drugs from its leading writers, academics and artists occasionally but almost never with real passion. . . . What can the intellectuals do? They can use the power of their names, contacts, wit and creativity to fight for the money needed for treatment, research, police, job training and education at home — and the planning needed to slow narcotics production abroad.

> *A.M. Rosenthal, "The Drug Train,"* New York Times, *February 3, 1989*

DUTY

You will always find those who think they know what your duty is better than you know it.

> *Emerson, "Self-Reliance,"* Essays, *1841*

The burning conviction that we have a holy duty toward others is often a way of attaching our drowning selves to a passing raft.

> *Eric Hoffer,* The True Believer, *1951*

Without duty, life is soft and boneless; it cannot hold itself together.

> *Joseph Joubert,* Pensées, *1842*

Duty is what one expects from others, it is not what one does oneself.

> *Oscar Wilde,* A Woman of No Importance, *1893*

When a stupid man is doing something he is ashamed of, he always declares that it's his duty.

> *G.B. Shaw,* Caesar and Cleopatra, *1898*

I know of only one duty, and that is to love.

> *Albert Camus,* Notebooks, *1935–1942*

The strongest is never strong enough to be always the master, unless he transforms his strength into right, and obedience into duty.

> *Rousseau,* The Social Contract, *1762*

It is not what a lawyer tells me I *may* do; but what humanity, reason, and justice tell me I ought to do.

> *Edmund Burke,* Second Speech on Conciliation, *1775*

Our duty is to be useful, not according to our desires but according to our powers.

> *Amiel,* Journal, *December 17, 1856*

Allah obligeth no man to more than he hath given him ability to perform.

> *The Koran*

Nobody is bound by any obligation unless it has first been freely accepted.

> *Ugo Betti,* The Fugitive, *1953*

If you are willing to forget that there is an element of duty in love and of love in duty, then it's easy to choose between them.

> *Jean Giraudoux,* Siegfried, *1928*

The paths of glory at least lead to the Grave, but the paths of duty may not get you Anywhere.

> *Thurber,* "The Patient Bloodhound," Fables for Our Time, *1940*

(*See also* **RESPONSIBILITY**)

EATING

As life's pleasures go, food is second only to sex. Except for salami and eggs. Now that's better than sex, but only if the salami is thickly sliced.

Alan King, New York Times, *October 28, 1981*

Seeing is deceiving. It's eating that's believing.

James Thurber, Further Fables for Our Time, *1956*

One cannot think well, love well, sleep well, if one has not dined well.

Virginia Woolf, A Room of One's Own, *1929*

Gluttony is mankind's exclusive prerogative.

Brillat-Savarin, Physiologie du goût, *1825*

He who keeps on eating after his stomach is full digs his grave with his teeth.

Turkish proverb

The one way to get thin is to reestablish a purpose in life. . . . Obesity is a mental state, a disease brought on by boredom and disappointment.

Cyril Connolly, The Unquiet Grave, *1945*

In a restaurant I order everything I don't want, so I have a lot to play around with while everybody else is eating.

Andy Warhol (d. 1987), From A to B and Back Again

78

How to eat [spinach] like a child: Divide into piles. Rearrange again into piles. After five or six maneuvers, sit back and say you are full.

Delia Ephron, New York Times, *1983*

ECOLOGY: *See* NATURAL RESOURCES.

ECONOMY

. . . The art of making the most of life; the love of economy is the root of all virtue.

G.B. Shaw, Man and Superman, *1905*

Political institutions are a superstructure resting on an economic foundation.

V.I. Lenin (d. 1924), Three Sources and Three Constituent
Parts of Marxism

Blessed are the young, for they shall inherit the national debt.

Herbert Hoover, attributed

Reaganomics, that makes sense to me. It means if you don't have enough money, it's because poor people are hoarding it.

Kevin Rooney, quoted in CQ, *1984*

The whole process of production . . . has been brought almost entirely under the power of a few, so that a very few rich and exceedingly rich men have laid a yoke of almost slavery on the unnumbered masses of non-owning workers.

Pope Leo XIII, De Rerum novarum, *1891*

The conflict in America is between two kinds of planning: . . . privately planned economic scarcity by companies for profits or publicly planned economic abundance for people.

Walter Reuther, The Nation, *December 3, 1952*

The interest of landlords is . . . opposed to the interests of every other class in the country.

David Ricardo, Political Economy and Taxation, *1817*

One can relish the varied idiocy of human action during a [financial] panic to the full, for, while it is a time of great tragedy, nothing is being lost but money.

J.K. Galbraith, The Great Crash, 1929.

I learned more about economics from one South Dakota dust storm than I did in all my years in college.

Hubert Humphrey, speech, 1960

Economic growth without social progress lets the great majority of the people remain in poverty while a privileged few reap the benefits of rising abundance.

John F. Kennedy, Message to Congress, March 14, 1961

We face the question whether a still higher "standard of living" is worth its cost in things natural, wild, and free.

Aldo Leopold, A Sand County Almanac, *1949*

the high cost of
living isnt so bad if you
dont have to pay for it.

Don Marquis, Archy and Mehitabel, *1927*

(*See also* **BUSINESS AND INDUSTRY**)

EDUCATION

Do not be puffed up because of your knowledge nor overconfident because you are a learned person. Take counsel with the ignorant as well as with the wise, for the limits of proficiency cannot be reached and no person is ever fully skilled.

Egyptian Magistrate Ptah-Hotep to his son, c. 2400 B.C.

When Aristotle was asked how much educated men were superior to the uneducated, he replied, "As much as the living are to the dead."

Dionysius of Halicarnassus, Aristotle, *20 B.C.*

Education is the taming or domestication of the soul's raw passions — not suppressing them or excising them, which would deprive the soul of its energy — but forming and informing them as art.

Allan Bloom, The Closing of the American Mind, *1987*

Education is an admirable thing, but it is well to remember from time to time that nothing worth knowing can be taught.

Oscar Wilde, "The Critic as Artist," *1890*

The preservation of the means of knowledge among the lowest ranks is of more importance to the public than all the property of the rich men in the country.

John Adams, Dissertation on the Canon . . . Law, *1765*

Respect for the fragility and importance of an individual life is still the mark of the educated man.

Norman Cousins, Saturday Review, *1954*

If you feel that you have both feet planted on level ground, then the university has failed you.

Robert Goheen, Time, *June 23, 1961*

It takes most men five years to recover from a college education, and to learn that poetry is as vital to thinking as knowledge.

Brooks Atkinson, Once Around the Sun, *1951*

No absurdity [is] so palpable but that it may be firmly planted in the human head if you only begin to inculcate it before age five, by constantly repeating it with an air of great solemnity.

Arthur Schopenhauer, Studies in Pessimism, *1851*

Human nature is not a machine to be built after a model, and set to do exactly the work prescribed for it, but a tree, which requires to grow and develop itself on all sides, according to the tendency of the inward forces which make it a living thing.

John Stuart Mill, On Liberty, *1859*

There is only one curriculum, no matter what the method of education: what is basic and universal in human experience and practice, the underlying structure of culture.

Paul Goodman, Growing Up Absurd, *1960*

The aim of the college, for the individual student, is to eliminate the need in his life for the college; the task is to help him become a self-educating man.

C. Wright Mills, Power, Politics and People, *1963*

Education, which was at first made universal in order that all might be able to read and write, has been found capable of serving quite other purposes. By instilling nonsense it unifies populations and generates collective enthusiasm.

Bertrand Russell, Unpopular Essays, *1950*

In the first place God made idiots. This was for practice. Then he made school boards.

Mark Twain, Following the Equator, *1897*

(*See also* **LEARNING; LITERACY, CULTURAL; TEACHING**)

EDUCATION: DISCIPLINE

Let early education be a sort of amusement; you will then be better able to discover the [child's] natural bent.

Plato, The Republic, *c. 375 B.C.*

With children, use force; with adults, reason; such is the natural order of things. Wise men need no laws at all.

Rousseau, Emile, *1762*

Perhaps the most valuable result of all education is the ability to make yourself do the thing you have to do, when it ought to be done, whether you like it or not.

Walter Bagehot, Physics and Politics, *1879*

Children have to be educated, but they have also to be left to educate themselves.

Abbé Dimnet, Art of Thinking, *1928*

(*See also* **SELF-CONTROL**)

EDUCATION, LIBERAL

What is desperately needed . . . is the skepticism and the sense of history that a liberal arts education provides.

Felix G. Rohatyn, New York Times, *June 3, 1987*

Knowledge of human nature is the beginning and end of political education.

Henry Adams, Education, *1907*

A faithful study of the liberal arts humanizes character and permits it not to be cruel.

Ovid, Epistolae ex Ponto, *c. A.D. 10*

(*See also* **KNOWLEDGE, SCHOLARS**)

EFFORT

Effort is only effort when it begins to hurt.

Ortega y Gasset, "In Search of Goethe," Partisan Review, *December 1949*

To travel hopefully is a better thing than to arrive, and the true success is to labor.

Robert Louis Stevenson, Virginibus puerisque, *1881*

Life has not taught me to expect nothing, but she has taught me not to expect success to be the inevitable result of my endeavors. She taught me to seek sustenance from the endeavor itself, but to leave the result to God.

Alan Paton, "The Challenge of Fear," Saturday Review, *September 9, 1967*

(*See also* **DIFFICULTY, WORK**)

ELOQUENCE

True eloquence consists in saying all that should be said, and that only.

La Rochefoucauld, Maxims, *1665*

Eloquence lies as much in the tone of the voice, in the eyes, and in the speaker's manner, as in his choice of words.

La Rochefoucauld, ibid.

Continuous eloquence wearies.

Pascal Pensées, *1670*

(*See also* **PERSUASION, PUBLIC SPEAKING**)

EMOTIONS

Let's not forget that the little emotions are the great captains of our lives and we obey them without realizing it.

Vincent Van Gogh to his brother Théo, 1889

All the knowledge I possess everyone else can acquire, but my heart is all my own.

Goethe, The Sorrows of Young Werther, *1774*

It is as healthy to enjoy sentiment as to enjoy jam.

G.K. Chesterton, Generally Speaking, *1928*

In a full heart there is room for everything, and in an empty heart there is room for nothing.

Antonio Porchia, Voces, *1968*

We know too much and feel too little. At least, we feel too little of those creative emotions from which a good life springs.

Bertrand Russell, Authority and the Individual, *1949*

(*See also* **PASSION, SENSIBILITY**)

ENDS AND MEANS

Whatsoever thou takest in hand, remember the end, and thou shalt never do amiss.

Apocrypha, *Ecclesiasticus 7:36*

A great politician has to concern himself less with the means than with the goal.

Adolf Hitler, Mein Kampf, *1932*

The end cannot justify the means for the simple and obvious reason that the means employed determine the nature of the ends produced.

Aldous Huxley, Ends and Means, *1937*

(*See also* **MOTIVES, PURPOSE**)

ENDURANCE

The man who sticks it out against his fate
shows spirit, but the spirit of a fool.

Euripides, Heracles, *c. 420 B.C.*

To endure what is unendurable is true endurance.

Japanese proverb

People are too durable, that's their main trouble. They can do too much to themselves, they last too long.

Bertolt Brecht, Jungle of Cities, *1924*

(*See also* **PATIENCE, RESIGNATION**)

ENEMIES

Love your enemies, do good to them that hate you, bless them that curse you, and pray for them that despitefully use you.

Jesus, Sermon on the Mount, Matthew 5:44

As society is now constituted, a literal adherence to the moral precepts scattered throughout the Gospels would mean sudden death.

Alfred North Whitehead, Dialogues, *1954*

If we are bound to forgive an enemy, we are not bound to trust him.

Thomas Fuller, Gnomologia, *1732*

Never ascribe to an opponent motives meaner than your own.

J.M. Barrie, Address, St. Andrew's, May 22, 1922

A man cannot be too careful in the choice of his enemies.

Oscar Wilde, The Picture of Dorian Gray, *1891*

Pay attention to your enemies, for they are the first to discover your mistakes.

Antisthenes (fl. 400 B.C.), in Diogenes Laertius, Lives.

We have met the enemy and they are us!

Walt Kelly, Pogo, *1971*

(*See also* **HATRED, STRANGERS**)

THE ENGLISH: HOW DIFFERENT!

It is not that the Englishman can't feel — it is that he is afraid to feel. He has been taught at his public school that feeling is bad form. He must not express great joy or sorrow, or even open his mouth too wide when he talks — his pipe might fall out.

E.M. Forster, Abinger Harvest, *1936*

The difference between the vanity of a Frenchman and an Englishman seems to be this: the one thinks everything right that is French, the other thinks everything wrong that is not English.

William Hazlitt, Characteristics, *1823*

One matter Englishmen don't think is the least funny is their happy consciousness of possessing a deep sense of humor.

Marshall McLuhan, The Mechanical Bride, *1951*

England is the paradise of individuality, eccentricity, heresy, anomalies, hobbies, and humours.

George Santayana, Soliloquies in England, *1922*

An Englishman thinks he is moral when he is only uncomfortable.

G.B. Shaw, Man and Superman, *1930*

(*See also* **LANGUAGE, LITERATURE**)

ENTERPRISE

Nothing will ever be attempted, if all possible objections must be first overcome.

Samuel Johnson, Rasselas, *1759*

The passion to get ahead is sometimes born of the fear lest we be left behind.

Eric Hoffer, The Passionate State of Mind, *1954*

None will improve your lot
If you yourself do not.

Bertolt Brecht, Roundheads and Peakheads, *1933*

If you don't crack the shell, you can't eat the nut.

Persian proverb

(*See also* **AMBITION, EFFORT**)

ENVY

Envy is a littleness of soul, which cannot see beyond a certain point, and if it does not occupy the whole space feels itself excluded.

William Hazlitt, Characteristics, *1823*

Whoever envies another confesses his superiority.

Samuel Johnson (fl. 1750), The Rambler, *No. 183*

Every other sin hath some pleasure annexed to it, or will admit of an excuse: envy alone wants both.

Robert Burton, The Anatomy of Melancholy, *1651*

How much better it is to be envied than pitied.

Herodotus (fl. 450 B.C.), Histories

(*See also* **JEALOUSY**)

EQUALITY

We hold these truths to be self-evident, that all men and women are created equal. . . .

Elizabeth Cady Stanton, Women's Rights Convention, Seneca Falls, NY, 1848

All animals are equal, but some are more equal than others.

George Orwell, Animal Farm, *1945*

Just as modern mass production requires the standardization of commodities, so the social process requires standardization of man, and this standardization is called equality.

Erich Fromm, The Art of Loving, *1956*

It is the American vice, the democratic disease which expresses its tyranny by reducing everything unique to the level of the herd.

Henry Miller, The Wisdom of the Heart, *1941*

Every individual of the community at large has an equal right to the protection of government.

Alexander Hamilton to the Constitutional Convention, June 29, 1787

The Lord so constituted everybody that no matter what color you are you require the same amount of food.

Will Rogers, Autobiography, *1949*

(*See also* **ARISTOCRACY, DEMOCRACY**)

ERA

In one era and out the other.

Sam Levenson, Title, *1973*

In every age "the good old days" were a myth. No one ever thought they were good at the time. For every age has consisted of crises that seemed intolerable to the people who lived through them.

Brooks Atkinson, Once Around the Sun, *1951*

If it is the great delusion of moralists to suppose that all previous ages were less sinful than their own, then it is the great delusion of intellectuals to suppose that all previous ages were less sick.

Louis Kronenberger, Contemporary Manners, *1954*

The reason for the sadness of this modern age [19th century] and the men who live in it is that it looks for the truth in everything and finds it.

E. and J. de Goncourt, Journal, *October 23, 1864*

(*See also* **PAST, TWENTIETH CENTURY**)

ERROR

An error is the more dangerous in proportion to the degree of truth contained in it.

Amiel, Journal, *1883*

No error is so monstrous that it fails to find defenders among the ablest men.

Lord Acton to Mary Gladstone, April 24, 1881

People still retain the errors of their childhood, their nation, and their age, long after they have accepted the truths needed to refute them.

> *Condorcet*, Progress of the Human Mind, *1794*

If you shut your door to all errors truth will be shut out.

> *Rabindranath Tagore*, Stray Birds, *1916*

The most powerful cause of error is the war existing between the senses and reason.

> *Pascal* Pensées, *1670*

Nothing is more damaging to a new truth than an old error.

> *Goethe (d. 1832)*, Proverbs in Prose

A man should never be ashamed to own he has been in the wrong, which is but saying . . . that he is wiser today than he was yesterday.

> *Alexander Pope, in Swift*, Miscellanies

Give me a fruitful error any time, full of seeds, bursting with its own corrections. You can keep your sterile truth for yourself.

> *Vilfredo Pareto (d. 1923), on Johann Kepler*

(*See also* **TRUTH VS. FALSEHOOD**)

ESCAPE

Those that fly may fight again,
Which he can never do that's slain.
Hence timely running's no mean part
Of conduct, in the martial art.

> *Samuel Butler*, Hudibras, *1663*

A runaway monk never speaks well of his monastery.

> *Italian Proverb*

(*See also* **COWARDS, ILLUSION**)

EVIL

God may still be in His Heaven, but there is more than sufficient evidence that all is not right with the world.

> *Irwin Edman*, Adam, the Baby, and the Man from Mars, *1929*

There is no explanation for evil. It must be looked upon as a necessary part of the order of the universe.

> *W. Somerset Maugham*, The Summing Up, *1938*

The evil that is in the world almost always comes of ignorance, and good intentions may do as much harm as malevolence if they lack understanding.

Albert Camus, The Plague, *1947*

The present evils of the world: its huge armaments, its vast accumulations of capital, its advancing materialism, and declining arts.

Henry Adams, Presidential Address, American Historical Association, 1894

Evil is not *merely* a by-product of unfavorable circumstances; it is too widespread and too deep-seated to admit of any such explanation; so widespread, so deep-seated that one can only conclude that what the religions have always taught is true, and that evil is endemic in the heart of man.

C.E.M. Joad, God and Evil, *1943*

Glory be to God, who determined, for reasons we know not, that wickedness and stupidity should rule the world.

Arthur de Gobineau, Nouvelles asiatiques, *1876*

When you choose the lesser of two evils, always remember that it is still an evil.

Max Lerner, Actions and Passions, *1949*

Between two evils, I always pick the one I never tried before.

Mae West, Klondike Annie, *movie, 1936*

(*See also* **CRIME, GOOD, SIN**)

EVOLUTION

The general theory of evolution . . . assumes that in nature there is a great, unital, continuous and everlasting process of development, and that all natural phenomena without exception . . . are subject to the same great law of causation.

Ernest Haeckel, Frei Wissenschaft und frei Lehre, *1878*

It is an error to imagine that evolution signifies a constant tendency to increased perfection. That process undoubtedly involves a constant . . . adaptation [of the organism] to new conditions whether the direction of the modifications . . . be upward or downward.

T.H. Huxley, The Struggle for Existence in Human Society, *1888*

Evolution is not a force but a process, not a cause but a law.

John Morley, On Compromise, *1874*

I don't believe your old bastard theory of evolution, . . . I believe it's pure jackass nonsense. . . . If a minister believes and teaches evolution, he is a skunk, a hypocrite, and a liar.

Billy Sunday, Revival Meeting, 1912

(*See also* **PROGRESS, STRUGGLE FOR SURVIVAL**)

EXAMPLE

. . . is always more efficacious than precept.

Samuel Johnson, Rasselas, *1759*

Few things are harder to put up with than the annoyance of a good example.

Mark Twain, Pudd'nhead Wilson, *1894*

EXCELLENCE

To enjoy the things we ought and hate the things we ought has the greatest bearing on excellence of character.

Aristotle, Nicomachean Ethics, *c. 300 B.C.*

There is none who cannot teach somebody something, and there is none so excellent that he cannot be excelled.

Baltasar Gracian, The Art of Worldly Wisdom, *1647*

(*See also* **ARTIST, GENIUS, SUPERIORITY**)

EXCESS

To go beyond is as wrong as to fall short.

Confucius (fl. 500 B.C.), Analects

The road of excess leads to the palace of wisdom.

William Blake, The Marriage of Heaven and Hell, *1790*

The archer that shoots over, misses as much as he that falls short.

Montaigne, Essays, *1588*

Too much work and too much energy kill a man just as effectively as too much assorted vice or too much drink.

Kipling, Plain Tales from the Hills, *1888*

Excess on occasion is exhilirating. It prevents moderation from deadening the effect of a habit.

W. Somerset Maugham, The Summing Up, *1938*

(*See also* **MODERATION**)

EXISTENCE

That I exist is a perpetual surprise which is life.

Rabindranath Tagore, Stray Birds, *1916*

At a given moment I open my eyes and exist. And before that, during all eternity, what was there? Nothing.

Ugo Betti, The Inquiry, *1945*

An atom tossed in a chaos made
Of yeasting worlds, which bubble and foam.
Whence have I come?
What would be my home?
I hear no answer. I am afraid!

Amy Lowell, Sword Blades and Poppy Seeds, 1914

(*See also* **IDENTITY, LIFE**)

EXISTENTIAL MAN

Man finally knows that he is alone in the indifferent immensity of the Universe, from which he emerged by accident.

Jacques Monod, Le Hasard et la nécessité, *1970*

Man is abandoned on earth in the midst of his infinite responsibilities, without help, with no aim but what he sets himself.

Jean Paul Sartre, Being and Nothingness, *1943*

There is no I as such but only the basic I-You and the I of the basic
    word I-It. . . .
The world as experience belongs to the basic word I-It.
The basic word I-You establishes the world of relation.

Martin Buber, I and Thou, *1923*

God is Being-Itself. God is not *a* being, not even the highest one. . . .
God as *a* being is below Being itself; [if] He has something above Himself, He is an idol.

Paul Tillich, Love, Power, and Justice, *1954*

(*See also* **ABSURD, EXISTENCE, RESPONSIBILITY**)

EXPERIENCE

Experience is a hard teacher because she gives the test first, the lesson after.

> *Vernon Law*, This Week, *August 14, 1960*

I have but one lamp by which my feet are guided, and that is the lamp of experience, [judging] the future by the past.

> *Patrick Henry, speech, Virginia Convention, 1775*

You cannot create experience, you undergo it.

> *Albert Camus*, Notebooks, 1935–1942, *1962*

Nothing ever becomes real till it is experienced — Even a proverb is no proverb to you till your Life is illustrated by it.

> *John to George and Georgina Keats, May 3, 1891*

Experience is not what happens to you; it is what you do with what happens to you.

> *Aldous Huxley*, Reader's Digest, *March 1956*

The knowledge of the world is only to be acquired in the world, and not in a closet.

> *Lord Chesterfield*, Letters to His Son, *October 4, 1746*

From their own experience or from the recorded experience of others (history), men learn only what their passions and their metaphysical prejudices allow them to learn.

> *Aldous Huxley*, Collected Essays, *1959*

Experience is a comb which nature gives us when we are bald.

> *Chinese proverb*

(*See also* **INVOLVEMENT, LIFE**)

EXPLANATION

"Are you lost, daddy," I asked tenderly.
"Shut up," he explained.

> *Ring Lardner (d. 1933)*, "The Young Immigrants."

"I can't explain myself, I'm afraid, sir," said Alice,
"because I'm not myself, you see."
"I don't see," said the Caterpillar.

> *Lewis Carroll*, Alice . . . in Wonderland, *1865*

Never explain. Your friends do not need it and your enemies will not believe you anyway.

Elbert Hubbard, The Note Book, *1927*

EXPLOITATION

No system has ever existed which did not in some form involve the exploitation of some human beings for the advantage of others.

John Dewey, The Quest for Certainty, *1929*

Of course I believe in free enterprise but the democratic principle is that there never was, never has been, never will be, room for the ruthless exploitation of the many for the benefit of the few.

Harry S. Truman, Congressional Record, *May 9, 1944*

(*See also* **ECONOMY**)

EXTREMISM

We must not overlook the role that extremists play. They are the gadflies that keep society from being too complacent. . . .

Abraham Flexner, Universities, *1930*

The world acquires value only through its extremists and endures only through its moderates; extremists make the world great, moderates keep it stable.

Paul Valéry, in The Nation, *January 5, 1957*

What is objectionable, what is dangerous about extremists is not that they are extreme, but that they are intolerant. The evil is not what they say about their cause, but what they say about their opponents.

Robert F. Kennedy, The Pursuit of Justice: Extremism,
Left and Right, *1964*

(*See also* **FANATICISM, ZEAL**)

FACTS

You can't make the Duchess of Windsor into Rebecca of Sunnybrook Farm. The facts of life are very stubborn things.
Cleveland Amory, Conversation, October 6, 1955

People in general have no notion of the sort and amount of evidence often needed to prove the simplest fact.
Peter Mere Latham (d. 1875), Collected Works *2:525*

Some circumstantial evidence is very strong, as when you find a trout in the milk.
Henry David Thoreau (d. 1862), Miscellanies

(*See also* **REALITY**)

FAILURE: *See* **SUCCESS**.

FAITH

'Tis not the dying for a faith that's so hard, . . . every man of every nation has done that—'tis the living up to it that's difficult.
William Makepeace Thackeray, Henry Esmond, *1852*

Faith is an excitement and an enthusiasm: it is a condition of intellectual magnificence to which we must cling as to a treasure and not squander [in] . . . priggish argument.

> *George Sand to Des Planches, May 25, 1866*

Life is doubt, and faith without doubt is nothing but death.

> *Miguel de Unamuno,* Poesias, *1907*

Faith may be defined briefly as an illogical belief in the occurrence of the improbable.

> *H.L. Mencken,* Prejudices, *Third Series, 1922*

If there was no faith there would be no living in this world. We couldn't even eat hash with safety.

> *Josh Billings,* His Complete Works, *1888*

In the Affairs of this World, Men are saved not by Faith but by the Want of it.

> *Benjamin Franklin,* Poor Richard's Almanack, *1754*

Faith always implies the disbelief of a lesser fact in favor of a greater.

> *Oliver Wendell Holmes,* The Autocrat of the Breakfast Table, *1858*

Reason is the greatest enemy that faith has.

> *Martin Luther,* Table Talk, *1569*

Proofs are the last things looked for by a truly religious mind which feels the imaginative fitness of its faith.

> *George Santayana,* Interpretations of Poetry and Religion, *1900*

(*See also* **BELIEF, DOUBT**)

FALSEHOOD: *See* LIES, TRUTH VS. FALSEHOOD.

FAMILY

The family is the association established by nature for the supply of man's everyday wants.

> *Aristotle (d. 322 B.C.),* Politics

The Family! Home of all social evils, a charitable institution for indolent women, a prison workshop for the slaving breadwinner, and a hell for children.

> *August Strindberg,* The Son of a Servant, *1886*

Big sisters are the crabgrass in the lawn of life.

Charles M. Schulz, Peanuts, *1952*

A man's womenfolk, whatever their outward show of respect for his merit and authority, always regard him secretly as an ass, and with something akin to pity.

H.L. Mencken, In Defense of Women, *1922*

To my way of thinking, the American family started to decline when parents began to communicate with their children. When we began to "rap," "feed into one another," "let things hang out" that mother didn't know about and would rather not.

Erma Bombeck, If Life Is a Bowl of Cherries—
What Am I Doing in the Pits? *1978*

(*See also* **CHILDREN, MARRIAGE, PARENTHOOD**)

FAMOUS

Mere wealth, I am above it.
It is the reputation wide,
The playwright's group, the poet's pride
That eagerly I covet.

Phyllis McGinley, "A Ballad of Anthologies," *1941*

I'm never going to be famous. My name will never be writ large on the roster of Those Who Do Things. I don't do anything. Not one single thing. I used to bite my nails, but I don't even do that any more.

Dorothy Parker, "The Little Hours," *1941*

I'm famous. That's my job.

Jerry Rubin, Growing (Up) at 37, *1976*

Some are born great, some achieve greatness, and some hire public relations officers.

Daniel Boorstin, The Image, *1962*

(*See also* **CELEBRITY**)

FANATICISM

. . . consists in redoubling your effort when you have forgotten your aim.

Santayana, Life of Reason, *1905*

Belief in a Divine mission is one of the many forms of certainty that have afflicted the human race.

> *Bertrand Russell,* Unpopular Essays, *1950*

If there is anything more dangerous to the life of the mind than having no independent commitment to ideas, it is having an excess of commitment to some special and constricting idea.

> *Richard Hofstadter,* Anti-Intellectualism in American Life, *1963*

Fanaticism is just one step away from barbarism.

> *Denis Diderot (fl. 1760),* Essai sur le mérite.

A fanatic is a man that does what he thinks the Lord wud do if He knew the facts iv the case.

> *Peter Finley Dunne,* Mr. Dooley's Opinions, *1901*

(*See also* **DOGMATISM, EXTREMISM**)

FASCISM

Liberty is not an end, it is a means. As a means, it needs to be controlled and dominated.

> *Benito Mussolini, speech, Undine, September 20, 1922*

Today the most striking of post-war experiences . . . are marked by the defeat of Liberalism.

> *Mussolini, in* Gerarchia, *March 1923*

Fascism conceives of the State as an absolute, in comparison with which all individuals or groups are relative. . . .

> *"The Doctrine of Fascism,"* Italian Encyclopedia, *1932*

The classic Fascist movements have represented the extremism of the center.

> *Seymour Lipset,* Political Man, *1963*

If Fascism came to America it would be on a program of 100 percent Americanism.

> *Huey P. Long, U.S. Army Talk, March 24, 1945*

Fascists can't argue, so they kill.

> *Victor Marguerite (d. 1942), speech, French Academy*

(*See also* **DESPOTISM, LIBERALISM, TYRANNY**)

FASHION: *See* DRESS

FATE

See how the Fates their gifts allot,
For A is happy—B is not.
Yet B is worthy, I dare say,
Of more prosperity than A!

W.S. Gilbert, The Mikado, *1885*

Unseen in the background, Fate was quietly slipping the lead into the boxing glove.

P.G. Wodehouse, Very Good, Jeeves, *1930*

They . . . who await
No gifts from Chance, have conquered Fate.

Matthew Arnold, "Resignation," 1849

Human reason has only to will more strongly than fate, and she *is* fate.

Thomas Mann, The Magic Mountain, *1924*

If fate means you to lose, give him a good fight anyhow.

William McFee, Casuals of the Sea, *1916*

(*See also* CHANCE, FORTUNE)

FATHERS: *See* PARENTS.

FAULTS

The greatest of faults, I should say, is to be conscious of none.

Thomas Carlyle, Heroes and Hero-worship, *1841*

Certain defects are necessary for the existence of individuality.

Goethe, Elective Affinities, *1809*

Misfortunes one can endure—they come from outside, they are accidents. But to suffer for one's own faults—ah! there is the sting of life.

Oscar Wilde, Lady Windermere's Fan, *1892*

(*See also* WEAKNESS)

FEAR

. . . The main source of superstition, and one of the main sources of cruelty. To conquer fear is the beginning of wisdom.

> *Bertrand Russell,* Outline of Intellectual Rubbish, *1950*

How does one kill fear, I wonder? How do you shoot a specter through the heart, slash off its spectral head, take it by its spectral throat?

> *Joseph Conrad,* Lord Jim, *1900*

The only permanent emotion of the inferior man is fear—fear of the unknown, the complex, the inexplicable.

> *H.L. Mencken,* Prejudices, *1919*

I am . . . afraid of airplanes, deep-sea diving, psychiatry. The earth alone comforts me, regardless of how much dirt it may contain.

> *Françoise Sagan,* La Garde du coeur, *1972*

Men fear thought as they fear nothing else on earth—more than ruin, more even than death.

> *Bertrand Russell (d. 1970),* Selected Papers

There are times when fear is good.
It must keep its watchful place
at the heart's controls. There is
advantage in the wisdom won from pain.

> *Aeschylus,* Eumenides, *458 B.C.*

A good scare is worth more to a man than good advice.

> *Edgar Watson Howe,* Country Town Sayings, *1911*

(*See also* **ANXIETY, COURAGE**)

FEMINISM: *See* WOMEN'S MOVEMENT.

FICTION: *See* NOVEL, WRITER.

FLATTERY

Of all the diseases of the mind there is not one more epidemical or more pernicious than the love of flattery.

> *Sir Richard Steele,* The Spectator, *December 3, 1711*

'Tis an old maxim in the schools,
That flattery's the food of fools;
Yet now and then your men of wit
Will condescend to take a bit.

> *Jonathan Swift (d. 1745), "Cadenas and Vanessa," 1713*

(*See also* **SELF-ESTEEM**)

FOLLY

Men are contented to be laughed at for their wit, but not for their folly.

> *Jonathan Swift,* Thoughts on Various Subjects, *1711*

If we're not foolish young, we're foolish old.

> *Chaucer, "The Knight's Tale,"* Canterbury Tales, *c. 1400*

The folly of one man is the fortune of another.

> *Francis Bacon,* Essays, *1625*

It is folly alone that stays the fugue of Youth and beats off louring Old Age.

> *Erasmus,* In Praise of Folly, *1509*

My only books
Were women's looks
And folly's all they've taught me.

> *Thomas Moore, "The Time I've Lost in Wooing," 1834*

Those who realize their folly are not true fools.

> *Chuang tzu,* Works, *fourth century* B.C.

What use is wisdom when folly reigns?

> *Hanan J. Ayalti, ed.,* Yiddish Proverbs, *1949*

(*See also* **STUPIDITY**)

FOOLS

A learned fool is more foolish than an ignorant one.

> *Molière,* Les Femmes savantes, *1672*

Fools have a great advantage over the wise: they are always self-satisfied.

> *Napoleon I (d. 1821), Correspondence*

There are two kinds of fools: those who suspect nothing and those who suspect everything.

Le Prince de Ligne (d. 1814), Mes Ecarts

Young men think old men are fools; but old men *know* young men are.

George Chapman, All Fools, *1605*

Even a fool, when he holdeth his peace, is counted wise.

Proverbs 17:28

The fool is a social type . . . Whereas the hero represents the victory of good over evil, the fool represents values . . . rejected by the group.

Orrin Klapp, "The Fool as a Social Type," 1953

FORCE

To win the easiest victory over reason, [use] terror and force.

Adolf Hitler, Mein Kampf, *1924*

Justice without force is impotent, force without justice is tyranny. We must reconcile them, either by making justice strong or force just.

Pascal, Pensées, *1670*

(*See also* **POWER, VIOLENCE**)

FORETHOUGHT

The man who knows when not to act
is wise. To my mind, bravery is forethought.

Euripides, The Suppliant Women, *c. 420 B.C.*

To fear the worst often cures the worse.

Shakespeare, Troilus and Cressida, *1601*

Look to the end, no matter what it is you are considering. Often enough God gives a man a glimpse of happiness and then utterly ruins him.

Solon, quoted in Herodotus, Histories, *fifth century B.C.*

(*See also* **PRUDENCE**)

FORGETTING: *See* MEMORY.

FORGIVENESS

Of course [God] will forgive me; that's His business.

Heinrich Heine's dying words, 1856

Our Father who art where thou art
Surrounded by unfaithful Angels
Sincerely don't suffer any more for us
You must take into account
That the gods are not infallible
And that we have come to forgive everything.

Nicanor Parra, Breathing Exercises, *1966*

The discoverer of the role of forgiveness in the realm of human affairs was Jesus of Nazareth.

Hannah Arendt, The Human Condition, *1958*

Only the brave know how to forgive. . . . A coward never, . . . it's not in his nature.

Laurence Sterne, Sermons, *1760*

It is easier to forgive an enemy than to forgive a friend.

William Blake, Jerusalem, *1804–20*

Nothing is harder to forgive than real merit.

Denis Diderot, Jack the Fatalist, *1770*

Amnesty: An act by which sovereigns commonly pardon injustices committed by themselves.

Graffiti, French student revolt, Paris, May 1968

(*See also* **JESUS, CHRISTIANITY**)

FORTUNE, GOOD/BAD

We are all quite capable of bearing up under other people's misfortunes.

La Rochefoucauld, Reflections, *1665*

It takes more strength of character to withstand good fortune than bad.

La Rochefoucauld, Ibid.

The power of fortune is confessed only by the miserable, for the happy impute all their success to prudence or merit.

Jonathan Swift, Thoughts on Various Subjects, *1711*

There are two tragedies in life: one is not to get your heart's desire; the other is to get it.

> *G.B. Shaw,* Man and Superman, *1905*

I can enjoy [Fortune] when she's kind;
But when she dances in the wind,
And shakes the wings and will not stay,
I puff the prostitute away.

> *John Dryden,* Imitation of Horace, *1685*

Luck never made a man wise.

> *Seneca,* Letters to Lucilius, *c. A.D. 50*

Fortune is not on the side of the faint-hearted.

> *Sophocles,* Phaedra, *c. 430 B.C.*

(*See also* **ADVERSITY, CHANCE**)

FRANKNESS

Of all plagues, good Heaven, thy wrath can send,
Save me, oh save me from the candid friend!

> *George Canning,* New Morality, *1798*

Honesty and wisdom are such a delightful pastime at another's expense!

> *Nathaniel Hawthorne,* The Blithedale Romance, *1852*

Lies kill love, it's been said. Well, what about frankness, then?

> *Abel Hermant,* Eloge du mensonge, *1925*

(*See also* **HONESTY, SINCERITY, TRUTH**)

FRAUD: *See* DECEPTION.

FREE

The spirit of liberty is the spirit of Him who, near two thousand years ago, taught mankind that lesson it has never learned, but never quite forgotten: that there is a kingdom where the least shall be heard and considered side by side with the greatest.

> *Judge Learned Hand,* The Faith We Fight for, *1952*

Men of faith know that throughout history the crimes committed in liberty's name have been exceeded only by those committed in God's name.

Mills E. Godwin, Governor of Virginia, speech, 1967, on the Klu Klux Klan's burning crosses.

[That man is free] who is self-reliant, . . . who masters his passions; who fears neither poverty nor death nor prison; who resists his appetites [and] despises worldly ambition.

Horace, Satires, 35 B.C.

I call that mind free which jealously guards its intellectual rights and powers, which calls no man master, which does not content itself with a passive or hereditary faith, [and] receives new truth as an angel from Heaven.

William Ellery Channing, "Spiritual Freedom," 1848

We have confused the free with the free and easy.

Adlai Stevenson, Putting First Things First, 1960

Freedom is the will to be responsible to ourselves.

Nietzsche, Twilight of the Idols, 1888

Let us forget such words, and all they mean,
as Hatred, Bitterness and Rancor, Greed,
Intolerance, Bigotry; let us renew
our faith and pledge to Man, his right to be
Himself, and free.

Edna St. Vincent Millay, "Poem and Prayer for an Invading Army"

True individual freedom cannot exist without economic security and independence. People who are hungry and out of a job are the stuff of which dictatorships are made.

Franklin D. Roosevelt, message to Congress, January 11, 1944.

(*See also* **FREE COUNTRY, FREEDOM VS. LICENSE**)

FREE COUNTRY

[Let any] who would wish to dissolve this Union or to change its republican form . . . stand undisturbed as monuments of the safety with which error of opinion may be tolerated where reason is left free to combat it.

Thomas Jefferson, First Inaugural Address, 1801

When the legislative and executive powers are united in the same person, or in the same body of magistrates, there can be no freedom.

Montesquieu, Spirit of the Laws, *1750*

I believe there are more instances of the abridgment of the freedom of the people by gradual and silent encroachments of those in power than by violent and sudden usurpations.

James Madison, speech, Virginia Convention, 1788

When men are brought face to face with their opponents, forced to listen and learn and mend their ideas, they cease to be children . . . and begin to live like civilized men.

Walter Lippmann, Atlantic Monthly, *August 1939*

The most certain test by which we judge whether a country is really free is the amount of security enjoyed by minorities.

Lord Acton, The History of Freedom in Antiquity, *1877*

The real guarantee of freedom is an equilibrium of social forces. . . . No one gang or group—neither the proletariat, nor the capitalists, nor the landowners, nor the bankers, nor the army, nor the church, nor the state itself—[should] have unlimited power.

Max Eastman, Reflections on the Failure of Socialism, *1955*

My definition of a free society is a society where it is safe to be unpopular.

Adlai Stevenson, speech, Detroit, 1952

Liberty is the possibility of doubting, of making a mistake, . . . of searching and experimenting, . . . of saying No to any authority— literary, artistic, philosophical, religious, social, and even political.

Ignazio Silone, The God That Failed, *1950*

There is danger from all men. The only maxim of a free government ought to be to trust no man living with power to endanger the public liberty.

John Adams, Notes for an Oration at Braintree, 1772

Freedom is an indivisible word. If we want to enjoy it, and fight for it, we must be prepared to extend it to everyone.

Wendell L. Willkie (d. 1944), One World.

(*See also* **GOVERNMENT**)

FREEDOM, ESCAPE FROM

O God . . . I am free, deliver me from freedom.
Paul Claudel, Cinq Grandes Odes, *1910*

Escape from Freedom.
Erich Fromm, Title, 1941

Maybe people are tired of Liberty. They have had a surfeit of it. Liberty is no longer a chaste and austere virgin. . . . Today's youth are moved by other slogans: Order, Hierarchy, Discipline.
Mussolini, speech, March 1923

The end result of [freedom] will always be . . . a dictatorship of the masses. Believe me, behind that word "freedom" demons lurk.
Bernhard Rust, Nazi Minister of Education, speech, Göttingen, 1937

The people never give up their liberties but under some delusion.
Edmund Burke, speech, Buckinghamshire, 1784

(*See also* **DISCIPLINE, ORDER**)

FREEDOM VS. LICENSE

The liberty of the individual to do as he pleases, even in innocent matters, is not absolute. It must frequently yield to the common good.
Justice George Sutherland, Atkins vs. Children's Hospital, 1925

Man's freedom consists solely in this: that he obeys the laws of nature because he himself recognizes them as such and not because they have been imposed on him.
Mikhail Bakunin, Dieu et l'état, *1882*

Only by unintermitted agitation can a people be kept sufficiently awake to principle, not to let liberty be smothered in material prosperity.
Wendell Phillips, Address, Anti-Slavery Society, Boston, 1852

The ideal changes, Nature remains; and the best use man can make of freedom—is to make no use of it whatsoever.
Jean Grenier (d. 1971), Le Bon Usage de la liberté

FREE SPEECH

Free speech is a tricky issue and cannot be taken too literally.

S. Norman Haq, "Salman Rushdie, Blame Yourself,"
New York Times, *February 23, 1989*

Almost nobody means precisely what he says when he makes the declaration, "I'm in favor of free speech."

Heywood Broun, "The Miracle of Debs,"
New York World, *October 23, 1926*

The sound of tireless voices is the price we pay for the right to hear the music of our own opinions.

Adlai Stevenson, speech, New York City, August 28, 1952

The right to be heard does not automatically include the right to be taken seriously.

Hubert Humphrey, speech, Madison, Wis., August 23, 1965

(*See also* **PRESS/MEDIA**)

FREE WILL

The greatest gift that God in His bounty made . . . was the freedom of the will, with which the intelligent creatures were and are endowed.

Dante, The Divine Comedy, *1321*

There is no such thing as free will. The mind is induced to wish this or that by some cause and that cause is determined by another cause, and so on back to infinity.

Spinoza, Ethics, *1677*

(*See also* **SELF-DETERMINATION**)

FRIENDSHIP

The friend is the man who knows all about you, and still likes you.

Elbert Hubbard, The Notebook, *1927*

A man of active and resilient mind outwears his friendships just as certainly as he outwears his love affairs, his politics and his epistemology.

H.L. Mencken, Prejudices, Third Series, *1922*

Every one that flatters thee
Is no friend in misery.
Words are easy, like the wind,
Faithful friends are hard to find.

Richard Barnfield, Poems, *1598*

Before the Flowers of Friendship Faded Friendship Faded.

Gertrude Stein, title, 1930

One friend in a lifetime is much; two are many; three are hardly possible.

Henry Adams, Education, *1907*

True friendship is like sound health; the value of it is seldom known until it is lost.

Charles Caleb Colton, Lacon, *1825*

(*See also* **COMPANY, LONELINESS, INTIMACY**)

FUNERALS: *See* **BURIALS.**

FUTURE

. . . That period of time in which our affairs prosper, our friends are true and our happiness is assured.

Ambrose Bierce, The Devil's Dictionary, *1911*

If a man examine carefully his thoughts he will be surprised to find how much he lives in the future. His well-being is always ahead.

Emerson, Journals, *1827*

Only mothers can think of the future—because they give birth to it in their children.

Maxim Gorky, Vassa Zheleznova, *1910*

The future is called "perhaps," which is the only possible thing to call the future. And the only important thing is not to allow that to scare you.

Tennessee Williams, Orpheus Descending, *1957*

The future you shall know when it has come; before then, forget it.

Aeschylus, Agamemnon, *458 B.C.*

I believe the future is only the past again, entered through another gate.

> *Arthur Wing Pinero,* The Second Mrs. Tanqueray, *1893*

Future shock: the shattering stress and disorientation that we induce in individuals by subjecting them to too much change in too short a time.

> *Alvin Toffler,* Future Shock, *1970*

(*See also* **PAST, PRESENT**)

GAMBLING

The best throw of the dice is to throw them away.

English proverb

A man's idee iv a card game is war—crool, devastatin', and pitiless.
A lady's idee iv it is a combynation iv larceny, embezzlement, an'
burglary.

Peter Finley Dunne, Mr. Dooley on Making a Will, *1919*

Adventure upon all the tickets in the lottery, and you lose for certain;
and the greater the number of your tickets the nearer you approach
to this certainty.

Adam Smith, The Wealth of Nations, *1776*

Whoever plays deep must necessarily lose his money or his character.

Lord Chesterfield, Letters to His Godson, *1773*

GENERALIZATION

All generalizations are false, including this one.

Alexander Chase, Perspectives, *1966*

To generalize is to be an idiot. To particularize is alone the distinction of merit—general knowledges are those knowledges that idiots
possess.

William Blake, Sir Joshua Reynolds' Discourses, *1798*

GENERATION GAP

... A chasm, amorphously situated in time and space, that separates those who have grown up absurd from those who will, with luck, grow up absurd.

> *Bernard Rosenberg*, Dictionary for the Disenchanted, *1972*

Men fight for liberty and win it with hard knocks. Their children, brought up easy, let it slip away again, poor fools. And their grandchildren are once more slaves.

> *D.H. Lawrence*, Classical American Literature, *1922*

Nothing so dates a man as to decry the younger generation.

> *Adlai Stevenson, speech, University of Wisconsin, 1952*

(*See also* **PARENTS, CHILDREN**)

GENEROSITY: *See* BENEVOLENCE, GIVING.

GENIUS

... An infinite capacity for taking pains.

> *Jane Ellice Hopkins*, Work Amongst Working Men, *1870*

Better beware of notions like genius and inspiration; they are a sort of magic wand and should be used sparingly by anybody who wants to see things clearly.

> *Ortega y Gasset*, Notes on the Novel, *1925*

Genius is the ability to see things invisible, to manipulate things intangible, to paint things that have no features.

> *Joseph Joubert*, Pensées, *1842*

[The source of genius] is imagination alone, or, what amounts to the same thing, the refinement of the senses that sees what others do not see, or sees them differently.

> *Eugène Delacroix*, Journal, *April 27, 1824*

The man of genius is he and he alone who finds such joy in his art that he will work at it come hell or high water.

> *Stendhal*, Life of Haydn, *1814*

A musician must make music, an artist must paint, a poet must write, if he is to be ultimately at peace with himself. What a man can be, he must be.

> *Abraham H. Maslow*, Motivation and Personality, *1954*

Talent is that which is in a man's power; genius is that in whose power a man is.

> *James Russell Lowell,* Literary Essays, II, *1870*

Men of genius are meteors destined to burn themselves out in lighting up their age.

> *Napoleon Bonaparte,* Discours de Lyon, *1771*

The greatest wrong of genius is in offending virtue and making modesty blush.

> *François Villemain (d. 1870),* Mélanges littéraires

God made me and broke the mold.

> *Rousseau,* Confessions, *1782*

We wish genius and morality were affectionate companions, but it is a fact that they are often bitter enemies.

> *Artemus Ward, "Morality and Genius," 1872*

The public is wonderfully tolerant. It forgives everything except genius.

> *Oscar Wilde, "The Critic as Artist," 1891*

(*See also* **TALENT**)

GENTLEMAN

It is almost a definition of a gentleman to say he is one who never inflicts pain.

> *John Henry Newman,* The Idea of a University, *1858*

A gentleman never insults anyone unintentionally.

> *Oscar Wilde, in conversation.*

The true gentleman does not advertise himself.

> *La Rochefoucauld (d. 1680),* Maxims

One can be a gentleman and still write bad verse.

> *Molière,* The Misanthrope, *1666*

GIVING

Magnanimity will not consider the prudence of its motives.

> *Vauvenargues,* Reflections and Maxims, *1746*

We do not quite forgive a giver. The hand that feeds us is in some danger of being bitten.

> *Emerson,* Essays: Second Series, *1844*

Not what we give, but what we share—
For the gift without the giver is bare;
Who gives himself with his alms feeds three—
Himself, his hungering neighbor, and me.

> *James Russell Lowell,* Vision of Sir Launfal, *1848*

You need more tact in the dangerous art of giving than in any other social action.

> *William Bolitho,* Twelve Against the Gods, *1929*

People who think they're generous to a fault usually think that's their only fault.

> *Sydney J. Harris,* On the Contrary, *1962*

(*See also* **BENEVOLENCE**)

GHOSTS: *See* **ILLUSION, IMAGINATION.**

GLORY

Glory ought to be the consequence, not the motive of our actions.

> *Pliny the Younger,* Letters, *c. A.D. 100*

The nearest way to glory—a shortcut, as it were—is to strive to be what you wish to be thought to be.

> *Socrates, quoted in Cicero,* De Officiis, *44 B.C.*

Glory is largely a theatrical concept. There is no striving for glory without a vivid awareness of an audience.

> *Eric Hoffer,* The True Believer, *1951*

The boast of heraldry, the pomp of pow'r,
And all that beauty, all that wealth e'er gave,
Awaits alike the inevitable hour,
The paths of glory lead but to the grave.

> *Thomas Gray,* "Elegy," *1750*

GLUTTONY: *See* **EATING.**

GOD

Hear, O Israel: the Lord our God is one Lord: and thou shalt love the Lord thy God with all thine heart, and with all thy soul, and with all thy might.

Deuteronomy 6:4–5

God is a child who amuses himself, going from laughing to crying for no reason, each day reinventing the world to the chagrin of hair-splitters, pedants, and preachers, who try to teach God his job as Creator.

Elie Faure, L'Esprit des formes, 1927

Teach us, good Lord, to serve Thee as Thou deservest:
To give and not to count the cost;
To fight and not to heed the wounds;
To toil and ask no reward. . . .

Ignatius Loyola, Prayer, 1548

Ministers [talk] of God as if they had a monopoly on the subject.

Henry David Thoreau, Walden, 1854

If God were not a necessary Being of Himself, He might almost seem to be made for the use and benefit of men.

John Tillotson (d. 1694), Sermon

Believe in no other God than the one who insists on justice and equality among men.

George Sand to Mme. d'Agoult, July 1836

Mankind have banned the Divinity from their presence; they have relegated him to a sanctuary; the walls of the temple restrict his view; he does not exist outside of it.

Diderot, Pensées philosophiques, 1746

The existence of a world without God seems to me less absurd than the presence of a God, existing in all his perfection, creating an imperfect man in order to make him run the risk of Hell.

Armand Salacrou, "Certitudes et incertitudes," 1943

It was subtle of God to learn Greek when he wished to become an author—and not to learn it better.

Nietzsche, Beyond Good and Evil, 1886

Seeing so much poverty everywhere makes me think that God is not rich. He gives the appearance of it, but I suspect some financial difficulties.

Victor Hugo, Les Misérables, 1862

All your Western theologies, the whole mythology of them, are based on the concept of God as a senile delinquent.

Tennessee Williams, The Night of the Iguana, *1961*

God is the immemorial refuge of the incompetent, the helpless, the miserable. They find not only sanctuary in His arms, but also a kind of superiority, soothing to their macerated egos: He will set them above their betters.

H.L. Mencken, Minority Report, *1956*

God without the devil is dead, being alone.

Samuel Butler, Note-Books, *1912*

God is our name for the last generalization to which we can arrive.

Emerson, Journals, *1836*

An honest God is the noblest work of man.

Robert C. Ingersoll, The Gods, *1872*

We need God, not in order to understand *why*, but in order to . . . give a meaning to the Universe.

Miguel Unamuno, The Tragic Sense of Life, *1913*

I am waiting for them to prove that God is really American.

Lawrence Ferlinghetti, A Coney Island of the Mind, *1958*

(*See also* **DEVIL, EXISTENTIAL MAN**)

GOLD

. . . The most useless thing in the world. I am not interested in money but in the things of which money is the symbol.

Henry Ford, quoted in Fortune.

Gold, which leads [us] everywhere, has become our national God. There is only one vice, poverty; one virtue, wealth. If you are not rich, you are scorned.

Diderot, Conversation of a Father with His Children, *1772*

Though wisdom cannot be gotten with gold, still less can it be gotten without it.

> *Samuel Butler (d. 1902)*, Note-Books.

GOLDEN RULE

All things whatsoever ye would that men should do to you, do ye even so to them: for this is the law and the prophets.

> *Matthew 7:12*

Do unto yourself as your neighbors do unto themselves and look pleasant.

> *George Ade*, Hand-Made Fables, *1920*

Do not do unto others as you would that they should do unto you. Their tastes may not be the same.

> *G.B. Shaw, "Maxims for Revolutionists," 1898*

The golden rule is that there is no golden rule.

> *Shaw*, Man and Superman, *1903*

GOOD VS. EVIL

Be not overcome of evil but overcome evil with good.

> *Paul to the Romans 12:20*

Whatever happens in accordance with nature should be accounted good.

> *Cicero*, De Senectute, *44 B.C.*

Nothing is good for everyone, but only relatively for some people.

> *André Gide*, The Counterfeiters, *1925*

There is nothing either good or bad but thinking makes it so.

> *Shakespeare*, Hamlet, *1600*

Goodness without wisdom always accomplishes evil.

> *Robert A. Heinlein*, Strangers in a Strange Land, *1961*

Desire persuades me one way, reason another. I see the better and approve it, but I follow the worse.

> *Ovid (d. A.D. 17)*, Metamorphoses

The omission of good is no less reprehensible than the commission of evil.

Plutarch, Moralia, *c. A.D. 100*

Good and evil . . . are not what popular opinion accounts them; many who seem to be struggling with adversity are happy; many, amid great affluence, are miserable.

Tacitus, Annals, *c. A.D. 115*

We cannot freely and wisely choose the right way for ourselves unless we know both good and evil.

Helen Keller, My Religion, *1927*

The character of human life, like the character of all life, is "ambiguity": the inseparable mixture of good and evil, the true and false, the creative and destructive forces—both individual and social.

Paul Tillich, Time, *May 17, 1963*

(*See also* **EVIL**)

GOOD NATURE

The teeth are smiling, but is the heart?

Congolese proverb

Good nature is worth more than knowledge, more than money, more than honor, to the persons who possess it.

Henry Ward Beecher, Proverbs from Plymouth Pulpit, *1887*

Of cheerfulness, or a good temper—the more it is spent, the more of it remains.

Emerson, The Conduct of Life, *1860*

Good-fellowship, unflagging, is the prime requisite for success in our society, and the man or woman who smiles only for reasons of humor or pleasure is a deviate.

Marya Mannes, More in Anger, *1958*

A good disposition is a virtue in itself, and it is lasting; the burden of the years cannot depress it, and love that is founded on it endures to the end.

Ovid, The Art of Beauty, *c. A.D. 8*

(*See also* **TEMPERAMENT**)

GOODNESS

It must be a good thing to be good or ivrybody wudden't be pretendin' he was.

Finley Peter Dunne, Observations by Mr. Dooley, *1902*

Goodness does not more certainly make men happy than happiness makes them good.

Walter Savage Landor, Imaginary Conversations, *1853*

Do good by stealth, and blush to find it fame.

Alexander Pope, Epilogue to the Satires, *1738*

No man can be good for long if goodness is not in demand.

Bertolt Brecht, The Good Woman of Setzuan, *1940*

Seek not goodness from without; seek it within yourselves, or you will never find it.

Epictetus, Discourses, *c. A.D. 100*

A good man isn't good for everything.

John W. Gardner, No Easy Victories, *1968*

It is from reason that justice springs, but goodness is born of wisdom.

Maurice Maeterlinck, Wisdom and Destiny, *1898*

Goodness is the only investment that never fails.

Thoreau, Walden, *1854*

(*See also* **CORRUPTION, EVIL**)

GOOD SENSE

Everybody thinks himself so well supplied with it that even those most difficult to please . . . never desire more of it than they already have.

René Descartes, Discourse on Method, *1637*

We rarely think that people have good sense unless they agree with us.

La Rochefoucauld, Reflections, *1678*

(*See also* **INTELLIGENCE, REASON**)

GOSSIP

I don't at all like knowing what people say of me behind my back. It makes one far too conceited.

Oscar Wilde, An Ideal Husband, *1895*

There are two kinds of people who blow through life like a breeze, And one kind is gossipers, and the other kind is gossipees. ·

Ogden Nash, "I Have It on Good Authority," Verses from 1929 On, *1949*

There is only one thing in the world worse than being talked about, and that is not being talked about.

Oscar Wilde, The Picture of Dorian Gray, *1891*

(*See also* **SLANDER, TALKING**)

GOVERNMENT

As long as I was in the White House I ran the executive branch of the government, and no one was ever allowed to act in the capacity of President . . . except [me].

Harry S. Truman, Democratic Digest, *1958*

The worst thing in this world, next to anarchy, is government.

Henry Ward Beecher, Proverbs from Plymouth Pulpit, *1887*

Administration, n. An ingenious abstraction in politics, designed to receive the kicks and cuffs due to the . . . president.

Ambrose Bierce, The Devil's Dictionary, *1911*

It is perfectly true that that government is best which governs least. It is equally true that that government is best which provides most.

Walter Lippmann, "The Red Herring," 1914

A compassionate government keeps faith with the trust of the people and cherishes the future of their children.

Lyndon B. Johnson, My Hopes for America, *1964*

No matter how noble the objectives of a government, if it blurs decency and kindness, cheapens human life, and breeds ill will and suspicion—it is an evil government.

Eric Hoffer, The Passionate State of Mind, *1954*

The test of any government is the extent to which it increases the good in the people.

Aristotle (d. 322 B.C.), Politics

Government is more than the sum of all the interests, it is the paramount interest, the public interest. It must be the efficient, effective agent of a responsible citizenry, not the shelter of the incompetent and the corrupt.

Adlai Stevenson, Speech, Bloomington, Ill., 1948

Governments are best classified by considering who are the "somebodies" they are in fact endeavoring to satisfy.

Alfred North Whitehead, Adventures in Ideas, *1933*

Any system of government will work well when everything is going well. It's the system that functions in the pinches that survives.

John F. Kennedy, Why England Slept, *1940*

Society in every state is a blessing, but Government even in its best state, is a necessary evil; in its worst state, an intolerable one.

Thomas Paine, Common Sense, *1776*

A people living under the . . . threat of war and invasion is very easy to govern. It demands no social reforms. It does not haggle over armaments and military expenditures. It pays without discussion, it ruins itself, and that is a fine thing for the financiers and manufacturers for whom patriotic terrors are an abundant source of gain.

Anatole France, Penguin Island, *1908*

(*See also* **BUREAUCRACY, DEMOCRACY, TYRANNY**)

GOVERNMENT FUNCTIONS

Government is a contrivance of human wisdom to provide for human wants. Men have a right that these wants should be provided for, [including] the want of a sufficient restraint upon their passions.

Edmund Burke, The Revolution in France, *1790*

Governments exist to protect the rights of minorities. The loved and the rich need no protection.

Wendell Phillips, speech, Boston, December 21, 1860

Many people consider the things which government does for them to be social progress, but they consider the things government does for others as socialism.

Earl Warren, speech, Madison, Wis., June 1955

That government is best which governs best.

John M. Hutchins, Address, New York, January 21, 1959

Certain things we cannot accomplish . . . by any process of government. We cannot legislate intelligence. We cannot legislate morality. No, and we cannot legislate loyalty, for loyalty is a kind of morality.

A. Whitney Griswold, Essays on Education, *1954*

The great security against a gradual concentration of the several powers in the same department, consists in giving to those who administer each department the necessary constitutional means and personal motives to resist encroachments of the others.

James Madison, The Federalist, *1788*

GRAFFITI

Poster: SAVE WATER—REMEMBER THE SHORTAGE
"Stop and think. As long as God water the earth there can be no shortage."
"God dint pipe it here."

Fort Monmouth, N.J., 1943

Man, preceded by the forest,
Is followed by the desert.

Latin Quarter, Paris, 1968

"God is dead."—Nietzsche.
"Nietzsche is dead."—God.

New York subway, 1972

"Cogito ergo sum."—Descartes.
"Coito ergo sum."—Freud.

Men's room, Adelphi University, 1982

"Christ is the answer."
"What was the question?"

New York subway, 1964

GRATITUDE

Next to ingratitude, the most painful thing to bear is gratitude.

Henry Ward Beecher, Proverbs, *1887*

Gratitude is a debt which usually goes on accumulating like blackmail; the more you pay, the more is exacted.

Mark Twain, Autobiography, *1924*

(*See also* **APPRECIATION**)

GREATNESS

Great men are but life-sized. Most of them, indeed, are rather short.

Max Beerbohm, And Even Now, *1920*

The greatest spirits are capable of the greatest vices as well as the greatest virtues.

Descartes, Discourse on Method, *1639*

I distrust great men. They produce a desert of uniformity around them and often a pool of blood too, and I always feel a little man's pleasure when they come a cropper.

E.M. Forster, Two Cheers for Democracy, *1951*

Great and good are seldom the same man.

Thomas Fuller, Gnomologia, *1732*

No man is truly great who is great only in his own lifetime. The test of greatness is the page of history.

William Hazlitt, Table Talk, *1822*

A great man need not be virtuous, nor his opinions right, but he must have a firm mind, a distinctive luminous character.

George Santayana, Winds of Doctrine, *1913*

It is easy in the world to live after the world's opinion; it is easy in solitude to live after our own; but the great man is he who in the midst of the crowd keeps with perfect sweetness the independence of solitude.

Emerson, "Self-Reliance," *1841*

"My name is Ozymandias, king of kings:
Look on my works, ye Mighty, and despair!"
Nothing beside remains. Round the decay
Of that colossal wreck, boundless and bare,
The lone and level sands stretch far way.

Percy Bysshe Shelley, "Ozymandias," *1817*

Great men are almost always bad men, even when they exercise influence and not authority, still more when you superadd the tendency . . . [to] corruption by authority.

Lord Acton to Mandell Creighton, April 5, 1887

The history of the world is but the biography of great men.

Thomas Carlyle, Heroes and Hero Worship, *1840*

In historical events great men—so-called—are but labels used for naming an event, and like labels, they have the least possible connection with the event itself.

Leo Tolstoy, War and Peace, *1865*

Great men help dazzle the people; . . . after that, they dazzle themselves even more dangerously.

Cardinal de Retz (d. 1679), Mémoires

FIGARO: Because you're a great nobleman, you think you're a gifted person. . . . Nobility, wealth, reputation, high office—that all makes you proud of yourself! But what did you do to deserve it? You took the trouble to be born, that's all.

Beaumarchais, The Marriage of Figaro, *1784*

(*See also* **HEROES**)

GREED

Yuppies' creed: "I want it all and I want it now."

Russell Baker, New York Times, *February 6, 1988*

I think the enemy is here before us. . . . I think the enemy is simple selfishness and compulsive greed. . . . I think he stole our earth from us, destroyed our wealth, and ravaged and despoiled our land.

Thomas Wolfe, You Can't Go Home Again, *1949*

each generation wastes a little more of the future with greed and lust for riches.

Don Marquis, archy and mehitable, *1927 [Archy, a cockroach, types by jumping on the keys, but he can't operate the shift key.]*

(*See also* **EXCESS**)

GRIEF/SORROW

There is no grief which time does not lessen and soften.

Cicero (d. 43 B.C.), Epistolae

Grief drives men into habits of serious reflection, sharpens the understanding and softens the heart.

John Adams to Thomas Jefferson, May 6, 1816

Great grief is a divine and terrible radiance which transfigures the wretched.

Victor Hugo, Les Misérables, *1862*

Let us remember that sorrow alone is the creator of great things.

Ernest Renan, La Réforme intellectuelle, *1871*

Happiness is salutary for the body, but it is sorrow that develops spiritual strength.

Marcel Proust, The Past Recaptured, *1927*

It is better to drink of deep griefs than to taste shallow pleasures.

William Hazlitt, Characteristics, *1823*

When a man or woman loves to brood over a sorrow and takes care to keep it green in their memory, you may be sure it is no longer a pain to them.

Jerome K. Jerome, The Idle Thoughts of an Idle Fellow, *1889*

Grief can't be shared. Everyone carries it alone, his own burden, his own way.

Anne Morrow Lindbergh, "Theodore," Dearly Beloved, *1962*

Happiness is beneficial for the body, but it is grief that develops the powers of the mind.

Marcel Proust, The Past Recaptured, *1927*

(*See also* **SAD/MELANCHOLY**)

GROWTH AND DEVELOPMENT

Growth is the only evidence of life.

John Henry Newman, Apologia pro vita sua, *1864*

There are few successful adults who were not at first successful children.

Alexander Chase, Perspectives, *1966*

Some people seem as if they can never have been children, and others seem as if they could never be anything else.

George Dennison Prentice, Prenticeana, *1860*

It is the highest creatures who take the longest to mature, and are the most helpless during their immaturity.

G.B. Shaw, Back to Methuselah, *1921*

One must be thrust out of a finished cycle in life, and that leap [is] the most difficult to make—to part with one's faith, one's love, when one would prefer to renew the faith and recreate the passion.

Anaïs Nin, Diary, *1932*

(*See also* **LEARNING, MATURITY**)

GUESTS

What is there more kindly than the feeling between host and guest?

Aeschylus, The Libation Bearers, *458 B.C.*

After three days men grow weary, of a wench, a guest, and weather rainy.

Franklin, Poor Richard's Almanack, *1833*

Unbidden guests are often welcomest when they are gone.

Shakespeare, Henry VI, Part I, *1591*

GUILTY/INNOCENT

Suspicion always haunts the guilty mind.

Shakespeare, Henry VI, Part III.

Rather let the crime of the guilty go unpunished than condemn the innocent.

Justinian I, Law Code, *A.D. 535*

We are all exceptional cases. . . . Each man insists on being innocent, even if it means accusing the whole human race, and heaven.

Albert Camus, The Fall, *1956*

We have no choice but to be guilty.
God is unthinkable if we are innocent.

Archibald MacLeish, JB, *1958*

'Tis e'er the lot of the innocent in the world to fly to the wolf for succor from the lion.

John Barth, The Sot-Weed Factor, *1960*

There is a sort of man who pays no attention to his good actions, but is tormented by his bad ones. This is the type that most often writes about himself.

W. Somerset Maugham, The Summing Up, *1938*

(*See also* **CONSCIENCE**)

 "H"

HABIT

The enormous flywheel of society, its most precious conservative agent.

>*William James,* The Principles of Psychology, *1890*

Habit rules the unreflecting herd.

>*William Wordsworth,* Ecclesiastical Sonnets, *1822*

Not in novelty but in habit and custom do we find the greatest pleasure.

>*Raymond Radiguet (d. 1923),* Le Diable au corps

Habit will reconcile us to everything but change.

>*C.C. Colton,* Lacon, *1825*

Habit is stronger than reason.

>*Santayana,* Interpretations of Poetry and Religion, *1900*

(*See also* **CUSTOM**)

HAPPINESS/UNHAPPINESS

Man's ultimate happiness lies not in this life.

>*Thomas Aquinas (d. 1274),* Summa contra Gentiles

There is only one duty: that is to be happy.

Diderot, Conversation with Catherine II, 1773

You shall have joy or you shall have power, said God; you shall not have both.

Emerson, Journal, *October 1842*

Human felicity is produced not so much by great pieces of good fortune that seldom happen, as by little advantages that occur every day.

Benjamin Franklin, Autobiography, *1731*

Ask yourself whether you are happy and you cease to be so.

John Stuart Mill, Autobiography, *1873*

A lifetime of happiness: no man alive could bear it; it would be hell on earth.

Shaw, Man and Superman, *1903*

All happiness is a work of art: the smallest error falsifies it, the slightest hesitation alters it, the least heaviness spoils it, the slightest stupidity brutalizes it.

Marguerite Yourcenar, Les Mémoires d'Hadrien, *1951*

The greatest happiness you can have is knowing that you do not necessarily require happiness.

William Saroyan, News summaries, *December 16, 1957*

Nothing blocks happiness like happiness remembered.

André Gide, The Immoralist, *1902*

I cannot help being happy. I've struggled against it but to no good. Apart from an odd five minutes here and there, I have been happy all my life. There is, I am well aware, no virtue whatever in this. It results from a combination of heredity, health, good fortune and shallow intellect.

Arthur Marshall, Taking Liberties, *1977*

To be happy we must not be too concerned with others.

Albert Camus, The Fall, *1956*

Can you learn to live? Yes, if you are not happy. There is no virtue in felicity.

Colette , Earthly Paradise, *1966*

The search for happiness is one of the chief sources of unhappiness.

Eric Hoffer, The Passionate State of Mind, *1954*

I am happy and content because I think I am.

Lesage, Histoire de Gil Blas, *1735*

There is nothing which has yet been contrived by man by which so much happiness is produced as by a good tavern.

Samuel Johnson, in Boswell's Life, *March 21, 1776*

I find my joy of living in the fierce and ruthless battles of life, and my pleasure comes from learning something.

Auguste Strindberg, Miss Julie, *1888*

Unquestionably, it is possible to do without happiness; it is done involuntarily by nineteen-twentieths of mankind.

John Stuart Mill, Utilitarianism, *1863*

The satisfied, the happy, do not live; they fall asleep in habit, near neighbor to annihilation.

Miguel de Unamuno, The Tragic Sense of Life, *1913*

The main thing today is shopping. Years ago a person, he was unhappy, didn't know what to do . . . he'd go to church, start a revolution—*something.* Today you're unhappy? Can't figure it out? . . . Go shopping.

Arthur Miller, The Price, *1958*

(*See also* **PAIN/PLEASURE, SAD/MELANCHOLY**)

HASTE

Ther n' is no werkman whatever he be
That may both werken wel and hastily.

Chaucer, The Canterbury Tales, *1400*

The greatest assassin of life is haste, the desire to reach things before the right time, which means overreaching them.

Juan Ramon Jiménez, Selected Writings, *1957*

People in a hurry cannot think, cannot grow, nor can they decay. They are preserved in a state of perpetual puerility.

Eric Hoffer, The Passionate State of Mind, *1954*

Do nothing hastily but catching of fleas.

Thomas Fuller, Gnomologia, *1732*

HATRED

... The anger of the weak.

> *Alphonse Daudet,* Lettres de mon moulin, *1866*

... The coward's revenge for being intimidated.

> *G.B. Shaw,* Major Barbara, *1905*

A precious liquid, a poison dearer than that of the Borgias—because it is made from our blood, our health, our sleep, and two-thirds of our love—we must be stingy with it.

> *Charles Baudelaire, "Advice to Young Writers," 1867*

I am too fond of myself to hate anyone. It would constrict . . . my life, which I prefer to expand over the whole universe.

> *Rousseau,* Les Reveries du promeneur solitaire, *1782*

The price of hating other human beings is loving oneself less.

> *Eldridge Cleaver,* Soul on Ice, *1968*

To wrong those we hate is to add fuel to our hatred. Conversely, to treat an enemy with magnanimity is to blunt our hatred for him.

> *Eric, Hoffer,* The Passionate State of Mind, *1954*

(*See also* **ENEMIES, LOVE**)

HEALTH

Healthy people are invalids who don't know it.

> *Jules Romains,* Dr. Knock, *1923*

The best part of health is fine disposition.

> *Emerson,* The Conduct of Life, *1860*

An imaginary ailment is worse than a disease.

> *Hanan J. Ayalti, ed.,* Yiddish Proverbs, *1949*

If you wish to keep as well as possible, the less you think about your health the better.

> *Oliver Wendell Holmes,* Over the Teacups, *1891*

What some call health, if purchased by perpetual anxiety about diet, isn't much better than tedious disease.

> *George Dennison Prentice,* Prenticeana, *1860*

There are more microbes *per person* than the entire population of the world. Imagine that. Per person!

> *Allen Bennett,* The Old Country, *Act I*

Digestion exists for health, and health exists for life, and life exists for the love of music or beautiful things.

> *G.K. Chesterton,* Generally Speaking, *1928*

When we are well, we all have good advice for those who are ill.

> *Terence,* The Woman of Andros, *166 B.C.*

(*See also* **PHYSICAL FITNESS, SICKNESS**)

HEART

One's head is invariably the dupe of one's heart.

> *La Rochefoucauld,* Reflections, *1665*

The heart has its reasons that reason knows nothing of.

> *Blaise Pascal,* Pensées, *1670*

We have hearts within,
Warm, live, improvident, indecent hearts.

> *Elizabeth Barrett Browning,* Aurora Leigh, *1856*

(*See also* **EMOTIONS**)

HEAVEN

The common man, who doesn't know what to do with this life, wants another which shall be endless.

> *Anatole France,* La Révolte des anges, *1914*

Do not ask God the way to heaven; He'll show you the hardest way.

> *Stanislaw Lec,* Unkempt Thoughts, *1962*

Heaven is large and affords space for all modes of love and fortitude.

> *Emerson,* Essays, *1841*

What they do in heaven we are ignorant of; what they do not we are told expressly, that they neither marry, nor are given in marriage.

> *Jonathan Swift,* Thoughts on Various Subjects, *1711*

(*See also* **HELL**)

HELL

Hell, Madame, is to love no longer.
> *George Bernanos,* The Diary of a Country Priest, *1936*

An intelligent hell would be better than a stupid paradise.
> *Victor Hugo,* Ninety-three, *1874*

Take away a Christian's fear of hell and you take away his faith.
> *Diderot,* Additions . . . , *1746*

Hell has three gates: lust, anger, and greed.
> Bhagavad-Gita

To work hard, to live hard, to die hard, and then to go to hell after all would be too damned hard.
> *Carl Sandburg,* The People, Yes, *1926*

Each of us bears his own Hell.
> *Virgil,* Aeneid, *c. 30 B.C.*

The Puritan's idea of hell is a place where everybody has to mind his own business.
> *Wendell Phillips (d. 1884), attributed*

Believing in hell must distort every judgment on this life.
> *Cyril Connolly,* The Unquiet Grave, *1945*

(*See also* **DEVIL, HEAVEN**)

HERESY

. . . is the lifeblood of religions. It is faith that begets heresies. There are no heresies in a dead religion.
> *André Suarès (d. 1948),* Péguy

Heresy is what the minority believe; it is the name given by the powerful to the doctrines of the weak.
> *Robert Ingersoll (d. 1899),* "Heretics and Heresies"

Heresies are experiments in man's unsatisfied search for truth.
> *H.G. Wells (d. 1946),* Crux Ansata

Heresy hunters are intolerant not only of unorthodox ideas; . . . they are intolerant of any ideas which are really alive and not empty cocoons.

> *Philip Lee Ralph*, Story of Civilization, *1954*

(*See also* **DISSENT**)

HEROES

There are no heroes of action, . . . only heroes of resignation and suffering.

> *Albert Schweitzer*, Out of My Life and Thought, *1932*

Heroism feels and never reasons and is therefore always right.

> *Emerson*, "Self-Reliance," *1841*

This thing of being a hero, about the main thing to do is to know when to die. Prolonged life has ruined more men than it ever made.

> *Will Rogers*, Autobiography, *1949*

Heroism does not require spiritual maturity.

> *Abel Hermant*, Xavier, *1923*

Formerly we used to canonize our heroes. The modern method is to vulgarize them. Cheap editions of great books may be delightful, but cheap editions of great men are absolutely detestable.

> *Oscar Wilde*, "The True Function and Value of Criticism," *1890*

The real hero is always a hero by mistake; he dreams of being an honest coward like everybody else.

> *Umberto Eco*, Travels in Hyper Reality, *1986*

Every hero becomes a bore at last.

> *Emerson*, "Uses of Great Men," *1850*

The chief business of the nation, as a nation, is the setting up of heroes, mainly bogus.

> *H.L. Mencken*, Prejudices: Third Series, *1922*

(*See also* **GLORY, GREATNESS**)

HEROES IN HISTORY

The face that launched a thousand ships,
And burnt the topless towers of Ilium . . .
Sweet Helen [of Troy]. . . .

> *Christopher Marlowe*, Dr. Faustus, *1604*

If Cleopatra's nose had been shorter, the whole face of the world would have changed.

> *Pascal,* Pensées, *1670*

Always remember, French people, that our nation was born in the breast of a woman, in her tenderness, her tears, her blood that she shed for us.

> *Jules Michelet,* Joan of Arc, *1853*

Louis XIV liked and trusted no one but himself. . . . He feared the minds, the abilities, even the noble sentiments of his generals and ministers.

> *Saint-Simon (d. 1755),* Mémoires

Here I stand; I can do no other. So help me God.

> *Martin Luther, speech before the Imperial Diet, 1521*

We (that's my ship and I) took off rather suddenly. We had a report, somewhere around 4 o'clock in the afternoon before, that the weather would be fine, so we thought that we would try it.

> *Lindbergh,* New York Times, *May 23, 1927*

I thank heaven for a man like Adolf Hitler, who built a front line of defence against the anti-Christ of Communism.

> *Frank Buchman,* New York World Telegram, *August 25, 1936*

Henry VIII was a strong king with a very strong sense of humor and VIII wives, memorable amongst whom are Katherine the Arrogant, Anne of Cloves, Lady Jane Austin and Ann Hathaway. His beard was, however, red.

> *Sellar and Yeatman,* 1066 and All That, *1931*

HISTORIAN

The first law is that the historian shall never dare utter an untruth. The second is that he shall suppress nothing that is true. Also, there must be no suspicion of partiality . . . or of malice.

> *Cicero (d. 43 B.C.),* De Oratore

A good writer of history is a guy who is suspicious. Suspicion marks the real difference between the man who wants to write honest history and the one who'd rather write a good story.

> *Jim Bishop,* New York Times, *February 5, 1955*

Never . . . use the word *gossip* in a pejorative sense. It's the stuff of biography and has to be woven in.

Joan Peyser, Publishers Weekly, *June 5, 1987*

No theologian could ever be a historian. History is essentially disinterested. The historian has only one concern: art and truth, which are inseparable, . . . whereas the theologian has something else at stake—his dogma.

Ernest Renan, Life of Jesus *(1863)*

HISTORY

Anybody can make history. Only a great man can write it.

Oscar Wilde, "The Critic as Artist," 1890

The history of the world is the record of the weakness, frailty, and death of public opinion.

Samuel Butler, Note-Books, *1912*

What experience and history teach is . . . that people and governments have never learned anything from history.

Georg F. Hegel, Philosophy of History, *1832*

We owe to the Middle Ages the two worst inventions of humanity—romantic love and gunpowder.

André Maurois, BBC-TV, January 1958

History never looks like history when you are living through it. It always looks confusing and messy, and it always feels uncomfortable.

John W. Gardner, No Easy Victories, *1968*

History studies not just facts and institutions, its real subject is the human spirit.

Fustel de Coulange, La Cité antique, *1864*

(*See also* **PAST**)

HOLIDAYS

From the sepulcher at sunrise to the fashion parade on Fifth Avenue is the boorish measure of our denial of Christ—from innocent wonder to cynical worldliness.

Brooks Atkinson, Once Around the Sun, *1951*

How many observe Christ's birthday! How few his precepts!
O! 'tis easier to keep holidays than commandments.

Benjamin Franklin, Poor Richard's Almanack, *1757*

April 1. This is the day upon which we are reminded of what we are
on the other three hundred and sixty-four.

Mark Twain, Pudd'nhead Wilson, *1894*

(*See also* **RELIGION**)

THE HOLOCAUST

The region . . . including the districts of Warsaw, Cracow, Lvov and
Radom, . . . contained some 2,284,000 Jews in 1939, according to the
Germans' own estimate. No one had ever conceived of murder on
such a scale before, and no sensible person would have thought it
possible.

Michael Marrus, New York Times Book Review, *June 28, 1987*

Another improvement [we made] was to build our gas chambers to
accommodate 2,000 people at a time, whereas the Treblinka chambers accommodated only 200.

Rudolf Hoess, Commander, Auschwitz: War Crimes Trials,
Document #3868-PS, Nuremberg, 1946

The Nazis came for the Communists and I didn't speak up because
I was not a Communist. They came for the Jews and I didn't speak
up for I was not a Jew. They came for the trade-unionists and I
didn't speak up because I was not a trade-unionist. They came for
the Catholics and I was a Protestant so I didn't speak up. Then they
came for me and by that time no one was left to speak up.

Pastor Martin Niemöller (d. 1984), attributed

The injury [to the survivors] cannot be healed; it extends through
time: the Furies, in whose existence we have to believe, not only rack
the tormentor . . . but perpetuate his work by denying peace to the
tormented.

Primo Levi, The Drowned and the Saved *[The author committed*
suicide in 1987.]

HOME

The house of everyone is to him as his castle and fortress, as well for
his defense against injury and violence as for his repose.

Sir Edward Coke (d. 1634), Semayne's Case

A man's home is his wife's castle.

Alexander Chase, Perspectives, *1966*

Every roof is agreeable to the eye, until it is lifted; then we find tragedy and moaning women, and hard-eyed husbands.

Emerson, Essays: Second Series, *1844*

Everybody's talking about people breaking into houses but there are more people in the world who want to break out of houses.

Thornton Wilder, The Matchmaker, *1955*

It's hard for women, you know,
To get away. There's so much to do.
Husbands to be patted and put in good tempers;
Servants to be poked out; Children washed
Or soothed with lullabies or fed with mouthfuls of pap.

Aristophanes, Lysistrata, *411 B.C.*

Home life as we understand it is no more natural to us than a cage is natural to a cockatoo.

G.B. Shaw, Getting Married, *1908*

(*See also* **FAMILY, PRIVACY**)

HOMOSEXUALITY

—My mother made me a homosexual.
—If I gave her the wool, would she make me one too?

Graffiti, London, 1978

Homosexuality is a sickness, just as are baby-rape or wanting to become head of General Motors.

Eldridge Cleaver, Soul on Ice, *1968*

Lesbianism has always seemed to me an extremely inventive response to the shortage of men, but otherwise not worth the trouble.

Nora Ephron, Heartburn, *1983*

I'd rather be black than gay because when you're black you don't have to tell your mother.

Charles Pierce, female impersonator, 1980

HONESTY/DISHONESTY

I have no idea what the mind of a low-life scoundrel is like, but I know what the mind of an honest man is like: it is terrifying.

Abel Hermant, Le Bourgeois, *1906*

There is no well-defined boundary between honesty and dishonesty. The frontiers of one blend with the outside limits of the other, and he who attempts to tread this dangerous ground may be sometimes in one domain and sometimes in the other.

O. Henry, Rolling Stones, *1912*

Many a time in the past, when an active operator in the Street, he had done things to the Small Investor which would have caused raised eyebrows on the fo'c's'le of a pirate sloop—and done them without a blush.

P.G. Wodehouse, The Heart of a Goof, *1926*

In keeping people straight, principle is not as powerful as a policeman.

Abel Hermant, Le Bourgeois, *1906*

HONOR: *See* INTEGRITY.

HOPE

He that lives upon hope will die fasting.

Benjamin Franklin, Poor Richard's Almanack, *c. 1750*

The virtue I like best, said God, is hope.

Charles Péguy, La Porche du mystère du deuxième vertu, *1911*

Hope deceives more men than cunning does.

Vauvenargues, Reflections and Maxims, *1746*

If it were not for hope, the heart would break.

Thomas Fuller, Gnomologia, *1732*

There is nothing so well known as that we should not expect something for nothing—but we all do and call it hope.

Edgar Watson Howe, Country Town Sayings, *1911*

In reality, hope is the worst of all evils, because it prolongs man's torments.

Nietzsche, Human, All Too Human, *1878*

HOSPITALITY: *See* GUESTS.

HOUSES

A man builds a fine house; and now he has a master, and a task for life; he is to furnish, watch, show it, and keep it in repair the rest of his days.

Emerson, Society and Solitude, *1870*

The worst of a modern stylish mansion is that it has no place for ghosts.

Oliver Wendell Holmes, The Poet at the Breakfast Table, *1872*

A man's house is his stage. Others walk on to play their bit parts. Now and again a soliloquy, a birth, an adultery.

Karl Shapiro, The Bourgeois Poet, *1964*

Small rooms or dwellings discipline the mind, large ones weaken it.

Leonardo da Vinci, Notebooks, *c. 1500*

(*See also* **ARCHITECTURE, HOME**)

HUMANISM

Man is the measure of all things.

Protagoras (d. 410 B.C.), in Plato, Theaetetus.

Nothing human is alien to me.

Terence (d. 159 B.C.), Heuton Timorumenos

A well-ordered humanism does not begin with the self, but puts the world ahead of life, life ahead of man, respect for others ahead of egotism.

Lévi-Strauss, L'Origine des manières de table, *1968*

It is better to be a human dissatisfied than a pig satisfied, better Socrates dissatisfied than a fool satisfied.

John Stuart Mill, Utilitarianism, *1863*

When men can no longer be theists, they must, if they are civilized, become humanists.

Walter Lippmann, A Preface to Morals, *1919*

Dead are the Gods: now do we expect the *Uebermensch* ("Overman") to live.

Nietzsche, Thus Spake Zarathustra, *1892*

From the failure of the humanist tradition to participate fully or to act decisively, civilizations may perhaps crumble or perish at the hands of barbarians. But unless the humanist tradition itself in some form survives, there can really be no civilization at all.

Louis Kronenberger, Company Manners, *1954*

(*See also* **HUMAN NATURE, MAN**)

HUMANITARIANISM

In abstract love of humanity one almost always loves oneself.

Dostoyevsky, The Idiot, *1868*

Humanitarianism is a manifestation of stupidity and cowardice.

Adolf Hitler, Mein Kampf, *1924*

The dignity of the individual requires that he not be reduced to vassalage by the largesse of others.

Saint-Exupéry, Flight to Arras, *1942*

Social work is a band-aid on the festering wounds of society.

Alexander Chase, Perspectives, *1966*

When you say you are in love with humanity, you are well satisfied with yourself.

Luigi Pirandello, Each in His Own Way, *1924*

He who is too busy doing good finds no time to be good.

Rabindranath Tagore, Stray Birds, *1916*

(*See also* **CHARITY**)

HUMANITY

. . . is a superhuman enterprise.

Jean Giraudoux, Intermezzo, *1933*

Love your country, O my brothers! . . . [But] your first duties . . . are towards humanity. You are *men* before you are either citizens or fathers.

Giuseppe Mazzini, Duties towards Your Country, *1844*

One cannot serve humanity at the expense of France.

Georges Clemenceau, speech, Chamber of Deputies, 1918

(*See also* **MAN**)

HUMAN NATURE

. . . has not changed and does not change; . . . inherent human beliefs stay the same [and] fundamental rules of human conduct continue to hold.

Lammont duPont, Forbes, *1956*

Human nature can be changed with the greatest ease and to the utmost possible extent. If huge . . . dangers lie in this, it also contains great [hope] for the future of mankind.

Bruce Bliven, Forbes, *1958*

A human being is not, in any proper sense, a human being till he is educated.

Horace Mann, Address, Antioch, 1859

The essence of being human is that one does not seek perfection.

George Orwell, Shooting an Elephant, *1950*

The thief and the murderer follow nature just as much as the philanthropist.

T.H. Huxley, "Evolution and Ethics," 1893

HUMILITY

We come nearest to the great when we are great in humility.

Rabindranath Tagore, Stray Birds, *1916*

He that humbleth himself wishes to be exalted.

Nietzsche, Human, All Too Human, *1878*

Plenty of people wish to become devout, but none wish to be humble.

La Rochefoucauld, Maxims, *1665*

A poor spirit is poorer than a poor purse.

Thomas Fuller, Gnomologia, *1732*

They are proud in humility; proud that they are not proud.

Robert Burton, Anatomy of Melancholy, *1621*

Humility is the first of virtues—for other people.

Oliver Wendell Holmes, The Professor at the Breakfast Table, *1858*

Man was created on the sixth day so that he could not be boastful, since he came after the flea in the order of creation.

> *Haggadah,* Palestinian Talmud, *4th century*

(*See also* **CONCEIT, PRIDE**)

HUMOR

Men will confess to treason, murder, arson, false teeth, or a wig. How many of them will own up to a lack of humor?

> *Frank Moore Colby,* The Colby Essays, *1926*

Everything is funny as long as it is happening to somebody else.

> *Will Rogers,* The Illiterate Digest, *1942*

Jester: I can make a joke about any subject.
King: Make a joke about me.
Jester: The king is not a subject.

> *Rogers, ibid.*

Humor is falling downstairs if you do it in the act of warning your wife not to.

> *Kenneth Bird, News Summaries, May 3, 1954*

The difficulty with humorists is that they will mix what they believe with what they don't; whichever seems likely to win an effect.

> *John Updike,* A Month of Sundays

Good taste and humor are a contradiction in terms, like a chaste whore.

> *Malcolm Muggeridge,* Time, *September 14, 1953*

Humor must have its background of seriousness. Without this contrast there comes none of that incongruity which is the mainspring of laughter.

> *Max Beerbohm (d. 1956), "A Conspectus of G.B.S."*

Nothing spoils a romance so much as a sense of humor in the woman—or the want of it in a man.

> *Oscar Wilde,* A Woman of No Importance, *1893*

Just when you think there's nothing to write about, Nixon says, "I am not a crook." Jimmy Carter says, "I have lusted after women in my heart." President Reagan says, "I have just taken a urinalysis test, and I am not on dope."

> *Art Buchwald,* Time, *September 29, 1986*

Humor [is] something that thrives between man's aspirations and his limitations. There is more logic in humor than in anything else. Because, you see, humor is truth.

Victor Borge, London Times, *January 3, 1984*

When we realize that we aren't God's given children, we'll understand satire. Humor is really laughing off a hurt, grinning at misery.

Bill Mauldin, Time, *July 21, 1961*

The secret of Humor . . . is not joy but sorrow. There is no humor in heaven.

Mark Twain, Pudd'nhead Wilson's New Calendar, *1894*

(*See also* **LAUGHTER, SENSE/NONSENSE, WIT**)

HUNGER

There's no sauce in the world like hunger.

Cervantes, Don Quixote, *1615*

Love and business and family and religion and art and patriotism are nothing but shadows of words when a man's starving.

O. Henry, Heart of the West, *1907*

Hunger does not breed reform; it breeds madness and all the ugly distempers that make an ordered life impossible.

Woodrow Wilson, Address to Congress, November 11, 1918

(*See also* **EATING**)

HUNTING

There is a passion for hunting something deeply implanted in the human breast.

Charles Dickens, Oliver Twist, *1837*

Wild animals never kill for sport. Man is the only one to whom the torture and death of his fellow creatures is amusing in itself.

James A. Froude (d. 1894), Oceana.

The English country gentleman galloping after a fox—the unspeakable in full pursuit of the uneatable.

Oscar Wilde, A Woman of No Importance, *1893*

HUSBAND

He tells you when you've got on too much lipstick,
And helps you with your girdle when your hips stick.

Ogden Nash, "The Perfect Husband,"
Verses from 1929 On, *1949*

Husbands are like fires. They go out if unattended.

Zsa Zsa Gabor, NBC TV, 1979

Men are horribly tedious when they are good husbands, and abominably conceited when they are not.

Oscar Wilde, A Woman of No Importance, *1893*

(*See also* **WIFE, WOMAN**)

HYPOCRISY

. . . The homage that vice pays to virtue.

La Rochefoucauld, Maxims, *1665*

No man, for any considerable period, can wear one face to himself, and another to the multitude, without finally getting bewildered as to which may be the true.

Nathaniel Hawthorne, The Scarlet Letter, *1850*

The hypocrite's crime is that he bears false witness against himself. What makes it so plausible to assume that hypocrisy is the vice of vices is that integrity can indeed exist under the cover of all vices except this one.

Lionel Trilling, On Revolution, *1963*

It is not uncommon to charge the difference between promise and performance . . . upon deep design and studied deceit; but the truth is that there is very little hypocrisy in the world.

Samuel Johnson, The Idler, *1760*

The true hypocrite is the one who ceases to perceive his deception, the one who lies with sincerity.

André Gide, The Counterfeiters, *1921*

It's a great comfort to me to know that I've always done what was right.

Douglass F. Camp, after his wife had divorced him for
mental cruelty, 1931

(*See also* **DECEPTION, SINCERITY**)

"I"

IDEALISM

Ideals are like stars; you will not succeed in touching them with your hands. But like the seafaring man on the desert of waters, you choose them as your guides, and following them you will reach your destiny.

Carl Schurz, Address, Faneuil Hall, Boston, 1859

Every form of addiction is bad, no matter whether the narcotic be alcohol or morphine or idealism.

C.G. Jung, Memories, Dreams, Reflections, *1968*

In no other country is the ideal side of public life so ignored by the mass and repudiated by its leaders.

James Bryce, The American Commonwealth, *1888*

It is not materialism that is the chief curse of the world, as pastors teach, but idealism. Men get into trouble by taking their visions and hallucinations too seriously.

H.L. Mencken, Minority Report, *1956*

IDEAS

The thinker dies, but his thoughts are beyond the reach of destruction. Men are mortal; but ideas are immortal.

Walter Lippmann, A Preface to Morals, *1929*

144

You cannot put a rope around the neck of an idea; you cannot put an idea up against a barrack square wall and riddle it with bullets; you cannot confine it in the strongest prison cell that your slaves could ever build.

Sean O'Casey, Death of Thomas Ashe, *1918*

Three ideas stand out above all others in the influence they have exerted and are destined to exert upon the development of the human race: The idea of the Golden Rule, the idea of natural law, and the idea of age-long growth, or evolution.

Robert A. Millikin, Forbes Magazine, *1940*

One of the greatest pains for human [beings] is the pain of a new idea.

Walter Bagehot, Physics and Politics, *1879*

Ideas are indeed the most dangerous weapons in the world. Our ideas of freedom are the most powerful political weapons man has ever forged.

Justice William O. Douglas (d. 1980), An Almanac of Liberty

All ideas are to some extent subversive. . . . Christianity was subversive to [Roman] paganism.

Albert Gérard, Testament of a Liberal, *1956*

An intellectual is not only a person for whom books are essential but one for whom an idea, however elementary, absorbs and orders his life.

André Malraux, The Walnut Trees of Altenburg, *1943*

Nothing is more dangerous than an idea if it's the only one you have.

Alain (d. 1951), Propos sur la religion

General and abstract ideas are the source of man's greatest errors.

Rousseau, Emile, *1762*

Every idea I get I have to deny, that's my way of testing it.

Alain, Histoire de mes pensées

Others go to bed with their mistresses; I with my ideas.

José Marti, letter, 1890

(*See also* **INTELLECT, THOUGHT**)

IDENTITY

Men can starve from a lack of self-realization as much as . . . from a lack of bread.

Richard Wright, Native Son, *1940*

It is thus with most of us; we are what other people say we are. We know ourselves chiefly by hearsay.

Eric Hoffer, The Passionate State of Mind, *1954*

We become what we are only by the radical and profound rejection of what others have said about us.

Jean Paul Sartre, preface to Fanon's Wretched of the Earth, *1961*

(*See also* **CHARACTER, INDIVIDUALISM, SELF**)

IDLENESS

To do nothing is the most difficult thing in the world—the most difficult and the most intellectual.

Oscar Wilde, The Critic as Artist, *1891*

Idleness, like kisses, to be sweet must be stolen.

Jerome K. Jerome, The Idle Thoughts of an Idle Fellow, *1889*

It is better to have loafed and lost than never to have loafed at all.

James Thurber, Fables for Our Time, *1943*

If a soldier or a laborer complain of the hardship of his lot, set him to doing nothing.

Pascal Pensées, *1670*

(*See also* **LAZINESS, LEISURE**)

IDOLS

Heathen, n. A benighted creature who has the folly to worship something that he can see and feel.

Ambrose Bierce, The Devil's Dictionary, *1911*

We boast our emancipation from many superstitions; but if we have broken any idols, it is [merely] through a transfer of idolatry.

Emerson, Essays, *1841*

Men are idolaters and want something to look at and kiss and hug, or throw themselves down before; they always did, they always will; and if you don't make it of wood, you must make it of words.

> *Oliver Wendell Holmes,* The Poet at the Breakfast Table, *1872*

(*See also* **WORSHIP**)

IGNORANCE

Nothing is more dreadful than ignorance in action.

> *Goethe (d. 1832),* Proverbs in Prose

To be conscious that you are ignorant is a great step to knowledge.

> *Benjamin Disraeli,* Sybil, *1845*

A learned bastard takes precedence over an ignorant high priest.

> *The Talmud, fifth century*

To be ignorant of what occurred before you were born is to remain a perennial child.

> *Cicero,* De Oratore, *c. 50 B.C.*

Nothing in the world is more dangerous than sincere ignorance and conscientious stupidity.

> *Martin Luther King, Jr.,* Strength to Love, *1963*

Ignorance is not bliss—it is oblivion.

> *Philip Wylie,* Generation of Vipers, *1942*

(*See also* **KNOWLEDGE, SIMPLICITY, STUPIDITY**)

ILLUSION

Man has always sacrificed truth to his vanity, comfort and advantage. He lives . . . by make-believe.

> *W. Somerset Maugham,* The Summing Up, *1938*

We must select the illusion which appeals to our temperament, and embrace it with passion, if we want to be happy.

> *Cyril Connolly,* The Unquiet Grave, *1945*

Rob the average man of his life-illusion and you rob him of his happiness at one stroke.

> *Henrik Ibsen,* The Wild Duck, *1884*

(*See also* **DREAM, REALITY**)

IMAGINATION

Heard melodies are sweet, but those unheard
Are sweeter.

> *Keats, "Ode on a Grecian Urn," 1819*

A lady's imagination is very rapid; it jumps from admiration to love, from love to matrimony in a moment.

> *Jane Austen,* Pride and Prejudice, *1813*

The gift of fantasy has meant more to me than my talent for absorbing positive knowledge.

> *Albert Einstein,* Washington Post, *March 6, 1985*

The lunatic, the lover, and the poet, are of imagination all compact.

> *Shakespeare,* Mid-Summer Night's Dream, *1595*

Society often forgives the criminal, . . . never the dreamer.

> *Oscar Wilde, "The Critic as Artist," 1891*

(*See also* **MIND, MYSTICISM, MYTHS**)

IMMIGRANTS AND FOREIGNERS

A nation, like a tree, does not thrive well till it is engrafted with a foreign stock.

> *Emerson,* Journals, *1823*

The great adventure of America is . . . the absorption of fifty different peoples.

> *Walter Lippmann,* A Preface to Politics, *1914*

My forefathers didn't come over on the *Mayflower*, but they met the boat.

> *Will Rogers (d. 1935), Comment [Rogers was of Indian descent.]*

America shudders at anything alien, and when it wants to shut its mind against any man's ideas, it calls him a foreigner.

> *Max Lerner,* Actions and Passions, *1949*

(*See also* **STRANGERS**)

IMMORTALITY

Immortality is not a gift,
Immortality is an achievement;

And only those who strive mightily
Shall possess it.

> *Edgar Lee Masters,* Spoon River Anthology, *1915*

Lead me from the unreal to the real!
Lead me from darkness to light!
Lead me from death to immortality!

> Brihadaranyaka Upanishad, *c. 500 B.C.*

I do not believe in revealed religion—I will have nothing to do with your immortality; we are miserable enough in this life without the absurdity of speculating upon another.

> *Lord Byron to Reverend Francis Hodgson, 1811*

(*See also* **DEATH AND DYING, MORTALITY**)

IMPOTENCE

The worst pain we can have is to know much and be impotent to act.

> *Herodotus (fl. 450 B.C.),* Histories

Powerlessness frustrates; absolute powerlessness frustrates absolutely. Absolute frustration is a dangerous emotion to run a world with.

> *Russell Baker,* New York Times, *May 1, 1969*

We look for some reward of our endeavours and are disappointed; not success, not happiness, not even peace of conscience, crowns our ineffectual efforts to do well.

> *Robert Louis Stevenson, "Pulvis et umbra," 1888*

(*See also* **POWER, WEAKNESS**)

IMPERIALISM: *See* VIOLENCE, COLONIAL.

INCOMPETENCE

Marriage laws, the police, armies and navies are the mark of human incompetence.

> *Dora Russell (b. 1894),* The Right to Be Happy

This world is a round gulf, and he who cannot swim must go to the bottom.

> *Spanish proverb*

The girl who can't dance says the band can't play.
>   *Hanan J. Ayalti,* Yiddish Proverbs, *1949*

(*See also* **TALENT**)

INCONSISTENCY

Do I contradict myself?
Very well then I contradict myself,
(I am large, I contain multitudes).
>   *Walt Whitman,* Leaves of Grass, *1892*

When someone accuses me of having contradicted myself, I reply:
Just because I've been wrong once, or even more than once, doesn't
mean that I aim to be wrong all the time.
>   *Vauvenargues,* Reflections and Maxims, *1746*

(*See also* **CHANGE, CONSISTENCY**)

INDECISION

Between two stools one sits on the ground.
>   *French proverb*

There is no more miserable human being than one in whom nothing
is habitual but indecision.
>   *William James,* The Principles of Psychology, *1892*

It is human nature to stand in the middle of a thing.
>   *Mariane Moore, "A Grave,"* Collected Poems, *1951*

He who hesitates is sometimes saved.
>   *James Thurber,* A Thurber Carnival, *1945*

(*See also* **DECISION, PURPOSE**)

INDEPENDENCE

. . . is for the very few; it is a privilege of the strong.
>   *Nietzsche,* Beyond Good and Evil, *1886*

"Independence" . . . [is] middle-class blasphemy. We are all dependent
on one another, every soul of us on earth.
>   *G.B. Shaw,* Pygmalion, *1912*

What man wants is simply independent choice, whatever that independence may cost and wherever it may lead.

> *Dostoyevski,* Notes from Underground, *1864*

(*See also* **LIBERTY, SELF-SUFFICIENCY**)

INDIFFERENCE

Indifference is a militant thing. It batters down the walls of cities and murders the women and children amid the flames and the purloining of altar vessels.

> *Stephen Crane (d. 1900),* "Death of the Child"

The opposite of love is not hate, it's indifference.
The opposite of art is not ugliness, it's indifference.
The opposite of faith is not heresy, it's indifference.
The opposite of life is not death, it's indifference.

> *Elie Wiesel,* U.S. News and World Report, *December 27, 1986*

To try may be to die, but not to care is never to be born.

> *William Redfield,* New York Times, *January 15, 1968*

Most people go on living their everyday life: half frightened, half indifferent, they behold the ghostly tragi-comedy that is being performed on the international stage before the eyes and ears of the world.

> *Einstein,* Out of My Later Life, *1950*

(*See also* **IGNORANCE, LOVE, NEGLECT**)

INDIGNATION

No one lies as much as the indignant do.

> *Nietzsche,* Beyond Good and Evil, *1886*

Indignation is the seducer of thought. No man can think clearly when his fists are clenched.

> *George Jean Nathan,* The World in Falseface, *1923*

A good indignation brings out all one's powers.

> *Emerson,* Journals, *1841*

(*See also* **ANGER**)

INDIVIDUALISM

How glorious it is—and how painful also—to be an exception.
Alfred de Musset, d. 1857

The whole theory of the universe is directed unerringly to one single individual—namely to You.
Walt Whitman, Leaves of Grass, *1892*

It is the lone worker who makes the first advance in a subject: the details may be worked out by a team, but the prime idea is due to the enterprise, thought and perception of an individual.
Sir Alexander Fleming, Address, Edinburgh, 1951

The man who walks alone is soon trailed by the F.B.I.
Wright Morris, A Bill of Rites . . . , *1967*

(*See also* **CONFORMITY, IDENTITY**)

INDOCTRINATION

The power of reiterated suggestion and consecrated platitude . . . has brought our entire civilization to imminent peril. . . . It is possible by these means to shape [one's] tastes, feelings, hopes . . . and convert him into a fanatical zealot, ready to torture and destroy and suffer mutilation and death for an obscene faith, baseless in fact, and morally monstrous.
Learned Hand, Address, Elizabethan Club, May 1951

When I transfer my knowledge, I teach. When I transfer my beliefs, I indoctrinate.
Arthur Danto, Analytic Philosophy of Knowledge, *1968*

(*See also* **PROPAGANDA**)

INFERIORITY AND INEQUALITY

The feeling of inferiority rules the mental life and can be clearly recognized as the sense of incompleteness and unfulfillment . . . both of individuals and of humanity.
Alfred Adler, The Neurotic Constitution, *1909*

Couldn't we even argue that it is because men are unequal that they have that much more need to be brothers?
Charles Du Bos, Journal, *February 27, 1918*

(*See also* **EQUALITY**)

INFIDELITY

Young men want to be faithful, and are not; old men want to be faithless, and cannot.

Oscar Wilde, The Picture of Dorian Gray, *1891*

Phyllis is my only joy,
Faithless as the winds or seas;
Sometimes cunning, sometimes coy,
Yet she never fails to please.

Sir Charles Sedley, "Song," *1702*

(*See also* **ADULTERY**)

INFLUENCE

Half our standards come from our first masters, and the other half from our first loves.

Santayana, The Life of Reason: Reason in Art, *1906*

Of all the pulpits from which human voice is ever sent forth, there is none from which it reaches so far as from the grave.

John Ruskin, The Seven Lamps of Architecture, *1849*

INGRATITUDE

A man is very apt to complain of the ingratitude of those who have risen far above him.

Samuel Johnson, in Boswell's Life, *March 28, 1776*

There are far fewer ungrateful people than we might think, because there are far fewer generous people than we believe.

Saint-Evremond, Sur les ingrats, *1705*

(*See also* **GRATITUDE**)

INHERITANCE

It is not only what we have inherited from our fathers that exists again in us, but all sorts of old dead ideas and . . . old dead beliefs and things of that kind. . . . and we can never be rid of them.

Henrik Ibsen, Ghosts, *1881*

A son can bear with composure the death of his father, but the loss of his inheritance might drive him to despair.

Machiavelli, The Prince, *1517*

INJURY

He that does you a very ill turn will never forgive you.

English proverb

There are some men whom a staggering emotional shock, so far from making them mental invalids for life, seems, on the other hand, to awaken, to galvanize, to arouse into an almost incredible activity of soul.

William McFee, Harbours of Memory, *1921*

'Tis better to suffer wrong than do it.

Thomas Fuller, Gnomologia, *1732*

(*See also* **INSULT, JUSTICE, REVENGE**)

INJUSTICE

To have a grievance is to have a purpose in life.

Alan Coren, The Sanity Inspector, *1974*

There is no social evil, no form of injustice whether of the feudal or capitalist order which has not been sanctified in some way or other by religious sentiment and thereby rendered more impervious to change.

Reinhold Niebuhr, Christian Realism and Political Problems, *1953*

(*See also* **JUSTICE**)

INNOCENCE: *See* GUILTY/INNOCENT.

INNOVATIONS

Innovators and men of genius have almost always been regarded as fools at the beginning (and very often at the end) of their careers.

Dostoyevski, The Idiot, *1868*

I say there can be no safety for these States without innovators— without free tongues, and ears willing to hear the tongues.

Walt Whitman, "To the States," 1872

The vast majority of human beings dislike and even actually dread all notions with which they are not familiar. . . . Hence innovators . . .

have generally been persecuted, and always derided as fools and madmen.

Aldous Huxley (d. 1963), Proper Studies

(*See also* **CHANGE, NOVELTY**)

INSECURITY

What can we take on trust
in this uncertain life? Happiness, greatness,
pride—nothing is secure, nothing keeps.

Euripides, Hecuba, *c. 425 B.C.*

People wish to be settled: only as far as they are unsettled is there any hope for them.

Emerson, Essays, *1841*

(*See also* **ANXIETY, SELF-DOUBT**)

INSPIRATION: *See* CREATIVITY.

INSTITUTIONS

The test of every religious, political, or educational system is the man which it forms. If it injures the intelligence, it is bad; if it injures the character, it is vicious; if it injures the conscience it is criminal.

Amiel, Journal, *June 17, 1852*

Wise and prudent men—intelligent conservatives—have long known that in a changing world worthy institutions can be conserved only by adjusting them to the changing time.

Franklin D. Roosevelt, speech, Syracuse, N.Y., September 29, 1936

(*See also* **BUREAUCRACY**)

INSULTS

No one can be as calculatedly rude as the British, which amazes Americans, who do not understand studied insult and can only offer abuse as a substitute.

Paul Gallico, New York Times, *January 14, 1962*

A wise man is superior to any insults which may be put upon him.

Molière, The Would-be Gentleman, *1670*

Insults should be well avenged or well endured.

Spanish proverb

INSURANCE

The Act of God designation on all insurance policies . . . means roughly that you cannot be insured for the accidents that are most likely to happen to you. If your ox kicks a hole in your neighbor's Maserati, however, indemnity is instantaneous.

Alan Coren, The Lady from Stalingrad Mansions, *1977*

I detest life-insurance agents. They always argue that I shall some day die, which is not so.

Stephen Leacock, Literary Lapses, *1910*

INTEGRITY

He has honor if he holds himself to an ideal of conduct though it is inconvenient, unprofitable, or dangerous to do so.

Walter Lippmann, A Preface to Morals, *1929*

Wisdom and virtue are like the two wheels of a cart.

Japanese proverb

(*See also* **CHARACTER, HONESTY**)

INTELLECTUALS

It is always the task of the intellectual to "think otherwise." This is not just a perverse idiosyncrasy. It is an absolutely essential feature of a society.

Harvey Cox, The Secular City, *1966*

In the modern riot of art and science and loving-kindness, Intellect has seen decline the virtues that make it what it is: unity, concentration, communicativeness, and knowledge of itself.

Jacques Barzun, The House of Intellect, *1959*

The intellectual is *engagé*—he is pledged, committed, enlisted. . . . [He feels imperatively] that ideas and abstractions are of signal importance in human life.

Richard Hofstadter, Anti-Intellectualism, *1963*

The intellectual is constantly betrayed by his vanity. God-like, he blandly assumes that he can express everything in words.

Anne Morrow Lindbergh, Wave of the Future, *1940*

Intellectuals should suffer a certain amount of persecution as early in life as possible. Not too much. That is bad for them. But a certain amount.

Bertrand Russell, conversation with Kenneth Harris.

Intellect is invisible to the person who hasn't any.

Arthur Schopenhauer, Essays

(*See also* **INTELLIGENCE, CULTURE**)

INTELLIGENCE

. . . Quickness to apprehend as distinct from ability, which is the capacity to act wisely on the thing apprehended.

Alfred North Whitehead, Dialogues, *December 15, 1939*

The sign of intelligent people is their ability to control emotions by the application of reason.

Marya Mannes, More in Anger, *1958*

Love is as necessary to human beings as food and shelter; [but] without intelligence, . . . love is impotent and freedom unattainable.

Aldous Huxley, Brave New World, *1958*

The true, strong, and sound mind is the mind that can embrace equally great things and small.

Samuel Johnson, in Boswell's Life, *April 29, 1778*

A person who doesn't lose his wits over certain things has no wits to lose.

G.F. Lessing, Emilia Galotti, *1772*

(*See also* **MIND, REASON**)

INTENTIONS

I may not always have done what was right, but at least I had good intentions.

Rousseau, Confessions

The road to Hell is paved with good intentions.

English Proverb

INTEREST

A man will fight harder for his interests than for his rights.

Napoleon I, Maxims, *1815*

Do not confuse your vested interests with ethics. Do not identify the enemies of your privilege with the enemies of humanity.

Max Lerner, Actions and Passions, *1949*

A world of vested interests is not a world which welcomes the disruptive force of candor.

Agnes Repplier, "Are Americans Timid?", 1924

Men are not against you; they are merely for themselves.

Gene Fowler, Skyline, *1961*

Interest speaks all sorts of languages, and plays all sorts of parts, even that of disinterestedness.

La Rochefoucauld, Maxims, *1665*

(*See also* **SELFISHNESS**)

INVOLVEMENT

Say "Yes" to the seedlings and a giant forest cleaves the sky. Say "Yes" to the universe and the planets become your neighbors. Say "Yes" to dreams of love and freedom. It is the password to utopia.

Brooks Atkinson, Once Around the Sun, *1951*

To say yes, you have to sweat and roll up your sleeves and plunge both hands into life up to the elbows. It is easy to say no, even if saying no means death.

Jean Anouilh, Antigone, *1942*

My trade and art is to live.

Montaigne, Essays, *1588*

The notion of looking on at life has always been hateful to me. What am I if I am not a participant? In order to be, I must participate.

Saint-Exupéry, Flight to Arras, *1942*

(*See also* **ACTION, EXPERIENCE**)

IRREVOCABLE

A word and a stone let go cannot be called back.

> *Thomas Fuller*, Gnomologia, *1732*

Of all sad words of tongue or pen,
The saddest are these: "It might have been!"

> *John Greenleaf Whittier, "Maud Muller," 1854*

It's over, and can't be helped, and that's one consolation, as they say in Turkey, ven they cuts off the wrong man's head.

> *Charles Dickens*, Pickwick Papers, *1837*

(*See also* **FATE, PAST**)

JEALOUSY

. . . That dragon which slays love under the pretense of keeping it alive.

Havelock Ellis, On Life and Sex: Essays of Love and Virtue, *1937*

In jealousy there is more self-love than love.

La Rochefoucauld, Reflections, *1678*

The jealous are the readiest of all to forgive, and all women know it.

Dostoyevski, The Brothers Karamazov, *1880*

It is not love that is blind, but jealousy.

Lawrence Durrell, Justine, *1957*

The jealous are troublesome to others, but a torment to themselves.

William Penn, Some Fruits of Solitude, *1693*

To jealousy, nothing is more frightful than laughter.

Françoise Sagan, La Chamade

(*See also* **ENVY**)

JESUS

The whole of history is incomprehensible without Him.

Ernest Renan, The Life of Jesus, *1863*

If Jesus Christ were to come today, people would not even crucify him. They would ask him to dinner, . . . hear what he had to say, and make fun of it.

Thomas Carlyle at His Zenith, *ed., D.A. Wilson*

Christ cannot possibly have been a Jew. I don't have to prove that scientifically. It's a fact.

Joseph Goebbels, The Nation, *February 6, 1935*

What is called the triumph of Christianity is more accurately the triumph of Judaism, and to Israel fell the singular privilege of giving a god to the world.

Anatole France (d. 1924), Epigrams

A man who was completely innocent, [Jesus] offered himself as a sacrifice for the good of others, including his enemies, and became the ransom of the world. It was a perfect act.

Gandhi, Non-Violence in Peace and War, *1948*

Jesus of Nazareth was the most scientific man that ever trod the globe. He plunged beneath the material surface of things, and found the spiritual cause.

Mary Baker Eddy, Science and Health with Key to the Scriptures, *1875*

Jesus said, Love; the Church says, Pay.

Victor Hugo, La Légende des siècles, *1859*

(*See also* **CHRISTIANITY**)

JEW(S)

I am a Jew. Hath not a Jew eyes? hath not a Jew hands, organs, dimensions, senses, affections, passions?

Shakespeare, The Merchant of Venice, *1596 with Jesus, 1972*

The Hebrews have done more to civilize men than any other nation.

John Adams to F.A. Van der Kamp, February 16, 1809

To the true Christian the Jew is the incomprehensibly obdurate man, who declines to see what has happened; and to the Jew the Christian is the incomprehensibly daring man, who affirms in an unredeemed world that its redemption has been accomplished.

Martin Buber, Paths in Utopia, *1986*

You are our dearly beloved brothers, and in a certain way, . . . our elder brothers.

Pope John Paul II, at the Synagogue of Rome, April 13, 1986

JOURNALISM

The public have an insatiable curiosity to know everything. Except what is worth knowing. Journalism, conscious of this, and having tradesman-like habits, supplies their demands.

Oscar Wilde, The Soul of Man under Socialism, *1891*

Nowhere can one find so miscellaneous, so various an amount of knowledge as is contained in a good newspaper.

Henry Ward Beecher, Proverbs from Plymouth Pulpit, *1887*

The evil that men do lives on the front pages of greedy newspapers, but the good is oft interred apathetically inside.

Brooks Atkinson, Once Around the Sun, *1951*

That ephemeral sheet, . . . the newspaper, is the natural enemy of the book, as the whore is of the decent woman.

E. and J. de Goncourt, Journal, *July 1858*

People everywhere confuse
What they read in newspapers with news.

A.J. Liebling, The New Yorker, *April 7, 1956*

Have you noticed that life, real honest-to-goodness life, with murders and catastrophes and fabulous inheritances, happens almost exclusively in the newspapers?

Jean Anouilh, The Rehearsal, *1950*

Adjectives do most of the work, smuggling in actual information under the guise of normal journalism. Thus the use of soft-spoken (mousy), loyal (dumb), high-minded (inept), hardworking (plodding), self-made (crooked), and pragmatic (totally immoral).

John Leo, "Journalism for the Lay Reader," Time, 1985

Cronyism is the curse of journalism. After many years I have reached the firm conclusion that it is impossible for any objective newspaperman to be a friend of a President.

Walter Lippmann, in conversation

(*See* **PRESS/MEDIA**)

JUDGING

The number of those who undergo the fatigue of judging for themselves is very small indeed.

Richard Brinsley Sheridan, The Critic, *1799*

When we come to judge others it is not by ourselves as we really are that we judge them, but by an image that we have formed of ourselves from which we have left out everything that offends our vanity or would discredit us in the eyes of the world.

W. Somerset Maugham, The Summing Up, *1938*

He hath a good judgment that relieth not wholly on his own.

Thomas Fuller, Gnomologia, *1732*

To judge a man means nothing more than to ask: What content does he give to the form of humanity? What concept of humanity should we have if he were its only representative?

Wilhelm von Humboldt, Uber den Geist der Menschheit, *1797*

Everyone complains of his memory, but no one complains of his judgment.

La Rochefoucauld, Maxims, *1665*

It is not true . . . that the more one thinks the less one feels, but it is true that the more one judges the less one loves.

Chamfort (d. 1794), Maxims and Thoughts

Judge not that ye be not judged.

Matthew 7:1

(*See also* **CRITICISM**)

JUDICIAL REVIEW

We are under a Constitution, but the Constitution is what the judges say it is, and the judiciary is the safeguard of our liberty and of our property under the Constitution.

Chief Justice Charles Evans Hughes, speech, Elmira, N.Y., 1907

I do not think the United States would come to an end if we lost our power to declare an Act of Congress void. I do think the Union would be imperiled if we could not make that declaration as to the laws of the several states.

Chief Justice Oliver Wendell Holmes, Jr., Law and the Court, *1913*

JUSTICE

I'll tell you a big secret, my friend: Don't wait for the Last Judgment. It happens every day.

Albert Camus, The Fall, *1956*

Men are too unstable to be just; they are crabbed because they have not passed water at the usual time, or testy because they have not been stroked or praised.

Edward Dahlberg, The Sorrows of Priapus, *1957*

[In America] a man is presoomed to be guilty ontil he's proved guilty an' afther that he's presoomed to be innocent.

Finley Peter Dooley, "On Criminal Trials," 1919

A great deal may be done by severity, more by love, but most by clear discernment and impartial justice.

Goethe, in Eckermann's Conversations, *March 22, 1825*

Justice is the tolerable accommodation of the conflicting interests of society, and I don't believe there is any royal road to attain such accommodation concretely.

Judge Learned Hand, in P. Hamburger, The Great Judge, *1946*

Even the most equitable of men is not permitted to be a judge in his own cause.

Pascal, Pensées, *1670*

I tremble for my country when I reflect that God is just.

Thomas Jefferson, Notes on the State of Virginia

Delay in justice is injustice.

Walter Savage Landor (d. 1864), Sinclair, the Cry for Justice

Injustice is relatively easy to bear; what stings is justice.

H.L. Mencken, Prejudices: Third Series, *1922*

In matters of government, justice means force as well as virtue.

Napoleon I, Maxims, *1815*

Justice is the very last thing of all wherewith the universe concerns itself. It is equilibrium that absorbs its attention.

Maurice Maeterlinck, Wisdom and Destiny, *1898*

"I'll be judge, I'll be jury," said cunning old Fury, "I'll try the whole cause, and condemn you to death."

Lewis Carroll, Alice . . . in Wonderland, *1865*

If a man destroy the eye of another man, they shall destroy his eye.

Hammurabi, Code, *c. 2040 B.C.*

(*See also* **INJUSTICE**)

KILLING

Assassination: the extreme form of censorship.

> *G.B. Shaw (d. 1950),* The Rejected Statement

Guns are neat little things, aren't they? They can kill extraordinary people with very little effort.

> *John W. Hinkley, Jr., quoted in* Time, *May 17, 1982*

To live without killing is a thought which could electrify the world, if men were only capable of staying awake long enough to let the idea soak in.

> *Henry Miller (d. 1980), "Reunion in Brooklyn"*

There are only about twenty murders a year in London and not all are serious—some are just husbands killing their wives.

> *G.H. Hatherill, Commander, Scotland Yard, News Summaries, July 1, 1954*

(*See also* **VIOLENCE**)

KINDNESS

Nature, in giving tears to man, confessed that he
Had a tender heart: this is our noblest quality.

> *Juvenal,* Satires, *c. A.D. 100*

Part of kindness is loving people more than they deserve.

> *Joseph Joubert*, Pensées, *1810*

Men are cruel, but Man is kind.

> *Rabindranath Tagore*, Stray Birds, *1916*

I have learned silence from the talkative, toleration from the intolerant, and kindness from the unkind; yet strange, I am ungrateful to those teachers.

> *Kahlil Gibran*, Sand and Foam, *1926*

(*See also* **BROTHERHOOD, CHARITY**)

KISS

Say I'm weary, say I'm sad,
Say that health and wealth have missed me,
Say I'm growing old, but add,
Jenny kissed me.

> *Leigh Hunt, "Rondeau," 1838*

Give me a kiss, and to that kiss a score;
Then to that twenty, add a hundred more:
A thousand to that hundred: so kiss on,
To make that thousand up a million.
Treble that million, and when that is done,
Let's kiss afresh, as when we first begun.

> *Robert Herrick, "To Althea: Ah, My Althea!" 1648*

A kiss can be a comma, a question mark or an exclamation point. That's basic spelling that every woman ought to know.

> *Mistinguett*, Theatre Arts, *December 1955*

KNOWLEDGE

Knowledge is the true organ of sight, not the eyes.

> *Panchatantra, fifth century* A.D.

The desire of knowledge, like the thirst of riches, increases ever with the acquisition of it.

> *Laurence Sterne*, Tristram Shandy, *1760*

Far more crucial than what we know or do not know is what we do not *want* to know.

> *Eric Hoffer*, The Passionate State of Mind, *1954*

Knowledge is not an abstract homogeneous good, of which there cannot be enough. Beyond the last flutter of actual or possible significance, pedantry begins.

Jacques Barzun, The House of Intellect, *1959*

The more I read, the more I meditate; and the more I acquire, the more certain I am that I know nothing.

Voltaire, Philosophical Dictionary, *1764*

There is no subject so old that something new cannot be said about it.

Dostoyevski, A Diary of a Writer, *1876*

Such is the constitution of the human mind, that any kind of knowledge, if it be really such, is its own reward.

John Henry Newman, The Idea of a University, *1853*

If a little knowledge is dangerous, where is the man who has so much as to be out of danger?

T.H. Huxley, "On Elementary Instruction in Physiology," 1877

(*See also* **LEARNING, SCHOLARS, WISDOM**)

KNOW THYSELF

Know then thyself, presume not God to scan:
The proper study of mankind is man.

Alexander Pope, Essay on Man, *1733*

"Know thyself"—a maxim as pernicious as it is odious. A person observing himself would arrest his own development. Any caterpillar who tried to "know himself" would never become a butterfly.

André Gide (d. 1951), Nouvelles Nourritures

The saying "Know thyself" is not well put. It would be more correct to say, "Know others."

Menander (fl. 375 B.C.), Thrasyleon

He who knows others is learned;
He who knows himself is wise.

Lao-tzu, Tao te Ching, *sixth century B.C.*

Whoever would know himself, let him open a book.

Jean Paulhan (d. 1918), Elements

Wherever we go, whatever we do, self is the sole subject we study and learn.

Emerson, Journals, *1833*

(*See also* **SELF, SELF-CRITICISM**)

LANGUAGE

Language is our body and our breath, our world and our thought, our perception and even our unconscious.

Philippe Sollers, Logiques, *1968*

Language is what makes people human, and it is the primary way we have of knowing who other people are.

Janet Malcolm, "Reflections," The New Yorker, *March 20, 1989*

Language,—human language,—after all is but little better than the croak and cackle of fowls, and other utterances of brute nature,— sometimes not so adequate.

Nathaniel Hawthorne, American Note-Books, *July 14, 1850*

I am under the spell of language, which has ruled me since I was ten.

V.S. Pritchett at age 80, New York Times, *December 14, 1980*

Language was given to man to conceal his thoughts.

Stendhal, Armance, *1827*

Language was not given to man: he seized it.

Louis Aragon (d. 1982), Le Libertinage.

Next in criminality to him who violates the laws of his country is he who violates the language.

Walter Savage Landor, Imaginary Conversations, *1853*

I am always sorry when any language is lost, because languages are the pedigree of nations.

> *Samuel Johnson, in Boswell's* Journal of a Tour to the Hebrides, *September 18, 1773*

The only living language is the language in which we think and have our being.

> *Antonio Machado,* Juan de Mairena, *1943*

Language is by its very nature a communal thing; that is, it expresses never the exact thing but a compromise—that which is common to you, me, and everybody.

> *Thomas Earnest Hulme,* Speculations, *1923*

Correct English is the slang of prigs who write history and essays. And the strongest slang of all is the slang of poets.

> *George Eliot,* Middlemarch, *1872*

This is the sort of nonsense up with which I refuse to put.

> *Winston Churchill (attributed), after having been criticized for ending a sentence with a preposition*

(*See also* **LITERATURE, WORDS**)

LANGUAGE: SLANG

Slang is a poor man's poetry.

> *John Moore,* You English Words, *1962*

Slang is a language that rolls up its sleeves, spits on its hands and goes to work.

> *Carl Sandburg,* New York Times, *February 13, 1959*

Dialect tempered with slang is an admirable medium of communication between persons who have nothing to say and persons who would not care for anything properly said.

> *Thomas Bailey Aldrich,* Ponkapog Papers, *1903*

LAUGHTER

I laugh about everything for fear of crying.

> *Beaumarchais,* The Barber of Seville, *1775*

Not by wrath does one kill but by laughter.

> *Nietzsche,* Thus Spake Zarathustra, *1892*

Laughter is not at all a bad beginning for a friendship, and it is far the best ending for one.

Oscar Wilde, The Picture of Dorian Gray, *1891*

We are in the world to laugh. In purgatory or in hell we shall no longer be able to do so. And in heaven it would not be proper.

Jules Renard, Journal, *June 1907*

No one is more profoundly sad than he who laughs too much.

Jean Paul Richter, Hesperus, *1795*

(*See also* **HUMOR, SENSE/NONSENSE, WIT**)

LAW AND ABOVE THE LAW

When the President does it, that means that it's not illegal.

Richard M. Nixon, interview with David Frost, May 19, 1977

You [Trajan] have made yourself subject to the laws. . . . Now, for the first time, I hear not Emperor above laws but laws above Emperor.

Pliny the Younger, Panegyric of the Emperor Trajan, A.D. 100.

Wherever law ends, tyranny begins.

John Locke, Treatise on Government, *1690*

In the whole history of law and order, the biggest step was taken by primitive man when . . . the tribe sat in a circle and allowed only one man to speak at a time. An accused who is shouted down has no rights whatever.

Curtis Bok, Saturday Review, *February 13, 1954*

The law is the true embodiment
Of everything that's excellent.
It has no kind of fault or flaw,
And I, my Lords, embody the Law.

W.S. Gilbert, Iolanthe, *1882*

The more laws the more offenders.

Thomas Fuller, Gnomologia, *1732*

Law will never be strong or respected unless it has the sentiment of the people behind it.

James Bryce, The American Commonwealth, *1888*

Good laws, if they are not obeyed, do not constitute good government.

> *Aristotle,* Politics, *c. 350 B.C.*

Laws are like spiders' webs which, if anything small falls into them they ensnare it, but large things break through and escape.

> *Solon (fl. 600 B.C.), in Diogenes Laertius,* Lives

Government can easily exist without law, but law cannot exist without government.

> *Bertrand Russell,* Unpopular Essays, *1950*

We must not make a scarecrow of the law.

> *Shakespeare,* Measure for Measure, *1605*

(*See also* **GOVERNMENT, JUSTICE**)

LAWYERS

The average lawyer is essentially a mechanic who works with a pen instead of a ball peen hammer.

> *Robert Schmitt, Americans for Legal Reform,* Newsletter, *spring 1984*

A criminal lawyer, like a trapeze performer, is seldom more than one slip from an awful fall.

> *Paul O'Neil,* Life, *June 22, 1959*

Lawyers as a group are no more dedicated to justice or public service than a private utility is dedicated to giving light.

> *David Milinkoff,* San Francisco Examiner, *June 22, 1973*

A lawyer has no business with the justice or injustice of the cause which he undertakes. . . . The justice or injustice of the cause is to be decided by the judge.

> *Samuel Johnson, in Boswell,* Tour of the Hebrides, *August 15, 1773*

They have no lawyers [in Utopia] for they consider them as a sort of people whose profession it is to disguise matters.

> *Sir Thomas More,* Utopia, *1516*

You're an attorney. It's your duty to lie, conceal and distort everything, and slander everybody.

> *Jean Giraudoux,* The Mad Woman of Chaillot, *1945*

An incompetent attorney can delay a trial for years or months. A competent attorney can delay one even longer.

Evelle J. Younger, Attorney General of California, Los Angeles Times, *March 3, 1971*

Legal reform is too serious a matter to be left to the legal profession.

Leslie Scarman, New York City Bar Association, Record, *January 1955*

(*See also* **CRIME, JUSTICE**)

LAZINESS

Go to the ant, thou sluggard; consider her ways and be wise.

Proverbs 6:6

Consider the lilies of the field, how they grow; they toil not, neither do they spin.

Matthew 6:28

Indolence is a delightful but distressing state: we must be doing something to be happy.

William Hazlitt, "On the Pleasure of Painting," 1821

What use is a good head if the legs won't carry it?

Hanan J. Ayalti, ed., Yiddish Proverbs, 1949

(*See also* **AMBITION, IDLENESS**)

LEADERSHIP

There are men who, by their sympathetic attractions, carry nations with them.

Emerson, The Conduct of Life, *1860*

Leadership is more likely to be assumed by the aggressive than by the able, and those who scramble to the top are more often motivated by their own inner torments.

Bergen Evans, The Spoor of the Spook, *1954*

The crowd will follow a leader who marches twenty paces ahead of them, but if he is a thousand paces ahead of them, they will neither see nor follow him.

Georg Brandes, Ferdinand Lasalle, *1881*

Why are you going along with those people?
I have to, I'm their leader.

> *Ledru-Rollin (attributed), French presidential campaign, 1848*

To lead means to direct and to exact, and no man dare do either. He might be unpopular.

> *Marya Mannes*, More in Anger, *1958*

(*See also* **AUTHORITY, DEMOCRACY**)

LEARNING

It takes the whole of life to learn how to live, and—even more surprising—it takes the whole of life to learn how to die.

> *Seneca (d. A.D. 65)*, De Brevitate Vitae

We live and learn, but not the wiser grow.

> *John Pomfret (d. 1702)*, Reason

I am convinced that it is of primordial importance to learn more every year than the year before. After all, what is education but a process by which a person begins to learn how to learn.

> *Peter Ustinov*, Dear Me, *1977*

Just as eating against one's will is injurious to health, so study without a liking for it spoils the memory, and it retains nothing it takes in.

> *Leonardo da Vinci*, Notebooks, *c. 1500*

To be fond of learning is to be near to knowledge.

> *Tze-sze*, The Doctrine of the Mean, *fifth century B.C.*

(*See also* **EDUCATION, GROWTH AND DEVELOPMENT**)

LEISURE

Increased means and increased leisure are the two civilizers of man.

> *Benjamin Disraeli, Speech, Manchester, 1872*

There can be no high civilization where there is not ample leisure.

> *Henry Ward Beecher*, Proverbs from Plymouth Pulpit, *1887*

Any notion of the serious life of leisure, as well as men's taste and capacity to live it, has disappeared. Leisure [has become] entertainment.

> *Allan Bloom*, The Closing of the American Mind, *1987*

More free time means more time to waste. The worker who used to have only a little time in which to get drunk and beat his wife now has time to get drunk, beat his wife—and watch TV.

Robert Hutchins, News summaries, January 2, 1954

If bread is the first necessity of life, recreation is a close second.

Edward Bellamy, Looking Backward, *1888*

(*See also* **IDLENESS, PLAY**)

LIBERALISM

Not . . . *what* opinions are held, but . . . *how* they are held: instead of being held dogmatically, [liberal] opinions are held tentatively, and with a consciousness that new evidence may at any moment lead to their abandonment.

Bertrand Russell, Unpopular Essays, *1950*

The chief characteristics of the [liberal] attitude are human sympathy, a receptivity to change, and a scientific willingness to follow reason rather than faith.

Chester Bowles, New Republic, *July 22, 1946*

Fascism . . . throws the noxious theories of so-called Liberalism on the rubbish heap.

Mussolini, Gerarchia, *March 1923*

The liberal . . . insists that the individual must remain so supreme as to make the state his servant.

Sen. Wayne Morse, New Republic, *July 22, 1946*

Liberal institutions straightway cease from being liberal the moment they are soundly established.

Nietzsche, Twilight of the Idols, *1888*

There are no liberals behind steering wheels.

Russell Baker, Poor Russell's Almanac, *1972*

(*See also* **CONSERVATISM, HUMANISM**)

LIBERATION

Armies under the control of . . . a sovereign State cannot bring freedom to anyone.

Simone Weil (d. 1943), Ecrits historiques . . .

We sure liberated the hell out of this place.

> *American soldier in the ruins of a French village, 1944, quoted in*
> *M. Miller,* The Far Shore, *1945*

LIBERTY: *See* FREE COUNTRY.

LIBRARIES

A man's library is a sort of harem.

> *Emerson,* The Conduct of Life, *1860*

Th' first thing to have in a libry is a shelf. Fr'm time to time this can be decorated with litrachure. But th' shelf is the main thing.

> *Peter Finley Dunne,* Mr. Dooley's Opinions, *1901*

(*See also* **BOOKS, READING**)

LIES

Any fool can tell the truth, but it requires a man of some wit to know how to tell a lie.

> *Samuel Butler,* Note-Books, *1912*

I don't mind lying, but I hate inaccuracy.

> *Butler, ibid.*

Anyone can tell word lies; but *body* lies require different skills. The art of faking desire or happiness or agreeable fatigue is not vouchsafed to everyone.

> *François Mauriac,* Thérèse Desqueyroux, *1927*

I like truth. I think mankind needs it; but people have a greater need of lies—lies that flatter, console, and open endless possibilities. Without lies, humanity would die of boredom and futility.

> *Anatole France,* La Vie en fleur, *1923*

Americans detest all lies except lies spoken in public or printed lies.

> *Edgar Watson Howe,* Ventures in Common Sense, *1919*

The great masses of the people . . . will more easily fall victim to a big lie than to a small one.

> *Adolf Hitler,* Mein Kampf, *1933*

The sergeant's widow told a lie when she said I flogged her. I never flogged her. She flogged herself.

> *Nickolai Gogol,* The Inspector General, *1836*

(*See also* **TRUTH VS. FALSEHOOD**)

LIFE

Life is either a daring adventure, or nothing. . . . Security is mostly a superstition. It does not exist in nature.

> *Helen Keller,* The Open Door, *1957*

The great business of life is to be, to do, to do without, and to depart.

> *John Morley, Address on aphorisms, Edinburgh, 1887*

Life is half spent before we know what it is.

> *George Herbert,* Jacula Prudentum, *1651*

That it will never come again
Is what makes life so sweet.

> *Emily Dickinson (d. 1886).*

It's a great thing to talk about or read in books, but when it comes to living it, life is pretty awful.

> *Jean Anouilh,* Time Remembered, *1939*

Life is a progress from want to want, not from enjoyment to enjoyment.

> *Samuel Johnson, in Boswell,* Life, *1791*

People hold on to life more than to anything else; it's really funny when you think of all the beautiful things there are in the world.

> *Romain Gary,* La Vie devant soi, *1975*

How amazing it is to be alive!
Anyone who lives and breathes and puts both feet on the ground,
What possible reason could he have for envying the gods?

> *Paul Claudel,* Tete d'or. *1890*

Life is like a B-picture script. It is that corny. If I had my life story offered to me to film, I'd turn it down.

> *Kirk Douglas,* Look, *October 4, 1955*

Life is like an onion that one peels crying.

> *French proverb*

It has always been difficult for man to realize that his life is all an art. It has been more difficult to conceive it so than to act it so.

Havelock Ellis, The Dance of Life, *1923*

The art of living is more like wrestling than dancing.

Marcus Aurelius, Meditations, *c. A.D. 150*

Life is a jest, and all things show it;
I thought so once, but now I know it.

John Gay, "My Own Epitaph," Fables, *1728*

Life is a tragedy—Hurrah!

Georges Duhamel, Scènes de la vie future, 1930

Life is the greatest bargain; we get it for nothing.

Hanan J. Ayalti, ed., Yiddish Proverbs, 1949

The only basis for living is believing in life, loving it, and applying the whole force of one's intellect to know it better.

Emile Zola, Le Docteur Pascal, *1893*

The moment one is on the side of life "peace and security" drop out of consciousness. The only peace, the only security, is in fulfillment.

Henry Miller, The Wisdom of the Heart, *1941*

Live all you can; it's a mistake not to. It doesn't so much matter what you do in particular, so long as you have your life. If you haven't had that, what have you had?

Henry James, The Ambassadors, *1923*

Hold it the greatest wrong to prefer life to honor and for the sake of life to lose the reason for living.

Juvenal, Satires, *c. 100*

(*See also* **LIFE AND DEATH, LONGEVITY**)

LIFE AND DEATH

I'm not afraid of death. It's the stake one puts up in order to play the game of life.

Jean Giraudoux, Amphitryon, *1929*

In the midst of life, we are in death.

Church of England, The Book of Common Prayer

If a man hasn't discovered something that he will die for, he isn't fit to live.

> *Martin Luther King, Jr., speech, Detroit, 1963*

It matters not how a man dies, but how he lives.

> *Samuel Johnson, in Boswell's* Life, *1791*

People living deeply have no fear of death.

> *Anaïs Nin,* Diary, *1967*

Death, my son, is a benefit for all of us; it is the night of this turbulent day that we call Life.

> *Bernardin de St. Pierre,* Paul et Virginie, *1788*

Life is a sickness which sleep relieves every sixteen hours; but it's [only] a palliative, death is the remedy.

> *Chamfort (d. 1794),* Maximes

If life must not be taken too seriously—then so neither must death.

> *Samuel Butler,* Note-Books, *1912*

I postpone death by living, by suffering, by error, by risking, by giving, by losing.

> *Anaïs Nin,* Diary, *March 1933*

(*See also* **DEATH AND DYING, RESIGNATION**)

LIMITS

O my soul, do not aspire to immortal life, but exhaust the limits of the possible.

> *Pindar,* Odes, *fifth century B.C.*

Our accepting what we are must always inhibit our being what we ought to be.

> *John Fowles,* The Magus, *1965*

Knowledge of what is possible is the beginning of happiness.

> *George Santayana,* Little Essays, *1920*

The thing I am most aware of is my limits. And this is natural; for I never, or almost never, occupy the middle of my cage; my whole being surges toward the bars.

> *André Gide,* Journals, *August 4, 1930*

The humorous man recognizes that absolute purity, absolute justice, absolute logic and perfection are beyond human achievement and that men have been able to live happily for thousands of years in a state of genial frailty.

Brooks Atkinson, Once Around the Sun, *1951*

(*See also* **MORTALITY, PERFECTION, RESIGNATION**)

LITERACY, CULTURAL

He that reads and grows no wiser seldom suspects his own deficiency, but complains of hard words and obscure sentences, and asks why books are written which cannot be understood.

Samuel Johnson, The Idler, *1760*

Cultural literacy lies *above* the everyday levels of knowledge that everyone possesses and *below* the expert level known only to specialists. It is that middle ground of cultural knowledge possessed by the "common reader." It includes information that we have traditionally expected our children to receive in school, but which they no longer do.

E.D. Hirsch, Jr., Cultural Literacy, *1987*

LITERATURE

Literature is my Utopia. Here I am not disfranchized. No barrier of the senses shuts me out from the sweet, gracious discourse of my book friends. They talk to me without embarrassment or awkwardness.

Helen Keller, The Story of My Life, *1902*

Literature transmits incontrovertible condensed experience . . . from generation to generation. In this way literature becomes the living memory of a nation.

Alexander Solzhenitsyn, Nobel Prize Lecture, 1972

What is so wonderful about great literature is that it transforms the man who reads it towards the condition of the man who wrote.

E.M. Forster, Two Cheers for Democracy, *1951*

Literature is the human activity that takes the fullest and most precise account of variousness, possibility, complexity, and difficulty.

Lionel Trilling, The Liberal Imagination, *1950*

The land of literature is a fairy land to those who view it at a distance, but, like all other landscapes, the charm fades on a nearer approach, and thorns and briars become visible.

> *Washington Irving,* Tales of a Traveler, *1824*

The illusion of art is to make one believe that great literature is very close to life, but exactly the opposite is true. Life is amorphous, literature is formal.

> *Françoise Sagan, interview,* Writers at Work, *1958*

The decline of literature indicates the decline of a nation.

> *Goethe, in Eckermann's* Conversations, *1836*

(*See also* **BOOKS, NOVEL, WRITING**)

LITERATURE AND POLITICS

Governments are suspicious of literature because it is a force that eludes them.

> *Emile Zola,* Le Roman expérimental, *1880*

A great writer is, so to speak, a second government in his country. And for that reason no regime has ever loved great writers, only minor ones.

> *Alexander Solzhenitsyn,* The First Circle, *1964*

LONELINESS

[D.H. Lawrence] was the first modern novelist to realize that men and women cannot solve one another's loneliness.

> *Anatole Broyard,* New York Times *Book Review, November 8, 1987*

Courage is the price that life exacts for granting peace.
The soul that knows it not, knows no release
From little things;
Knows not the livid loneliness of fear.

> *Amelia Earhart (d. 1937), "Courage"*

—Are you in trouble?—Do you need advice?—Write-to-Miss-Lonelyhearts-ι nd-she-will-help-you. . . .
The Miss Lonelyι earts are the priests of twentieth century America.

> *Nathanael West,* Miss Lonelyhearts, *1933*

(*See also* **SOLITUl E**)

LONGEVITY

People do not care how nobly they live, only how long, despite the fact that it is within everyone's reach to live nobly, but within no one's reach to live long.

> *Seneca (d. 65 B.C.),* Epistles

The fundamental precept of the fight for longevity is avoidance of satiation. One must not lose desires. They are mighty stimulants to creativeness, to love and to long life.

> *Dr. Alexander Bogomoletz,* Prolongation of Life, *1946*

Every man desires to live long, but no man would be old.

> *Jonathan Swift,* Thoughts on Various Subjects, *1711*

Life protracted is protacted woe.

> *Samuel Johnson,* The Vanity of Human Wishes, *1749*

(*See also* **AGE, AGING**)

LOSERS

In life [unlike a game] the loser's score is always zero.

> *W.H. Auden,* The Dyer's Hand, *1962*

Some people are so fond of ill-luck that they run half-way to meet it.

> *Douglas Jerrold, "Meeting Troubles Half-Way," 1859*

The schlemiehl lands on his back and bruises his nose.

> *Hanan J. Ayalti, ed.,* Yiddish Proverbs, *1949*

(*See also* **SUCCESS/FAILURE**)

LOSS

You must lose a fly to catch a trout.

> *George Herbert,* Jacula prudentum, *1651*

Loss is nothing else but change, and change is Nature's delight.

> *Marcus Aurelius,* Meditations, *c. 150*

No man can lose what he never had.

> *Izaak Walton,* The Compleat Angler, *1653*

There are occasions when it is undoubtedly better to incur loss than to make gain.

Plautus, The Captives, *c. 280 B.C.*

Whatever you lose, reckon of no account.

Publius Syrus, Moral Sayings, *c. 50 B.C.*

(*See also* **ADVERSITY**)

LOVE

There is a law that man should love his neighbor as himself. In a few hundred years it should be as natural to mankind as breathing or the upright gait; but if he does not learn it he must perish.

Alfred Adler (d. 1937), Social Interest

Come live with me, and be my love,
And we will some new pleasures prove
Of golden sands, and crystal brooks,
With silken lines, and silver hooks.

John Donne, "The Bait," *c. 1600*

Love is the miracle of civilization.

Stendhal, On Love, *1822*

Loving is not just looking at each other, it's looking in the same direction.

Antoine de St.-Exupéry, Wind, Sand, and Stars, *1939*

The supreme happiness in life is the conviction that we are loved.

Victor Hugo, Les Misérables, *1862*

Loving is not just caring deeply, it's, above all, understanding.

Françoise Sagan, Le Soir, *April 20, 1960*

Are we ever our own master when it comes to falling in love? and if we are in love, can we act as if we were not?

Diderot, Jack the Fatalist and His Master, *1770*

Like everybody who is not in love, he thought one chose the person to be loved after endless deliberations and on the basis of particular qualities or advantages.

Marcel Proust, Remembrance of Things Past: Cities of the Plain, *1922*

Love is an irresistible desire to be irresistibly desired.

> *Robert Frost, in conversation*

Love looks not with the eyes, but with the mind,
And therefore is winged Cupid painted blind.

> *Shakespeare,* Mid-Summer Night's Dream, *1595*

The big question in life is the unhappiness one has caused; . . . the most ingenious rationalizations will not help the man who has broken the heart he loved.

> *Benjamin Constant,* Adolphe, *1816*

Shall I compare thee to a summer's day?
Thou art more lovely and more temperate. . . .

> *Shakespeare,* Sonnet No. 18

God made coitus; man made love.

> *E. and J. de Goncourt,* Journal, *July 19, 1855*

Love is not all: it is not meat nor drink
Nor slumber nor a roof against the rain;
Nor yet a floating spar to men that sink. . . .

> *Edna St. Vincent Millay, "Fatal Interview," 1931*

Love, [Emma] believed, had to come suddenly with great thunderclaps and lightning flashes—a storm from the heavens upon a life, turning it upside down, blowing away its petty wills like leaves, and carrying one's heart to the edge of the abyss.

> *Gustave Flaubert,* Madame Bovary, *1857*

To be able to say how much you love is to love but little.

> *Petrarch (fl. 1300), "To Laura in Death"*

Love, all alike, no season knows, nor clime,
Nor hours, days, months, which are the range of time.

> *John Donne, "The Sun Rising," 1595*

Love is the emotion that a woman feels always for a poodle dog and sometimes for a man.

> *George Jean Nathan,* The Theatre, the Drama, the Girls, *1921*

It seems that it is madder never to abandon one's self than often to be infatuated; better to be wounded, a captive and a slave, than always to walk in armor.

> *Margaret Fuller,* Summer on the Lakes, *1844*

(*See also* **COURTSHIP, LOVERS, SEXUAL RELATIONS**)

LOVE, LOSS OF

We are never so defenseless against suffering as when we love, never so helplessly unhappy as when we have lost our love object or its love.

Sigmund Freud, Civilization and Its Discontents, *1930*

The great tragedy of life is not that men perish, but that they cease to love.

W. Somerset Maugham, The Summing Up, *1938*

The heart that can no longer
Love passionately, must with fury hate.

Jean Racine, Andromache, *1667*

Yet each man kills the thing he loves,
By each let this be heard,
Some do it with a bitter look,
Some with a flattering word.
The coward does it with a kiss,
The brave man with a sword.

Oscar Wilde, The Ballad of Reading Gaol, *1898*

(*See also* **INFIDELITY, REJECTION**)

LOVE AND SCANDAL

. . . are the best sweeteners of tea.

Henry Fielding, Love in Several Masques, *1743*

A girl's loving adoration is stronger than society's disapproval.

Balzac, Modeste Mignon, *1834*

Christianity, by making love a sin, did Love a great service.

Anatole France, The Garden of Epicurus, *1894*

LOVERS

The first symptom of love in a young man is timidity; in a girl boldness.

Victor Hugo, Les Misérables, *1862*

Who would give a law to lovers? Love is unto itself a higher law.

Boethius, The Consolation of Philosophy, A.D. *524*

It is easier to be a lover than a husband for the simple reason that it is more difficult to be witty every day than to say pretty things from time to time.

> *Balzac,* Physiologie du mariage, *1829*

When I lie tangled in her hair
And fettered to her eye,
The gods that wanton in the air
Know no such liberty.

> *Richard Lovelace, "To Althea from Prison," 1649*

The lover is a monotheist who knows that other people worship different gods but cannot himself imagine that there could be other gods.

> *Theodor Reik,* Of Love and Lust, *1957*

The reason lovers never tire of each other is this: they're always talking about themselves.

> *La Rochefoucauld,* Maxims, *1665*

Come my Celia, let us prove
While we can, the sport of love;
Time will not be ours forever,
He at length our good will sever. . . .

> *Ben Jonson, "Song to Celia," 1607*

Send home my long-strayed eyes to me,
Which (Oh) too long have dwelt on thee.

> *John Donne, "The Message," c. 1595*

The lover knows much more about absolute good and universal beauty than any logician or theologian, unless the latter, too, be lovers in disguise.

> *George Santayana,* The Life of Reason: Reason in Society, *1906*

She lived unknown, and few would know
When Lucy ceased to be;
But she is in her grave, and oh,
The difference to me!

> *William Wordsworth, "She Dwelt Among the Untrodden Ways,"*
> *1800*

LOVE, TRUE

True love always makes a man better, no matter what woman inspires it.

> *Alexandre Dumas fils,* Camille, *1852*

Let me not to the marriage of true minds
Admit impediments. Love is not love
Which alters when it alteration finds.

Shakespeare, Sonnet No. 116

All things to their destruction draw,
Only our love hath no decay;
This, no tomorrow hath, no yesterday.

John Donne, "The Anniversary," c. 1595

In love there are no vacations. . . . No such thing. Love has to be lived
fully with its boredom and all that.

Marguerite Duras, Les Petits Chevaux de Tarquinia, *1953*

LOYAL/DISLOYAL

My kind of loyalty was loyalty to one's country, not to its institutions
or its office-holders.

Mark Twain, A Connecticut Yankee in King Arthur's Court, *1889*

Loyalty in a free society depends upon the toleration of disloyalty.

Alan Barth, The Loyalty of Free Man, *1951*

LUST

[The] common men-in-the-street and women-in-the-street . . . have
as great a hate and contempt of sex as the greyest Puritan. . . . They
insist that a film-heroine shall be a neuter, . . . that real sex feelings
shall only be shown by the villain or villainess . . .

D.H. Lawrence, "Pornography and Obscenity," This Quarter, *Paris,
1929*

Lust for power is the most flagrant of all the passions.

Tacitus, Annals, *c. A.D. 100*

LUXURY

. . . The lust for comfort, that stealthy thing that enters the house as
a guest, and then becomes a host, and then a master.

Kahlil Gibran, The Prophet, *1923*

Minds, like bodies, will often fall into a pimpled, ill-conditioned state
from mere excess of comfort.

Charles Dickens, Barnaby Rudge, *1842*

They must know but little of mankind who imagine that, having once been seduced by luxury, they can ever renounce it.

Rousseau, Lettre à d'Alembert sur les spectacles, *1758*

Luxury . . . corrupts at once rich and poor, the rich by possession and the poor by covetousness.

Rousseau, The Social Contract, *1762*

Give me the luxuries of life and I will willingly do without the necessities.

Frank Lloyd Wright, obituary, 1959

(*See also* **EXCESS**)

MACHINE AGE

We sensed the devil in the machine and we were right. To a believer, it signifies God dethroned.

Oswald Spengler, The Decline of the West, *1918*

Many remarkable discoveries and inventions were made [in the nineteenth century]. Most memorable among these was the discovery . . . that women and children could work for 25 hours a day . . . without many of them dying or becoming excessively deformed. This was known as the Industrial Revelation.

W. Sellar and R. Yeatman, 1066 and All That, 1931

Case No. 14—Isabella Read, 12 years old, coal bearer:
"I carry about 125 pounds on my back. Have to stoop much and am frequently in water up to calves of my legs. When first went down, fell frequently asleep while waiting for coal and from heat and [fatique]. I do not like the work nor do the lassies, but they are made to like it. When the weather is warm, there is [difficulty] breathing and frequently the lights go out."

Great Britain, Parliamentary Report, Ashley Mines Commission,
1842

The future offers very little hope for those who expect that our new mechanical slaves will offer us a world in which we may rest from thinking. Help us they may, but at the cost of supreme demands upon our honesty and our intelligence. The world of the future will be an ever more demanding struggle against the limitations of our intelligence, not a comfortable hammock in which we can lie down to be waited upon by our robot slaves.

> *Norbert Wiener,* God and Golem, Inc., *1964*

The machine has conquered man [and] man has become a machine, working but no longer living.

> *Mahatma Gandhi,* Autobiography, *1924*

Kitty Hawk: Success. Four flights Thursday morning. All against 21–mile wind. Started from level with engine power alone. Average speed through air 31 miles. Longest 59 seconds. Inform press. Home Christmas.

> *Orville and Wilbur Wright, telegram to the Reverend Milton Wright, December 17, 1903*

What is it that makes a man willing to sit on top of an enormous Roman candle, such as a Redstone, Atlas, Titan or Saturn rocket, and wait for someone to light the fuse?

> *Tom Wolfe,* The Right Stuff, *1979*

(*See also* **PROGRESS**)

MAJORITY

The power of the majority . . . is not unlimited. Above it in the moral world are humanity, justice, and reason; and in the political world, vested rights.

> *Alexis de Tocqueville,* Democracy in America, *1835*

Nor is the people's judgment always true:
The most may err as grossly as the few.

> *John Dryden,* Absalom and Achitophel, *1680*

That which has always been accepted by everyone, everywhere, is almost certain to be false.

> *Paul Valéry,* Tel Quel, *1943*

Politically I believe in democracy, but culturally, not at all. . . . Whenever a cultural matter rolls up a majority I know it is wrong.

> *John Sloan (d. 1951), American artist.*

A majority can never replace the individual. . . Just as a hundred fools do not make one wise man, a heroic decision is not likely to come from a hundred cowards.

> *Adolf Hitler,* Mein Kampf, *1933*

MAN

So God created man in his own image, in the image of God created he him; male and female created he them.

Genesis 1:27

Good Lord, what is man! for as simple as he looks,
Do but try to develop his hooks and his crooks,
With his depths and his shallows, his good and his evil,
All in all, he's a problem must puzzle the devil.

Robert Burns (d. 1796), Sketch

Man may be considered as a superior species of animal who produces philosophies and poems in about the same way that silkworms produce their cocoons and bees their hives.

Hippolyte Taine, La Fontaine et ses fables, *1853*

Man is the only animal that laughs and weeps; for he is the only animal that is struck with the difference between what things are and what they ought to be.

William Hazlitt, The English Comic Writers, *1819*

Drinking without being thirsty and making love at any time, Madame, are the only things that distinguish us from other animals.

Beaumarchais, The Marriage of Figaro, *1784*

Man . . . is simply the most formidable of all the beasts of prey, and, indeed, the only one that preys systematically on his own species.

William James, Memories and Studies, *1911*

Man is the only animal that blushes or needs to.

Mark Twain, Pudd'nhead Wilson's New Calendar, *1894*

Oh, how I love the Earth and everything in it, life and death. And men. One can think of nothing finer, or nicer, than men . . . their wars, their concentration camps, their justice.

Marcel Aymé, Uranus, *1948*

I am more and more convinced that man is a dangerous creature; and that power, whether vested in many or a few, is ever grasping, and like the grave, cries, "Give, give!"

Abigail to John Adams, November 27, 1775

Man is only a reed, the weakest thing in nature, but he is a thinking reed, and from that comes all his dignity.

Pascal, Pensées, *1670*

Man is a creature adapted for life under circumstances which are very narrowly limited. A few degrees of temperature more or less, a slight variation in the composition of air, the precise suitability of food, make all the difference between health and sickness, . . . life and death.

Sir Robert S Ball, The Story of the Heavens, *1885*

(*See also* **HUMANISM, HUMAN NATURE**)

MANNERS

Etiquette is what you are doing when people are looking and listening. What you are thinking is your business.

Hudson, Virginia Cary, O Ye Jigs and Juleps! *1962*

Under bad manners, as under graver faults, lies very commonly an overestimate of our special individuality, as distinguished from our generic humanity.

Oliver Wendell Holmes, The Professor at the Breakfast Table, *1858*

A bad manner spoils everything, even reason and justice; a good one supplies everything, gilds a No, sweetens truth, and adds a touch of beauty to old age itself.

Baltasar Gracian, The Art of Worldly Wisdom, *1647*

MARRIAGE

Therefore shall a man leave his father and his mother, and shall cleave unto his wife: and they shall be one flesh.

Genesis 2:24

Marriage, n. A community consisting of a master, a mistress, and two slaves, making in all two.

Ambrose Bierce, The Devil's Dictionary, *1911*

Is not marriage an open question, when it is alleged, from the beginning of the world, that such as are in the institution wish to get out, and such as are out wish to get in?

Emerson, Representative Men, *1850*

Marriage is the only evil that men pray for.

Greek proverb

Get married, in any case. If you happen to get a good mate, you will be happy; if a bad one, you will become philosophical, which is a fine thing in itself.

Socrates (d. 399 B.C.,) in Diogenes Laertius, Lives.

Marriage has many pains, but celibacy has no pleasures.

Samuel Johnson, Rasselas, *1759*

His designs were strictly honorable, as the phrase is: that is, to rob a lady of her fortune by way of marriage.

Henry Fielding, Tom Jones, *1749*

Of all serious things, marriage is the funniest.

Beaumarchais, The Marriage of Figaro, *1784*

The best part of married life is the fights. The rest is only so–so.

Thornton Wilder, The Matchmaker, *1954*

I married beneath me—all women do.

Nancy Astor, M.P., speech, Oldham, England, 1951

In order to keep something sacred here below, it would be better if a marriage had one slave, instead of two strong-willed people.

Madame de Staël, Germany, *1810*

The people people have for friends
Your common sense appall,
But the people people marry
Are the queerest folk of all.

Charlotte Perkins Gilman, "Queer People", *1899*

Seldom, or perhaps never, does a marriage develop into an individual relationship smoothly and without crises; there is no coming to consciousness without pain.

C.G. Jung, Analytical Psychology, *1928*

In every house of marriage
there's room for an interpreter.

Stanley Kunitz, "Route Six,"
The Poems of Stanley Kunitz, 1928–1978, *1976*

Lexicon for marital fighting:
   Amnesia: "Who do you think you ARE?"
   Apology: "PARdon me for LIVing!"
   Family Tree: "She's YOUR mother, not mine."
   Hearing impairment: "Could you speak up a little? They can't hear you in Europe."
   Language barrier: "What's the matter, don't you understand English?"
   Mining: "I hadn't realized we'd descended to that level."

Wildlife: "That's right, use physical violence. That's all an animal like you knows anyway."

> *Dan Greenburg and Suzanne O'Malley,* How to Avoid Love and Marriage, *1983*

To keep marriage brimming
With love in the marriage cup,
Whenever you're wrong, admit it;
Whenever you're right, shut up.

> *Ogden Nash, "A Word to Husbands,"* Everyone but Thee and Me, *1962*

The number of women in London who flirt with their own husbands is perfectly scandalous. It looks so bad. It is simply washing one's clean linen in public.

> *Oscar Wilde,* The Importance of Being Earnest, *1895*

MARTYRDOM

To die for a religion is easier than to live it absolutely.

> *Jorge Luis Borges,* Labyrinthes, *1962*

Martyrdom has always been a proof of the intensity, never the correctness, of a belief.

> *Arthur Schweitzer,* Out of My Life and Thought, *1932*

Perhaps there is no happiness in life so perfect as the martyr's.

> *O Henry,* The Trimmed Lamp, *1907*

It is often pleasant to stone a martyr, no matter how much we may admire him.

> *John Barth,* The Floating Opera, *1956*

In the history of the world it is the Absurd that has claimed the most martyrs.

> *E. and J. de Goncourt,* Journal, *October 31, 1860*

MATERIALISM

We live in a world of things, and our only connection with them is that we know how to manipulate or consume them.

> *Erich Fromm,* The Sane Society, *1948*

What is at the heart of all our national problems? It is that we have seen the hand of material interest sometimes about to close upon our dearest rights and possessions.

Woodrow Wilson, speech, *October 27, 1913*

MATHEMATICS

. . . takes us into the world region of absolute necessity, to which not only the actual world, but every possible world, must conform.

Bertrand Russell, The Study of Mathematics, *1902*

Mathematics . . . possesses not only truth, but supreme beauty—a beauty cold and austere, like that of a sculpture, without appeal to any part of our weaker nature, without the gorgeous trappings of painting or music, yet sublimely pure, and capable of a stern perfection such as only the greatest art can show.

Ibid.

The union of the mathematician with the poet, fervor with measure, passion with correctness, this surely is the ideal.

William James, Collected Essays and Reviews, *1920*

The perfection of mathematical beauty is such. . . that whatsoever is most beautiful and regular is also found to be the most useful and excellent.

Sir D'Arcy Wentworth Thompson, On Growth and Form, *1917*

One has to be able to count if only so that, at fifty, one doesn't marry a girl of twenty.

Maxim Gorky, The Zykovs, *1914*

The true spirit of delight, the exaltation, the sense of being more than Man, which is the touchstone of the highest excellence, is to be found in mathematics as surely as in poetry.

Bertrand Russell, Mysticism and Logic, *1917*

She was a crazy mathematics major from the Wharton School of Business who could not count to twenty-eight each month without getting into trouble.

Joseph Heller, Catch-22, *1955*

Mathematicians who are only mathematicians have exact minds, provided all things are explained to them by means of definitions and axioms; otherwise they are inaccurate and insufferable, for they are only right when the principles are quite clear.

Pascal, Pensées, *1670*

MATURITY

How do you know the fruit is ripe?—Simple: When it leaves the branch.

André Gide, Pretexts, *1903*

The turning point in the process of growing up is when you discover the core of strength within you that survives all hurt.

Max Lerner, The Unfinished Country, *1950*

The process of maturing is an art to be learned, an effort to be sustained. By the age of fifty you have made yourself what you are, and if it is good, it is better than your youth.

Marya Mannes, More in Anger, *1958*

A person's maturity consists in having found again the seriousness one had as a child, at play.

Nietzsche, Beyond Good and Evil, *1886*

To live with fear and not be afraid is the final test of maturity.

Edward Weeks, Look, *July 18, 1961*

(*See also* **YOUTH**)

MEANING

The meaning of things lies not in the things themselves but in our attitude towards them.

Saint-Exupéry, The Wisdom of the Sands, *1948*

There is no meaning to life except the meaning man gives his life by the unfolding of his powers, by living productively.

Erich Fromm, Man for Himself, *1947*

MEDIOCRITY

Some men are born mediocre, some men achieve mediocrity, and some men have mediocrity thrust upon them. With Major Major it had been all three.

Joseph Heller, Catch-22, *1961*

Things in which mediocrity is insupportable—poetry, music, painting, public speaking.

La Bruyère, Characters, *1694*

As a rule, the man who can do all things equally well is a very mediocre individual.

> *Elbert Hubbard (d. 1915)*, The Philistine

In the republic of mediocrity genius is dangerous.

> *Robert G. Ingersoll*, Prose-Poems and Selections, *1884*

Solitude, the safeguard of mediocrity. . . .

> *Emerson*, The Conduct of Life, *1860*

MEMORY

Memory is the thing you forget with.

> *Alexander Chase*, Perspectives, *1966*

"The horror of that moment," the King went on, "I shall never, *never* forget!"
"You will, though," the Queen said, "if you don't make a memorandum of it."

> *Lewis Carroll*, Through the Looking-Glass, *1872*

Memory performs the impossible for man; holds together past and present, gives continuity and dignity to human life.

> *Mark Van Doren*, Liberal Education, *1943*

When to the sessions of sweet silent thought
I summon up remembrance of things past,
I sigh the lack of many a thing I sought,
And with old woes new wail my dear times' waste.

> *Shakespeare*, Sonnet No. 30

Not the power to remember, but its very opposite, the power to forget, is a necessary condition for our existence.

> *Sholem Asch*, The Nazarene, *1939*

Women and elephants never forget.

> *Dorothy Parker*, Death and Taxes, *1931*

MEN VS. WOMEN

Male, n. A member of the unconsidered or negligible sex. The male of the human race is commonly known (to the female) as Mere Man. The genus has two varieties: good providers and bad providers.

> *Ambrose Bierce*, The Devil's Dictionary, *1911*

There was, I think, never any reason to believe in any innate superiority of the male, except his superior muscle.

Bertrand Russell, Unpopular Essays, *1950*

To deny the fundamental antagonism between [men and women], their mutual and eternal hostility; to dream . . . of equal rights, equal education, equal obligations . . . —such are the signs of a shallow mind; one so shallow in this area . . . will probably be too "short" for the [larger] problems of life.

Nietzsche, Beyond Good and Evil, *1886*

Man is the hunter; woman is his game.
The sleek and shining creatures of the chase,
We hunt them for the beauty of their skins;
They love us for it, and we ride them down.

Alfred, Lord Tennyson, The Princess, *1847*

God created women for the unique purpose of domesticating men.

Voltaire, L'Ingénu, *1767*

The common study of mankind is woman and . . . it is the most complex and arduous.

Henry Adams, Mont Saint Michel and Chartres, *1904*

Man's love is of man's life a thing apart,
'Tis woman's whole existence.

Lord Byron, Don Juan, *1818*

Women are not men's equals in anything except responsibility. We are not their inferiors, either, or even their superiors. We are quite simply different races.

Phyllis McGinley, The Province of the Heart, *1959*

Women [have] a special talent for understanding a man better than he understands himself.

Victor Hugo, Les Misérables, *1862*

Women like silent men. They think they're listening.

Marcel Achard, Quote, *November 4, 1956*

'Tis strange what a man may do, and a woman yet think him an angel.

William Makepeace Thackeray, Henry Esmond, *1852*

Women are never disarmed by compliments; men always are.

Oscar Wilde, An Ideal Husband, *1899*

In the lower classes, the woman is not only superior to the man, she almost always controls him as well.

Balzac, Cousine Bette, *1847*

"My clichés about men: as vain as a man, as selfish as a man, as tricky as a man, as two-faced as a man."
"What have men ever done to you?"
"Nothing. But they have caused all the trouble in the world and they brag about it."

Elsa Triolet (d. 1970), Les Fantomes armés

Men are what their mothers made them.

Emerson, The Conduct of Life, *1860*

Women speak because they wish to speak, whereas a man speaks only when driven to speech by something outside himself—like, for instance, he can't find any clean socks.

Jean Kerr, The Snake Has All the Lines, *1960*

Men are the reason that women do not love one another.

La Bruyère, Characters, 1688

When a man's in love he at once makes a pedestal of the Ten Commandments and stands on the top of them with his arms akimbo. When a woman's in love she doesn't care two straws for Thou Shalt and Thou Shalt Not.

W. Somerset Maugham, Lady Frederick, *1907*

Women want mediocre men, and men are working hard to be as mediocre as possible.

Margaret Mead, Quote, *May 15, 1958*

Women, as they grow older, rely more and more on cosmetics. Men, as they grow older, rely more and more on a sense of humor.

George Jean Nathan, American Mercury, *July 1925*

Woman understands children better than man does, but man is more childlike than woman.

Nietzsche, Thus Spake Zarathustra, *1892*

Women are not so sentimental as men, and are not so easily touched with the unspoken poetry of nature; being less poetical, and having less imagination, they are more fitted for practical affairs, and would make less failures in business.

Charles Dudley Warner, Backlog Studies, *1873*

There is trouble with a wife, but it's even worse with a woman who is not a wife.

Leo Tolstoy, Anna Karenina, *1876*

A man in the house is worth two in the street.

Mae West, in Belle of the Nineties, *movie, 1934*

The male is a domestic animal which, if treated with firmness and kindness, can be trained to do most things.

Jilly Cooper, Cosmopolitan, *1972*

Every man who is high up loves to think he has done it all himself; and the wife smiles, and lets it go at that. It's our only joke. Every woman knows that.

J.M. Barrie, What Every Woman Knows, *1908*

I require only three things of a man:
He must be handsome, ruthless, and stupid.

Dorothy Parker, You Might As Well Live, *1971*

MERIT

The world more often rewards the appearance of merit than merit itself.

La Rochefoucauld, Maxims, *1665*

Charms strike the sight, but merit wins the soul.

Alexander Pope, The Rape of the Lock, *1712*

The assumption of merit is easier, less embarrassing, and more effectual than the actual attainment of it.

William Hazlitt, Characteristics, *1823*

METHOD

There is always a best way of doing everything, if it be to boil an egg. Manners are the happy ways of doing things.

Emerson, The Conduct of Life, *1860*

It is not always by plugging away at a difficulty and sticking to it that one overcomes it; often it is by working on the one next to it. Some things and some people have to be approached obliquely, at an angle.

André Gide, Journals, *October 26, 1924*

There is time enough for everything in the course of the day if you do but one thing at once; but there is not time enough in the year if you will do two things at a time.

> *Lord Chesterfield*, Letters to His Son, *April 14, 1747*

MIDDLE CLASS

The middle class is always a firm champion of equality when it comes to a class above it; but it is its inveterate foe when it concerns elevating a class below it.

> *Orestes A. Brownson*, The Laboring Classes, *1840*

I have to live for others and not for myself; that's middle-class morality.

> *G.B. Shaw*, Pygmalion, *1912*

Most Americans want to be . . . only comfortably cultivated. They dabble with the intellectual just enough to avoid being lowbrow and escape being highbrow.

> *Alan Valentine (b. 1901)*, The Age of Conformity

(*See also* **BOURGEOIS**)

MILITARY / MILITARISM

What fosters militarism makes for barbarism; what fosters peace makes for civilization.

> *Herbert Spencer*, Social Statics, *1850*

Overgrown military establishments are, under any form of government, inauspicious to liberty, and are to be regarded as particularly hostile to republican liberty.

> *George Washington*, Farewell Address, *1796*

We must guard against the acquisition of unwarranted influence . . . by the military-industrial complex. The potential for the disastrous rise of misplaced power exists and will persist.

> *Dwight D. Eisenhower, Farewell Address, 1961*

The professional military mind is by necessity an inferior and unimaginative mind; no man of high intellectual quality would willingly imprison his gifts in such a calling.

> *H.G. Wells*, The Outline of History, *1920*

Military intelligence—a contradiction in terms.

> *Oswald Garrison Villard, Lecture, 1920*

MIND

My mind to me a kingdom is;
Such present joys therein I find
That it excels all other bliss
The earth affords or grows by kind.
Sir Edward Dyer (d. 1607), Rawlinson Poetry MS 85

Curiosity is one of the permanent and certain characteristics of a vigorous mind.
Samuel Johnson, The Rambler, *1751*

Iron rusts from disuse, stagnant water loses its purity and in cold weather becomes frozen; even so does inaction sap the vigor of the mind.
Leonardo da Vinci, Notebooks, *1508*

Every man has seen the wall that limits his mind.
Alfred de Vigny, Les Destinées, *1864*

The direction of the mind is more important that its progress.
Joseph Joubert, Pensées, *1842*

I know of no country in which there is so little independence of mind . . . as in America.
Alexis de Tocqueville, Democracy in America, *1835*

(*See also* **INTELLIGENCE**)

MIRACLES

Real miracles are created by men when they use their God-given courage and intelligence.
Jean Anouilh, The Lark, *1955*

We must remember that Satan has his miracles, too.
John Calvin, Institutes of the Christian Religion, *1536*

Miracles happen to those who believe in them. Otherwise, why does the Virgin Mary not appear to Lamaists, Mohammedans, or Hindus?
Bernard Berenson (d. 1959), New York Times Book Review

MISERS

Thief: Don't make a move, this is a stick-up!
Jack Benny: What?

Thief: You heard me.
Benny: Mister . . . Mister, put down that gun.
Thief: Shut up . . . Now, come on . . . your money or your life. (*Long pause.*) Look bud, I said: Your money or your life.
Benny: I'm thinking . . .

"The Jack Benny Show," NBC-Radio, 1948

The miser puts all his gold pieces in a coffer; but as soon as the coffer is closed, it's the same as if it were empty.

André Gide, Pretexts, *1903*

MODERATION

The best is the enemy of the good.

Voltaire, Philosophical Dictionary, *1764*

Moderation is a fatal thing; nothing succeeds like excess.

Oscar Wilde, A Woman of No Importance, *1894*

Moderation in temper is always a virtue; but moderation in principle is always a vice.

Thomas Paine, The Rights of Man, *1791*

Perfect reason avoids all extremes,
And requires that one be good, in moderation.

Molière, The Misanthrope, *1666*

I have not been afraid of excess: excess on occasion is exhilirating. It prevents moderation from acquiring the deadening effect of a habit.

W. Somerset Maugham, The Summing Up, *1938*

(*See also* **EXCESS, EXTREMISM**)

MODESTY

. . . The art of encouraging people to find out for themselves how wonderful you are.

Anonymous

He's a modest little man with much to be modest about.

Re: Clement Atlee, quoted in M. Foote, Aneurin Bevan

Who would succeed in the world should be wise in the use of his pronouns.
Utter the You twenty times, where you once utter the I.

John Hay, "Distichs," c. 1870

For people of average ability, modesty is merely candor; but for men of great talent, it is hypocrisy.

> *Schopenhauer*, Parerga and Paralipomena, *1851*

A modest man is usually admired—if people ever hear of him.

> *Edgar Watson Howe*, Ventures in Common Sense, *1919*

MONEY

A cynic knows the price of everything and the value of nothing.

> *Oscar Wilde*, Lady Windermere's Fan, *1893*

I cannot afford to waste my time making money.

> *Louis Agassiz (d. 1873)*, declining an offer to teach

They who are of the opinion that Money will do everything, may very well be suspected to do everything for Money.

> *George Savile, (d. 1695)*, Complete Works, *1912*

I know of no country ... where the love of money has taken stronger hold on the affections of men and where a profounder contempt is expressed for the theory of the permanent equality of property.

> *Tocqueville*, Democracy in America, *1835*

Young people nowadays imagine that money is everything; when they get older they *know* it.

> *Oscar Wilde*, Picture of Dorian Grey, *1891*

Love of money is the root of all evil.

> *1 Timothy 6:17*

Lack of money is the root of all evil.

> *G.B. Shaw*, Man and Superman, *1903*

Do not value money for any more nor any less than its worth; it is a good servant but a bad master.

> *Alexandre Dumas fils*, Camille, *1852*

The methods that help a man acquire a fortune are the very ones that keep him from enjoying it.

> *Antoine de Rivarol (d. 1801)*, Discours sur l'homme ...

(*See also* **RICHES**)

MOON-LANDING

Stepping on the moon, I begin
the gay pilgrimage to new
Jerusalems
in foreign galaxies.
Heat. Cold. Craters of silence.
The Sea of Tranquillity
rolling on the shores of entropy.

> *Stanley Kunitz, "The Flight of Apollo,"*
> The Testing-Tree, *1969*

So there he is at last. Man on the moon. The poor magnificent bungler! He can't even get to the office without undergoing the agonies of the damned, but give him a little metal, a few chemicals, some wire and twenty or thirty billion dollars and vroom! there he is, up on a rock a quarter of a million miles up in the sky.

> *Russell Baker*, New York Times, *July 21, 1969*

MORALITY

. . . cannot be legislated but behavior can be regulated. Judicial decrees may not change the heart, but they can restrain the heartless.

> *Martin Luther King, Jr. (d. 1968),* Strength to Love.

Morality knows nothing of geographical boundaries or distinctions of race.

> *Herbert Spencer*, Social Statics, *1851*

What is morality in any given time or place? It is what the majority then and there happen to like, and immorality is what they dislike.

> *Alfred North Whitehead,* Dialogues, *August 30, 1941*

Two things fill my mind with ever-increasing wonder and awe: . . . the starry skies above me and the moral law within me.

> *Immanuel Kant,* Critique of Practical Reason, *1788*

Act only on that maxim which you can at the same time will that it should become a universal law.

> *Kant, "The Categorical Imperative," 1797*

Do not do an immoral thing for moral reasons.

> *Thomas Hardy,* Jude the Obscure, *1875*

We know no spectacle so ridiculous as the British public in one of its periodical fits of morality.

> *Thomas Babington Macauley,* Edinburgh Review, *1830*

It is not reason that gives us our moral orientation, it is sensitivity.
Maurice Barrès, La Grande Pitié des églises de France, *1914*

People are very inclined to set moral standards for others.
Elizabeth Drew, The New Yorker, *February 16, 1987*

MORTALITY

God is becoming bitter, he envies man his mortality.
Jacques Rigaut (d. 1929), Pensées

Man comes and tills the field and lies beneath,
And after many a summer dies the swan.
Alfred, Lord Tennyson, "Tithonus," *1860*

We thank with brief thanksgiving
Whatever gods may be
That no life lives forever;
That dead men rise up never;
That even the weariest river
Winds somewhere safe to sea.
Algernon C. Swinburne, "Garden of Prosperine," *1866*

(*See also* **DEATH AND DYING**)

MOTION

A body remains in a state of rest or . . . motion unless acted upon by an external force.
Sir Isaac Newton, Principia mathematica, *1687*

The mind-expanding discovery of quantum mechanics is that Newtonian physics does not apply to subatomic phenomena. . . . We cannot know both the position *and* the momentum of a particle with absolute precision. . . . This is Werner Heisenberg's uncertainty principle.
Gary Zukav, The Dancing Wu Li Masters, *1979*

MOTIVES

We would frequently be ashamed of our good deeds if people saw all of the motives that produced them.
La Rochefoucauld, Maxims, *1665*

All we do is done with an eye to something else.
Aristotle (fl. 350 B.C.) Nichomachean Ethics,

MUNDANE

Many eyes go through the meadow, but few see the flowers in it.
Emerson, Journals, 1834

A mind too proud to unbend over the small ridiculosa of life is as painful as a library with no trash in it.
Christopher Morley, Inward Ho! *1923*

MUSIC

If music could be translated into human speech, it would no longer need to exist.
Ned Rorem, Music from the Inside Out, *1967*

Music must take rank as the highest of the fine arts—as the one which, more than any other, ministers to human welfare.
Herbert Spencer, Essays on Education, *1866*

It is from the blues that all that may be called American music derives its most distinctive characteristics.
James Weldon Johnson, Black Manhattan, *1930*

In music the passions enjoy themselves.
Nietzsche, Beyond Good and Evil, *1886*

If I don't practice one day, I know it: two days, the critics know it: three days, the public knows it.
Jascha Heifetz, San Francisco Examiner & Chronicle, *April 18, 1971*

I never practice; I always play.
Wanda Landowska, Time, *December 1, 1952*

One of the greatest sounds of them all . . . is utter, complete silence.
André Kostelanetz, New York Journal-American, *February 8, 1955*

Nothing is capable of being set to music that is not nonsense.
Joseph Addison, The Spectator, *March 21, 1711*

No operatic star has yet died soon enough for me.
Sir Thomas Beecham, BBC-TV, August 22, 1958

We can't expect you to be with us all the time, but perhaps you could be good enough to keep in touch now and again.
Beecham to a musician at rehearsal (attributed)

[Mozart's] G-minor Symphony consists of eight remarkable measures . . . surrounded by a half-hour of banality.

> *Glenn Gould,* The Glenn Gould Reader, *1984*

The one true comment on a piece of music is another piece of music.

> *Stravinsky,* New York Review of Books, *May 12, 1966*

We're now more popular than Jesus Christ.

> *John Lennon, re: the Beatles,* Time, *August 21, 1966*

MYSTERY

We cannot kindle when we will
The fire that in the heart resides,
The spirit bloweth and is still,
In mystery our soul abides.

> *Matthew Arnold, "Morality," 1852*

The most beautiful thing we can experience is the mysterious. It is the source of all true art and science.

> *Albert Einstein (d. 1955),* What I Believe.

MYSTICISM

Without mysticism man can achieve nothing great.

> *André Gide,* The Counterfeiters, *1925*

Mysticism is, in essence, little more than a certain intensity and depth of feeling in regard to what is believed about the universe.

> *Bertrand Russell,* Mysticism and Logic, *1918*

Mystics always hope that science will some day overtake them.

> *Booth Tarkington,* Looking Forward to the Great Adventure, *1926*

MYTHS

A man is always a teller of tales, he lives surrounded by his stories and the stories of others, he sees everything that happens to him through them; and he tries to live his life as if he were recounting it.

> *J.P. Sartre,* Nausea, *1938*

The Indian . . . feels for his village as no white man for his country. . . . The myths are the village, and the winds and rains. The river is the village, and . . . the talking bird, the owl, who calls the name of the man who is going to die.

> *Margaret Craven,* I Heard the Owl Call My Name, *1933*

Science must begin with myths and the criticism of myths.

Sir Karl Popper, Philosophy of Science, *1950*

Men and societies need myths, not science, by which to live.

Allan Bloom, The Closing of the American Mind, *1987*

Both dreams and myths are important communications from ourselves to ourselves. If we do not understand the language in which they are written, we miss a great deal of what we know and tell ourselves in those hours when we are not busy manipulating the outside world.

Erich Fromm, New York Times, *January 5, 1964*

People don't like the true and simple; they like fairy tales and humbug.

Edmond and Jules de Goncourt, Journal, *March 2, 1861*

"N"

NARROW-MINDED VS. OPEN-MINDED

Poverty of goods is easily cured; poverty of the mind is irreparable.

Montaigne, Essays, *1588*

The most fatal illusion is the settled point of view. Since life is growth and motion, a fixed point of view kills anybody who has one.

Brooks Atkinson, Once Around the Sun, *1951*

He who knows only his own side of the case, knows little of that.

John Stuart Mill, On Liberty, *1859*

The only means of strenthening one's intellect is to make up one's mind about nothing—to let the mind be a thoroughfare for all thoughts.

John Keats to George and Georgina Keats, September 1819

Ah, snug lie those that slumber
Beneath Conviction's roof.
Their floors are sturdy lumber,
Their windows weatherproof.
But I sleep cold forever
And cold sleep all my kind,
For I was born to shiver
In the draft from an open mind.

Phyllis McGinley, "Lament for a Wavering Viewpoint," A Pocketful of Wry, *1940*

NATION/NATIONALISM

The United States is the only great and populous nation-state and world power whose people are not cemented by ties of blood, race, or original language.

Dorothy Thompson, Ladies Home Journal, *October 1954*

A nation is a spirit. . . . It manifests itself in . . . the consent of the people and their clearly expressed desire to continue life in common.

Ernest Renan, "What Is a Nation?," 1882

Borders are scratched across the hearts of men
By strangers with a calm, judicial pen,
And when the borders bleed we watch with dread
The lines of ink across the map turn red.

Marya Mannes, Subverse: Rhymes for Our Times, *1959*

Nationalism is an infantile disease. It is the measles of mankind.

Albert Einstein, The World As I See It, *1934*

Let us create rational human beings, capable of crushing under foot the futile magnificence of barbaric glories, and of resisting those bloody ambitions of nationalism and imperialism.

Anatole France, speech, Tours, August 1919

To wish the greatness of our own country is often to wish evil to our neighbors. He who could bring himself to wish that his country should always remain as it is, would be a citizen of the universe.

Voltaire, Philosophical Dictionary, *1764*

The State, which is not God, . . . must nevertheless imitate God in its thinking, its patience, its universal protection, its humanity, and its foresight.

George Sand to Maurice Sand, September 1861

NATURAL RESOURCES

To waste, to destroy our natural resources, to skin and exhaust the land instead of using it so as to increase its usefulness, will result in undermining in the days of our children the very prosperity which we ought by right to hand down to them amplified and developed.

Theodore Roosevelt, Message to Congress, 1907

America today stands poised on a pinnacle of wealth and power, yet we live in a land of vanishing beauty, of increasing ugliness, of shrinking open space, and of an over-all environment that is diminished daily by pollution and noise and blight.

Stewart L. Udall, The Quiet Crisis, *1963*

A land ethic for tomorrow should be as honest as Thoreau's *Walden,* and as comprehensive as the sensitive science of ecology. It should stress the oneness of our resources and the live-and-help-live logic of the great chain of life. If, in our haste to "progress," the economics of ecology are disregarded by citizens and policy makers alike, the result will be an ugly America.

Ibid.

NATURE

When a man says to me, "I have the intensest love of nature," at once I know that he has none.

Emerson, Journals, *1857*

To see a World in a Grain of Sand
And a Heaven in a wild Flower,
Hold Infinity in the palm of your hand
And Eternity in an hour.

William Blake, "Auguries of Innocence," 1810

All nature is but art unknown to thee,
All chance, direction which thou canst not see;
All discord, harmony not understood;
All partial evil, universal good.

Alexander Pope, "Essay on Man," 1733

Nature wants us to enjoy life to the full and die without giving it a second thought; Christianity wants the opposite.

Sainte-Beuve (d. 1869), Les Cahiers

We are a spectacular manifestation of life. We have language. . . . We have affection. We have genes for usefulness, and usefulness is about as close to a "common goal" of nature as I can guess at. And finally, and perhaps best of all, we have music.

Dr. Lewis Thomas, The Medusa and the Snail, *1979*

The chessboard is the world, the pieces are the phenomena of the universe, the rules of the game are what we call the laws of Nature. The player on the other side of the board is hidden from us. We know that his play is always fair, just, and patient. But also we know, to our cost, that he never overlooks a mistake, or makes the smallest allowance for ignorance.

T.H. Huxley, A Liberal Education, *1868*

Nature is trying very hard to make us succeed, but nature does not depend on us. We are not the only experiment.

Buckminster Fuller, Synergetics, *1975*

Education is the instruction of the intellect in the laws of Nature, under which name I include not merely things and their forces but men and their ways, and the fashioning of the affections and the will into an earnest and loving desire to move in harmony with these laws.

T.H. Huxley, Science and Education, *1868*

One impulse from a vernal wood
May teach you more of man,
Of moral evil and of good,
Than all the sages can.

William Wordsworth, "The Tables Turned," 1798

The insufferable arrogance of human beings to think that Nature was made solely for their benefit, as if it was conceivable that the sun had been set afire merely to ripen men's apples and head their cabbages.

Cyrano de Bergerac (d. 1655), Trip to the Moon

We understand nature by resisting it.

Gaston Bachelard, La Formation de l'esprit scientifique, *1938*

We need the tonic of wildness [and] . . . nature.

Henry David Thoreau, Walden

There is a pleasure in the pathless woods,
There is a rapture on the lonely shore,
There is society, where none intrudes,
By the deep Sea, and Music in its roar:
I love not Man the less, but Nature more.

Lord Byron, Childe Harold's Pilgrimage, *1818*

How doth the little busy bee
Improve each shining hour,
And gather honey all the day
From every opening flower!

Isaac Watts, "Against Idleness and Mischief," 1706

That's the wise thrush; he sings each song twice over,
Lest you should think he never could recapture
The first fine careless rapture!

Robert Browning, Home Thoughts from Abroad, *1845*

Tiger, Tiger, burning bright
In the forests of the night,
What immortal hand or eye
Could frame thy fearful symmetry?

William Blake, "The Tiger," 1791

How doth the little crocodile
· Improve his shining tail,
And pour the waters of the Nile
On every golden scale!

Lewis Carroll, Alice . . . in Wonderland, *1865*

NECESSITY

There is no good in arguing with the inevitable. The only argument available with an east wind is to put on your overcoat.

James Russell Lowell, Democracy and Other Addresses, *1887*

I don't think necessity is the mother of invention—invention, in my opinion, arises directly from idleness, possibly also from laziness. To save oneself trouble.

Agatha Christie, An Autobiography, *1977*

Necessity is the plea for every infringement of human freedom. . . . the argument of tyrants, . . . the creed of slaves.

William Pitt, addressing the Commons, 1783

NEGLECT

A little neglect may breed great mischief: . . . for want of a nail the shoe was lost; for want of a shoe the horse was lost; and for want of a horse the rider was lost.

Benjamin Franklin, Poor Richard's Almanack, *1758*

Through a wise and salutary neglect [of the colonies], a generous nature has been suffered [allowed] to take her own way to perfection.

Edmund Burke, Second Speech on Conciliation, *1775*

Perpetual devotion to what a man calls his business, is only to be sustained by perpetual neglect of many other things.

Robert Louis Stevenson, Virginibus puerisque, *1881*

NEUROSES

A neurotic is the person who builds a castle in the air; a psychotic is the person who lives in it; and a psychiatrist is the person who collects the rent.

Anonymous

Equilibrium is the profoundest tendency of all human activity.
Jean Piaget (d. 1980), Six Etudes de psychologie

Work and love—these are the basics. Without them there is neurosis.
Theodor Reik, Of Love and Lust, *1957*

The poet is in command of his fantasy, while it is exactly the mark of the neurotic that he is possessed by his fantasy.
Lionel Trilling, The Liberal Imagination, *1950*

NEWSPAPERS: *See* JOURNALISM.

NIGHT

The night
Shows stars and women in a better light.
Byron, Don Juan, *1824*

The day is done, and the darkness
Falls from the wings of Night,
As a feather is wafted downward
From an eagle in his flight.
Longfellow, "The Day is Done," *1844*

An angel robed in spotless white
Bent down and kissed the sleeping night.
Night woke to blush; the sprite was gone.
Men saw the blush and called it dawn.
Paul Laurence Dunbar, "Dawn," *1899*

To make ourselves invisible to creditors or to the envious, and even to our own worries, we can take advantage here on earth of a great democratic institution—the night.
Jean Giraudoux, Amphitryon, *1929*

NOISE

. . . The most impertinent of all forms of interruption.
Arthur Schopenhauer, Studies in Pessimism, *1851*

Nowadays most men lead lives of noisy desperation.
James Thurber, Further Fables for Our Time, *1956*

People who make no noise are dangerous.
Jean de La Fontaine, Fables, *1678*

Beethoven's Fifth Symphony is the most sublime noise that has ever penetrated into the ear of man.

E.M. Forster, Howards End, *1910*

NONCONFORMITY

In every human soul there is a socialist and an individualist, an authoritarian and a fanatic for liberty, as in each there is a Catholic and a Protestant.

R.H. Tawney, Religion and the Rise of Capitalism, *1926*

It is probable that democracy owes more to nonconformity than to any other single movement.

Ibid.

Safe upon the solid rock the ugly houses stand:
Come and see my shining palace built upon the sand!

Edna St. Vincent Millay, A Few Figs from Thistles, *1920*

NOVEL/NOVELIST

"And what are you reading, Miss ——?" "Oh! it is only a novel" ... or, in short, only some work in which the most thorough knowledge of human nature, the happiest delineation of its varieties, the liveliest effusions of wit and humour are conveyed to the world in the best chosen language.

Jane Austen, Northanger Abbey, *1818*

The love of novels is the preference of sentiment to the senses.

Emerson, Journals, *1831*

People think that because a novel's invented, it isn't true. Exactly the reverse is the case. Biography and memoirs can never be wholly true, since they cannot include every conceivable circumstance of what happened. The novel can do that.

Anthony Powell, Hearing Secret Harmonies, *1964*

A novel ... tells us that for every human being there is a diversity of existences, that the single existence is itself an illusion in part, that these many existences signify something, tend to something, fulfill something; it promises us meaning, harmony, and even justice.

Saul Bellow, speech, Nobel Prize, 1976

I am a man, and alive ... For this reason I am a novelist. And being a novelist, I consider myself superior to the saint, the scientist, the philosopher, and the poet, who are all great masters of different bits of man alive, but never get the whole hog.

D.H. Lawrence, preface to Shestov, All Things Are Possible, *1938*

A novel is balanced between a few true impressions and the multitude of false ones that make up most of what we call life.

Saul Bellow, accepting Nobel Prize, 1976

The novel remains for me one of the few forms where we can record man's complexity and the strength and decency of his longings. Where we can describe, step by step, minute by minute, our not altogether unpleasant struggle to put ourselves into a viable and devout relationship to our beloved and mistaken world.

John Cheever, accepting the National Book Award, The Writer, *September 1958*

When a writer becomes the center of his [own] attention, he has become a nudnick, and a nudnick who believes he is profound is even worse than just a plain nudnick.

Isaac Bashevis Singer, New York Times, *November 26, 1978*

There are many reasons why novelists write, but they all have one thing in common—a need to create an alternative world.

John Fowles, interview, October 2, 1977

Fiction is not a dream. Nor is it guesswork. It is imagining based on facts, and the facts must be accurate or the work of imagining will not stand up.

Margaret Culkin Banning, The Writer, *March 1960*

Fiction is like a spider's web, attached ever so slightly perhaps, but still attached to life at all four corners.

Virginia Woolf, A Room of One's Own, *1929*

The "New Novel" takes in all those who are seeking new forms to express . . . new relationships between man and the world, all those who have decided to invent the novel or, in other words, to invent man.

Alain Robbe-Grillet, For a New Novel, *1963*

(*See also* **LITERATURE**)

NOVELTY

Only God and some few rare geniuses can keep forging ahead into novelty.

Diderot, Rameau's Nephew, *1762*

Novelties *please* less than they *impress.*

Byron, Don Juan, *1824*

A brand new mediocrity is thought more of than accustomed excellence.

Baltasar Gracián, The Art of Worldly Wisdom, *1947*

Homer is new this morning, and perhaps nothing is as old as today's newspaper.

Charles Péguy, Les Cahiers de la quinzaine, *April 8, 1914*

The one thing the public dislikes is novelty. Any attempt to extend the subject-matter of art is extremely distasteful to the public; and yet the vitality and progress of art depends in a large measure on the continual extension of subject-matter. The public dislikes novelty because it . . . represents to them a mode of Individualism, an assertion on the part of the artist that he selects his own subject, and treats is as he chooses.

Oscar Wilde, "The Soul of Man under Socialism," 1891

We have learned so well how to absorb novelty that receptivity itself has turned into a kind of tradition—"the tradition of the new." Yesterday's avant-garde experience is today's chic and tomorrow's cliché.

Richard Hofstadter, Anti-Intellectualism in American Life, *1963*

Our minds . . . grow in spots; and like grease spots, the spots spread. But we let them spread as little as possible: we keep unaltered as much of our old prejudices and beliefs, as we can. We patch and tinker more than we renew. The novelty soaks in; it stains the ancient mass; but it is also tinged by what absorbs it.

William James, Pragmatism, *1907*

OBJECT(S)

Inanimate objects are classified scientifically into three major categories—those that don't work, those that break down and those that get lost.

Russell Baker, New York Times, *June 18, 1968*

We are the slaves of objects around us, and appear of little or no importance as these contract or give us room to expand.

Goethe, in Eckermann's Conversations, *September 11, 1828*

The superior gratification derived from the use and contemplation of costly and supposedly beautiful products is, commonly, in great measure a gratification of our sense of costliness masquerading under the name of beauty.

Thorstein Veblen, The Theory of the Leisure Class, *1899*

Things have their laws as well as men, and things refuse to be trifled with.

Emerson, Essays: Second Series, *1844*

(*See also* **MATERIALISM**)

OBJECTIVITY

I can promise to be frank, I cannot promise to be impartial.

Goethe, Proverbs in Prose, *1819*

There are only two ways to be . . . impartial. One is to be completely ignorant. The other is to be completely indifferent.

Bias and prejudice are attitudes to be kept in hand, not attitudes to be avoided.

Charles P. Curtis, A Commonplace Book, *1957*

In the last analysis, we see only what we are prepared to see, what we have been taught to see. We eliminate and ignore everything that is not part of our prejudices.

Jean Martin Charcot, De l'Expectation, *1857*

OBSCURITY/OBSCURANTISM

Untruth being unacceptable to the mind of man, there is no other defence left for absurdity but obscurity.

Locke, An Essay Concerning Human Understanding, *1690*

Where misunderstanding serves others as an advantage, one is helpless to make oneself understood.

Lionel Trilling, The Liberal Imagination, *1950*

Sanity, soundness, and sincerity, of which gleams and strains can still be found in the human brain under powerful microscopes, flourish only in a culture of clarification, which is now becoming harder to detect with the naked eye.

James Thurber, Lanterns and Lances, *1961*

OBSTINACY

He has one of those terribly weak natures that are not susceptible to influence.

Oscar Wilde, An Ideal Husband, *1895*

The obstinacy of human beings is exceeded only by the obstinacy of inanimate objects.

Alexander Chase, Perspectives, *1966*

There are some men who turn a deaf ear to reason and good advice, and willfully go wrong for fear of being controlled.

La Bruyère, Characters, *1688*

A man will do more for his stubbornness than for his religion or his country.

Edgar Watson Howe, Country Town Sayings, *1911*

No man is good for anything who has not some particle of obstinacy to use upon occasion.

> *Henry Ward Beecher*, Proverbs, *1887*

Obstinacy and dogmatism are the surest signs of stupidity. Is there anything more confident, resolute, disdainful, grave and serious than an ass?

> *Montaigne*, Essays, *1588*

He can never be good that is not obstinate.

> *Thomas Wilson*, Maxims of Piety and Christianity, *c. 1780*

I am firm; *you* are obstinate; *he* is a pigheaded fool.

> *Bertrand Russell, "Brain Trust," BBC-Radio*

(*See also* **DOGMATISM**)

OLD AGE: *See* AGE, AGING.

OPERA

An opera may be allowed to be extravagantly lavish in its decorations, as its only design is to gratify the senses and keep up an indolent attention in the audience.

> *Joseph Addison*, The Spectator, *March 6, 1911*

The opera is like a husband with a foreign title: expensive to support, hard to understand, and therefore a supreme social challenge.

> *Cleveland Amory, NBC-TV, 1961*

People are wrong when they say that opera is not what it used to be. It *is* what it used to be. That is what's wrong with it.

> *Noël Coward, in conversation*

No good opera plot can be sensible: . . . people do not sing when they are feeling sensible.

> *W.H. Auden*, Time, *December 29, 1961*

Whenever I go to an opera, I leave my sense and reason at the door . . . and deliver myself up to my eyes and ears.

> *Lord Chesterfield*, Letters to His Son, *January 23, 1752*

(*See also* **MUSIC**)

OPINION, PERSONAL

Everyone has the right . . . to hold opinions without interference and to seek, receive and impart information and ideas through any media regardless of frontiers.

> Universal Declaration of Human Rights, *art. 19, 1948*

Every new opinion, at its starting, is precisely a minority of one.

> *Thomas Carlyle,* Heroes and Hero Worship, *1841*

Opinions cannot survive if one has no chance to fight for them.

> *Thomas Mann,* The Magic Mountain, *1924*

Nora: While I was home with father, he used to tell me his opinions and I had the same ones. If I had other opinions, I concealed them, because he wouldn't have liked it.

> *Ibsen,* A Doll's House, *1879*

Few people are capable of expressing with equanimity opinions which differ from the prejudices of their social environment. Most people are even incapable of forming such opinions.

> *Albert Einstein,* Ideas and Opinions, *1954*

Men get opinions as boys learn to spell,
By reiteration chiefly.

> *Elizabeth Barrett Browning,* Aurora Leigh, *1856*

In the human mind one-sidedness has always been the rule, and many-sidedness the exception. Hence, even in revolutions of opinion, one part of the truth usually sets while the other rises.

> *John Stuart Mill,* On Liberty, *1859*

Even good opinions are worth very little unless we hold them in a broad, intelligent, and spacious way.

> *John Morley,* Critical Miscellanies, *1908*

It were not best that we should all think alike; it is difference of opinion that makes horse-races.

> *Mark Twain,* Pudd'nhead Wilson, *1894*

(*See also* **ARGUMENT**)

OPINION, PUBLIC

Public opinion is stronger than the legislature, and nearly as strong as the Ten Commandments.

Charles Dudley Warner, My Summer in a Garden, *1870*

Public opinion ... requires us to think other men's thoughts, to speak other men's words, to follow other men's habits.

Walter Bagehot, Biographical Studies, *1907*

It is a besetting vice of democracies to substitute public opinion for law. This is the usual form in which masses of men exhibit their tyranny.

James Fenimore Cooper, The American Democrat, *1838*

(*See also* **PROPAGANDA**)

OPPORTUNITY

A wise man will make more opportunities than he finds.

Francis Bacon, Essays, *1625*

The opportunity that God sends does not wake up him who sleeps.

Senegalese proverb

There is no security on this earth; there is only opportunity.

Gen. Douglas MacArthur, in C. Whitney, MacArthur, *1955*

(*See also* **FATE**)

OPPOSITION

He that struggles with us strengthens our nerves, and sharpens our skill. Our antagonist is our helper.

Edmund Burke, The Revolution in France, *1790*

The opposition is indispensable. A good statesman, like any other sensible human being, always learns more from his opponents than from his fervent supporters.

Walter Lippmann, Atlantic Monthly, *August 1939*

The State is a great and noble steed, which is dilatory in movement because of his very size, and has to be goaded into action. I am the gadfly, all day long, everywhere, always fastening on you the people, arousing, persuading, reproaching you.

Socrates, in Plato's "Apology," 399 B.C.

I respect only those who resist me, but I cannot tolerate them.

> *Charles de Gaulle,* New York Times, *May 12, 1968*

The cry has been that when war is declared, all opposition should therefore be hushed. A sentiment more unworthy of a free country could hardly be propagated. If the doctrine be admitted, rulers have only to declare war and they are screened at once from scrutiny.

> *William Ellery Channing, in W.H. Channing, ed.,* Life, *1848*

We are willing enough to praise freedom when she is safely tucked away in the past and cannot be a nuisance. In the present, amidst dangers whose outcome we cannot foresee, we get nervous about her, and admit censorship.

> *E.M. Forster,* Two Cheers for Democracy, *1951*

What country can preserve its liberties, if its rulers are not warned from time to time, that this people preserve the spirit of resistance?

> *Thomas Jefferson to Col. William S. Smith, November 13, 1787*

(*See also* **DISSENT**)

OPPRESSION

It is bad to be oppressed by a minority, but it is worse to be oppressed by a majority.

> *Lord Acton,* History of Freedom, *1907*

Reason has never failed men. Only force and oppression have made the wrecks in this world.

> *William Allen White,* Emporia Gazette, *July 27, 1922*

Resistance to tyrants is obedience to God.

> *Thomas Jefferson, motto*

The slave begins by demanding justice and ends by wanting to wear a crown. He must dominate in his turn.

> *Albert Camus,* The Rebel, *1951*

(*See also* **DESPOTISM, TYRANNY**)

OPTIMISM/PESSIMISM

Optimism is the folly of maintaining that everything is all right when we are wretched.

> *Voltaire,* Candide, *1759*

The place where optimism most flourishes is the lunatic asylum.
Havelock Ellis, The Dance of Life, *1923*

The optimist proclaims that we live in the best of all possible worlds; and the pessimist fears this is true.
James Branch Cabell, The Silver Stallion, *1926*

an optimist is a guy
that has never had
much experience.
Don Marquis, archy and mehitabel, *1927*

An optimist is a person who sees a green light everywhere, while the pessimist sees only the red light. . . . The truly wise person is colorblind.
Albert Schweitzer, News Summaries, *January 14, 1955*

Pessimism comes from the temperament, optimism from the will.
Alain, Propos sur le bonheur, *1928*

A pessimist is a man who has been compelled to live with an optimist.
Elbert Hubbard, The Note-Book, *1927*

ORATORY: *See* PUBLIC SPEAKING.

ORDER

The desire for order is the only order in the world.
Georges Duhamel, The Pasquier Chronicles, *1933*

Life creates order, but order does not create life.
Saint-Exupéry, Letter to a Hostage, *1942*

Order marches with weighty and measured strides; disorder is always in a hurry.
Napoleon I, Maxims, *1815*

(*See also* LAW)

ORIGINALITY

All good things which exist are the fruits of originality.
John Stuart Mill, On Liberty, *1959*

An original writer is not one who imitates nobody, but one whom nobody can imitate.

Chateaubriand, Le Génie du Christianisme, *1802*

Nothing is ever said that has not been said before.

Terence (d. 159 B.C.), Eunuchus

Wilde: I wish I'd said that!
Whistler: You will, Oscar, you will.

D.C. Seitz, Whistler Stories, *1913*

A thought is often original, though you have uttered it a hundred times.

Oliver Wendell Holmes, The Autocrat of the Breakfast Table, 1858

It is perfectly easy to be original by violating the laws of decency and the canons of good taste.

Oliver Wendell Holmes, Over the Teacups, *1891*

Originality is not seen in single words or even sentences.
Originality is the sum total of a man's thinking and writing.

Isaac Bashevis Singer, interview with Richard Burgin,
New York Times Magazine, *December 3, 1978*

(*See also* **CREATIVITY, INDIVIDUALISM**)

ORTHODOX/UNORTHODOX

Orthodoxy: That peculiar condition where the patient can neither eliminate an old idea nor absorb a new one.

Elbert Hubbard, The Note-Book, *1927*

If there is any fixed star in our constitutional constellation, it is that no official, high or petty, can prescribe what shall be orthodox in politics, nationalism, religion, or other matters of opinion, or force citizens to confess by word or act their faith therein.

Justice Robert H. Jackson, Minersville School District v. Gobitis,
1940

The great and invigorating influences in American life have been the *un*orthodox: the people who challenge an existing institution or way of life, or say and do things that make people think.

Justice William O. Douglas, interview with Mike Wallace, 1958

The heresy of one age becomes the orthodoxy of the next.
Helen Keller, Optimism, *1903*

(*See also* **HERESY**)

OWNERSHIP: *See* **POSSESSION, PROPERTY.**

PACIFISM/NONVIOLENCE

Pacifism is simply undisguised cowardice.

Adolf Hitler, speech, August 21, 1926

Join the Army, see the world, meet interesting people—and kill them.

Pacifist badge, 1978

Ahimsa [nonviolence] means the largest love. It is the supreme law. By it alone can mankind be saved. He who believes in nonviolence believes in a living God.

Mahatma Gandhi, Sayings, ed. S. Hobhouse, 1939

Nonviolence is the answer to the crucial political and moral questions of our time; the need for men to overcome oppression and violence without resorting to oppression and violence.

Martin Luther King, speech, Nobel Peace Prize, December 11, 1964

Nonviolence is a flop. The only bigger flop is violence.

Joan Baez, London Observer, 1967

(*See also* **FORCE, PEACE**)

PAIN/PLEASURE

Nature has placed man under the governance of two sovereign masters, *pain* and *pleasure*.

> *Jeremy Bentham,* Principles of Morals and Legislation, *1789*

The pleasures to which we have given ourselves without let or hindrance become our most implacable enemies.

> *Charles Nodier,* La Fée aux miettes, *1832*

There is no pain as great as being alive,
no burden heavier than that of conscious life.

> *Rubén Darío,* The Swans and Other Poems, *1905*

Pains of love be sweeter far
Than all other pleasures are.

> *John Dryden,* Tyrannic Love, *1669*

Rich the treasure,
Sweet the pleasure—
Sweet is pleasure after pain.

> *Dryden,* Alexander's Feast, *1697*

The Puritan hated bear-baiting, not because it gave pain to the bear, but because it gave pleasure to the spectators.

> *Thomas Babington Macaulay,* History of England, *1849*

(*See also* **HAPPINESS, SUFFERING**)

PARADISE

Two cities have been formed by two loves: the earthly city by the love of self, even to the contempt of God, and the heavenly city by the love of God, even to the contempt of self.

> *Augustine,* City of God, *415*

Of man's first disobedience, and the fruit
Of that forbidden tree whose mortal taste
Brought death into the world, and all our woe,
With loss of Eden.

> *John Milton,* Paradise Lost, *1667*

When our first parents were driven out of Paradise, Adam is believed to have remarked to Eve: "My dear, we live in an age of transition."

> *Dean W.R. Inge (d. 1954),* Assessments and Anticipations

If there is a paradise on the face of the earth,
It is this, oh! it is this, oh! it is this.

—Mogul inscription in the Red Fort, Delhi, 1640

Paradise is wherever I am.

Voltaire, Le Mondain, 1736

Where choice begins, Paradise ends, innocence ends, for what is Paradise but the absence of any need to choose this action?

Arthur Miller, After the Fall, 1964

(*See also* **HEAVEN**)

PARDON

Love truth, but pardon error.

Voltaire to Frederick the Great, 1740

We pardon to the extent that we love.

La Rochefoucauld, Maxims, 1665

Amnesty: an act by which sovereigns commonly pardon injustices committed by themselves.

Graffito during Paris student revolt, 1968

The offender never pardons.

George Herbert, Jacula Prudentum, 1651

Sleep; and if life was bitter to thee, pardon;
If sweet, give thanks; thou hast no more to live;
And to give thanks is good, and to forgive.

Swinburne, "Ave Atque Vale: In Memory of Charles Baudelaire,"
1878

(*See also* **FORGIVENESS**)

PARENTHOOD

Speak roughly to your little boy,
And beat him when he sneezes:
He only does it to annoy,
Because he knows it teases.

Lewis Carroll, Alice . . . in Wonderland, 1865

A Jewish man with parents alive is a 15-year-old boy and will remain a 15-year-old boy till they die.

> *Philip Roth*, Portnoy's Complaint, *1969*

Children begin by loving their parents: after a time they judge them; rarely, if ever, do they forgive them.

> *Oscar Wilde*, The Picture of Dorian Gray, *1891*

The most important thing a father can do for his children is to love their mother.

> *Theodore M. Hesburgh*, Reader's Digest, *January 1963*

It is not a bad thing that children should occasionally, and politely, put parents in their place.

> *Colette*, My Mother's House, *1922*

The real menace in dealing with a five-year-old is that in no time at all you begin to sound like a five-year-old.

> *Joan Kerr*, Please Don't Eat the Daisies, *1957*

When you are dealing with a child, keep all your wits about you, and sit on the floor.

> *Austin O'Malley*, Keystones of Thought, *1915*

How often do we not see children ruined through the virtues, real or supposed, of their parents.

> *Samuel Butler*, Note-Books, *1912*

To make a child in your own image is a capital crime, for your image is not worth repeating. The child knows this and you know it. Consequently you hate each other.

> *Karl Shapiro*, The Bourgeois Poet, *1964*

Few parents nowadays pay any regard to what their children say to them. The old-fashioned respect for the young is fast dying.

> *Oscar Wilde*, The Importance of Being Earnest, *1899*

(*See also* **CHILDREN, CHILDHOOD**)

PARENTS: MOTHERS

God could not be everywhere, so he created mothers.

> *Jewish proverb*

Most American children suffer too much mother and too little father.

> *Gloria Steinem*, New York Times, *August 26, 1971*

Few misfortunes can befall a boy which bring worse consequences than to have a really affectionate mother.

W. Somerset Maugham (d. 1965), A Writer's Notebook

A man who has been the indisputable favorite of his mother keeps for life the feeling of a conqueror, that confidence of success that often induces real success.

Sigmund Freud, in E. Jones, Life, *1953*

A mother is not a person to lean on but a person to make leaning unnecessary.

Dorothy Canfield Fisher, Her Son's Wife, *1926*

No woman can shake off her mother. There should be no mothers, only women.

G.B. Shaw, Too True to be Good, *1934*

PARENTS: FATHERS

You don't have to deserve your mother's love. You have to deserve your father's. He's more particular.

Robert Frost, Writers at Work, *1963*

He that will have his son have a respect for him and his orders must have a great reverence for his son.

John Locke, Some Thoughts Concerning Education, *1693*

We cannot carry our father's corpse with us everywhere we go.

Guillaume Apollinaire, The Cubist Painters, *1913*

The fundamental defect of fathers is that they want their children to be a credit to them.

Bertrand Russell, New York Times, *June 9, 1963*

Providing for one's family as a good husband and father is a watertight excuse for making money hand over fist. Greed may be a sin, exploitation of other people might ... look rather nasty, but who can blame a man for "doing the best" for his children?

Eva Figes, Nova, *1973*

Fathers should neither be seen nor heard. That is the only basis for family life.

Oscar Wilde, An Ideal Husband, *1895*

(*See also* **BABIES, BOYS, CHILDREN**)

PART

The way a crow
Shook down on me
The dust of snow
From a hemlock tree

Has given my heart
A change of mood
And saved some part
Of a day I had rued.

Robert Frost, "Dust of Snow," 1923

O World, thou choosest not the better part!
It is not wisdom to be only wise,
And on the inward vision close the eyes,
But it is wisdom to believe the heart.

Santayana, "O World, Thou Choosest Not," 1894

I am part of the sun as my eye is part of me. That I am part of the earth my feet know perfectly, and by blood is part of the sea. My soul knows that I am part of the human race, my soul is an organic part of the great human race, as my spirit is part of my nation. In my very own self, I am part of my family.

D.H. Lawrence, Apocalypse, 1931

PARTING

Maid of Athens ere we part,
Give, oh give me back my heart.

Lord Byron, "Maid of Athens," 1810

Forever, Fortune, wilt thou prove
An unrelenting foe to love,
And, when we meet a mutual heart,
Come in between and bid us part?

James Thomson, "To Fortune," 1730

None shall part us from each other,
One in life and death are we:
All in all to one another—
I to thee and thou to me!

W.S. Gilbert, Iolanthe, 1882

Take hand and part with laughter;
Touch lips and part with tears;
Once more and no more after,
Whatever comes with years.

Swinburne, "Rococo," 1886

PASS

Loveliest of lovely things are they,
On earth, that soonest pass away,
The rose that lives its little hour
Is prized beyond the sculptured flower.
 William Cullen Bryant, "A Scene on the Banks of the Hudson," 1828

I expect to pass through this world but once; any good thing therefore that I can do, or any kindness that I can show to any fellow creature, let me do it now; let me not defer or neglect it, for I shall not pass this way again.
 Stephen Grellet (d. 1855), attributed

They are not long, the weeping and the laughter,
Love and desire and hate:
I think they have no portion in us after
We pass the gate.
 Ernest Dowson, "Vitae summa brevis . . . ," 1896

PASSION(S)

Only passions, great passions, can elevate the soul to great things.
 Diderot, Pensées philosophiques, *1746*

Man is only truly great when he acts from the passions.
 Benjamin Disraeli, Coningsby, *1844*

It is by no means self-evident that human beings are most real when most violently excited; violent physical passions do not in themselves differentiate men from each other, but rather tend to reduce them to the same state.
 T.S. Eliot, "After Strange Gods," 1934

Serving one's own passions is the greatest slavery.
 Thomas Fuller, Gnomologia, *1732*

The mind is the soul's eye, not its source of power. That lies in the heart, in other words, in the passions.
 Vauvenarges, Reflections and Maxims, *1746*

Without passion man is a mere latent force and possibility, like the flint which awaits the shock of the iron before it can give forth its spark.
 Amiel, Journal, *December 17, 1856*

All humanity is passion; without passion, religion, history, novels, art would be ineffectual.

Balzac, La Comédie humaine, *1841*

Three passions, simple but overwhelming, have governed my life: the longing for love, the search for knowledge, and unbearable pity for the suffering of mankind.

Bertrand Russell, Autobiography, *1967*

Passions . . . are less harmful than boredom, because passions tend to decrease, boredom to increase.

Barbey d'Aurevilly, Une Vieille Maîtresse, *1851*

It may be called the Master Passion, the hunger for self-approval.

Mark Twain, What Is Man?, *1906*

(*See also* **DESIRES, EMOTIONS, LOVE**)

PAST

Nothing changes more consistently than the past; . . . the past that influences our lives [is] not what actually happened but what [we] believe happened.

Gerald W. Johnson, Heroes and Hero-Worship, *1943*

The past, with its pleasure, its rewards, its foolishness, its punishments, is there for each of us forever, and it should be.

Lillian Hellman, Scoundrel Time, *1976*

In books lies the soul of the whole Past Time; the articulate audible voice of the Past, when the body and material substance of it has altogether vanished like a dream.

Carlyle, Heroes and Hero Worship, *1840*

The past is but the beginning of a beginning, and all that is and has been is but the twilight of the dawn.

H.G. Wells, The Discovery of the Future, *1901*

Things always seem fairer when we look back at them, and it is out of that inaccessible tower of the past that Longing leans and beckons.

James Russell Lowell, Literary Essays, *1864*

We two kept house, the Past and I,
The Past and I;

I tended while it hovered nigh,
Leaving me never alone.
Thomas Hardy, "The Ghost of the Past," 1912

Build thee more stately mansions, O my soul,
As the swift seasons roll!
Leave thy low-vaulted past!
Oliver Wendell Holmes, "The Chambered Nautilus, 1858

People will not look forward to posterity who never look backward
to their ancestors.
Edmund Burke, The Revolution in France, *1790*

If we open a quarrel between the past and the present, we shall find
that we have lost the future.
Winston Churchill, speech, House of Commons, June 18, 1940

The past is a foreign country; they do things differently there.
Lesley P. Hartley, The Go-Between, *1953*

The past is a work of art, free of irrelevancies and loose ends.
Sir Max Beerbohm, Zuleika Dobson, *1911*

(*See also* **HISTORY, TRADITION**)

PATIENCE

. . . A minor form of despair, disguised as a virtue.
Ambrose Bierce, The Devil's Dictionary, *1911*

How poor are they that have not patience!
What wound did ever heal but by degrees?
Shakespeare, Othello, *1604*

Patience, that blending of moral courage with physical timidity.
Thomas Hardy, Tess of the D'Urbervilles, *1891*

Even this shall pass away.

Arab proverb

Patience is the virtue of asses.

French proverb

(*See also* **RESIGNATION**)

PATRIOT/PATRIOTISM

No man can be a patriot on an empty stomach.
William Cowper Brann, The Iconoclast, Old Glory, *July 4, 1893*

Patriots always talk of dying for their country and never of killing for their country.
Bertrand Russell, attributed

In the beginning of a change, the patriot is a scarce man, and brave, and hated and scorned. When his cause succeeds, the timid join him, for then it costs nothing to be a patriot.
Mark Twain, Notebook, *1935*

He [had] majored in English history, which was a mistake. "*English history!*" roared the silver-maned Senator . . . indignantly. "What's the matter with American history? American history is as good as any history in the world!"
Joseph Heller, Catch-22, *1961*

"My country, right or wrong," is a thing no patriot would think of saying except in a desperate case. It is like saying, "My mother, drunk or sober."
G.K. Chesterton (d. 1936), The Defendant

Breathes there a man, with soul so dead,
Who never to himself hath said,
This is my own, my native land!
Sir Walter Scott, The Lay of the Last Minstrel, *1805*

If I should die, think only this of me
That there's some corner of a foreign field
That is forever England.
Rupert Brooke, "The Soldier," 1914

Guard against the impostures of pretended patriotism.
George Washington, Farewell Address, *1796*

Patriotism is the last refuge of a scoundrel.
Samuel Johnson to Lord Chesterfield, 1775

France cannot be France without greatness.
Charles de Gaulle, War Memoirs, *1955*

I am the fellow citizen of every being that thinks; my country is Truth.

> *Alphonse de Lamartine, "Marseillaise of Peace," 1841*

Love of country, the ruling virtue of noble souls, seizes me whenever I spy a bottle of burgundy.

> *President de Brosses to MM. Tourney and Neuilly, 1739*

If I had to choose between betraying my country and betraying my friend, I hope I should have the guts to betray my country.

> *E.M. Forster,* Two Cheers for Democracy, *1951*

(*See also* **NATION/NATIONALISM**)

PAY

Nowadays we are all of us so hard up that the only pleasant things to pay are compliments. They're the only things we can pay.

> *Oscar Wilde,* Lady Windermere's Fan, *1892*

Money does not pay for anything, never has, never will. It is an economic axiom as old as the hills that goods and services can be paid for only with goods and services.

> *Albert Jay Nock,* Memoirs of a Superfluous Man, *1943*

I have known no man of genius who had not to pay, in some affliction or defect, either physical or spiritual, for what the gods had given him.

> *Sir Max Beerbohm,* Zuleika Dobson, *1911*

PEACE

The name of peace is sweet and the thing itself good, but between peace and slavery there is the greatest difference.

> *Cicero,* Philippics, *44 B.C.*

Where they make a desert, they call it peace.

> *Tacitus,* Agricola, *c. A.D. 100*

No one can have peace longer than his neighbor pleases.

> *Dutch proverb*

Peace, like charity, begins at home.

> *Franklin D. Roosevelt, speech, Chatauqua, NY, August 14, 1936*

"Peace" is meaningless; what we want is a *glorious* peace.

> *Napoleon I to Prince Joseph Bonaparte, December 13, 1805*

It is easier to lead men to combat, stirring up their passions, than to restrain them and direct them toward the patient labors of peace.

André Gide, Journals, *September 13, 1938*

Who would ever prefer peace to the glory of sloshing through mud, suffering the agonies of hunger and thirst, and dying in the service of their country?

Jean Giraudoux, Amphitryon, *1929*

(*See also* **PACIFICISM, WAR**)

PEDANTRY: *See* **KNOWLEDGE, SCHOLARS**

PEOPLE

The individual person is more interesting than people in general; he and not they is the one whom God created in His image.

André Gide, Journal, *1943*

I'm sure that President Johnson would never have pursued the war in Vietnam if he'd ever had a Fulbright to Japan, or say Bangkok, or had any feeling for what these people are like and why they acted the way they did. He was completely ignorant.

Senator J. William Fulbright, Chairman, Senate Foreign Relations Committee, New York Times, *June 26, 1986*

Office seekers . . . hold their peace, [while] men of sound understanding, . . . who perceive the Delusion of the times, [doubt] the impartiality or the capacity of the People [and] resign themselves to unmanly despair. . . .

Rufus King, quoted in Robert Ernest, Rufus King, American Federalist, *1968*

It's absurd to divide people into good and bad. People are either charming or tedious.

Oscar Wilde, Lady Windermere's Fan, *1892*

(*See also* **CLASSES, DEMOCRACY, SOCIETY**)

PERCEPTION

A fool sees not the same tree that a wise man sees.

William Blake, The Marriage of Heaven and Hell, *1790*

We must always tell what we see. Above all, and this is more difficult, we must always see what we see.

Charles Péguy, Basic Verities, *1943*

No object is mysterious. The mystery is your eye.

> *Elizabeth Bowen*, The House in Paris, *1935*

(*See also* **SENSES, SENSIBILITY**)

PERFECTION

Culture is . . . properly described not as having its origin in curiosity, but as having its origin in the love of perfection; it is *a study of perfection.*

> *Matthew Arnold,* Culture and Anarchy, *1869*

I am little concerned with beauty or perfection. I don't care for the great centuries. All I care about is life, struggle, intensity. I am at ease in my generation.

> *Emile Zola,* My Hates, *1866*

Believing as I do that man in the distant future will be a far more perfect creature than he now is, it is an intolerable thought that he and all other sentient beings are doomed to complete annihilation after such long-continued slow progress.

> *Charles Darwin,* Life and Letters, ed. Francis Darwin, *1887*

The chimerical pursuit of perfection is always linked to some important deficiency, frequently the inability to love.

> *Bernard Grasset (d. 1955),* Les Chemins de l'écriture

A good garden may have some weeds.

> *Thomas Fuller,* Gnomologia, *1732*

The indefatigable pursuit of an unattainable perfection, even though it consist in nothing more than in the pounding of an old piano, is what alone gives a meaning to our life on this unavailing star.

> *Logan Pearsall Smith,* Afterthoughts, *1931*

The perfection preached in the Gospels never yet built up an empire. Every man of action has a strong dose of egotism, pride, hardness, and cunning. But all those things will be forgiven him, indeed, they will be regarded as high qualities, if he can make of them the means to achieve great ends.

> *Charles de Gaulle,* Le Fil de l'épée, *1934*

If thou wouldst be perfect, go and sell that thou hast, and give to the poor, and thou shalt have treasure in heaven.

> *Matthew 19:21*

(*See also* **ERROR, FAULTS**)

PERSEVERANCE: *See* EFFORT, ENDURANCE

PERSONALTIY: *See* CHARACTER, INDIVIDUALISM

PERSUASION

People are generally better persuaded by the reasons which they have themselves discovered than by those which have come to the minds of others.

Pascal, Pensées, *1670*

To please people is the greatest step toward persuading them.

Lord Chesterfield, Letters to His Son, *November 1, 1739*

Most people have ears but few have judgment; tickle those ears and, depend upon it, you will catch their judgments, such as they are.

Ibid., December 9, 1749

Soft words are hard arguments.

Thomas Fuller, Gnomologia, *1732*

(*See also* ARGUMENT, PROPAGANDA)

PERVERSITY

The good that I would do I do not; but the evil which I would not, that I do.

Paul to the Romans 7:19

Look around the habitable world: how few
Know their own good, or knowing it, pursue.

Juvenal, Satires, *c. 100*

Such is the blindness, nay, the insanity of mankind, that some men are driven to death by the fear of it.

Seneca (d. A.D. 65) to Lucullus

The heart *prefers* to move against the grain of circumstance; perversity is the soul's very life.

John Updike, "More Love in the Western World," 1965

Man never knows what he wants; he aspires to penetrate mysteries and as soon as he has, he wants to reestablish them. Ignorance irritates him and knowledge cloys.

Amiel, Journal, *1884*

PETS, HOUSE

Know one false step is ne'er retrieved,
And be with caution bold.

> *Thomas Gray, "Ode to a Favorite Cat," 1747*

What female heart can gold despise?
What cat's averse to fish?

> *Ibid.*

When I play with my cat, who knows if I am not a pastime to her more than she is to me?

> *Montaigne,* Essays, *1580*

Of all God's creatures there is only one that cannot be made the slave of the lash. That one is the cat. If man could be crossed with the cat it would improve man, but it would deteriorate the cat.

> *Mark Twain,* Notebooks, *1935*

Those who play with cats must expect to get scratched.

> *Miguel de Cervantes,* Don Quixote, *1605–1615*

Confound all cats! All cats—alway—
Cats of all colors, black, white, grey;
by night a nuisance and by day—
    Confound the cats!

> *Orlando Dobbin (fl. 1870), "A Dithyramb on Cats."*

I've got a little cat,
And I'm mighty fond of that,
But I'd rather have a bowwow, wow.

> *Joseph Tabrar, "Daddy Wouldn't Buy Me a Bowwow," 1892*

He that lieth with dogs, riseth with fleas.

> *George Herbert,* Jacula Prudentum, *1651*

The old dog barks backward without getting up.
I can remember when he was a pup.

> *Robert Frost, "The Span of Life," 1936*

A door is what a dog is perpetually on the wrong side of.

> *Ogden Nash, "A Dog's Best Friend Is His Illiteracy,"*
> Verses from 1929 On, *1949*

PHILOSOPHER

A true philosopher is like an elephant: he never puts the second foot down until the first one is solidly in place.

Fontenelle, Histoire des miracles, *1687*

There is nothing so strange and so unbelievable that it has not been said by one philosopher or another.

Descartes, Discourse of Method, *1639*

My definition [of a philosopher] is of a man up in a balloon, with his family and friends holding the ropes which confine him to earth and trying to haul him down.

Louisa May Alcott, in Life, Letters, and Journals, *ed. E.D. Cheney, 1889*

To be a philosopher is not merely to have subtle thoughts, nor even to found a school, but so to love wisdom as to live according to its dictates, a life of simplicity, independence, magnanimity, and trust.

Thoreau, Walden, *1854*

My husband, T.S. Eliot, loved to recount how late one evening he stopped a taxi. As he got in, the driver said: "You're T.S. Eliot." When asked how he knew, he replied, "Ah, I've got an eye for a celebrity. Only the other evening I picked up Bertrand Russell, and I said to him: 'Well, Lord Russell, what's it all about?' and do you know, he couldn't tell me."

Valerie Eliot to the London Times, *1970*

What is it to be a philosopher? Is it not to be prepared against events?

Epictetus (fl. 100), Discourses

I much prefer Sartre's plays to his philosophy. Existentialism works much better in the theatre than in theory.

A.J. Ayer, in K. Tynan, Show People, *1980*

A married philosopher belongs to comedy.

Nietzsche, The Geneology of Morals, *1887*

Mankind will never see an end of trouble until . . . lovers of wisdom come to hold political power, or the holders of power . . . become lovers of wisdom.

Plato, The Republic, *c. 400 B.C.*

(*See also* **SCHOLAR, WISE PERSON**)

PHILOSOPHY

The unexamined life is not worth living.

> *Socrates, in Plato's* Apology, *c. 399 B.C.*

Philosophy is not a body of doctrine but an activity.

> *Ludwig Wittgenstein,* Tractatus Logico-philosophicus, *1919*

The object of studying philosophy is to know one's own mind, not other people's.

> *Dean W.R. Inge,* Outspoken Essays, *1922*

Philosophy will clip an angel's wings,
Conquer all mysteries by rule and line,
Empty the haunted air, and gnomed mine—
Unweave a rainbow.

> *John Keats, "Lamia," 1819*

Making fun of philosophy is really philosophizing.

> *Pascal,* Pensées, *1670*

The philosophy of one century is the common sense of the next.

> *Henry Ward Beecher,* Life Thoughts, *1858*

Philosophy triumphs easily over past evils and future evils; but present evils triumph over it.

> *LaRochefoucauld,* Maxims, *1678*

For the learning of every virtue there is an appropriate discipline, and for the learning of suspended judgment the best discipline is philosophy.

> *Bertrand Russell,* Unpopular Essays, *1950*

In philosophy it is not the attainment of the goal that matters, it is the things that are met with by the way.

> *Havelock Ellis,* The Dance of Life, *1923*

Psychiatry's chief contribution to philosophy is the discovery that the toilet is the seat of the soul.

> *Alexander Chase,* Perspectives, *1966*

(*See also* **ARGUMENT, THINKING, THOUGHT**)

PHYSICAL FITNESS

Bodily exercise profiteth little, but godliness is profitable to all things.

1 Timothy 4:8

We are under-exercised as a nation. We look instead of play. We ride instead of walk. Our existence deprives us of the minimum of physical activity essential for healthy living.

John F. Kennedy, Address, New York City, December 5, 1961

Oh, the wild joy of living! the leaping from rock to rock,
The strong rending of boughs from the fir-tree, the cool silver shock
Of the plunge in a pool's living water.

Robert Browning, Men and Women, *1855*

(*See also* **HEALTH, SPORTS**)

PITY

. . . The feeling which arrests the mind in the presence of whatsoever is grave and constant in human sufferings and unites it with the human sufferer.

James Joyce, A Portrait of the Artist as a Young Man, *1916*

The hardest sentiment to tolerate is pity, especially when it's deserved. Hatred is a tonic, it vitalizes us, it inspires vengeance, but pity deadens, it makes our weakness weaker.

Balzac, La Peau de chagrin, *1831*

Self-pity is easily the most destructive of the nonpharmaceutical narcotics; it is addictive, gives momentary pleasure and separates the victim from reality.

John W. Gardner, The Recovery of Confidence, *1970*

(*See also* **SUFFERING, SYMPATHY**)

PLAY

The true object of all human life is play. Earth is a task garden; heaven is a playground.

G.K. Chesterton, All Things Considered, *1908*

There are toys for all ages.

English proverb

In our play we reveal what kind of people we are.

Ovid, The Art of Love, *c. A.D. 8*

Game, n. Any serious activity designed for the relaxation of busy people and the distraction of idle ones; useful for taking people off our hands when we have nothing to say to them, and sometimes even ourselves.

Abbé de Condillac, Dictionnaire de synonymes, *1751*

(*See also* **LEISURE, SPORTS, WORK**)

PLAYS: *See* **CINEMA, THEATER**

PLEASURE

There are two things to aim at in life: first, to get what you want; and after that, to enjoy it. Only the wisest of mankind achieve the second.

Logan Peasall Smith, Afterthoughts, *1931*

Mankind is safer when men seek pleasure than when they seek the power and the glory.

Geoffrey Gorer, New York Times Magazine, *November 27, 1966*

After pleasant scratching comes unpleasant itching.

Danish proverb

I take it as a prime cause of the present confusion of society that it is too sickly and too doubtful frankly to use pleasure as a test of value.

Rebecca West, in C. Fadiman, ed., I Believe, *1939*

(*See also* **PAIN/PLEASURE**)

POET

Each man carries within him the soul of a poet who died young.

Sainte-Beuve, Portraits littéraires, *1862*

Poets treat their experiences shamelessly: they exploit them.

Nietzsche, Beyond Good and Evil, *1886*

The poet . . . may be used as a barometer, but let us not forget that he is also part of the weather.

Lionel Trilling, The Liberal Imagination, *1950*

Poets help us to love: that is their only function. And a fine use of their delightful vanity.

> *Anatole France (d. 1924),* The Garden of Epicurus

The worst fate for a poet is to be admired without being understood.

> *Jean Cocteau,* Le Rappel á l'ordre, *1926*

Poetry is not a career, but a mug's game. No honest poet can ever feel quite sure of the permanent value of what he has written: he may have wasted his time and messed up his life for nothing.

> *T.S. Eliot,* The Use of Poetry and the Use of Criticism, *1933*

To be a wit, intelligence is enough; to be a poet takes imagination.

> *Cardinal de Bernis (d. 1794),* La poésie

The poet's function is to make his imagination . . . become the light in the mind of others. His role, in short, is to help people to live their lives.

> *Wallace Stevens,* The Necessary Angel, *1951*

You don't have to suffer to be a poet. Adolescence is enough suffering for anyone.

> *John Ciardi,* Simmons Review, *Fall 1962*

The poet never asks for admiration; he wants to be believed.

> *Jean Cocteau,* Newsweek, *April 7, 1958*

A poet's autobiography is his poetry. Anything else is just a footnote.

> *Yevgeny Yentushenko,* The Sole Survivor, *1982*

I may as well tell you that if you are going about the place thinking things pretty, you will never make a modern poet. Be poignant, man, be poignant!

> *P.G. Wodehouse,* The Small Bachelor, *1927*

The works of the great poets have never yet been read by mankind, for only great poets can read them.

> *Thoreau,* Walden, *1854*

Young poet (to Voltaire, who had berated him for writing and
> publishing trash): "I've gotta live, don't I?"
Voltaire: "I don't see the necessity."

> *Voltaire,* attributed

(*See also* **FANTASY, IMAGINATION, WORDS**)

POETRY

. . . Simply the most beautiful, impressive and wisely effective way of saying things.

Matthew Arnold, Essays in Criticism, *1865*

The grand style arises in poetry, when a noble nature, poetically gifted, treats with simplicity or with severity a serious subject.

Arnold, On Translating Homer, *1861*

Poetry is a counterfeit creation, and makes things that are not, as though they were.

John Donne, Sermons, *1622*

Genuine poetry can communicate before it is understood.

T.S. Eliot, Dante, *1920*

A poet looks at the world the way a man looks at a woman.

Wallace Stevens, Opus Posthumous, *1957*

Poetry is certainly something more than good sense, but it must be good sense at all events; just as a palace is more than a house, but it must be a house, at least.

Coleridge, Table Talk, *May 9, 1830*

Any healthy man can go without food for two days—but not without poetry.

Baudelaire, "Advice to Young Writers," 1867

If I read a book and it makes my whole body so cold no fire can ever warm me, I know that is poetry. If I feel physically as if the top of my head were taken off, I know that is poetry.

Emily Dickinson, in M. Bianchi's Life, *1924*

You don't make a poem with ideas, but with words.

Stéphane Mallarmé, Poésies complètes, *1887*

Poetry is not a turning loose of emotion, but an escape from emotion; it is not the expression of personality, but an escape from personality.

T.S. Eliot, Tradition and Individual Talent, *1919*

Each memorable verse of a true poet has two or three times the written content.

Alfred de Musset, Le Poète déchu, *1839*

Poetry is ordinary language raised to the nth power. Poetry is boned with ideas, nerved and blooded with emotions, all held together by the delicate, tough skin of words.

> *Paul Engle,* New York Times, *February 17, 1957*

No good poem, however confessional it may be, is just a self-expression. Who on earth would claim that the pearl *expresses* the oyster?

> *C.D. Lewis,* Christian Science Monitor, *May 24, 1966*

I come here to speak poetry. It will always be in the grass. It will also be necessary to bend down to hear it [and] it will always be too simple to be discussed in assemblies.

> *Boris Pasternak, speech, International Congress of Writers, 1935*

Poetry is poetry, and one's objective as a poet is to achieve poetry precisely as one's objective in music is to achieve music.

> *Wallace Stevens, on selecting "Domination of Black" as his best poem, 1957*

Poetry is a rich, full-bodied whistle, cracked ice crunching in pails, the night that numbs the leaf, the duel of two nightingales, the sweet pea that has run wild, Creation's tears in shoulder blades.

> *Stevens, quoted in* Life, *June 13, 1960*

To *name* an object is to deprive a poem of three–fourths of its pleasure, which consists in a little-by-little guessing game; the ideal is to *suggest.*

> *Stephane Mallarmé, "Réponse à une enquête sur l'évolution littéraire," 1891*

Japanese poetry has as its subject the human heart. It may seem to be of no practical use and just as well left uncomposed, but when one knows poetry well, one understands also without explanation the reasons governing order and disorder in the world.

> *Kamo Mabuchi (d. 1769),* Writings

The poem . . . is a little myth of man's capacity of making life meaningful. And in the end, the poem is not a thing we see—it is, rather, a light by which we may see—and what we see is life.

> *Robert Penn Warren,* Saturday Review, *March 22, 1958*

Generally speaking, the more civilized and polished a people become, the less poetic its ways; everything weakens as it mellows.

> *Diderot (d. 1784),* On Dramatic Poetry

(*See also* **CREATIVITY, LANGUAGE, WRITING**)

POETRY: INTERPRETATION

A poem should not mean
But be.

Archibald MacLeish, Ars Poetica, *1926*

You can tear a poem apart to see what makes it tick. . . . You're back with the mystery of having been moved by words. The best craftsmanship always leaves holes and gaps . . . so that something that is *not* in the poem can creep, crawl, flash or thunder in.

Dylan Thomas, Poetic Manifesto, *1961*

Here is a verbal contraption, how does it work? What kind of a guy inhabits this poem? What is his notion of the Good Life? What is his notion of the Evil One? What does he conceal from the reader? . . . even from himself?

W.H. Auden, The Dyer's Hand, *1962*

The poet should seize the Particular, and he should, if there be anything sound in it, thus represent the Universal.

Goethe, in Eckermann's Conversations, *June 11, 1825*

People fancy they hate poetry, and they are all poets and mystics.

Emerson, Essays: Second Series, *1844*

Before people complain of the obscurity of modern poetry, they should first examine their consciences and ask themselves with how many people and on how many occasions they have genuinely and profoundly shared some experience with another.

W.H. Auden, Newsweek, *March 17, 1958*

POETRY VS. PROSE

Poetry is to prose as dancing is to walking.

John Wain, BBC-radio, January 13, 1976

The poet thinks in disconnected terms, unrelated ideas, juxtaposed images. Prose writers develop a succession of ideas . . . logically connected, that just flow out.

Pierre Reverdy, Le Livre de mon bord, *1948*

"All that's prose isn't verse, and all that isn't verse is prose. . . . "
"Good Heavens! I've been speaking prose for the last forty years and didn't even know it!"

Molière, The Would-Be Gentleman, *1670*

Poetry is not the proper antithesis to prose, but to science. Poetry is opposed to science, and prose to meter. The proper and immediate object of science is the acquirement, or communication of truth; the proper and immediate object of poetry is the communication of immediate pleasure.

Coleridge, Definitions of Poetry, *1811*

POLICE: *See* LAW, ORDER

POLITICAL PARTIES

Men are naturally divided into two parties: (1) those who fear and distrust the people, . . . (2) those who identify themselves with the people, have confidence in them, cherish and consider them as the most honest and safe.

Thomas Jefferson to Henry Lee, August 10, 1824

What good is a political party to people without bread?

Jean-Paul Marat to Camille Desmoulins, June 24, 1790

Political campaigns are designedly made into emotional orgies which endeavor to distract attention from the real issues involved, and they actually paralyze what slight powers of cerebration man can normally muster.

James Harvey Robinson, The Human Comedy, *1937*

Party spirit: the madness of the many for the gain of a few.

Alexander Pope to E. Blount, August 27, 1714

I'd call [the Republican Party platform] a new version of voodoo economics, but I'm afraid that would give witch doctors a bad name.

Geraldine A. Ferraro, Vice-Presidential candidate, August 25, 1984

(*See also* CONSERVATISM, LIBERALISM, POLITICS)

POLITICIAN

A politician must often talk and act before he has thought and read.

Thomas Babington Macaulay (d. 1859), Gladstone

A politician thinks of the next election; a statesman thinks of the next generation.

James Freeman Clarke (d. 1888), Sermon

In the course of a political lifetime, Ronald Reagan innocently squirrels away tidbits of misinformation and then, sometimes years later, casually drops them into his public discourse, like gum balls in a quiche.

Lucy Howard, Newsweek, *November 11, 1985*

Through his mastery of storytelling techniques, [Ronald Reagan] has managed to separate his character, in the public mind, from his action as president. . . . He has, in short, mesmerized us with that steady gaze.

Jean Nathan Miller, "Ronald Reagan and the Techniques of Deception," Atlantic, *February 1984*

Our great democracies still tend to think that a stupid man is more likely to be honest than a clever man, and our politicians take advantage of this prejudice by pretending to be even more stupid than nature made them.

Bertrand Russell, New Hopes for a Changing World, *1951*

A politician is . . . trained in the art of inexactitude. His words tend to be blunt or rounded, because if they have a cutting edge they may later return to wound him.

Edward R. Murrow, Address, London Guildhall, October 19, 1959

The *press conference* is a politician's way of being informative without saying anything. Should he accidentally say something, he has at his side a *press officer* who immediately explains it away by "clarifying" it.

Emery Kelen, Platypus at Large, *1960*

Political language—and with variations this is true of all political parties, from Conservatives to Anarchists—is designed to make lies sound truthful and murder respectable, and to give an appearance of solidity to pure wind.

George Orwell, Shooting an Elephant, *1950*

My constituency is the desperate, the damned, the disinherited, the disrespected, and the despised.

Jesse Jackson, Address, Democratic National Convention, July 17, 1984

Politicians . . . rise predominantly from . . . the "lower middle class"; most are self-made men . . . ; most depend on their political jobs for a livelihood and most have little time, inclination, or opportunity for adult education; hence the dominating qualities of so many are greed, vulgarity, attention to special interest, avarice, and selfishness.

John Gunther, Inside U.S.A., *1947*

Successful . . . politicians are insecure and intimidated men. They advance politically only as they placate, appease, bribe, seduce, bamboozle or otherwise manage to manipulate the demanding and threatening elements in their constituencies.

Walter Lippmann, The Public Philosophy, *1955*

(*See also* **DEMAGOGUE, GOVERNMENT, PUBLIC OFFICE**)

POLITICS

. . . The conduct of public affairs for private advantage.

Ambrose Bierce, The Devil's Dictionary, *1911*

Practical politics consists in ignoring facts.

Henry Adams, Education, *1907*

Politics is perhaps the only profession for which no preparation is thought necessary.

Robert Louis Stevenson (d. 1894), Familiar Studies

Politics is the art of looking for trouble, finding it everywhere, diagnosing it incorrectly and applying the wrong remedies.

Groucho Marx, recalled on the occasion of his death,
August 19, 1977

Nowhere are prejudices more mistaken for truth, passion for reason, and invective for documentation than in politics.

John Mason Brown, Through These Men, *1952*

I offer my opponents a bargain: if they will stop telling lies about us, I will stop telling the truth about them.

Adlai Stevenson, Campaign speech, 1952

POLLUTION

The meadow is poisonous but pretty in the fall.
The cows browsing there
Slowly poison themselves.

Guillaume Apollinaire, Alcools, *1913*

What the West has thrown on the waters of the world drifts back to us on a tide of cultural pollution appalling to behold.

Arthur C. Erickson, speech, International Congress of Architects,
Iran, 1974

As crude a weapon as the caveman's club, the chemical barrage has been hurled against the fabric of life.

Rachel Carson, Silent Spring, *1962*

(*See also* **NATURE**)

POPULARITY: *See* CELEBRITY

POPULATION

Population, when unchecked, increases in a geometrical ratio; subsistence . . . only in an arithmetrical ratio.

Thomas Robert Malthus, Essay on Population, *1798*

Overpopulation . . . has created conditions favorable to the survival of the unfit and the elimination of the fit.

William Ralph Inge, Outspoken Essays, *1922*

Each organic being . . . has to struggle for life and to suffer great destruction. . . . The vigorous, the healthy, and the happy survive and multiply.

Charles Darwin, Origin of Species, *1859*

Europe is overpopulated, the world soon will be. . . . If the self-reproduction of man is not "rationalized," . . . we shall have war.

Henri Bergson, Creative Evolution, *1907*

We have been God-like in our planned breeding of our domesticated plants and animals, but we have been rabbit-like in our unplanned breeding of ourselves.

Arnold Toynbee, National Observer, *June 10, 1963*

(*See also* **BIRTH, DEATH, STRUGGLE FOR SURVIVAL**)

PORNOGRAPHY

A taste for dirty stories may be said to be inherent in the human animal.

George Moore, Confessions of a Young Man, *1888*

At last, an unprintable book that is readable.

Ezra Pound, re: Henry Miller's Tropic of Cancer, *1934*

Nine–tenths of the appeal of pornography is due to the indecent feelings concerning sex which moralists inculcate in the young; the other tenth is physiological, and will occur in one way or another whatever the state of the law may be.

Bertrand Russell, Marriage and Morals, *1929*

A Word about Pornography: You'll need it. Lots of it. The dirty, filthy, degrading kind. But keep it *well hidden!* Don't discount secret wall panels, trick drawers, holes in the yard, etc., especially if you have teenage boys or a Baptist wife with a housekeeping obsession.

John Hughes, "Very Married Sex," National Lampoon, *1979*

The worst that can be said about pornography is that it leads not to "antisocial" acts but to the reading of more pornography.

Gore Vidal, Reflections upon a Sinking Ship, *1969*

Perhaps it would help . . . to compose a letter to the [London] *Times:* Dear Sir: I hope I am not a prude, but I feel compelled to lodge a protest against the ever-increasing flood of obscenity in dreams. Many of my friends have been as shocked and sickened as myself by the filth that is poured nightly as soon as our eyes are closed. It is certainly not my idea of home "entertainment."

Kenneth Tynan, The Sound of Two Hands Clapping, *1975*

We are unalterably opposed to the presentation of the female body being stripped, bound, raped, tortured, mutilated, and murdered in the name of commercial entertainment and free speech.

Susan Brownmiller, Against Our Will, *1975*

(*See also* **CENSORSHIP, PRUDERY, PURITANISM**)

POSSESSION

What a man has honestly acquired is absolutely his own, which may be freely given, but cannot be taken from him without his consent.

Samuel Adams, Massachusetts circular letter, 1768

It is preoccupation with possession, more than anything else, that prevents men from living freely and nobly.

Bertrand Russell, Principles of Social Reconstruction, *1917*

It is disastrous to own more of anything than you can possess, and it is one of the fundamental laws of human nature that our power actually to possess is limited.

Joseph Wood Krutch, If You Don't Mind My Saying So, *1964*

I like to walk about among the beautiful things that adorn the world; but private wealth I should decline, or any sort of personal possessions, because they would take away my liberty.

> *Santayana (d. 1952), "The Irony of Liberalism"*

There is radicalism in all getting, and conservatism in all keeping. Lovemaking is radical, while marriage is conservative.

> *Eric Hoffer,* The Passionate State of Mind, *1954*

It is as unjust to possess a woman exclusively as to possess slaves.

> *The Marquis de Sade,* La Philosophie dans le boudoir, *1795*

(*See also* **PROPERTY**)

POSSIBILITIES

Knowledge of what is possible is the beginning of happiness.

> *Santayana,* Little Essays, *1920*

Ah Christ, that it were possible
For one short hour to see
The souls we loved, that they might tell us
What and where they be.

> *Tennyson, "Maud," 1855*

It is a most mortifying reflection for a man to consider what he has done, compared to what he might have done.

> *Samuel Johnson, in Boswell's* Life, *1770*

I beseech you, in the bowels of Christ, think it possible you may be mistaken.

> *Oliver Cromwell to the General Assembly of the Church of Scotland, August 3, 1650*

All things are possible until they are proved impossible—and even the impossible may only be so, as of now.

> *Pearl S. Buck,* A Bridge for Passing, *1937*

The world is the sum-total of our vital possibilities.

> *Ortega y Gasset,* The Revolt of the Masses, *1930*

(*See also* **PROBABILITIES**)

POVERTY

Poverty is no disgrace to a man, but it is confoundedly inconvenient.
Sydney Smith, His Wit and Wisdom, *1900*

I used to think I was poor. Then they told me I wasn't poor, I was needy. They told me it was self-defeating to think of myself as needy, I was deprived. Then they told me underprivileged was overused. I was disadvantaged. I still don't have a dime. But I have a great vocabulary.
Jules Feiffer, Safire's Political Dictionary, *1978*

Boredom is the keynote of poverty . . . for when there is no money there is no change of any kind, not of scene or of routine.
Moss Hart, Act One, *1959*

The trouble with being poor is that it takes up all your time.
Willem de Kooning, in conversation

To be poor and independent is very nearly an impossibility.
William Cobbett (d. 1835), Advice to Young Men

Poverty keeps together more homes than it breaks up.
Saki, The Chronicles of Clovis, *1911*

Mendoza: I am a brigand: I live by robbing the rich.
Tanner: I am a gentleman: I live by robbing the poor.
G.B. Shaw, Man and Superman, *1903*

If a free society cannot help the many who are poor, it cannot save the few who are rich.
John F. Kennedy, Inaugural Address, January 20, 1961

We have the means of removing starvation and disease. . . . One thing is lacking: good will and understanding.
Vannevar Bush, Address, Columbia University, 1947

Poverty is the great reality. That is why the artist seeks it.
Anaïs Nin, Diary, *Summer 1937*

The fields were fruitful, and starving men moved on the roads. The granaries were full and the children of the poor grew up rachitic.
John Steinbeck, The Grapes of Wrath, *1939*

The other America, the America of poverty, is hidden today in a way it never was before.... The poor are increasingly slipping out of the very experience and consciousness of the nation.

Michael Harrington, The Other America, *1962*

People who are much too sensitive to demand of cripples that they run races ask of the poor that they get up and act like everyone else in the society.

Ibid.

There is only one class in the community that thinks more about money than the rich, and that is the poor. The poor can think of nothing else.

Oscar Wilde, "The Soul of Man under Socialism," 1891

We who are liberal and progressive know that the poor are our equals in every sense except that of being equal to us.

Lionel Trilling, The Liberal Imagination, *1950*

The poor shall inherit the earth, but not the mineral rights.

J. Paul Getty, attributed

POWER

... The great aphrodisiac.

Henry Kissinger, New York Times, *January 19, 1971*

The effect of power and publicity on all men is the aggravation of self, a sort of tumor that ends by killing the victim's sympathy.

Henry Adams, Education, *1907*

Power that controls the economy should be in the hands of elected representatives of the people, not in the hands of an industrial oligarchy.

William O. Douglas, dissent, U.S. v. Columbia Steel, *1948*

Power tends to corrupt and absolute power corrupts absolutely.

Lord Acton to Bishop Mandell Creighton, 1887

Power corrupts, but lack of power corrupts absolutely.

Adlai Stevenson, New York Times, *February 10, 1987*

No man is fit to be trusted with power.... Any man who has lived at all knows the follies and wickedness he's capable of.

C.P. Snow, The Light and the Dark, *1961*

(*See also* **AUTHORITY, IMPOTENCE, TYRANNY**)

PRACTICALITY: *See* COMMON SENSE, PRUDENCE

PRAISE

The advantage of doing one's praising to oneself is that one can lay it on so thick and exactly in the right places.
Samuel Butler, The Way of All Flesh, *1903*

Praise, like gold and diamonds, owes its value only to its scarcity.
Samuel Johnson, The Rambler, *June 6, 1751*

Praise shames me, for I secretly beg for it.
Rabindranath Tagore, Stray Birds, *1916*

(*See also* APPRECIATION, MERIT)

PRAYER

When thou prayest, enter into thy closet and when thou has shut the door, pray to thy Father which is in secret, and thy Father which seest in secret shall reward thee openly.
Jesus, Sermon on the Mount, Matthew 6:6

[We want] a constitutional amendment to permit voluntary school prayer. God should never have been expelled from America's classrooms in the first place.
Ronald Reagan, State of the Union message, January 25, 1983

The wish to pray is prayer in itself.
Georges Bernanos, Diary of a Country Priest, *1887*

Certain thoughts are prayers. There are moments when, whatever be the attitude of the body, the soul is on its knees.
Victor Hugo, Les Misérables, *1862*

My words fly up, my thoughts remain below.
Words without thoughts never to heaven go.
Shakespeare, Hamlet, *1600*

Pray, v. To ask that the laws of the universe be annulled in behalf of a single petitioner confessedly unworthy.
Ambrose Bierce, The Devil's Dictionary, *1911*

Prayer gives a man the opportunity of getting to know a gentleman he hardly ever meets. I do not mean his maker, but himself.
William Inge (d. 1954), Dean of St. Paul's Cathedral

Pray to God but keep on rowing the boat ashore.

Russian proverb

Forgive us for turning our churches into private clubs; for loving familiar hymns and religious feelings more than we love You; for pasting stained glass on our eyes and our ears to shut out the cry of the hungry and the hurt of the world.

United Presbyterian Church, Litany for Holy Communion, *1968*

(*See also* **JESUS, WORSHIP**)

PREJUDICE

. . . A vagrant opinion without visible means of support.

Ambrose Bierce, The Devil's Dictionary, *1911*

It is so much easier to assume than to prove, . . . less painful to believe than to doubt, such a charm in the repose of prejudice, when no discordant voice jars upon . . . belief.

W.E.H. Lecky, A History of Rationalism, *1900*

Knowledge humanizes mankind, and reason inclines to mildness; but prejudices destroy every tender disposition.

Montesquieu, Spirit of the Laws, *1748*

Fear and ignorance about AIDS can so weaken people's senses as to make them susceptible to an equally virulent threat: bigotry.

Editorial, New York Times, *October 7, 1985*

I hang onto my prejudices; they are the testicles of my mind.

Eric Hoffer, Before the Sabbath, *1979*

PRESENT

Every situation—nay, every moment—is of infinite worth, for it is the representative of a whole eternity.

Goethe, in Eckermann's Conversations, *November 3, 1823*

Real generosity toward the future lies in giving all to the present.

Albert Camus, The Rebel, *1951*

With the Past, as past, I have nothing to do; nor with the Future as future. I live now, and will verify all past history in my own moments.

Emerson, Journals, *1839*

Ah, take the Cash, and let the Credit go,
Nor heed the rumble of a distant Drum!

Omar Khayyam, Rubáiyát, *c. 1200*

The word "now" is like a bomb through the window, and it ticks.

Arthur Miller, After the Fall, *1964*

(*See also* **FUTURE, PAST, TWENTIETH CENTURY**)

PRESIDENCY

A President either is constantly on top of events or, if he hesitates, events will soon be on top of him. I never felt that I could let up for a single moment.

Harry S. Truman, Memoirs, *1955*

I was not fully informed.

Ronald Reagan, News conference, November 19, 1986

No *easy* problems ever come to the President. . . . If they are easy to solve, somebody else has solved them.

Dwight D. Eisenhower, Parade, *April 8, 1962*

A president's hardest task is not to do what is right, but to *know* what is right.

Lyndon B. Johnson, State of the Union, January 4, 1965

The progress of evolution from President Washington to President Grant [is] alone enough to upset Darwin.

Henry Adams, Education, *1907*

(*See also* **STATE, HEADS OF**)

PRESS/MEDIA

The newspapers! Sir, they are the most villainous—licentious—abominable—infernal—Not that I ever read them—No—I make it a rule never to look into a newspaper.

Richard Brinsley Sheridan, The Critic, *1779*

Were it left to me to decide whether we should have a government without newspapers, or newspapers without government, I should . . . prefer the latter. But I should mean that every man should receive those papers and be capable of reading them.

Thomas Jefferson to Colonel Carrington, 1787

The crux is not the publisher's "freedom" to print; it is rather, the citizen's "right to know."

Arthur Hays Sulzberger, Address, 1956

The press must be free; it has always been so and much evil has been corrected by it. If Government finds itself annoyed by it, let it examine its own conduct [to] find the cause.

Thomas Erskine, Lord Chancellor of England, Rex v. Paine, 1792

Our press laws are such that differences of opinion among members of the Government are no longer open to the public; they are none of the press's business.

Adolf Hitler, Secret Conversations, *1953*

The press is our chief ideological weapon. Its duty is to strike down the enemies of the working class, the foes of the working people.

Nikita S. Khrushchev, New York Times *Magazine, September 29, 1957*

The bigger the information media, the less courage and freedom they allow. Bigness means weakness.

Eric Sevareid, "The Press and the People," TV Program, 1959

Today intimidation of the press is a standard item on the agenda of the organized political right. There are self-appointed monitors who circulate denunciations of articles and television programs that depart from their ideology. There are groups that support libel suits. And there is Jesse Helms, threatening to buy up a network that is not far enough to the right for his taste.

Anthony Lewis, "The Intimidated Press," New York Review of Books, *January 19, 1989*

(*See also* **CENSORSHIP, JOURNALISM**)

PRETENSION

Affectation is a greater enemy to the face than smallpox.

English proverb

All human beings have gray little souls—and they all want to rouge them up.

Maxim Gorky, The Lower Depths, *1903*

Some degree of affectation is as necessary to the mind as dress is to the body; we must overact our part in some measure, in order to produce any effect at all.

William Hazlitt, Sketches and Essays, *1839*

Pretending is a virtue. If you can't pretend, you can't be king.

Luigi Pirandello, Liolà, *1916*

(*See also* **HYPOCRISY**)

PRIDE

. . . goeth before destruction, and a haughty spirit before a fall.

Proverbs 16:18

We should not deny people their pride; it is their only compensation for their misery.

Charles Nodier, La Fée aux miettes, *1832*

Pride is the mask of one's own faults.

Hebrew proverb

(*See also* **CONCEIT, HUMILITY, SELF-IMPORTANCE**)

PRINCIPLES

A man is usually more careful of his money than of his principles.

Oliver Wendell Holmes, Jr., speech, Boston, January 8, 1897

Men of principle are sure to be bold, but those who are bold may not always be men of principle.

Confucius, Analects, *sixth century* B.C.

Principle never forgives and its logic is to kill.

Jacques Barzun, The House of Intellect, *1959*

It is often easier to fight for principles than to live up to them.

Adlai Stevenson, speech, New York City, August 27, 1952

(*See also* **INTEGRITY**)

PRISON

Self is the only prison that can ever bind the soul.

Henry Van Dyke (d. 1933), "The Prison and the Angel"

A prison is a house of care, a place where none can thrive;
A touchstone true to try a friend, a grave for one alive.
Sometimes a place of right, sometimes a place of wrong,
Sometimes a place of rogues and thieves and honest men among.

Inscription, Edinburgh's old Tolbooth prison, 1817

Prison is a Socialist's Paradise, where equality prevails, everything is supplied and competition is eliminated.

Elbert Hubbard, The Note Book, *1927*

Lennie. . . . "Human weakness takes many forms. Desire, greed, lust—we're all here for different reasons aren't we?"
Fletcher: "With respect, Godber, we're all here for the same reason—we got caught."

Dick Clement and Ian La Fresnais, "Poetic Justice," BBC-TV, 1976

That is the whole beauty of prisons—the benefit is not to the prisoner, of being reformed or rehabilitated, but to the public. Prisons give those outside a resting period from town bullies and horrible characters, and for this we should be very grateful.

Roy Kerridge, The Lone Conformist, *1984*

I know not whether Laws be right,
Or whether Laws be wrong;
All that we know who lie in gaol
Is that the wall is strong;
And that each day is like a year,
A year whose days are long.

Oscar Wilde, The Ballad of Reading Gaol, *1898*

PRIVACY

Civilization is the progress toward a society of privacy. The savage's whole existence is public, ruled by the laws of the tribe.

Ayn Rand, The Fountainhead, *1943*

The free state offers what a police state denies—the privacy of the home, the dignity and peace of mind of the individual.

Justice William O. Douglas, Address, 1953

There is no right of privacy in the [U.S.] Constitution.

Judge Robert H. Bork, testimony before the Senate Judiciary Committee, September 16, 1987

(*See also* **HOME, SOLITUDE**)

PRIVILEGE: *See* CLASSES, DEMOCRACY, INEQUALITY

PROBABILITIES

A reasonable probability is the only certainty.

Edgar Watson Howe, Country Town Sayings, *1911*

The laws of probability, so true in general, so fallacious in particular.
Edward Gibbon (d. 1794), Autobiography

There is nothing impossible in the existence of the supernatural: its existence seems to me decidedly probable.
Santayana, The Genteel Tradition at Bay, *1931*

As for a future life, every man must judge for himself between conflicting vague probabilities.
Darwin, Life and Letters, *ed. Francis Darwin, 1887*

The theory of probabilities is at bottom nothing but common sense reduced to calculus.
Laplace, Théorie analytique des probabilités, *1820*

(*See also* **POSSIBILITIES**)

PROBLEMS

Our problems are man-made, therefore they may be solved by man. . . . No problem of human destiny is beyond human beings.
John F. Kennedy, Address, American University, June 10, 1963

She probably labored under the common delusion that you made things better by talking about them.
Rose Macauley, Crewe Train, *1926*

There are two problems in my life. The political ones are insoluble and the economic ones are incomprehensible.
Sir Alec Douglas-Home, the Earl of Home, speech, 1964

In my experience, the worst thing you can do to an important problem is to discuss it.
Simon Gray, Otherwise Engaged, *1975*

We don't solve our problems, we simply learn to live with them.
Anonymous

PROFIT

The engine which drives Enterprise is not thrift, but profit.
John Maynard Keynes, A Treatise on Money, *1930*

Without development there is no profit, without profit no development. For the capitalist system it must be added that without profit there would be no accumulation of wealth.

Joseph A. Schumpeter, The Theory of Economic Development, *1934*

I have made my mistakes, but in all my years of public life I have never profited, *never* profited from public service. I have earned every cent. . . . I welcome this kind of examination because people have got to know whether or not their President is a crook. Well, I'm not a crook.

Richard M. Nixon, Press conference, November 11, 1973

PROFITEERING

Prefer a loss to a dishonest gain: the one brings pain at the moment, the other for all time.

Chilon (sixth century B.C.), in Diogenes Laetius, Lives

He that maketh haste to be rich shall not be innocent.

Proverbs 28:20

The smell of profit is clean
And sweet, whatever the source.

Juvenal, Satires, *c. A.D. 100*

Not even a collapsing world looks dark to a man who is about to make his fortune.

E.B. White, One Man's Meat, *1944*

PROFLIGACY

Now is the time to get drunk! To stop being the martyred slaves of time, to get absolutely drunk—on wine, poetry, or on virtue, as you please.

Charles Baudelaire, "Enivrez-vous," Paris Spleen, *1869*

An unrestricted satisfaction of every need presents itself as the most enticing method of conducting one's life, but it means putting enjoyment before caution, and soon brings its own punishment.

Sigmund Freud, Civilization and Its Discontents, *1930*

Not joy but joylessness is the mother of debauchery.

Nietzsche, Miscellaneous Maxims and Opinions, *1879*

An orgy looks particularly alluring seen through the mists of righteous indignation.

Malcolm Muggeridge, "Dolce Vita in a Cold Climate," 1966

PROFUNDITY

There's no one so transparent as the person who thinks he's devilish deep.

Somerset Maugham, Lady Frederick, *1907*

The profound thinker always suspects that he is superficial.

Disraeli, Contarini Fleming, *1832*

(*See also* **WISDOM**)

PROGRESS

All progress is based on a universal innate desire on the part of every organism to live beyond its income.

Samuel Butler, The Way of All Flesh, *1903*

The progress, order, security, and peace of each country are necessarily connected with the social progress, order, security and peace of all other countries.

Pope John XXIII, Pacem in terris, *Encyclical, 1963*

All progress has resulted from people who took unpopular positions.

Adlai Stevenson, speech, Princeton, 1954

I do not believe in the indefinite progress of Societies; I believe in man's progress over himself.

Balzac, La Comédie humaine, *1841*

Progress itself increases the urgency of the warning that . . . *Natura non facit saltum* [Nature does not make jumps]. Progress must be slow.

Alfred Marshall, Principles of Economics, *1890*

The test of our progress is not whether we add more to the abundance of those who have much; it is whether we provide enough for those who have too little.

Franklin D. Roosevelt, Inaugural Address, 1937

So long as all the increased wealth which modern progress brings goes but to build up great fortunes, to increase luxury and make sharper the contrast between the House of Have and the House of Want, progress is not real and cannot be permanent.

Henry George, Progress and Poverty, *1879*

The whole history of the progress of human liberty shows that all concessions yet made . . . have been born of earnest struggle. . . . If there is no struggle there is no progress.

Frederick Douglass (former slave), Narrative of His Life, *1845*

The progress of an artist is a continual self-sacrifice, a continual extinction of personality.

T.S. Eliot, Tradition and the Individual Talent, *1919*

There can be no progress—real, moral progress—except in the individual and by the individual himself.

Baudelaire, Mon Coeur mis à nu, *1887*

Progress, man's distinctive mark alone,
Not God's, and not the beasts'. . . .

Robert Browning, "A Death in the Desert," *1864*

Progress . . . is not an accident, but a necessity. . . . It is a part of nature.

Herbert Spencer, Social Statics, *1851*

Till women are more rationally educated, the progress in human virtue and improvement in knowledge must receive continual check.

Mary Wollstonecraft, A Vindication of the Rights of Women, *1792*

(*See also* **MACHINE AGE, TECHNOLOGY**)

PROMISCUITY

"Has it ever occurred to you that in your promiscuous pursuit of women you are merely trying to assuage your subconscious fears of sexual impotence?"
"Yes, sir, it has."
"Then why do you do it?"
"To assuage my fears of sexual impotence."

Joseph Heller, Catch-22, *1961*

Lady Capricorn, he understood, was still keeping open bed.

Aldous Huxley, Antic Hay, *1923*

Like the bee sting, the promiscuous leave behind them in each encounter something of themselves by which they are made to suffer.

Cyril Connolly, The Unquiet Grave, *1945*

You were born with your legs apart. They'll send you to your grave in a Y-shaped coffin.

Joe Orton, What the Butler Saw, *1969*

What is a promiscuous person? It is usually someone who is getting more sex than you are.

Victor Lownes, Playboy, *1985*

(*See also* **PROFLIGACY, INFIDELITY**)

PROPAGANDA

The real struggle is not between East and West, or capitalism and communism, but between education and propaganda.

Martin Buber (d. 1965), in A. Hodes, Encounter

Through clever and constant propaganda, people can be made to see paradise as hell and vice versa, to consider the most wretched sort of life as heaven itself.

Adolf Hitler, Mein Kampf, *1933*

The biggest lesson I learned from Vietnam is not to trust [our] government's statements. I had no idea until then that you could not rely on them.

Sen. William Fulbright, New York Times, *April 30, 1985*

Propaganda must be so popular and on such an intellectual level that even the most stupid will understand it. . . . It should be limited to a very few points which, in turn, should be used as slogans until the very last person can get the message.

Hitler, Mein Kampf, *1933*

The propagandist's purpose is to make one set of people forget that certain other sets of people are human.

Aldous Huxley, The Olive Tree, *1937*

The United States . . . is a country where public opinion plays an important role. . . . Nothing can be achieved or endure without it, and its veto is final. It is more spontaneous than anywhere else in the world and also more easily directed by efficient propaganda than in any other country.

> *André Siegfried,* America at Mid–Century, *1955*

(*See also* **ADVERTISING, DEMAGOGUE, OPINION**)

PROPERTY

He that hath nothing is frightened at nothing.

> *Thomas Fuller,* Gnomologia, *1732*

The first person who, having enclosed a piece of ground, . . . said, "This is mine," and found people simple enough to believe him, was the real founder of civil society.

> *Rousseau,* Origins of Social Inequality, *1755*

Private property was the original source of freedom. It still is its main bulwark.

> *Walter Lippmann,* The Good Society, *1937*

Private property is a natural fruit of labor, a product of intense activity of man, acquired through his energetic determination to ensure and develop with his own strength his own existence and that of his family, and to create for himself and his own an existence of just freedom, not only economic, but also political, cultural, and religious.

> *Pius XII, Radio broadcast, September 1, 1944*

The true conservative is he who insists that property shall be the servant and not master of the commonwealth. . . . The citizens of the United States must effectively control the mighty commercial forces which they have themselves called into being.

> *Theodore Roosevelt,* The New Nationalism, *1910*

Every man holds his property subject to the general right of the community to regulate its use to whatever degree the public welfare may require it.

> *T. Roosevelt, speech, Osawatomie, August 31, 1910*

Upon the sacredness of property civilization itself depends—the right of the laborer to his hundred dollars in the savings bank, and equally the legal right of the millionaire to his millions.

> *Andrew Carnegie, "Wealth,"* North American Review, *June 1899*

The most common and durable source of factions has been the various and unequal distribution of property.

James Madison, The Federalist, *1787*

Property, like liberty, though immune from destruction, . . . , is not immune from regulation . . . for the common good. What the regulation should be, every generation must work out for himself.

Justice Benjamin Cardozo, Helvering et al. v. Davis, *1937*

(*See also* **POSSESSION, POVERTY, WEALTH**)

PROPHETS

Beware of false prophets, which come to you in sheep's clothing, but inwardly they are ravening wolves.

Matthew 7:15

Men reject their prophets and slay them, but they love their martyrs and honor those whom they have slain.

Fyodor Dostoyevski, The Brothers Karamazov, *1880*

Prognostics do not always prove prophecies—at least the wisest prophets make sure of the event first.

Horace Walpole to Thomas Walpole, February 19, 1785

(*See also* **THE BIBLE, JESUS, THE KORAN**)

PROSPERITY

. . . is the blessing of the Old Testament; adversity is the blessing of the New.

Francis Bacon, "Of Adversity," 1625

Armaments, universal debt and planned obsolescence—those are the three pillars of Western prosperity.

Aldous Huxley (d. 1963), Island

If you don't want prosperity to falter, then Buy, Buy, Buy—on credit, of course. In other words, the surest way of bringing on a rainy day is to prepare for it.

Joseph Wood Krutch, Human Nature and the Human Condition, *1959*

We have produced a world of contented bodies and discontented minds.

Adam Clayton Powell, Keep the Faith, Baby! *1967*

(*See also* **ADVERSITY, SUCCESS, WEALTH**)

PROSTITUTION

The big difference between sex for money and sex for free is that sex for money usually costs less.

Brendan Francis, Playboy, *1985*

Prostitution gives her an opportunity to meet people. It provides fresh air and wholesome exercise, and it keeps her out of trouble.

Joseph Heller, Catch-22, *1961*

Prisons are built with stones of law,
brothels with bricks of religion.

William Blake, The Marriage of Heaven and Hell, *1790*

PROTEST

I want every American free to stand up for his rights, even if sometimes he has to sit down for them.

John F. Kennedy, Campaign speech, Philadelphia, October 31, 1960

Agitators are a set of interfering meddling people, who come down to some perfectly contented class of the community and sow the seeds of discontent among them. That is the reason why agitators are so absolutely necessary.

Oscar Wilde, "The Soul of Man under Socialism," 1891

It is not difficult to be unconventional in the eyes of the world when your unconventionality is but the convention of your set.

W. Somerset Maugham, The Moon and Sixpence, *1919*

(*See also* **DISSENT, OPPOSITION**)

PROVERBS: *See* APHORISMS, QUOTATIONS

PROVIDENCE

God will provide—if only God would provide until he provides.

Hanan J. Ayalti, ed., Yiddish Proverbs, *1949*

To put one's trust in God is only a longer way of saying that one will chance it.

Samuel Butler, Note-Books, *1912 (posth.)*

God gives, but man must open his hand.

German proverb

How dark are the ways of god to man!

Euripides, Heracles, *c. 420 B.C.*

(*See also* **FATE, FORTUNE**)

PRUDENCE

No one tests the depth of a river with both feet.

Ashanti proverb

Tell not all you know, believe not all you hear, do not do all you can.

Italian proverb

So soon as prudence has begun to grow up in the brain, like a dismal fungus, it finds its first expression in a paralysis of generous acts.

Robert Louis Stevenson, Virginibus puerisque, *1881*

The prudent man does himself good; the virtuous man does good to others.

Voltaire, Philosophical Dictionary, *1764*

(*See also* **COMMON SENSE, FOLLY, MODERATION**)

PRUDERY

I'm an intensely shy and vulnerable woman. My husband has never seen me naked. Nor has he expressed the least desire to do so.

Dame Edna Everage (Barry Humphries), "Housewife Superstar," one-man show, 1976

The peculiarity of prudery is to multiply sentinels in proportion as the fortress is less threatened.

Victor Hugo, Les Misérables, *1862*

Nature knows no indecencies; man invents them.

Mark Twain, Notebook, *1935*

(*See also* **CENSORSHIP, PORNOGRAPHY, PURITANISM**)

PSYCHIATRY

. . . The care of the id by the odd.

Anonymous

You go to a psychiatrist when you're slightly cracked and keep going until you're completely broke.

Anonymous

My psychiatrist and I have decided that when we both think I'm ready, I'm going to get in my car and drive off the Verrazano Bridge.

Neil Simon, The Last of the Red Hot Lovers, *1969*

A psychiatrist is a man who goes to the Folies Bergère and looks at the audience.

Dr. Mervyn Stockwood, Anglican bishop, quoted in the London Observer, *1961*

(*See also* **NEUROSES, PSYCHOANALYSIS, PSYCHOLOGY**)

PSYCHOANALYSIS

A psychoanalyst is one who pretends he doesn't know everything.

Anonymous

Look into the depths of your own soul and learn first to know yourself, then you will understand why this illness was bound to come upon you and perhaps you will thenceforth avoid falling ill.

Sigmund Freud, Collected Papers, *1950*

I was in group analysis 'cause I couldn't afford private. I was captain of the Latent–Paranoid Softball Team. We played all the neurotics on a Sunday morning. The Nail–Biters against the Bed–Wetters.

Woody Allen, The Nightclub Years, 1964–1968, *recording, 1972*

You will . . . be able to utilize the special words and phrases you have learned in therapy. Your mate will find these particularly grating. For example:
 1. "Will you stop ACTING OUT and start RELATING?"
 2. "You know what this is about? TRANSFERENCE."
 3. "What's the psychological PAYOFF in all this for you?"
 4. "Boy, do you have a lot of REPRESSED RAGE."
 5. "You're a classic example of ANAL-RETENTIVE behavior."

Dan Greenburg and Suzanne O'Malley, How to Avoid Love and Marriage, *1983*

All cases are unique, and very similar to others.

T.S. Eliot, The Cocktail Party, *1949*

The man who once cursed his fate, now curses himself—and pays his psychoanalyst.

John W. Gardner, No Easy Victories, *1968*

(*See also* **ANXIETY, SELF-DOUBT, SELF-SUFFICIENCY**)

PSYCHOLOGY

A large part of the popularity and persuasiveness of psychology comes from its being a sublimated spiritualism: a secular, ostensibly scientific way of affirming the primacy of "spirit" over matter.

Susan Sontag, Illness as Metaphor, *1977*

There is no psychology; there is only biography and autobiography.

Thomas Szasz, The Second Sin: Psychology, *1973*

The purpose of psychology is to give us a completely different idea of the things we know best.

Paul Valéry, Tel Quel, *1943*

It seems a pity that psychology has destroyed all our knowledge of human nature.

G.K. Chesterton, London Observer, *December 9, 1934*

(*See also* **MIND**)

PUBLIC

The public, which is feebleminded, . . . will never be able to preserve its individual reactions from the tricks of the exploiter. The public is and always will be exploited.

D.H. Lawrence, Pornography and Obscenity, *1929*

The public be damned!

William A. Vanderbilt (d. 1885), railroad magnate.

People on the whole are very simpleminded, in whatever country one finds them. They are so simple as to take literally, more often than not, the things their leaders tell them.

Pearl S. Buck, What America Means to Me, *1943*

Why should there not be a patient confidence in the ultimate justice of the people? Is there any better or equal hope in the world?

Abraham Lincoln, Inaugural Address, 1861

In a community where public services have failed to keep abreast of private consumption. . . . in an atmosphere of private opulence and public squalor, the private goods have full sway.

> *John Kenneth Galbraith,* The Affluent Society, *1958*

The public buys its opinions as it buys its meat, or takes in its milk, on the principle that it is cheaper to do this than to keep a cow. So it is, but the milk is more likely to be watered.

> *Samuel Butler,* Notebooks, *1912*

(*See also* **PEOPLE**)

PUBLICITY

Formerly a public man needed a *private* secretary for a barrier between himself and the public. Nowadays he has a *press* secretary, to keep him properly in the public eye.

> *Daniel J. Boorstin,* The Image, *1962*

We march through life an' behind us marches th' phottygrafter an' th' rayporther. There are no such things as private citizens.

> *Finley Peter Dunne,* Observations by Mr. Dooley, *1902*

(*See also* **ADVERTISING, PRIVACY, PROPAGANDA**)

PUBLIC OFFICE

The very essence of a free government consists in considering offices as public trusts, bestowed for the good of the country, and not for the benefit of an individual or party.

> *John C. Calhoun, speech, February 13, 1835*

Your public servants serve you right; indeed often they serve you better than your apathy and indifference deserve.

> *Adlai Stevenson, speech, Los Angeles, September 11, 1952*

(*See also* **GOVERNMENT, POLITICIAN**)

PUBLIC SPEAKING

Whereas logic is the art of demonstrating truth, eloquence is the gift of winning over people's hearts and minds so that you may inspire them and persuade them in whatever way you choose.

> *La Bruyère,* Characters, *1688*

An orator can hardly get beyond commonplaces: if he does he gets beyond his hearers.

William Hazlitt, The Plain Speaker, *1826*

Nothing is so unbelievable that oratory cannot make it acceptable.

Cicero, Paradoxa Stoicorum, *46 B.C.*

Once you get 'em laughing and their mouths open, you can stuff something in.

Francis Harvey Green, The Pennington School, *1932*

It is terrible to speak well and be wrong.

Sophocles, Electra, *c. 415 B.C.*

Everyone may speak truly, but to speak logically, prudently, and adequately is a talent few possess.

Montaigne, Essays, *1588*

There can be no fairer ambition than to excel in talk: to be affable, gay, ready, clear, and welcome.

Robert Louis Stevenson, "Talk and Talkers," 1882

Eloquence is the language of nature and cannot be learned in the schools; but rhetoric is the creature of art, which he who feels least will most excel in.

C.C. Colton, Lacon, *1825*

There is no more sovereign eloquence than the truth [told] with indignation.

Victor Hugo, Les Misérables, *1862*

Oratory is like prostitution: you have to have a few tricks.

Vittorio Emanuele Orlando, Time, *December 8, 1952*

There are some people who speak well but write badly. However, the audience and the situation stimulate them and draw from their minds more than they could think of without such a challenge.

Pascal, Pensées, *1670*

If you have to make an unpopular speech, give it all the sincerity you can muster; that's the only way to sweeten it.

Cardinal de Retz, Memoirs, *1718*

In oratory the greatest art is to hide art.

Jonathan Swift, A Critical Essay upon the Faculties of the Mind, *1707*

What orators lack in depth they make up in length.

> *Montesquieu,* Lettres persanes, *1721*

Lecturer, n. One with his hand in your pocket, his tongue in your ear, and his faith in your patience.

> *Ambrose Bierce,* The Devil's Dictionary, *1911*

(*See also* **ELOQUENCE, STYLE, WORDS**)

PUNCTUALITY

I have noticed that the people who are late are often jollier than the people who have to wait for them.

> *E.V. Lucas,* Reading, Writing and Remembering, *1932*

I've been on a calendar, but never on time.

> *Marilyn Monroe,* Look, *1962*

He was always late on principle, his principle being that punctuality is the thief of time.

> *Oscar Wilde,* Picture of Dorian Gray, *1891*

(*See also* **DELAY**)

PUNISHMENT

In nature there are neither rewards nor punishment—there are consequences.

> *Robert Ingersoll, Address, New York, October 29, 1896*

My object all sublime
I shall achieve in time—
To make the punishment fit the crime.

> *W.S. Gilbert,* The Mikado, *1885*

Speaking generally, punishment hardens and numbs, it produces obstinacy, it sharpens the sense of alienation and strengthens the power of resistance.

> *Nietzsche,* The Geneology of Morals, *1887*

He alone may chastise who loves.

> *Rabindranath Tagore,* The Crescent Moon, *1913*

(*See also* **HELL, PRISON**)

PUNISHMENT, CAPITAL

When a man knows he is to be hanged, it concentrates his mind wonderfully.

Samuel Johnson, in Boswell's Life, *September 19, 1777*

It is fairly obvious that those who favor the death penalty have more affinity with assassins than those who do not.

Rémy de Gourmont, Pensées inédites, *1924*

The compensation for a death sentence is knowledge of the exact hour when one is to die. A great luxury, but one that is well earned.

Vladimir Nabokov, Invitation to a Beheading, *1934*

Executions, far from being useful to the survivors, have . . . a quite contrary effect, by hardening the heart they ought to terrify.

Mary Wollstonecraft, Letter, 1796

If a barmaid . . . has demanded silver in excessive amount, . . . she shall be prosecuted, [bound], and thrown in the river.

Hammurabi's Code, c. 2040 B.C.

[Moosbrugger] was not afraid of death. There is a great deal that one has to put up with in life that hurts more than being hanged. . . . The passive pride of a person who has been in prison many times kept him from fearing his punishment; but even apart from that he had no reason to cling to life.

Robert Musil, The Man without Qualities, *1930*

(*See also* **LIFE AND DEATH, SUICIDE**)

PUNS

There is no kind of false wit which has been so recommended by the practice of all ages, as that which consists of a jingle of words, and is comprehended under the general name of *Punning.*

Joseph Addison, The Spectator, *1712*

The goodness of the true pun is in the direct ratio of its intolerability.

Edgar Allan Poe, Marginalia, *1849*

A pun is the lowest form of humor—if you didn't think of it first.

Oscar Levant, attributed

(*See also* **HUMOR, WIT**)

PURITANISM

. . . The haunting fear that someone, somewhere may be happy.

H.L. Mencken, A Book of Burlesques, *1920*

We are descended from the Puritan, who nobly fled from a land of despotism to a land of freedom, where they could not only enjoy their own religion, but prevent everybody else from enjoyin' *his.*

Artemis Ward in London, 1872

The prig is a very interesting psychological study, and though of all poses a moral pose is the most offensive, still to have a pose at all is something.

Oscar Wilde, The Critic as Artist, *1890*

PURITY

No one is more dangerous than he who imagines himself pure in heart: for his purity, by definition, is unassailable.

James Baldwin, Nobody Knows My Name, *1961*

My strength is as the strength of ten,
Because my heart is pure.

Alfred, Lord Tennyson, "Sir Galahad," *1824*

(*See also* **GUILTY/INNOCENT**)

PURPOSE

Nothing contributes so much to tranquilize the mind as a steady purpose—a point on which the soul may fix its intellectual eye.

Mary Wollstonecraft Shelley, Frankenstein, *1818*

There is one quality more important than "know-how" and we cannot accuse the United States of any undue amount of it. This is "know-what" by which we determine not only how to accomplish our purposes, but what our purposes are to be.

Norbert Wiener, The Human Use of Human Beings, *1954*

Many persons have a wrong idea of what constitutes true happiness. It is not attained through self-gratification but through fidelity to a worthy purpose.

Helen Keller, Journal, *1938*

QUALITIES

We never love a person, only qualities.

Pascal, Pensées, *1670*

We don't love qualities, we love persons, sometimes for their defects as well as for their qualities.

Jacques Maritain, Reflections on America, *1958*

A Man without Qualities.

Robert Musil, Title of novel, 1930

It is easier to confess a defect than to claim a quality.

Max Beerbohm, And Even Now, *1920*

One shining quality lends luster to another, or hides some glaring defect.

William Hazlitt, Characteristics, *1823*

(*See also* **SELF-ESTEEM**)

QUARRELS

Make sure to be in with your equals if you're going to fall out with your superiors.

H.J. Ayalti, ed., Yiddish Proverbs, *1949*

You can make up a quarrel, but it will always show where it was patched.

> *Edgar Watson Howe,* Country Town Sayings, *1911*

For souls in growth, great quarrels are great emancipations.

> *Logan Pearsall Smith,* Afterthoughts, *1931*

In France quarrels strengthen a love affair, in America they end it.

> *Ned Rorem,* The Paris Diary of Ned Rorem, *1966*

It takes in reality only one to make a quarrel. It is useless for the sheep to pass resolutions in favor of vegetarianism, while the wolf remains of a different opinion.

> *William Ralph Inge,* Outspoken Essays, *1919*

(*See also* **ARGUMENT, DIFFERENCES, SEXUAL RELATIONS**)

QUESTIONS

It is easier to judge a person's mental capacity by his questions than by his answers.

> *Le Duc de Lévis (d. 1830),* Maxims

A sudden, bold, and unexpected question doth many times surprise a man and lay him open.

> *Francis Bacon,* Essays, *1625*

The scientist is not a person who gives the right answers, he's one who asks the right questions.

> *Claude Lévi-Strauss,* Le Cru et le cuit, *1964*

The first key to wisdom is this—constant and frequent questioning . . . for by doubting we are led to question and by questioning we arrive at the truth.

> *Peter Abelard,* Sic et non, *c. 1120*

'Tis not every question that deserves an answer.

> *Thomas Fuller,* Gnomologia, *1732*

To question a wise man is the beginning of wisdom.

> *German proverb*

(*See also* **DOGMATISM, DOUBT/CERTAINTY**)

QUIET

An inability to stay quiet . . . is one of the most conspicuous failures of mankind.

Walter Bagehot, Physics and Politics, *1869*

A calm despair, without angry convulsions or reproaches directed at heaven, is the essence of wisdom.

Alfred de Vigny, Journal d'un poète, *1832*

(*See also* **PEACE, RESIGNATION**)

QUOTATIONS

Next to the originator of a good sentence is the first quoter of it.

Emerson, Letters and Social Aims, *1875*

Most people who put together collections of verse or epigrams resemble those who eat cherries or oysters: they begin by choosing the best and end by eating everything.

Chamfort, Maxims, *1825*

A writer expresses himself in words that have been used before because they give his meaning better than he can give it himself, or becaue they are beautiful or witty, or because he expects them to touch a chord of association in his reader, or because he wishes to show that he is learned and well read.

H.W. Fowler, "*Quotation*," Dictionary of Modern English Usage

A fine quotation is a diamond on the finger of a witty person, but a pebble in the hands of a fool.

Joseph Roux, Meditations of a Parish Priest, *1886*

(*See also* **APHORISMS**)

RACE/RACISM

. . . The dogma that one ethnic group is condemned by nature to congenital inferiority and another group is destined to congenital superiority.

Ruth Benedict, Race: Science and Politics, *1940*

[The black history] of rope, fire, torture, castration, infanticide, rape; death and humiliation; fear by day and night, fear as deep as the marrow of the bone, doubt that he was worthy of life, since everyone around him denied it; sorrow for his women, for his kinfolk, for his children, who needed his protection, and whom he could not protect; rage, hatred and murder, hatred for white men so deep that it often turned against him and his own, and made all love, all trust, all joy impossible.

James Baldwin, The Fire Next Time, *1963*

All who are not of good race in this world are chaff.

Adolf Hitler, Mein Kampf, *1932*

The Nordic race has a right to rule the world. We must make this right the guiding star of our foreign policy.

Hitler to Otto Strasser, May 21, 1930

At the core of these aristocratic races the beast of prey is not to be mistaken, the magnificent *blond beast,* avidly rampant for spoil and victory.

Nietzsche, Geneology of Morals, *1887*

Purity of race does not exist. Europe is a continent of energetic mongrels.

H.A.L. Fisher, A History of Europe, *1934*

There is no evidence that there is any advantage in belonging to a pure race. The purest races now in existence are the Pygmies, the Hottentots, and the Australian aborigines; The Tasmanians, who were probably even purer, are extinct. They were not the bearers of a brilliant culture.

Bertrand Russell, Unpopular Essays, *1950*

The Ku Klux Klan. They wear white sheets and their hats have a point—which is more than can be said for their beliefs.

Robert Frost and Michael Shea, A Mid-Atlantic Companion, *1986*

Absolute equality, that's the thing; and throughout the ages we have always defended to the death the sacred right of every Black man, no matter how lowly, to be equal to every other Black man.

Hugh Leonard, Time Was, *1976*

"Segregation" is such an active word that it suggests someone is trying to segregate somebody else. So the word "apartheid" was introduced. Now it has such a stench in the nostrils of the world, they are referring to "autogeneous development."

Alan Paton, New York Times, *October 24, 1960*

Race prejudice is not only a shadow over the colored—it is a shadow over all of us, and the shadow is darkest over those who feel it least and allow its evil effects to go on.

Pearl S. Buck, What America Means to Me, *1943*

Forgive us for not wanting to recognize our relatives in Your family who are black or red or yellow or white, whose children's children may be our grandchildren; for accepting people we like, but rejecting those we do not like because they are not of our class or color.

United Presbyterian Church, Litany for Holy Communion, *1968*

RADICALISM: *See* EXTREMISM.

RAIN

It is one of the secrets of Nature in its mood of mockery that fine weather lays heavier weight on the mind and hearts of the depressed and the inwardly tormented than does a really bad day with dark rain sniveling continuously and sympathetically from a dirty sky.

Muriel Spark, Territorial Rights, *1979*

When the hounds of spring are on winter's traces,
The mother of months in meadow or plain
Fills the shadows and windy places
With lisp of leaves and ripple of rain.

Algernon Charles Swinburne, Atalanta in Calydon, *1865*

Monotonously the lorries sway, monotonously come the calls, monotonously falls the rain. It falls on our heads and on the heads of the dead up the line, on the body of the little recruit with the wound that is so much too big for his hip; it falls . . . in our hearts.

Erich Maria Remarque, All Quiet on the Western Front, *1929*

RANK

To call a king "Prince" is pleasing because it diminishes his rank.

Pascal, Pensées, *1670*

Emperors, kings, artisans, peasants, big people, little people—at bottom we are all alike and all the same; all just alike on the inside, and when our clothes are off, nobody can tell which of us is which.

Mark Twain, North American Review, *April 1902*

My philosophy aims at a new order of rank. . . . The terrible consequences of "equality"—in the end everybody thinks he has a right to every problem.

Nietzsche, The Will to Power, *1889*

There is merit without rank, but there is no rank without some merit.

La Rochefoucauld, Maxims, *1665*

The greatest monarch on the proudest throne
is obliged to sit upon his own arse.

Benjamin Franklin, Poor Richard's Almanack, *1757*

Detestation of the high is the involuntary homage of the low.

Charles Dickens, A Tale of Two Cities, *1859*

The higher an ape mounts, the more he shows his breech.

Thomas Fuller, Gnomologia, *1732*

When everyone is somebodee,
Then no one's anybody.

W.S. Gilbert, The Gondoliers, *1889*

He who occupies the first place seldom plays the principal role.

Goethe, Sorrows of Young Werther, *1774*

Bottom is bottom even if it is turned upside down.

Stanislaw Lec, Unkempt Thoughts, *1962*

There may be as much nobility in being last as in being first, because the two positions are equally necessary in the world, the one to complement the other.

Ortega y Gasset, Meditations on Quixote, *1914*

(*See also* **ARISTOCRACY, CLASSES, SOCIETY**)

RATIONALIZATION

To give a reason for anything is to breed a doubt of it.

William Hazlitt, The Plain Speaker, *1826*

We do what we can and then make a theory to prove our performance the best.

Emerson, Journals, *1834*

(*See also* **EXPLANATION**)

READER

'Tis the good reader that makes the good book; in every book he finds passages which seem confidences or asides hidden from all else and unmistakenly meant for his ear; the profit of books is according to the sensibility of the reader; the profoundest thought or passion sleeps as in a mine, until it is discovered by an equal mind and heart.

Emerson, Society and Solitude, *1870*

It is absurd to think that the only way to tell if a poem is lasting is to wait and see if it lasts. The right reader of a good poem can tell the moment it strikes him that he has taken an immortal wound—and that he will never get over it.

Robert Frost, "The Poetry of Amy Lowell," Christian Science Monitor, *May 16, 1925*

The two cardinal points of poetry, the power of exciting the sympathy of the reader by a faithful adherence to the truth of nature, and the power of giving the interest of novelty by the modifying colors of imagination.

> *Samuel Taylor Coleridge,* Biographia Literaria, *1817*

READING

Reading is to the mind what exercise is to the body.

> *Sir Richard Steele,* Tatler, *1710*

People do not understand what it costs in time and suffering to learn how to read. I have been working at it for eighty years, and I still can't say that I've succeeded.

> *Goethe, in Eckermann's* Conversations, *1836*

Life being very short, and the quiet hours of it few, we ought to waste none of them in reading useless books.

> *John Ruskin,* Sesame and Lilies, *1865*

People say that life is the thing, but I prefer reading.

> *Logan Pearsall Smith,* Trivia, *1917*

It is curious how tyrannical the habit of reading is, and what shifts we make to escape thinking. There is no bore we dread being left with so much as our own minds.

> *Robert Lowell,* Literary Essays, *1864–1890*

Magazines all too frequently lead to books and should be regarded by the prudent as the heavy petting of literature.

> *Fran Lebowitz,* Metropolitan Life, *1978*

There are two motives for reading a book: one, that you enjoy it; the other, that you can boast about it.

> *Bertrand Russell, in conversation*

Much reading is an oppression of the mind, and extinguishes the natural candle, which is the reason of so many senseless scholars in the world.

> *William Penn,* Advice to His Children, *1799*

(*See also* **BOOKS, LITERATURE**)

REALITY

If it were possible to talk to the unborn, one could never explain to them how it feels to be alive, for life is washed in the speechless real.
Jacques Barzun, The House of Intellect, *1959*

What was once called the objective world is a sort of Rorschach ink blot, into which each culture, each type of personality, reads a meaning only remotely derived from the shape and color of the blot itself.
Lewis Mumford, The Conduct of Life, *1959*

Reality is a staircase going neither up nor down, we don't move, today is today, always is today.
Octavio Paz, "The Endless Instant," Modern European Poetry, *1966*

You . . . must not count overmuch on your reality as you feel it today, since, like that of yesterday, it may prove an illusion for you tomorrow.
Luigi Pirandello, Six Characters in Search of an Author, *1921*

The masses think that it is easy to flee from reality, when it is the most difficult thing in the world.
Ortega y Gasset, The Dehumanization of Art, *1948*

I saw reality, which is the most powerful of hallucinogens.
Romain Gary (d. 1980), Pseudo

(*See also* **DREAM, ILLUSION, IMAGINATION**)

REASON/REASONABLE

A wise man is not governed by others, nor does he try to govern them; he prefers that reason alone prevail.
La Bruyère, Characters, *1688*

The man who listens to Reason is lost: Reason enslaves all whose minds are not strong enough to master her.
G.B. Shaw, Man and Superman, *1903*

Two extremes: Trusting to reason, or leaving reason out of account.
Pascal, Pensées, *1670*

The last function of reason is to recognize that there are an infinity of things which surpass it.
Ibid.

The reasonable man adapts himself to the world; the unreasonable one persists in trying to adapt the world to himself. Therefore all progress depends on the unreasonable man.

G.B. Shaw, Man and Superman, *1903*

I have said the world is absurd but I spoke too soon. All we can say is that this world in and of itself is not reasonable. What is absurd, though, is the conflict between this irrationality and man's desperate wish for intelligibility.

Albert Camus, The Myth of Sisyphus, *1942*

The mind resorts to reason for want of training.

Henry Adams, Education, *1907*

Analysis kills spontaneity.

Amiel, Journal, *November 7, 1878*

Man has such a predilection for systems and abstract deductions that he is ready to distort the truth intentionally, he is ready to deny the evidence of his senses only to justify his logic.

Dostoyevski, Notes from Underground, *1864*

Reason cannot save us. Nothing can; but reason can mitigate the cruelty of living.

Philip Rieff, Freud: The Mind and the Man, *1959*

Reason is the life of the law; nay, the common law itself is nothing else but reason. . . . The law is perfection of reason.

Sir Edward Coke, First Institute, *1628*

If we would guide by the light of reason, we must let our minds be bold.

Justice Louis Brandeis, New State Ice Co. v. Liebmann, *1932*

If men are to be precluded from offering their sentiments on a matter which may involve the most serious and alarming consequences that can invite the consideration of mankind, reason is of no use; the freedom of speech may be taken away, and dumb and silent we may be led, like sheep to the slaughter.

George Washington, Address to officers of the Army,
March 15, 1783

I'll not listen to reason. . . . Reason always means what someone else has got to say.

Elizabeth Gaskell, Cranford, *1853*

Ah, when to the heart of man
Was it ever less than a treason
To go with the drift of things,
To yield with grade to reason. . . .

Robert Frost, Reluctance, *1913*

(*See also* **ARGUMENT, THOUGHT**)

REBELLION

The objector and the rebel who raises his voice against what he believes to be the injustice of the present and the wrongs of the past is the one who hunches the world along.

Clarence Darrow, Address to the jury, Chicago, 1920

I hold that a little rebellion, now and then, is a good thing, and as necessary in the political world as storms in the physical.

Thomas Jefferson to James Madison, January 30, 1787

Every conquered people should have a revolt. I would regard a revolt in Naples the way a father regards a case of smallpox in his child, provided it did not weaken the patient too seriously.

Napoleon I to Joseph Bonaparte, King of Naples, 1806

No one can go on being a rebel too long without turning into an autocrat.

Lawrence Durrell, Balthazar, *1958*

(*See also* **DISOBEDIENCE, DISSENT, REVOLUTION**)

RECOGNITION: *See* APPRECIATION, GRATITUDE.

REFORMERS

It is madness beyond compare
To try to reform the world.

Molière, The Misanthrope, *1666*

The urge to save humanity is almost always only a false-face for the urge to rule it.

H.L. Mencken, Minority Report, *1956*

Cautious, careful people, always casting about to preserve their reputation, . . . can never effect a reform.

Susan B. Anthony, "Reform of the Divorce Laws," 1860

The eager and often inconsiderate appeals of reformers and revolutionists are indispensable to counterbalance the inertia and fossilism marking so large a part of human institutions.

Walt Whitman, Democratic Vistas, *1871*

A man that'd expict to thrain lobsters to fly . . . is called a loonytic; but a man that thinks men can be tur-rned into angels by an iliction is called a rayformer an' remains at large.

Finley Peter Dunne, Mr. Dooley's Philosophy, *1900*

Every man is a reformer until reform tramps on his toes.

Edgar Watson Howe, Country Town Sayings, *1911*

All reformers are bachelors.

George Moore, The Bending of the Bough, *1900*

Nobody expects to find comfort and companionability in reformers.

Heywood Broun, New York World, *February 6, 1928*

I can think of few important movements for reform in which success was won by any method other than that of an energetic minority presenting the indifferent majority with a *fait accompli*, which was then accepted.

Vera Brittain, Humiliation with Honor, *1943*

Attempts at reform, when they fail, strengthen despotism, as he that struggles tightens those cords he does not succeed in breaking.

C.C. Colton, Lacon, *1825*

To give up the task of reforming society is to give up one's responsibility as a free man.

Alan Paton, Saturday Review, *September 9, 1967*

There are a thousand hacking at the branches of evil to one who is striking at the root.

Thoreau, Walden, *1854*

[I] put the question directly to myself: "Suppose that all your objects in life were realized; that all the changes in institutions and opinions which you are looking forward to, could be completely effected at this very instant: would this be a great joy and happiness to you?" And an irrepressible self-consciousness distinctly answered, "No!"

John Stuart Mill, Autobiography, *1909*

(*See also* **HUMANITARIANISM, IDEALISM**)

REGRET

We often repent the good we have done as well as the ill.
William Hazlitt, Characteristics, *1823*

To regret deeply is to live afresh.
Thoreau, Journal, *November 13, 1839*

Opportunities fly by while we sit regretting the chances we have lost, and the happiness that comes to us we heed not, because of the happiness that is gone.
Jerome K. Jerome, The Idle Thoughts of an Idle Fellow, *1889*

(*See also* **REPENTANCE**)

REJECTION

Heaven has no rage like love to hatred turned,
Nor hell a fury like a woman scorned.
William Congreve, The Mourning Bride, *1697*

Being jilted is a blow to one's pride. You must do your best to forget it but if you cannot, then at least, pretend to.
Molière, Tartuffe, *1664*

Spurn not the nobly-born
With love affected,
Nor treat with virtuous scorn
The well-connected.

W.S. Gilbert, Iolanthe, *1882*

(*See also* **LOVE, LOSS OF**)

RELATIONSHIPS, SOCIAL

Without wearing any mask we are conscious of, we have a special face for each friend.
Oliver Wendell Holmes, Journals, *1843*

There is no hope of joy except in human relations.
Saint-Exupéry, Wind, Sand, and Stars, *1939*

The opinions we hold of one another, our relations with friends and kinfolk are in no sense permanent, save in appearance, but are as eternally fluid as the sea itself.

Marcel Proust, The Guermantes Way, *1923*

(*See also* **FAMILY, SEXUAL RELATIONS**)

RELATIVES

Relations are simply a tedious pack of people, who haven't got the remotest knowledge of how to live, nor the smallest instinct about when to die.

Oscar Wilde, The Importance of Being Earnest, *1895*

There is no greater bugbear than a strong-willed relative in the circle of his own connections.

Nathaniel Hawthorne, The House of Seven Gables, *1851*

It is a melancholy truth that even great men have their poor relations.

Charles Dickens, Bleak House, *1852*

When our relatives are at home, we have to think of all their good points or it would be impossible to endure them.

G.B. Shaw, Heartbreak House, *1929*

(*See also* **FAMILY, PARENTS, CHILDREN**)

RELIGION

A life without religion is a life without principles, and a life without principles is like a ship without a rudder.

Mahatma Gandhi, Autobiography, 1924

The various religions are like different roads converging on the same point. What difference does it make if we follow different routes, provided we arrive at the same destination.

Ibid.

Everyday people are straying away from the church and going back to God.

Lennie Bruce, The Essential Lennie Bruce, *1972*

He represented what any minister will tell you is the bane of parish work: somebody who has got religion. It's as embarrassing to a cleric of sensibility as "poetry lovers" are to a poet.

Peter De Vries, The Mackerel Plaza, *1958*

After coming in contact with a religious man, I always feel that I must wash my hands.

Nietzsche, The Antichrist, *1888*

God made everything out of the void, but the void shows through.

Paul Valéry, Mauvaises Pensées et autres, *1941*

Religion is not a popular error. It is a great instinctive truth, sensed by the people, expressed by the people.

Ernest Renan, Les Apôtres, *1866*

All the steam in the world could not, like the Virgin, build Chartres [Cathedral]. . . . Symbol or energy, the Virgin had acted as the greatest force the Western world ever felt. . . .

Henry Adams, Education, *1907*

[The] men of the technostructure are the new and universal priesthood. Their religion is business success; their test of virtue is growth and profit. Their bible is the computer printout; their communion bench is the committee room.

J.K. Galbraith, The Age of Uncertainty, *1977*

The greatest vicissitude of things among men is the vicissitude of sects and religions.

Francis Bacon, Essays, *1597*

Men will wrangle for religion, write for it, fight for it, die for it; anything but live for it.

C.C. Colton, Lacon, *1825*

I want nothing to do with any religion concerned with keeping the masses satisfied to live in hunger, filth and ignorance.

Jawaharlal Nehru, New York Times, *September 7, 1958*

Intellectually, religious emotions are not creative but conservative. They attach themselves readily to the current view of the world and consecrate it.

John Dewey, "The Influence of Darwinism on Philosophy," 1909

The cosmic religious experience is the strongest and the noblest driving force behind scientific research.

Einstein, quoted in his obituary, 1955

We have just enough religion to make us hate, but not enough to make us love one another.

Jonathan Swift, Miscellanies, *1711*

Nothing shocks me more in the men of religion and their flocks than their . . . pretensions to be the only religious people.

Jean Guéhenno (d. 1978), Changer la vie

One's religion is whatever he is most interested in, and yours is Success.

James M. Barrie, The Twelve-Pound Look, *1910*

Writing for a penny a word is ridiculous. If a man wants to make a million dollars, the best way would be to start a new religion.

L. Ron Hubbard, founder of Scientology, quoted in New York Times, *July 11, 1984*

Nobody can have the consolations of religion or philosophy unless he has first experienced their desolations.

Aldous Huxley, Themes and Variations, *1950*

Even the weakest disputant is made so conceited by what he calls religion, as to think himself wiser than the wisest who thinks differently from him.

Walter Savage Landor, Imaginary Conversations, *1853*

Religion is the sign of the oppressed creature, the sentiment of a heartless world, and the soul of soul-less conditions. It is the opium of the people.

Karl Marx, "Contribution to the Critique of Hegel's Philosophy of Right," 1884

Man is certainly stark mad: he cannot make a flea, yet he makes gods by the dozens.

Montaigne, Essays, *1588*

Religion indeed enlightens, terrifies, subdues; it gives faith, it inflicts remorse, it inspires resolutions, it draws tears, it inflames devotion, but only for the occasion.

John Henry (Cardinal) Newman, The Idea of a University, *1858*

Matters of religion should never be matters of controversy. We neither argue with a lover about his taste, nor condemn him, if we are just, for knowing so human a passion.

George Santayana, The Life of Reason: Reason in Religion, *1906*

Religion cannot be kept within the bounds of sermons and scriptures. It is a force in itself and it calls for the integration of lands and peoples in harmonious unity. The lands [of the earth] wait for those who can discern their rhythms. The peculiar genius of each continent, the placid lakes, all call for relief from the constant burdens of exploitation.

> *Vine Victor Deloria, Jr.,* God Is Red, *1973. [The author is a Sioux Indian.]*

(*See also* **THE BIBLE, PRAYER, WORSHIP**)

RELIGION AND POLITICS

God has decreed that there be sick and poor in this world, but in the next it will be the other way around.

> *Napoleon I, Diary, August 13, 1800*

A state must have a religion and that religion should be under the control of the government.

> *Napoleon to Count Thibaudeau, 1801*

We are now again in an epoch of wars of religion, but a religion is now called an "ideology."

> *Bertrand Russell,* Unpopular Essays, *1950*

Leave the matter of religion to the family, . . . the church, and the private schools, supported entirely by private contributions. Keep the Church and the State forever separate.

> *Ulysses S. Grant, speech, Des Moines, Iowa, 1875*

RELIGION AND SUPERSTITION

Superstition is the religion of feeble minds.

> *Edmund Burke,* The Revolution in France, *1790*

No sooner had Jesus knocked over the dragon of superstition than Paul boldly set it on its legs again in the name of Jesus.

> *G.B. Shaw,* Androcles and the Lion, *1912*

I maintain that superstition is more hurtful to God than atheism is.

> *Diderot,* Pensées philosophiques, *1746*

Superstition is the poetry of life.

> *Goethe,* Proverbs in Prose, *1819*

In all superstition wise men follow fools.

> *Francis Bacon,* Essays, *1625*

The superstition in which we grew up,
Though we may recognize it, does not lose
Its power over us.—Not all are free
Who would make mock of their chains.

> *Gotthold Lessing,* Nathan the Wise, *1779*

[Let us oppose] one species of superstition to another, set them a-quarreling; while we ourselves . . . happily make our escape into the calm, though obscure, regions of philosophy.

> *David Hume,* The Natural History of Religion, *1757*

RELIGIOUS COERCION

What has been the effect of religious coercion? To make half the world fools, and the other half hypocrites.

> *Thomas Jefferson,* Notes on the State of Virginia, *1785*

The day that this country ceases to be free for irreligion, it will cease to be free for religion.

> *Justice Jackson, dissent, Zorach v. Clausor, 1952*

Religion is the masterpiece of the art of animal training, for it trains people as to how they shall think.

> *Arthur Schopenhauer,* Studies in Pessimism, *1851*

RELIGIOUS DISPUTES

Religion is less a matter of holiness than an excuse for dispute.

> *Montesquieu,* Persian Letters, *1721*

Religion condemns religion. It is not the school that is without God, it is the Church that is without God.

> *Alain (d. 1951),* Propos sur la religion

(*See also* **HERESY**)

RELIGIOUS PERSECUTION

We forbid our Protestant subjects to meet . . for the exercise of their [religion] in any public place or any private home, under any pretext whatever.

> *Louis XIV, Edict, 1685*

"I, _____, do declare that I do believe that there is not any transubstantiation in the sacrament of the Lord's Supper, or in the elements of bread and wine, at or after the consecration by any person what-soever."

England, Test Act, 1673

The unbelievers shall have garments of fire fitted unto them; boiling water shall be poured on their heads; their bowels shall be dissolved thereby, and also their skins, and they shall be beaten with maces of iron.

The Koran

(*See also* **NONCONFORMITY, TOLERANCE**)

REPENTANCE

The sinning is the best part of repentance.

Arab proverb

Our repentance is not so much regret for the evil we have done as fear of what may happen to us because of it.

La Rochefoucauld, Maxims, *1665*

Remorse is impotent; it will sin again. Only repentance is strong; it can end everything.

Henry Miller, The Wisdom of the Heart, *1941*

(*See also* **REGRET, SIN/SINNERS**)

REPRESENTATIVES

In a democratic society like ours, relief must come through an aroused popular conscience that sears the conscience of the people's representatives.

Justice Felix Frankfurter, Baker v. Carr, *1962*

Instead of the function of governing, for which it is radically unfit, the proper office of a representative assembly is to watch and control the government.

John Stuart Mill, Dissertations, *1859*

(*See also* **CONGRESS, DEMOCRACY**)

REPROACH

The sting of a reproach is the truth of it.

Thomas Fuller, Gnomologia, *1732*

Fear not the anger of the wise to raise;
Those best can bear reproof who merit praise.

> *Alexander Pope*, An Essay on Criticism, *1711*

The correction of silence is what kills; when you know you have transgressed, and your friend says nothing and avoids your eye.

> *Robert Louis Stevenson, "Talk and Talkers," 1882*

Reprove not a scorner, lest he hate thee; rebuke a wise man, and he will love thee.

> *Proverbs 9:8*

REPRODUCTION: *See* BIRTHS, DEATH, POPULATION.

REPUTATION

There are many who dare not kill themselves for fear of what the neighbors will say.

> *Cyril Connolly*, The Unquiet Grave, *1945*

There are two modes of establishing our reputation: to be praised by honest men, and to be abused by rogues.

> *C.C. Colton*, Lacon, *1825*

The Englishman wants to be recognized as a gentleman, or as some other suitable species of human being; the American wants to be considered a "good guy."

> *Louis Kronenberger*, Company Manners, *1954*

One can survive everything nowadays, except death, and live down anything except a good reputation.

> *Oscar Wilde*, A Woman of No Importance, *1893*

(*See also* **MERIT, SLANDER**)

RESIGNATION

A calm despair, without angry convulsions or reproaches directed at heaven, is the essence of wisdom.

> *Alfred de Vigny*, Journal d'un poète, *1832*

I am not resigned to the shutting away of loving hearts in the hard ground.
So it is, and so it will be, for so it has been, time out of mind:

Into the darkness they go, the wise and the lovely. Crowned
With lilies and with laurel they go; but I am not resigned.

Edna St. Vincent Millay, "Dirge without Music," 1928

(*See also* **PATIENCE, STOICISM**)

RESPECT

Without feelings of respect, what is there to distinguish men from
beasts?

Confucius, Analects, *sixth century* B.C.

We can always make ourselves liked provided we are likable, but we
cannot always make ourselves esteemed, no matter what our merits
are.

Nicolas Malebranche, Traité de la morale, *1867*

(*See also* **MERIT**)

RESPONSIBILITY

. . . A detachable burden easily shifted to the shoulders of God, Fate,
Fortune, Luck or one's neighbor. In the days of astrology it was
customary to unload it upon a star.

Ambrose Bierce, The Devil's Dictionary, *1911*

Responsibility's like a string we can only see the middle of. Both ends
are out of sight.

William McFee, Casuals of the Sea, *1916*

Unto whomsoever much is given, of him shall much be required.

Luke 12:48

Liberty trains for liberty. Responsibility is the first step in responsibility.

W.E.B. DuBois, John Brown, *1909*

Life always gets harder toward the summit—the cold increases, responsibility increases.

Nietzsche, The Antichrist, *1888*

The responsibility of the great states is to serve and not to dominate
the world.

Harry S. Truman, Message to Congress, April 16, 1945

(*See also* **DUTY**)

REST/REPOSE

In all things rest is sweet; there is surfeit even in honey, even in Aphrodite's lovely flowers.

Pindar, Odes, *c. 400 B.C.*

One cannot rest except after steady practice.

George Ade, "The Man Who Was Going to Retire," 1901

Rest is not a word for free peoples—Rest is a monarchial word.

Carl Sandburg, "Is There Any Easy Road to Freedom?" 1950

Restfulness is a quality for cattle; the virtues are all active, life is alert.

Robert Louis Stevenson, "Talk and Talkers," 1882

Certainty generally is illusion, and repose is not the destiny of man.

Oliver Wendell Holmes, Jr., The Path of the Law, *1897*

We combat obstacles in order to get repose, and, when got, the respose is insupportable.

Henry Adams, Education, *1907*

Me this uncharted freedom tires;
I feel the weight of chance desires;
My hopes no more much change their name,
I long for a repose that ever is the same.

Wordsworth, "Ode to Duty," 1807

(*See also* **LEISURE, SLEEP**)

RESTLESS

Never have I been able to settle in life. Always seated askew, as if on the arm of a chair; ready to get up, to leave.

André Gide, Journals, *July 14, 1930*

Unrest of spirit is a mark of life.

Karl Menninger, This Week, *October 16, 1958*

A wanderer is man from his birth.
He was born in a ship
On the breast of the river of Time.

Matthew Arnold, "The Future," 1852

(*See also* **PATIENCE**)

RETIREMENT

Few men of action have been able to make a graceful exit at the appropriate time.

Malcolm Muggeridge, The Most of Malcolm Muggeridge, *1966*

I married him for better or for worse, but not for lunch.

Hazel Weiss, after her husband retired as general manager of the New York Yankees in 1960

Dismiss the old horse in good time, lest he fail in the lists and the spectators laugh.

Horace, Epistles, *c. 8 B.C.*

(*See also* **IDLENESS, LEISURE**)

RETRIBUTION

Whatsoever a man soweth, that shall he also reap.

Paul to the Galatians 6:7

Our fathers and ourselves sowed dragon's teeth.
Our children know and suffer the armed men.

Stephen Vincent Benét, Litany for Dictatorship, *1935*

The gods visit the sins of the fathers upon the children.

Euripides, Electra, *413 B.C.*

As he brews, so shall he drink.

Ben Johnson, Every Man in His Humour, *1598*

(*See also* **PUNISHMENT**)

REVENGE

Vengeance always springs from weakness of spirit, which is incapable of enduring insults and injuries.

La Rochefoucauld, Maximes, *1665*

By paying our other debts, we are equal with mankind; but in refusing to pay a debt of revenge, we are superior.

C.C. Colton, Lacon, *1825*

Blood cannot be washed out with blood.

Persian proverb

Vengeance is mine, . . . saith the Lord. Therefore if thine enemy hunger, feed him; if he thirst, give him drink: for in so doing thou shalt heap coals of fire upon his head.

Paul to the Romans 12:19–20

Upon surprising his wife and her lover, a man is not avenged by killing them in each other's arms; that is the greatest service he can render them.

Balzac, Physiologie du mariage

(*See also* **INSULTS**)

REVERIE

To make a prairie it takes a clover and one bee,
One clover, and a bee,
And revery.
The revery alone will do,
If bees are few.

Emily Dickinson, Poems, *c. 1862–1886*

Reverie is the groundwork of creative imagination; it is the privilege of the artist that with him it is not as with other men an escape from reality, but the means by which he accedes to it.

Somerset Maugham, The Summing Up, *1938*

Thought is the labor of the intellect, reverie is its pleasure.

Victor Hugo, Les Misérables, *1862*

Let us leave every man free to search within himself and lose himself in his ideas.

Voltaire, "Soul," Philosophical Dictionary, *1764*

(*See also* **DREAM, IMAGINATION**)

REVOLUTION

In any revolution there are two kinds of people: those who make the revolution and those who profit from it.

Napoleon I, attributed

Thinkers prepare the revolution, bandits carry it out.

Mariano Azuela, The Flies, *1918*

Revolutions are not made: they come. A revolution is as natural as an oak tree. It comes out of the past; its foundations are laid far back.

Wendell Phillips, Address, Anti-Slavery Society, 1852

If we trace the history of most revolutions, we shall find that the first inroads upon the laws have been made by the governors, as often as by the governed.

C.C. Colton, Lacon, *1825*

The overwhelming pressure of mediocrity, sluggish and indomitable as a glacier, will mitigate the most violent, and depress the most exalted revolution.

T.S. Eliot, "The Idea of a Christian Society," 1939

The successful revolutionary is a statesman, the unsuccessful one a criminal.

Erich Fromm, Escape from Freedom, *1941*

Though a revolution may call itself "national," it always marks the victory of a single party.

André Gide, Journals, *October 27, 1941*

Every social war is a battle between the very few on both sides who care and who fire their shots across a crowd of spectators.

Murray Kempton, Part of Our Time, *1955*

Women hate revolutions and revolutionists. They like men who are docile, and well-regarded at the bank, and never late at meals.

H.L. Mencken, Prejudices: Fourth Series, *1924*

Revolutions have never lightened the burden of tyranny; they have only shifted it to another shoulder.

G.B. Shaw, Man and Superman, *1903*

Every political good carried to extreme must be productive of evil.

Mary Wollstonecraft, The French Revolution, *1794*

It was left for the Germans to bring about a revolution of a kind never seen before: [the Nazi] revolution, devoid of ideas . . . and opposed to everything that is higher, better, and decent; opposed to liberty, truth, and justice.

Thomas Mann, Diary, *1946*

(*See also* **TERROR, VIOLENCE**)

REWARD

Good and evil, reward and punishment, are the only motives to a rational creature: these are the spur and reins whereby all mankind are set on work, and guided.

> *John Locke,* Some Thoughts Concerning Education, *1693*

The reward of a thing well done is to have done it.

> *Emerson,* Essays: Second Series, *1844*

The only reward of virtue is virtue; the only way to have a friend is to be one.

> *Emerson, "Self-Reliance"*

(*See also* **PUNISHMENT**)

RICHES

A shortcut to riches is to subtract from one's desires.

> *Plutarch (fl. A.D. 100),* Epistolae de rebus familiaribus

Few rich men own their own property; the property owns them.

> *Robert Ingersoll, speech, New York, October 29, 1896*

Ordinary riches can be stolen; real riches cannot. In your soul are infinitely precious things that cannot be taken from you.

> *Oscar Wilde,* The Soul of Man under Socialism, *1891*

He mocks the people who proposes that the Government shall protect the rich and that they in turn will care for the laboring poor.

> *Grover Cleveland,* Message to Congress, *1888*

I believe . . . that all the measures of the Government are directed to the purpose of making the rich richer and the poor poorer.

> *William Henry Harrison, U.S. president, October 10, 1840*

It is absurd and disgraceful to live magnificently and luxuriously when so many are hungry.

> *Clement of Alexandria (fl. A.D. 200),* Who Is the Rich Man
> That Is Saved?

His best companions, innocence and health;
And his best riches, ignorance of wealth.

> *Oliver Goldsmith,* The Good-Natured Man, *1768*

The things which . . . are esteemed as the greatest good of all . . . can be reduced to three headings: Riches, Fame, and Pleasure. With these the mind is so engrossed that it can scarcely think of any other good.

> *Spinoza,* Tractatus de Intellectus Emendatione, *1677*

Industrialized communities neglect the very objects for which it is worth while to acquire riches in their feverish preoccupation with the means by which riches can be acquired.

> *R.H. Tawney,* The Acquisitive Society, *1920*

(*See also* **MONEY, WEALTH**)

RIDDLES

What walks on four feet in the morning, two at noon, and three in the evening? Answer: Man, crawling on all fours in his infancy, walking upright in his prime, and using a cane in his old age.

> *Oedipus, The Riddle of the Sphinx, Greek legend*

When Oedipus met the Sphinx, who asked him her riddle, he replied, *Man.* This simple word destroyed the monster. We have many monsters to destroy: let us remember Oedipus's answer.

> *George Seferis, on receiving the Nobel Prize, 1963*

Life's perhaps the only riddle
That we shrink from giving up.

> *W.S. Gilbert,* The Gondoliers, *1889*

RIDICULE

Mockery is often the result of a poverty of wit.

> *La Bruyère,* Characters, *1688*

The most effective way of attacking vice is to expose it to ridicule. We can stand rebukes, but not laughter; we don't mind seeming wicked, but we hate to look silly.

> *Molière,* Tartuffe, *1664*

The greatest type of heroism an individual, or a people, can attain is being able to face ridicule.

> *Miguel de Unamuno,* Tragic Sense of Life, *1913*

(*See also* **ABSURD, HUMOR, LAUGHTER**)

RIGHT

From a worldly point of view there is no mistake so great as that of being always right.

Samuel Butler, Note-Books, *1912*

We uniformly applaud what is right and condemn what is wrong— when it costs us nothing but the sentiment.

William Hazlitt, Characteristics, *1823*

May God prevent us from becoming "right-thinking men"—that is to say, men who agree perfectly with their own police.

Thomas Merton, quoted in his obituary, New York Times,
December 11, 1968

(*See also* **CONSCIENCE, ERROR, GOODNESS**)

RIGHT VS. WRONG

Alceste: "I'm either right or wrong."
Philinthe: "Don't be too sure of that."

Molière, The Misanthrope, *1666*

Right You Are If You Think You Are [Cosi è se vi pare].

Pirandello, Title of play, 1917

Women have, commonly, a very positive moral sense; that which they will, is right; that which they reject, is wrong; and their will, in most cases, ends by settling the moral.

Henry Adams, Education, *1907*

Habit with him was all the test of truth,
"It must be right: I've done it from my youth."

George Crabbe, The Borough, *1810*

Ezra [Pound] was right half the time, and when he was wrong, he was so wrong you were never in any doubt about it. Gertrude Stein was never wrong.

Ernest Hemingway to John Peale Bishop, November 11, 1936

How dreadful it is when the right judge judges wrong.

Sophocles, Antigone, *442 B.C.*

The fact that man knows right from wrong proves his *intellectual* superiority to the other creatures; but the fact that he can *do* wrong proves his *moral* inferiority to any creatures that *cannot.*

Mark Twain, What Is Man, *1906*

I think that we should be men first, and subjects afterward. It is not so desirable to cultivate a respect for the law, so much as for the right.

Thoreau, Civil Disobedience, *1849*

(*See also* **WRONG**)

RIGHTS, HUMAN

People have no special rights because they belong to one race or another: the word *human* defines all rights.

José Marti, My Race, *1893*

All, too, will bear in mind this sacred principle, that though the will of the majority is in all cases to prevail, that will to be rightful must be reasonable; that the minority possess their equal rights, which equal law must protect, and to violate would be oppression.

Thomas Jefferson, Inaugural Address, March 4, 1801

They have rights who dare maintain them.

James Russell Lowell, "The Present Crisis," 1844

The suppression of civil liberties is to many less a matter for horror than the curtailment of the freedom to profit.

Marya Mannes, But Will It Sell? *1964*

In the [Universal] Declaration of Human Rights the dignity of a person is acknowledged to all human beings; and . . . there is proclaimed, as a fundamental right, the right of free movement in search for truth and in the attainment of moral good and of justice, and also the right to a dignified life.

Pope John XXIII, Pacem in terris, *April 11, 1963*

The greatest achievement of the civil-rights movement is that it has restored the dignity of indignation.

Frederic Wertham, A Sign for Cain: An Exploration in Human Violence, *1966*

(*See also* **EQUALITY, JUSTICE, PRESS/MEDIA**)

RIVERS

I do not know much about gods; but I think that the river Is a strong brown god—sullen, untamed and intractable.

T.S. Eliot, "The Dry Salvages," Four Quartets, *1941*

We catched fish and talked, and we took a swim now and then to keep off sleepiness. It was kind of solemn, drifting down the big, still river, laying on our backs looking up at the stars, we didn't ever feel like talking loud, and it warn't often that we laughed—only a little kind of a low chuckle.

Mark Twain, Adventures of Huckleberry Finn, *1884*

Your true [river] pilot cares nothing about anything on earth but the river, and his pride in his occupation surpasses the pride of kings.

Twain, Life on the Mississippi, *1883*

In Xanadu did Kubla Khan
A stately pleasure dome decree;
Where Alph, the sacred river, ran
Through caverns measureless to man
Down to a sunless sea.

Samuel Taylor Coleridge, Kubla Khan, *1798*

ROADS

Does the road wind up-hill all the way?
Yes, to the very end.
Will the day's journey take the whole long day?
From morn to night, my friend.

Christina Rosetti, "Up-Hill," 1861

The tortuous road that had led from Montgomery to Oslo is a road over which millions of Negroes are traveling to find a new sense of dignity. It will, I am convinced, be widened into a superhighway of justice.

Martin Luther King., Jr., on receiving the Nobel Peace Prize, 1964

As life runs on, the road grows strange
With faces new, and near the end
The milestones into headstones change,
'Neath every one a friend.

James Russell Lowell, "Sixty-eighth Birthday," 1889

The untended Kosmos my abode,
I pass, a willful stranger;
My mistress still the open road
And the bright eyes of danger.

Robert Louis Stevenson, "Youth and Love," 1887

Times are changed with him who marries; there are no more bypath meadows, where you may innocently linger, but the road lies long and straight and dusty to the grave.

Stevenson, Virginibus puerisque, *1881*

There is no road to wealth so easy and respectable as that of matrimony.

Anthony Trollope, Doctor Thorne, *1858*

The road was new to me, as roads always are going back.

Sarah Orne Jewett, The Country Road of Pointed Firs, *1896*

Improvement makes straight roads; but the crooked roads without improvement are roads of genius.

William Blake, The Marriage of Heaven and Hell, *1793*

I shall be telling this with a sigh
Somewhere ages and ages hence:
Two roads diverged in a wood, and I—
I took the one less traveled by,
And that has made all the difference.

Robert Frost, "The Road Not Taken," 1916

Like one that on a lonesome road
Doth walk in fear and dread,
And having once turned round walks on,
And turns no more his head;
Because he knows a frightful fiend
Doth close behind him tread.

Coleridge, The Ancient Mariner, *1798*

The safest road to Hell is the gradual one—the gentle slope, soft underfoot, without sudden turnings, without milestones, without signposts.

C.S. Lewis, The Screwtape Letters, *1941*

ROMANCE: *See* COURTSHIP, LOVE.

ROYALTY

A prince is a gr-reat man in th' ol' country, but he niver is as gr-reat over there as he is here [in America].

Finley Peter Dunne, "Prince Henry's Reception," Observations by Mr. Dooley, *1902*

PETE: Do you know, at this very moment, Her Majesty is probably exercising the royal prerogative.

DUD: What's that then, Pete?

PETE: Don't you know the royal prerogative? It's a wonderful animal, Dud. It's a legendary beast, half bird, half fish, half unicorn, and it's being exercised at this very moment. Do you know that legend has it that e'er so long as the royal prerogative lives, happiness and laughter will reign throughout this green and pleasant land.

> *Peter Cook and Dudley Moore*, The Dagenham Dialogues, *1971*

We're the envy of the world, we are, having a Royal Family. It's the one thing in the world no one else has got. An' don't talk to me about Norway, and Holland, and Sweden and all that rubbish. I'm talking about *Royalty*. Not bloody cloth-cap kings riding about on bikes. I mean, that's not Royalty. You'll never see our Queen on a bike. She wouldn't demean herself.

> *Johnny Speight*, Alf Garnett's Little Blue Book, *1973*

The kingly office is entitled to no respect. It was originally procured by highwayman's methods; it remains a perpetuated crime, can never be anything but the symbol of a crime. It is no more entitled to respect than is the flag of a pirate.

> *Mark Twain*, Notebook, *1935*

Good kings are the only dangerous enemies that modern democracy has.

> *Oscar Wilde*, Vera, or The Nihilists, *1883*

Royalty is a government in which the attention of the nation is concentrated on one person doing interesting things. A Republic is a government in which that attention is divided between many, who are all doing uninteresting things. Accordingly, so long as the human heart is strong and the human reason weak, Royalty will be strong because it appeals to diffused feeling, and Republics weak because they appeal to the understanding.

> *Walter Bagehot*, The English Constitution, *1864*

(*See also* **RULER**)

RUDENESS: *See* COURTESY, TACT.

RULE/RULER

For us, with the rule of right and wrong given us by Christ, there is nothing for which we have no standard. And there is no greatness where there is not simplicity, goodness, and truth.

> *Tolstoy*, War and Peace, *1869*

He who would rule must hear and be deaf, see and be blind.

German proverb

I am the first servant of the State.

Frederick II (the Great), Prussia, Memoirs, *1758*

Where princes are concerned, a man who is able to do good is as dangerous and almost as criminal as a man who intends to do evil.

Cardinal de Retz, Mémoires, *1718*

If you have but a single ruler, you are under the discretion of a master who has no reason to love you; if you have several, you will have to endure their tyranny and their disagreements.

Rousseau, Discourse on Political Economy, *1758*

[The people] have a right, an indisputable, an unalienable, indefeasible, divine right to that most dreaded and envied kind of knowledge, the character and conduct of their rulers.

John Adams, Dissertation on the Canon . . . Law, *1765*

One cannot reign and be innocent.

Saint-Just, speech to the Convention, November 13, 1792

To know nor faith, nor love, nor law; to be
Omnipotent but friendless is to reign.

Shelley, Prometheus Unbound, *1819*

For estimating the intelligence of a ruler . . . look at the men he has around him.

Machiavelli, The Prince, *1513*

[A ruler] cannot and should not keep his word when to do so would go against his interests or when the reason he pledged it no longer holds.

Ibid.

(*See also* **GOVERNMENT, LEADERSHIP, ROYALTY**)

SACRIFICE

Greater love hath no man than this, that a man lay down his life for his friends.

John 15:13

Drown not thyself to save a drowning man.

Thomas Fuller, Gnomologia, *1732*

Self-sacrifice enables us to sacrifice other people without blushing.

G.B. Shaw, "Maxims for Revolutionists," 1903

Those who are certain to gain by the offering
Demand a spirit of sacrifice.

Bertolt Brecht, "Those Who Deprive the Table of Meat," Modern European Poetry, *1966*

For the sake of a family an individual may be sacrificed; for the sake of a village a family may be sacrificed; for the sake of a nation a village may be sacrificed; for the sake of one's self the world may be sacrificed.

Panchatantra, fifth century A.D.

(*See also* **MARTYRDOM**)

SAD/MELANCHOLY

All my joys to this are folly,
Naught so sweet as melancholy.

> *Robert Burton,* The Anatomy of Melancholy, *1651*

We can stand only a certain amount of unhappiness; anything beyond that annihilates us or passes us by, leaving us apathetic.

> *Goethe,* Elective Affinities, *1809*

The sovereign source of melancholy is repletion. Need and struggle are what excite and inspire us; our hour of triumph is what brings the void.

> *William James,* The Will to Believe, *1896*

True melancholy breeds your perfect, fine wit, sir.

> *Ben Jonson,* Every Man in His Humour, *1598*

You're lovely as a flower,
So pure and fair to see;
I look at you, and sadness
Comes stealing over me.

> *Heinrich Heine (d. 1856),* Du Bist wie eine Blume

When the melancholy fit shall fall
Sudden from heaven like a weeping cloud,
That fosters the droop-headed flowers all,
And hides the green hill in an April shroud;
Then glut thy sorrow on a morning rose.

> *John Keats,* "Ode on Melancholy," *1819*

Life is a well of joy; but for those of whom an upset stomach speaks, which is the father of melancholy, all wells are poisoned.

> *Nietzsche,* Thus Spake Zarathustra, *1892*

All man's troubles come from not knowing how to sit still in one room.

> *Pascal,* Pensées, *1670*

Since unhappiness excites interest, many, in order to render themselves interesting, feign unhappiness.

> *Joseph Roux,* Meditations of a Parish Priest, *1886*

If you are bitter at heart, sugar in the mouth will not help you.

> *Hanan J. Ayalti, ed.,* Yiddish Proverbs, *1949*

Listen! you hear the grating roar
Of pebbles which the waves draw back, and fling,
At their return, up the high strand,
Begin, and cease, and then again begin,
With tremulous cadence slow, and bring
The eternal note of sadness in.

Matthew Arnold, Dover Beach, *1867*

(*See also* **HAPPINESS/UNHAPPINESS**)

SADISM/CRUELTY

Cruelty is the law pervading all nature and society; and we can't get out of it if we would.

Thomas Hardy, Jude the Obscure, *1895*

Pity is not natural to man. Children always are cruel. Savages [also].

Samuel Johnson, in Boswell's Life, *July 20, 1763*

Pleasure is sweetest when 'tis paid for by another's pain.

Ovid, The Art of Love, *c. A.D. 8*

The vast majority of the race, whether savage or civilized, are secretly kind-hearted and shrink from inflicting pain, but in the presence of the aggressive and pitiless minority they don't dare to assert themselves.

Mark Twain, The Mysterious Stranger, *1916*

Man is the cruelest animal. At tragedies, bullfights, and crucifixions he has so far felt best on earth; and when he invented hell for himself, behold, that was his very heaven.

Nietzsche, Thus Spake Zarathustra, *1892*

Cruelty is perhaps the worst kind of sin. Intellectual cruelty is certainly the worst kind of cruelty.

G.K. Chesterton, All Things Considered, *1908*

We know well enough when we're being unjust and despicable. But we don't restrain ourselves because we experience a certain pleasure, a primitive sort of satisfaction in moments like that.

Ugo Betti, Landslide, *1936*

(*See also* **VIOLENCE**)

SAFE/SECURE

Most people want security in this world, not liberty.

> *H.L. Mencken*, Minority Report, *1956*

Even in the common affairs of life, in love, friendship, and marriage, how little security have we when we trust our happiness in the hands of others.

> *William Hazlitt*, Table Talk, *1822*

Every compulsion is put upon writers to become safe, polite, obedient, and sterile. In protest, I declined election to the National Institute of Arts and Letters some years ago, and now I must decline the Pulitzer Prize.

> *Sinclair Lewis, declining the prize for* Arrowsmith, *1926*

'Tis man's perdition to be safe,
When for the truth he ought to die.

> *Emerson, "Sacrifice,"* Poems, *1867*

Uncertainty and expectation are the joys of life. Security is an insipid thing, and the overtaking and possessing of a wish discovers the folly of the chase.

> *William Congreve*, Love for Love, *1695*

Only in growth, reform, and change, paradoxically enough, is true security to be found.

> *Anne Morrow Lindbergh*, The Wave of the Future, *1940*

They that can give up essential liberty to obtain a little temporary safety deserve neither liberty nor safety.

> *Benjamin Franklin*, Historical Review of Pennsylvania, *1759*

Security is when I'm very much in love with somebody extraordinary who loves me back.

> *Shelley Winters, in conversation, July 9, 1954*

SAINTS AND SAINTHOOD

Saint, n. A dead sinner revised and edited.

> *Ambrose Bierce*, The Devil's Dictionary, *1911*

The world will never be ready for its saints.

> *G.B. Shaw*, Saint Joan, *1923*

Heaven preserve us from saints!

> *Georges Bernanos,* Diary of a Country Priest, *1936*

And thus I clothe my naked villainy
With odd old ends stolen forth of Holy Writ,
And seem a saint when most I play the devil.

> *Shakespeare,* Richard III, *1593*

No doubt alcohol, tobacco, and so forth, are things that a saint must avoid, but sainthood is also a thing that human beings must avoid.

> *George Orwell, "Reflections on Gandhi,"* Shooting an Elephant, *1950*

Saints should always be judged guilty until they are proved innocent.

> *Ibid.*

It is easier to make a saint out of a libertine than out of a prig.

> *George Santayana,* The Life of Reason: Reason in Religion, *1906*

Can one be a saint if God does not exist? That is the only concrete problem I know of today.

> *Albert Camus,* The Plague, *1947*

The only difference between the saint and the sinner is that every saint has a past and every sinner has a future.

> *Oscar Wilde,* A Woman of No Importance, *1893*

[Saint Joan's] ideal biographer must be free from nineteenth century prejudices and biases; must understand the Middle Ages, the Roman Catholic Church, and the Holy Roman Empire much more intimately than our Whig historians have ever understood them; and must be capable of throwing off sex partialities and their romance, and regarding woman as the female of the human species, and not as a different kind of animal with specific charms and specific imbecilities.

> *G.B. Shaw,* Saint Joan, *1923*

We are content to place a statue of Francis of Assisi in the middle of a bird bath and let the whole business of the Saints go at that.

> *Bishop C. Kilmer Myers,* New York Times, *March 19, 1962*

(*See also* **MARTYRDOM, SIN/SINNERS**)

SAMENESS

Selfness is an essential fact of life. The thought of nonselfness, precise sameness is terrifying.

> *Dr. Lewis Thomas, "On Cloning a Human Being," 1974*

When two people do the same thing, it is not the same thing after all.

Publius Syrus, Moral Sayings, *c. 50 B.C.*

After you've done a thing the same way for two years, look it over carefully. After five years, look at it with suspicion. And after ten years, throw it away and start all over.

Alfred Edward Perlman, New York Times, *July 3, 1958*

SANITY/INSANITY

Who then is sane?

Horace, Satires II, *29 B.C.*

Our health is our sound relation to external objects; our sympathy with external being.

Emerson, Journals, *1836*

Sanity is madness put to good uses.

George Santayana (d. 1952), Little Essays

She: It's like intelligence, insanity. . . . You can't explain it. Just like intelligence. It comes over you, fills you up, and then you understand. But after it leaves, you can't understand it at all.

Marguerite Duras, Hiroshima mon amour, *1960*

There is a pleasure sure
In being mad which none but madmen know.

John Dryden, The Spanish Friar, *1681*

The "sane" person is not so much a person who has eliminated all contradictions, but one who uses them and applies them in his work.

Maurice Merleau-Ponty, Signes, *1960*

The madman who knows that he is mad is close to sanity.

Ruiz de Alarcón (d. 1639), La Amistad castigada

Insane people are always sure they're just fine. It's only the sane people who are willing to admit they're crazy.

Nora Ephron, Heartburn, *1983*

Madness is rare in individuals—but in groups, political parties, nations, and eras it's the rule.

Nietzsche, Beyond Good and Evil, *1886*

(*See also* **HEALTH, NEUROSES**)

SARCASM: *See* HUMOR, INSULTS, WIT

SATIRE

I wear my pen as others do their sword.
To each offending sot I meet, the word
Is *satisfaction*: straight to thrusts I go,
And pointed satire runs him through and through.

> *John Oldham (d. 1683), "Satire upon a Printer."*

Satire is a sort of glass, wherein beholders do generally discover everybody's face but their own.

> *Jonathan Swift,* The Battle of the Books, *1704*

Satire should, like a polished razor keen,
Wound with a touch that's scarcely felt or seen.

> *Lady Mary Wortley Montagu (d. 1762),* A Summary of
> Lord Lyttelton's Advice

(*See also* **HUMOR, RIDICULE**)

SATISFACTION

The superior man is satisfied and composed; the mean man is always full of distress.

> *Confucius (d. 479 B.C.),* Analects

It is the nature of desire not to be satisfied, and most men live only for the gratification of it. The beginning of reform is not so much to equalize property as to train the noble sort of natures not to desire more, and to prevent the lower from getting more.

> *Aristotle,* Ethics, *fourth century B.C.*

What do you suppose will satisfy the soul, except to walk free and own no superior?

> *Walt Whitman,* Leaves of Grass, *1892*

The return from your work must be the satisfaction which that work brings you and the world's need of that work. With this, life is heaven. ... Without this—with work which you despise, which bores you, and which the world does not need—this life is hell.

> *W.E.B. Du Bois, "To His Newborn Great-Grandson": Address on his*
> *ninetieth birthday, 1958*

If I can any way contribute to the diversion or improvement of the country in which I live, I shall leave it, when I am summoned out of it, with the secret satisfaction of thinking that I have not lived in vain.

Addison, The Spectator, No. 1, *March 1, 1711*

The one fact I would cry from every housetop is this: the Good Life is waiting for us—here and now! . . . At this very moment we have the necessary techniques, both material and psychological, to create a full and satisfying life.

B.F. Skinner, Walden Two, *1948*

He is rich that is satisfied.

Thomas Fuller, Gnomologia, *1732*

Greatest fools are oft most satisfied.

Nicolas Boileau, Art poétique, *1674*

From the satisfaction of desire there may arise, accompanying joy and as it were sheltering behind it, something not unlike despair.

André Gide, The Counterfeiters, *1925*

When we reside in an attic we enjoy a supper of fried fish and stout. When we occupy the first floor it takes an elaborate dinner at the Continental to give us the same amount of satisfaction.

Jerome K. Jerome, The Idle Thoughts of an Idle Fellow, *1889*

(*See also* **CONTENTMENT, WANTS/DESIRES**)

SAVAGES

There are many humorous things in the world, among them the white man's notion that he is less savage than the other savages.

Mark Twain, Following the Equator, *1897*

Is man a savage at heart, skinned o'er with fragile Manners? Or is savagery but a faint taint in the natural man's gentility, which erupts now and again like pimples on an angel's arse?

John Barth, The Sot-Weed Factor, *1960*

Men have been barbarians much longer than they have been civilized. They are only precariously civilized, and within us there is the propensity, persistent as the force of gravity, to revert under stress and strain, under neglect or temptation, to our first natures.

Walter Lippmann, The Public Philosophy, *1955*

Since barbarism has its pleasures it naturally has its apologists.
                    Santayana, The Life of Reason: Reason in Society, *1906*

(*See also* **BARBARISM, CIVILIZATION**)

SCANDAL: *See* GOSSIP, SLANDER

SCHOLARS AND SCHOLARSHIP

We can make majors and [other] officers every year but not scholars.
                    Robert Burton, The Anatomy of Melancholy, *1621*

No man is wiser for his learning.
                    John Selden, Table Talk, *1689*

A scholar who loves comfort is not fit to be called a scholar.
                    Confucius (d. 479 B.C.), Analects

The world's great men have not commonly been great scholars, nor its great scholars great men.
     Oliver Wendell Holmes, The Autocrat of the Breakfast Table, *1858*

This is the great vice of academicism, that it is concerned with ideas rather than with thinking.
                    Lionel Trilling, The Liberal Imagination, *1950*

Erudition, n. Dust shaken out of a book into an empty skull.
                    Ambrose Bierce, The Devil's Dictionary, *1911*

The office of the scholar is to cheer, to raise, and to guide men by showing them facts amidst appearances.
                    Emerson, The American Scholar, *1837*

The determined scholar and the man of virtue will not seek to live at the expense of injuring their virtue. They will even sacrifice their lives to preserve their virtue.
                    Confucius (d. 479 B.C.), Analects

When nature exceeds culture, we have the rustic. When culture exceeds nature, we have the pedant.

                    Ibid.

We want a Society for the Suppression of Erudite Research and the Decent Burial of the Past.
                    Samuel Butler, Note-Books, *1912*

Learning is the knowledge of that which none but the learned know.
William Hazlitt, Table Talk, *1822*

Two evils, of almost equal weight, may befall the man of erudition: never to be listened to, and to be listened to always.
Walter Savage Landor, Imaginary Conversations, *1853*

Don't appear so scholarly, pray. Humanize your talk, and speak to be understood.
Molière, The Critique of the School for Wives, *1663*

(*See also* **EDUCATION, KNOWLEDGE, TEACHING**)

SCHOOLS

High School is closer to the core of the American experience than anything else I can think of.
Kurt Vonnegut, Jr., Our Time is Now, *ed. J. Birmingham, 1970*

School days, I believe, are the unhappiest in the whole span of human existence. They are full of dull, unintelligible tasks, new and unpleasant ordinances, brutal violations of common sense and common decency.
H.L. Mencken, The Baltimore Evening Sun, *1928*

The founding fathers . . . provided jails called schools, equipped with tortures called education. School is where you go between when your parents can't take you and industry can't take you.
John Updike, The Centaur, *1963*

O vain futile frivolous boy. Smirking. I won't have it. I won't have. I won't have it. Go find the headmaster and ask him to beat you within an inch of your life. And say please.
Alan Bennett, Forty Years On, *1968*

Show me a man who has enjoyed his [English public] school days and I will show you a bully and a bore.
Robert Morley, Robert Morley: Responsible Gentleman, *1966*

(*See also* **EDUCATION, LEARNING, UNIVERSITY**)

SCIENCE

. . . The great antidote to the poison of enthusiasm and superstition.
Adam Smith, The Wealth of Nations, *1776*

Science is a cemetery of dead ideas.
> *Miguel de Unamuno,* The Tragic Sense of Life, *1913*

The quick harvest of applied science is the usable process, the medicine, the machine. The shy fruit of pure science is Understanding.
> *Lincoln Barnett,* Life, *January 9, 1950*

The theory of our modern technic shows that nothing is as practical as theory.
> *J. Robert Oppenheimer,* Reflex, *July 1977*

The whole of science is nothing more than a refinement of everyday thinking.
> *Einstein,* Out of My Later Years, *1950*

Common sense is the very antipodes of science.
> *E.B. Titchener,* Systematic Psychology, *1929*

Every scientific fulfillment raises new questions; it asks to be surpassed and outdated.
> *Max Weber (d. 1920),* Methodology of the Social Sciences

The construction of hypotheses is a creative act of inspiration, intuition, invention; its essence is the vision of something new in familiar material.
> *Milton Friedman,* Essays in Positive Economics, *1953*

A drug is a substance which when injected into a guinea pig produces a scientific paper.
> *Anonymous*

Most institutions demand unqualified faith; but the institution of science makes skepticism a virtue.
> *Robert K. Merton,* Social Theory, *1957*

Science is what you know; philosophy is what you don't know.
> *Bertrand Russell, in A. Wood,* Bertrand Russell, *1958*

There are in fact two things, science and opinion; the former begets knowledge, the latter ignorance.
> *Hippocrates (d. 400 B.C.),* Law

Nominally a great age of scientific inquiry, ours has actually become an age of superstition about the infallibility of science, of almost mystical faith in its nonmystical methods . . . of eternal verities, of traffic-cop morality, [of] rabbit-test truth.

Louis Kronenberger, Company Manners, *1954*

[Whereas] in art nothing worth doing can be done without genius, in science even a very moderate capacity can contribute to a supreme achievement.

Bertrand Russell, Mysticism and Logic, *1917*

Science is always simple and always profound. It is only the half-truths that are dangerous.

G.B. Shaw, The Doctor's Dilemma, *1913*

Familiar things happen, and mankind does not bother about them. It requires a very unusual mind to undertake the analysis of the obvious.

Whitehead, Science and the Modern World, *1925*

I have seen the science I worshipped, and the aircraft I loved, destroying the civilization I expected them to serve.

Charles A. Lindbergh, Time, *May 26, 1967*

It was through the Second World War that most of us suddenly appreciated for the first time the power of man's concentrated efforts to understand and control the forces of nature. We were appalled by what we saw.

Vannevar Bush, Science Is Not Enough, *1967*

SCIENCE AND CONSCIENCE

Science without conscience is the soul's perdition.

François Rabelais, Pantagruel, *1572*

People must understand that science is inherently neither a potential for good nor for evil. It is a potential to be harnessed by man to do his bidding.

Glenn T. Seaborg, interview with Alton Blakeslee,
September 29, 1964

(*See also* **CONSCIENCE, SELF-ESTEEM**)

SCIENCE AND DOUBT

Every sentence I utter must be understood not as an affirmation, but as a question.

Niels Bohr, New York Times Book Review, *October 20, 1957*

True science teaches, above all, to doubt and be ignorant.

Miguel de Unamuno, Tragic Sense of Life, *1913*

In making one discovery we never fail to get an incomplete knowledge of others of which we previously had no idea, so that we cannot solve one problem without finding new ones.

Joseph Priestly, Experiments and Observations, *1774*

(*See also* **SELF-DOUBT, KNOWLEDGE, THEORY**)

SCIENCE AND RELIGION

Science and religion, religion and science, put it as I may, they are two sides of the same glass, through which we see darkly until these two, focusing together, reveal the truth.

Pearl S. Buck, A Bridge for Passing, *1962*

Science without religion is lame, religion without science is blind.

Einstein, Out of My Later Years, *1950*

Every formula which expresses a law of nature is a hymn of praise to God.

Maria Mitchell (d. 1889), inscription, Hall of Fame

Science investigates; religion interprets. Science gives man knowledge which is power; religion gives man wisdom which is control.

Martin Luther King., Jr., Strength to Love, *1963*

The means by which we live have outdistanced the ends for which we live. Our scientific power has outrun our spiritual power. We have guided missiles and misguided men.

Ibid.

Religion will not regain its old power until it can face change in the same spirit as does science.

Whitehead, Science and the Modern World, *1925*

SCIENCE, RESISTANCE TO

There is a lurking fear that some things are not meant "to be known," that some inquiries are too dangerous for human beings to make.

Carl Sagan, Broca's Brain, *1979*

Sir, I do not like specialists. As far as I am concerned, to specialize is to limit one's universe.

Claude Debussy, M. Croche, antidilettante, *1921*

Sweet is the lore which Nature brings;
Our meddling intellect
Mis-shapes the beauteous form of things:—
We murder to dissect.

William Wordsworth, "The Tables Turned," 1798

(*See also* **HUMANISM, IGNORANCE, PREJUDICE**)

SCIENCE TRAINING

Would you like to learn science? Begin by learning your own language.

Abbé de Condillac, Human Understanding, *1749*

One cannot know a science completely without knowing its history.

Auguste Comte, Cours de philosophie positive, *1830*

It is not enough to say: I made a mistake. You must explain *how*.

Claude Bernard, Experimental Medicine, *1865*

(*See also* **EXPERIENCE, LANGUAGE, THEORY**)

SCIENTIFIC REVOLUTION

The Scientific Revolution outshines everything since the rise of Christianity and reduces the Renaissance and Reformation to the rank of mere episodes . . . of Medieval Christendom.

Herbert Butterfield, Origins of Modern Science, *1949*

The simplest schoolboy is now familiar with truths for which Archimedes would have given his life.

Ernest Renan, Souvenirs d'enfance et de jeunesse, *1883*

Literary intellectuals at one pole—at the other scientists.—. . . Between the two a gulf of mutual incomprehension.

C.P. Snow, The Two Cultures and the Scientific Revolution, *1959*

We must embark on a bold new program for making the benefit of our scientific and industrial progress available for the improvement and growth of underdeveloped areas.

Harry S. Truman, Inaugural Address, 1949

SEASONS: *See* WINTER/SUMMER

SECRETS

The most difficult secret for a man to keep is his own opinion of himself.

> *Marcel Pagnol, conversation, March 15, 1954*

A secret is not something unrevealed, but something told privately, in a whisper.

> *Pagnol,* César, *1936*

Three may keep a secret, if two of them are dead.

> *Benjamin Franklin,* Poor Richard's Almanack, *1735*

To whom you tell your secrets, to him you resign your liberty.

> *Spanish proverb*

It is much easier to tell intimate things in the dark.

> *William McFee,* Casuals of the Sea, *1916*

Love, pain, and money cannot be kept secret. They soon betray themselves.

> *Spanish proverb*

(*See also* **CONFESSION, PRIVACY, SELF**)

SECURITY: *See* SAFE/SECURE

SEDUCTION

Every maiden's weak and willin'
When she meets the proper villain.

> *Clarence Day,* Thoughts without Words, *1928*

All really great lovers are articulate, and verbal seduction is the surest road to actual seduction.

> *Marya Mannes,* More in Anger, *1958*

To win a woman in the first place you must please her, then undress her, and then somehow get her clothes back on her. Finally, so that she will let you leave her, you've got to antagonize her.

> *Jean Giraudoux,* Amphitryon, *1929*

(*See also* **CHARM, TEMPTATION**)

SELF

Trust yourself, then you will know how to live.

Goethe, Proverbs in Prose, *1828*

The "self" is hateful.

Pascal, Pensées, *1670*

Egotism: The art of seeing in yourself what others cannot see.

George Higgins, Minister, Congregational Church, March 2, 1986

People often say that this or that person has not yet found himself. But the self is not something that one finds. It is something that one creates.

Thomas Szasz, The Second Sin, *1973*

Risk! Risk anything! Care no more for the opinion of others, for those voices. Do the hardest thing on earth for you. Act for yourself. Face the truth.

Katherine Mansfield (d. 1932), Journals

One must raise the self by the self
And not let the self sink down
For the self's only friend is the self
And the self is the self's one enemy.

Bhagavad-Gita, c. 1050 B.C.

Self-reliance, the height and perfection of man, is reliance on God.

Emerson, The Fugitive Slave Law, *1854*

I have seen no more evident monstrosity and miracle in the world than myself.

Montaigne, Essays, *1580*

Our entire life, with our fine moral code and our precious freedom, consists ultimately in accepting ourselves as we are.

Jean Anouilh, Traveler without Luggage, *1936*

I say *me,* knowing all the while it's not me.

Samuel Beckett, The Unnamable, *1953*

One may understand the cosmos, but never the ego; the self is more distant than any star.

G.K. Chesterton, Orthodoxy, *1908*

What other dungeon is so dark as one's own heart! What jailer so inexorable as one's self!

> *Nathaniel Hawthorne*, The House of Seven Gables, *1822*

My thought is *me;* that is why I can't stop. I exist by what I think . . . and I can't stop thinking.

> *J.P. Sartre*, Nausea, *1938*

Self-reverence, self-knowledge, self-control,
These three alone lead life to sovereign power.

> *Alfred, Lord Tennyson, "Oenone," 1842*

In its widest possible sense . . . a man's self is the sum total of all that he *can* call his, not only his body and his psychic powers, but his clothes and his house, his wife and children, his ancestors and friends, his reputation and works, his lands and horses, and yacht and bank account. All these things give him the same emotions. If they wax and prosper, he feels triumphant; if they dwindle and die away, he feels cast down.

> *William James*, The Principles of Psychology, *1890*

(*See also* **CHARACTER, IDENTITY, INDIVIDUALISM**)

SELF-ASSERTION

The perfection preached in the Gospels never yet built an empire. Every man of action has a strong dose of egotism, pride, hardness, and cunning.

> *Charles de Gaulle*, New York Times Magazine, *May 12, 1968*

There is always room for a man of force, and he makes room for many.

> *Emerson, "Power,"* The Conduct of Life, *1860*

Nobody can give you freedom. Nobody can give you equality or justice or anything. If you're a man, you take it.

> *Malcolm X,* Malcolm X Speaks, *1965*

(*See also* **COURAGE, SELF-DETERMINATION**)

SELF-CONFIDENCE

Self-trust is the essence of heroism.

> *Emerson,* Essays, *1841*

[Self-]assurance is contemptible and fatal unless it is self-knowledge.
George Santayana, Character and Opinion in the United States,
1921

Angels can fly because they take themselves lightly.
G.K. Chesterton, Orthodoxy, *1908*

(*See also* **SELF-DOUBT**)

SELF-CONTROL

For better or for worse, man is the tool-using animal, and as such he has become the lord of creation. When he is lord also of himself, he will deserve his self-chosen title of *homo sapiens.*
William Ralph Inge, Outspoken Essays, *1922*

He who is allowed to do as he likes will soon run his head into a brick wall out of sheer frustration.
Robert Musil, The Man without Qualities, *1930*

Freedom is obtained not by the enjoyment of what is desired but by controlling desire itself.
Epictetus (fl. 100 A.D.), Discourses

Not being able to govern events, I govern myself, and apply myself to them, if they will not apply themselves to me.
Montaigne, Essays, *1588*

I am,
indeed,
a king,
because I know how
to rule myself.
Pietro Aretino to Agostino Ricchi, May 10, 1537

(*See also* **DISCIPLINE**)

SELF-CRITICISM

Americans are, if not the most self-critical, at least the most anxiously self-conscious people in the world, forever concerned about the inadequacy of something or other—their national morality, their national culture, their national purpose.
Richard Hofstadter, Anti-intellectualism, *1963*

I believe it is harder to be fair to oneself than to others.

> *André Gide,* Journals, *September 4, 1940*

How shall we expect charity towards others, when we are uncharitable to ourselves?

> *Sir Thomas Browne,* Religio Medici, *1642*

(*See also* **OBJECTIVITY**)

SELF-DENIAL

Refrain tonight,
And that shall lend a kind of easiness
To the next abstinence; the next more easy;
For use almost can change the stamp of nature.

> *Shakespeare,* Hamlet, *1600*

Abstainer, n. A weak person who yields to the temptation of denying himself a pleasure.

> *Ambrose Bierce,* The Devil's Dictionary, *1911*

Self-denial is not a virtue; it is only the effect of prudence on rascality.

> *G.B. Shaw,* Man and Superman, *1903*

To refuse the sweets of life because they once must leave us, is as preposterous as to wish to have been born old, because we one day must be old.

> *William Congreve,* The Way of the World, *1700*

(*See also* **CHASTITY, DISCIPLINE**)

SELF-DETERMINATION

Every man is the son of his own works.

> *Cervantes,* Dox Quixote, *1615*

You may fetter my leg, but Zeus himself cannot get the better of my free will.

> *Epictetus,* Discourses, *second century* A.D.

Some minds seem almost to create themselves, springing up under every disadvantage and working their solitary but irresistible way through a thousand obstacles.

> *Washington Irving,* The Sketch Book, *1820*

If we must accept Fate, we are no less compelled to affirm liberty, the significance of the individual, the grandeur of duty, the power of character.

Emerson, The Conduct of Life, *1860*

(*See also* **RESPONSIBILITY**)

SELF-DOUBT

He who undervalues himself is justly undervalued by others.

William Hazlitt, "On the Knowledge of Character," 1821

It is easy—terribly easy—to shake a man's faith in himself. To take advantage of that to break a man's spirit is devil's work.

G.B. Shaw, Candida, *1903*

He that listens after what people say of him shall never have peace.

Thomas Fuller, Gnomologia, *1732*

(*See also* **ANXIETY, INSECURITY**)

SELF-ESTEEM

Be a friend to thyself, and others will be so too.

Thomas Fuller, Gnomologia, *1732*

It is easy to live for others; everybody does. I call on you to live for yourselves.

Emerson, Journals, *1845*

If you love yourself meanly, childishly, timidly, even so shall you love your neighbor.

Maeterlinck, Wisdom and Destiny, *1898*

Self-respect will keep a man from being abject when he is in the power of enemies, and will enable him to feel that he may be in the right when the world is against him.

Bertrand Russell, Authority and the Individual, *1949*

A man cannot be comfortable without his own approval.

Mark Twain, "What is Man?", 1906

SELF-IMPORTANCE

Man desires to be free and he desires to feel important. This places him in a dilemma, for the more he emancipates himself from necessity the less important he feels.

W.H. Auden, The Dyer's Hand, *1962*

Egotism is the anesthetic that dulls the pain of stupidity.

Frank Leahy, Look, *January 10, 1955*

A sick man that gets talking about himself, a woman that gets talking about her baby, and an author that begins reading out of his own book, never know when to stop.

Oliver Wendel Holmes, The Poet at the Breakfast Table

It astounds us to come upon other egotists, as though we alone had the right to be selfish and full of the eagerness to live.

Jules Renard, Journal, *November 18, 1887*

(See also **CONCEIT, HUMILITY, VANITY***)*

SELFISHNESS/UNSELFISHNESS

Whosoever will save his life shall lose it: and whosoever will lose his life for my sake shall find it.

Matthew 16:23

Human history is the sad result of each one looking out for himself.

Julio Cortázar, The Winners, *1960*

Selfish persons are incapable of loving others, but they are not capable of loving themselves either.

Erich Fromm, Man for Himself, *1947*

The small share of happiness attainable by man exists only insofar as he is able to cease to think of himself.

Theodor Reik, Of Love and Lust, *1957*

To reach perfection, we must all pass, one by one, through the death of self-effacement.

Dag Hammarskjöld, Markings, *1964*

In every part and corner of our life, to lose oneself is to be gainer; for to forget oneself is to be happy.

Robert Louis Stevenson, "Old Mortality," 1884

I have been a selfish being all my life, in practice, though not in principle.

Jane Austen, Pride and Prejudice, *1813*

Selfishness is the greatest curse of the human race.

William E. Gladstone, speech, Hawarden, May 28, 1890

(*See also* **GREED, INTEREST**)

SELF-LOVE

He who is in love with himself has at least this advantage—he won't encounter many rivals.

Georg Christoph Lichtenberg, Aphorisms, *1799*

Simple narcissism gives the power of beasts to politicians, professional wrestlers and female movie stars.

Norman Mailer, Miami and the Siege of Chicago, *1968*

One must learn to love oneself . . . with a wholesome and healthy love, so that one can bear to be with oneself and need not roam.

Nietzsche, Thus Spake Zarathustra, *1892*

Self-love is the instrument of our preservation; it resembles that provision for the perpetuity of mankind; it is necessary, it is dear to us, it gives us pleasure, but we must conceal it.

Voltaire, Philosophical Dictionary, *1764*

Everyone gives himself credit for more brains than he has and less money.

Italian proverb

To love oneself is the beginning of a life-long romance.

Oscar Wilde, An Ideal Husband, *1895*

(*See also* **SELF-ESTEEM, VANITY**)

SELF-PITY

God put self-pity by the side of despair like the cure by the side of the disease.

Albert Camus, Notebooks 1935–1942, *1962*

Every man supposes himself not to be fully understood.

Emerson, Journals, *1840*

Self-pity comes so naturally to all of us, that the most solid happiness can be shaken by the compassion of a fool.

André Maurois, Ariel, *1924*

(*See also* **PITY**)

SELF-RIGHTEOUSNESS

Why beholdest thou the mote that is in thy brother's eye, but considereth not the beam that is in thine own eye?

Matthew 7:3

Righteous people have no sense of humor.

Bertolt Brecht, Baal, *1926*

Forgive us [Lord] for cheering legislators who promise low taxes, but deny homes and schools and help to those in need; for self-righteousness that blames the poor for their poverty or the oppressed for their oppression.

United Presbyterian Church, Litany for Holy Communion, *1968*

(*See also* **DOGMATISM, FANATICISM, HYPOCRISY**)

SELF-SUFFICIENCY

Every tub must stand upon its own bottom.

Thomas Fuller, Gnomologia, *1732*

Who to himself is law no law doth need,
Offends no law, and is a king indeed.

George Chapman, Bussy D'Ambois, *c. 1600*

We must be our own before we can be another's.

Emerson, "Friendship," Essays, *1841*

I care not so much what I am in the opinion of others, as what I am in my own; I would be rich of myself, and not by borrowing.

Montaigne, Essays, *1588*

Any man who is really a man must learn to be alone in the midst of others, to think alone for others, and if necessary against others.

Romain Rolland, Clérambault, *1919*

(*See also* **SELF-DETERMINATION**)

SENSATION(S)

O for a life of Sensations rather than of Thoughts!

> *John Keats to Benjamin Bailey, November 22, 1817*

I want to reach that condensation of sensations that constitutes a picture.

> *Henri Matisse,* Notes d'un peintre, *1908*

It is a peculiar sensation, this double-consciousness, this sense of always looking at one's self through the eyes of another.... One feels his two-ness—an American, a Negro; two souls, two thoughts, two unreconciled strivings; two warring ideals in one dark body, whose dogged strength alone keeps it from being torn asunder.

> *W.E.B. Du Bois,* The Souls of Black Folks, *1900*

SENSE/NONSENSE

The pendulum of the mind oscillates between sense and nonsense, not between right and wrong.

> *C.G. Jung,* Memories, Dreams, Reflections, *1968*

I conclude that there is as much sense in nonsense as there is non-sense in sense.

> *Anthony Burgess,* New York Times Book Review, *August 9, 1987*

Nonsense is the end result of all sense.

> *Georges Bataille (d. 1962),* Somme athéologique

I wish either my father or my mother, or indeed both of them, as they were in duty both equally bound to it, had minded what they were about when they begot me.

> *Laurence Sterne,* Tristram Shandy, *1760*

As soon as I stepped out of my mother's womb onto dry land, I realized that I had made a mistake—that I should not have come, but the trouble with children is that they are not returnable.

> *Quentin Crisp,* The Naked Civil Servant, *1966*

There was a young man from Quebec,
Who was buried in snow to his neck;
When they asked, "Is you friz?"
He replied, "Yes, I iz,
But we don't call this cold in Quebec."

> *Edward Lear,* Book of Nonsense, *1846*

"It takes all the running you can do just to keep in the same place,"
... said the Queen.

> *Lewis Carroll,* Through the Looking-Glass, *1872*

I do not like thee, Dr. Fell.
The reason why I cannot tell;
But this I know and know full well,
I do not like thee, Dr. Fell.

> *Tom Brown (d. 1704), written while at Oxford*

You can lead a whore to culture but you can't make her think.

> *Dorothy Thompson (d. 1961), speech, American Horticulture Society*

Mirrors should reflect a little before throwing back images.

> *Jean Cocteau (d. 1963),* Essai de critique indirecte

What is Matter?—Never mind.
What is Mind?—No matter.

> *Punch 29:19 (1855)*

If the Creator had a purpose in equipping us with a neck, he surely
meant for us to stick it out.

> *Arthur Koestler,* Encounter, *May 1970*

(*See also* **HUMOR**)

SENSES

All credibility, all good conscience, all evidence of truth come only
from the senses.

> *Nietzsche,* Beyond Good and Evil, *1886*

The ear tends to be lazy, craves the familiar, and is shocked by the
unexpected; the eye, on the other hand, tends to be impatient, craves
the novel and is bored by repetition.

> *W.H. Auden,* The Dyer's Hand, *1962*

We are astonished at thought, but sensation is equally wonderful.

> *Voltaire,* Philosophical Dictionary, *1764*

The modern nose, like the modern eye, has developed a sort of
microscopic, intercellular intensity which makes our human contacts
painful and revolting.

> *Marshall McLuhan,* The Mechanical Bride, *1951*

(*See also* **PERCEPTION**)

SENSIBILITY

If we had keen vision and feeling of all ordinary human life, it would be like hearing the grass grow and the squirrel's heart beat, and we should die of that roar which lies on the other side of silence.

George Eliot, Middlemarch, *1872*

Nothing is little to him that feels it with great sensibility.

Samuel Johnson, in Boswell's Life, *July 20, 1762*

The sensibility of man to trifles, and his insensibility to great things, indicates a strange inversion.

Pascal, Pensées, *1670*

The two pioneering forces of modern sensibility are Jewish moral seriousness and homosexual estheticism and irony.

Susan Sontag, "Notes on Camp," Against Interpretation, *1961*

(*See also* EMOTIONS, SYMPATHY)

SENTIMENTALITY

. . . The emotional promiscuity of those who have no sentiment.

Norman Mailer, Cannibals and Christians, *1966*

. . . The only sentiment that rubs you up the wrong way.

W. Somerset Maugham, A Writer's Notebook, *1941*

I hope my tongue in prune juice smothers
If I belittle dogs and mothers.

Ogden Nash, "Compliments of a Friend,"
Verses from 1929 On, *1949*

SERIOUSNESS

Almost everything serious is difficult, and everything is serious.

Rainer Maria Rilke, Letters to a Young Poet, *July 16, 1903*

Earnest people are often people who habitually look on the serious side of things that have no serious side.

Van Wyck Brooks, From a Writer's Notebook, *1958*

There are people who think that everything one does with a serious face is sensible.

Georg Christoph Lichtenberg, Aphorisms, *1799*

Solemnity is the shield of idiots.

> *Montesquieu (d. 1755),* Pensées et jugements

(*See also* **HUMOR, PROFUNDITY**)

SERVANTS

Few men have been admired by their servants.

> *Montaigne,* Essays, *1588*

Before the cleaning lady arrives, it is necessary to vacuum the entire house and straighten up all the rooms, because she works for friends of yours the other six days of the week and you don't want her to tell them how you really live.

> *P.J. O'Rourke,* Modern Manners, *1983*

It is perfectly all right to ask your cleaning lady to iron, wash windows, polish silver, do the grocery shopping, and clean up after the dog. You can also ask her to jump through a flaming hoop with a cold leg of mutton in her mouth for all the good it will do. She's going to dust a little, and that's it, no matter what.

> *Ibid.*

The cook was a good cook as cooks go; but as cooks go, she went.

> *Saki,* Reginald, *1904*

It has been my experience, sir, that no lady can ever forgive another lady for taking a really good cook away from her.

> *P.G. Wodehouse,* Carry on, Jeeves, *1925*

Cecily: I'm afraid I disapprove of servants.
Carr: You are quite right to do so. Most of them are without scruples.

> *Tom Stoppard,* Travesties, *1974*

SEXUAL RELATIONS

There is no greater nor keener pleasure than that of bodily love—and none which is more irrational.

> *Plato (fl. 400 B.C.),* The Republic

The relation of the sexes . . . is really the invisible central point of all action and conduct. . . . the cause of war and the end of peace.

> *Arthur Schopenhauer,* The World as Will and Idea, *1818*

Sex is the lyricism of the masses.

> *Charles Baudelaire,* Intimate Journals, *1887*

Sex is the great amateur art.
David Cort, Social Astonishments, *1963*

The sexual embrace can only be compared with music and with prayer.
Havelock Ellis, On Life and Sex, *1937*

Aphrodite spoke and loosened from her bosom the embroidered girdle of many colors into which all her allurements were fashioned. In it was love and in it desire and in it blandishing persuasion which steals the mind even of the wise.
Homer, The Iliad, *c. 700 B.C.*

The orgasm has replaced the Cross as the focus of longing and the image of fulfillment.
Malcolm Muggeridge, "Down with Sex," 1966

Women complain about sex more often than men. Their gripes fall into two major categories: 1) Not enough, 2) Too much.
Ann Landers, Ann Landers Says Truth is Stranger . . . , *1968*

The degree and kind of a man's sexuality reach up into the ultimate pinnacle of his spirit.
Nietzsche, Beyond Good and Evil, *1886*

My own view . . . is that sexuality is lovely, there cannot be too much of it, it is self-limiting . . . and satisfaction diminishes tension and clears the mind for attention and learning.
Paul Goodman, Compulsory Miseducation, *1964*

If a woman hasn't got a tiny streak of a harlot in her, she's a dry stick as a rule.
D.H. Lawrence, Pornography and Obscenity, *1930*

The truly erotic sensibility, in evoking the image of woman, never omits to clothe it. The robing and disrobing: that is the true traffic of love.
Antonio Machado, Juan de Mairena, *1943*

(*See also* **HOMOSEXUALITY, PROSTITUTION**)

SHAME

The more things a man is ashamed of, the more respectable he is.
G.B. Shaw, Man and Superman, *1905*

Better a red face than a black heart.

Portuguese proverb

One of the misfortunes of our time is that in getting rid of false shame we have killed off so much of real shame as well.

Louis Kronenberger, Company Manners, *1954*

(*See also* **GUILT/INNOCENCE, SELF**)

SICKNESS

I reckon being ill as one of the great pleasures of life, provided one is not too ill.

Samuel Butler, The Way of All Flesh, *1903*

How a sickness enlarges the dimensions of a man's self to himself! He is his own exclusive object. Supreme selfishness is inculcated upon him as his only duty.

Charles Lamb, "The Convalescent," *1833*

(*See also* **HEALTH, MICROBES**)

SILENCE

. . . One of the hardest arguments to refute.

The Complete Works of Josh Billings, *1919*

He knew the precise psychological moment when to say nothing.

Oscar Wilde, The Picture of Dorian Gray, *1891*

Man . . . is only too glad to have woman hold strictly to the Christian principle of suffering [in] silence.

George Sand, Letters to Marcie, *1837*

The Framers [of the Constitution] . . . created the federally protected right of silence and decreed that the law could not be used to pry open one's lips and make him a witness against himself.

Justice William O. Douglas, dissent, Ullman vs. U.S., *1956*

(*See also* **NOISE, SPEECH, TALKING**)

SIMPLICITY

Seek simplicity and distrust it.

Alfred North Whitehead, The Concept of Nature, *1920*

To be simple is the best thing in the world; to be modest is the next best thing. I am not sure about being quiet.

G.K. Chesterton, All Things Considered, *1908*

Thou canst not adorn simplicity. What is naked or defective is susceptible of decoration; what is decorated is simplicity no longer.

Walter Savage Landor, Imaginary Conversations, *1853*

Simplicity is the mean between ostentation and rusticity.

Alexander Pope, preface to the Iliad, 1720

Give me a look, give me a face,
That makes simplicity a grace;
Robes loosely flowing, hair as free,
Such sweet neglect more taketh me
Than all the adulteries of art:
They strike mine eyes, but not my heart.

Ben Jonson, Epicene, or The Silent Woman, *1609*

Art . . . should simplify. That, indeed, is very nearly the whole of the higher artistic process; finding what conventions of form and what detail one can do without and yet preserve the spirit of the whole.

Willa Cather, On the Art of Fiction, *1920*

SIN, ORIGINAL

When the woman saw that the tree was good for food, and that it was pleasant to the eyes, and a tree to be desired to make one wise, she took of the fruit thereof, and did eat, and gave also unto her husband with her; and he did eat.

Genesis 3:6

Her rash hand in evil hour
Forth reaching to the fruit, she plucked, she eat:
Earth felt the wound, and Nature from her seat,
Sighing through all her works, gave signs of woe
That all was lost.

John Milton, Paradise Lost, *1667*

When Eve upon the first of Men
The apple press'd with specious cant,
Oh! what a thousand pities then
That Adam was not Adamant!

Thomas Hood (d. 1835), "A Reflection"

SIN/SINNERS

Two kinds of people: the just, who consider themselves sinners, and the sinners, who consider themselves just.

Pascal, Pensées, *1670*

Pleasure's a sin, and sometimes sin's a pleasure.

Lord Byron, Don Juan, *1824*

Without the spice of guilt, sin cannot be fully savored.

Alexander Chase, Perspectives, *1966*

In seventeenth-century Italy, a princess, tasting ice cream on a warm day, remarked "A pity this isn't a sin!"

Stendhal, Chroniques italiennes, *1839*

Q. What kind of sins are the greatest?
A. Adultery, fornication, murder, theft, swearing, witchcraft, sedition, heresies, or any the like.

John Bunyan, Instructions for the Ignorant, *1675*

Oh, Lord, it is not the sins I have committed that I regret, but those which I've had no opportunity to commit.

Ghalib, Prayer, *c. 1800*

The physicists have known sin; and that is a knowledge they cannot lose.

J. Robert Oppenheimer, lecture, MIT, 1947

There is no sin but ignorance.

Christopher Marlowe, The Jew of Malta, *c. 1589*

In best understandings, sin began,
Angels sinned first, then Devils, and then Man.

John Donne, Letters to Several Personages, *1651*

Sin is a dangerous toy in the hands of the virtuous. It should be left to the congenitally sinful, who know when to play with it and when to let it alone.

H.L. Mencken, The American Mercury, *February 1929*

The twin concepts of sin and vindictive punishment seem to be at the root of much that is most vigorous, both in religion and politics.

Bertrand Russell, Unpopular Essays, *1950*

People are no longer sinful, they are only immature or underprivileged or frightened or, more particularly, sick.

> *Phyllis McGinley, "In Defense of Sin,"* The Province of the Heart, *1959*

I have found . . . that it may be well to choose one sin in order that another may be shunned.

> *Anthony Trollope,* Doctor Wortle's School, *1879*

The only deadly sin I know is cynicism.

> *Henry L. Stimson,* On Active Service in Peace and War, *1948*

We presume none sins unless he stands to profit by it.

> *The Talmud, sixth century*

(*See also* **EVIL, TEMPTATION**)

SINCERITY

The secret of success is sincerity: once you can fake that, you've got it made.

> *Jean Giraudoux, in A. Bloch,* Murphy's Law, Book Two, *1980*

It is dangerous to be sincere unless you are also stupid.

> *G.B. Shaw,* Man and Superman, *1905*

I am not sincere even when I say I'm not sincere.

> *Jules Renard (d. 1910),* Journal

How could sincerity be a condition of friendship? A taste for truth at any cost is a passion which spares nothing.

> *Albert Camus,* The Fall, *1956*

I have, all my life long, [lain in bed] till noon; yet I tell all young men, and tell them with great sincerity, that nobody who does not rise early will ever do any good.

> *Samuel Johnson, in Boswell's* Journal, *September 14, 1773*

Sincerity is an opening of the heart, found in very few people. What we usually see is merely a cunning deceit to gain another's confidence.

> *La Rochefoucauld,* Maxims, *1665*

A little sincerity is a dangerous thing, and a great deal of it is absolutely fatal.

> *Oscar Wilde, "The Critic as Artist," 1890*

The spontaneity of a slap is sincerity, whereas the ceremony of a caress is largely conventional.

Ugo Betti, The Gambler, *1950*

Sincerity is not a spontaneous flower, nor is modesty either.

Colette, Earthly Paradise, *1960*

The way I see it, it doesn't matter what you believe just so you're sincere.

Charles M. Schulz, Go Fly a Kite, Charlie Brown, *1963*

(*See also* **FRANKNESS, HYPOCRISY, INTEGRITY**)

SKEPTICISM

. . . The first step toward truth.

Diderot, Pensées philosophiques, *1746*

Skepticism is more easily understood by asking, "What do I know?"

Montaigne, Essays, *1580*

Man's most valuable trait
is a judicious sense of what not to believe.

Euripides, Helen, *412 B.C.*

Skeptic does not mean him who doubts, but him who investigates or researches, as opposed to him who asserts and thinks that he has found.

Miguel de Unamuno, Essays and Soliloquies, *1924*

The improver of knowledge absolutely refuses to acknowledge authority, as such. For him, skepticism is the highest of duties, blind faith the one unpardonable sin.

T.H. Huxley, On the Advisableness of Improving Natural Knowledge, *1866*

Skepticism is not below knowledge, but above it.

Alain, Libres-propos, *1914*

If a man have a strong faith he can indulge in the luxury of skepticism.

Nietzsche, The Twilight of the Idols, *1888*

(*See also* **DOUBT**)

SLANDER

He that flings dirt at another dirtieth himself most.

Thomas Fuller, Gnomologia, *1732*

There are different ways of assassinating a man—by pistol, sword, poison, or moral assassination. They are the same in their results except that the last is more cruel.

Napoleon I, Maxims, *1815*

If a man could say nothing against a character but what he can prove, history could not be written.

Samuel Boswell, in Boswell's Life, *April 3, 1776*

(*See also* **GOSSIP, SCANDAL**)

SLAVERY

God made freedom, man made slavery.

Marie-Joseph Chénier (d. 1811), Epître sur la calomnie, *1795*

No man can put a chain about the ankle of his fellow man without at last finding the other end fastened about his own neck.

Frederick Douglass, speech, Civil Rights Mass Meeting,
Washington, D.C., 1883

A slave has just one master; an ambitious person has as many masters as there are people useful to him.

La Bruyère, Characters, *1688*

He who is by nature not his own but another's, is by nature a slave.

Aristotle, Politics, *fourth century B.C.*

Art thou less a slave by being loved and favored by thy master? Thou art indeed well off, slave. Thy master favors thee; he will soon beat thee.

Pascal, Pensées, *1670*

Slaves lose everything in their chains, even the desire of escaping from them.

Rousseau, The Social Contract, *1762*

(*See also* **DESPOTISM, TYRANNY**)

SLEEP

Oh sleep! it is a gentle thing,
Beloved from pole to pole. . . .

> *Samuel Taylor Coleridge*, The Ancient Mariner, *1798*

Cut if you will, with Sleep's dull knife,
Each day to half its length, my friend,—
The years that Time takes off *my* life,
He'll take off from the other end!

> *Edna St. Vincent Millay, "Midnight Oil," 1920*

Even where sleep is concerned, too much is a bad thing.

> *Homer*, Odyssey, *ninth century* B.C.

Sleeping is no mean art: for its sake one has to stay awake all day.

> *Nietzsche*, Thus Spake Zarathustra, *1892*

(*See also* **BED, DREAM**)

SNOBBISHNESS

Levellers wish to level *down* as far as themselves; but they cannot bear levelling *up* to themselves.

> *Samuel Johnson, in Boswell's* Life, *July 21, 1763*

His hatred of snobs stemmed from his snobbishness, and made the simpletons (i.e., everybody else) believe that he was free from snobbishness.

> *Proust*, the Guermantes Way, *1920*

The true snob never rests; there is always a higher goal to attain, and there are, by the same token, always more and more people to look down upon.

> *Russell Lynes*, Harper's, *November 1950*

(*See also* **CLASSES, PRIDE, SOCIETY**)

SOCIALISM

. . . A condition of society in which there should be neither rich nor poor, . . . in which all men would be living in equality of condition, and would manage their affairs unwastefully, and with the full consciousness that harm to one would mean harm to all—the realization at last of the meaning of the word *commonwealth*.

> *William Morris, "Justice," 1884*

Socialism relieves us of the necessity of living for others.

> *Oscar Wilde,* "The Soul of Man under Socialism," *1891*

I am a firm believer in socialism and I know that the quicker you have monopoly in this country the quicker we will have socialism.

> *Charles P. Steinmetz, Congressional Record, January 27, 1949*

I am opposed to socialism because it dreams ingenuously of good, truth, beauty, and equal rights.

> *Nietzsche,* Will to Power, *1883*

The present state of affairs offends [many Socialists] not because it causes misery [or] makes freedom impossible, but because it is untidy; what they desire . . . is to reduce the world to something resembling a chessboard.

> *George Orwell,* The Road to Wigan Pier, *1937*

The fact is that life has become a sweepstake. Millions of people who have lost the sense of being able to make anything of the collective effort of shaping their economic society, now expect fortune to descend like pie from the sky.

> *Max Lerner,* "I'm Dreaming of a Bright Sweepstake," *1949*

Marxian Socialism must always remain a portent to historians—. . . how such a doctrine so illogical and so dull can have exercised so powerful and enduring an influence over the minds of men, and through them, the events of history.

> *John Maynard Keynes,* The End of Laissez-Faire, *1925*

(*See also* **COMMUNISM, DEMOCRACY, GOVERNMENT**)

SOCIETY

Man did not enter into society to become worse than he was before, nor to have fewer rights than he had before, but to have those rights better secured.

> *Thomas Paine,* The Rights of Man, *1791*

Society exists for the benefit of its members, not the members for the benefit of society.

> *Herbert Spencer,* Social Statics, *1850*

Society is immoral and immortal; it can afford to commit any kind of folly, and indulge in any sort of vice; it cannot be killed, and the fragments that survive can always laugh at the dead.

> *Henry Adams,* Education, *1907*

Since society exists, we have to believe that man wants to live in it, but from the beginning he has used a fair share of his energy to fight against it.

Georges Simenon (d. 1987), Le Grand Bob

One cannot raise the bottom of society without benefiting everyone above.

Michael Harrington, The Older America, *1962*

Society is always trying in some way or other to grind us down to a single flat surface.

Oliver Wendell Holmes, The Professor at the Breakfast Table, *1860*

Everyone who receives the protection of society owes a return for the benefit.

John Stuart Mill, On Liberty, *1859*

What makes a multitude of individuals a society rather than a crowd is a commonly held ideal. While such an ideal is always a fiction, ... it is men's ability to believe in such fictions that enables them to act together as part of a group.

Melvin Lyon, Symbol and Ideal in Henry Adams, *1970*

What man loses by the social contract is his natural liberty and an unlimited right to everything he tries to get and succeeds in getting; what he gains is civil liberty and the proprietorship of all he possesses.

Rousseau, The Social Contract, *1762*

The principles of the good society call for a concern with an order of being—which cannot be proved existentially to the sense organs— where it matters supremely that the human person is inviolable, that reason shall regulate the will, that truth shall prevail over error.

Walter Lippmann, The Public Philosophy, *1955*

Nature holds no brief for the human experiment: it must stand or fall by its results.

G.B. Shaw, Back to Methuselah, *1921*

Cursed be the social lies that warp us from the truth.

Alfred, Lord Tennyson, "Locksley Hall," *1842*

The chaos of our society is the product of the dishevelment of our ideas.

Philip Wylie, Generation of Vipers, *1942*

(*See also* **CIVILIZATION, CLASSES, GOVERNMENT**)

SOCIETY, POLITE

There is a toad in every social dish, however well they cook it.
Logan Pearsall Smith, Afterthoughts, *1931*

I love London Society! I think it has immensely improved. It is entirely composed now of beautiful idiots and brilliant lunatics.
Oscar Wilde, An Ideal Husband, *1895*

Human society is founded on mutual deceit: few friendships would endure if each knew what his friend said of him in his absence.
Pascal, Pensées, *1670*

Society is a more level surface than we imagine. Wise men or absolute fools are hard to be met with, as there are few giants or dwarfs.
William Hazlitt, Characteristics, *1823*

To get into the best society nowadays, one has either to feed people, amuse people, or shock people.
Oscar Wilde, A Woman of No Importance, *1893*

To be in [society] is merely a bore. But to be out of it simply tragedy.
Ibid.

So you want to be a social climber? Of all the occupations dealt with here, this is undoubtedly the easiest to crack. It is also, alas, the hardest to stomach—a fact that seems to have had surprisingly little effect upon the hordes that crowd the field.
Fran Lebowitz, Metropolitan Life, *1978*

Dear Miss Manners,
   If you had a single piece of advice to offer a couple who want to break into society, what would it be?
Gentle Reader:
   Don't bother.
Judith Martin, Miss Manner's Guide to Excruciatingly Correct Behavior, *1982*

(*See also* **MANNERS, SNOBBISHNESS**)

SOLITUDE

. . . is as needful to the imagination as society is wholesome for the character.
James Russell Lowell, Literary Essays, *1890*

Solitude, though it may be silent as light, is, like light, the mightiest of agencies; for solitude is essential to man. All men come into this world *alone;* all will leave it alone.

> *Thomas De Quincey,* Confessions of an English Opium-Eater, sequel, *1822*

He who is unable to live in society, or who has no need because he is sufficient for himself, must be either a beast or a god.

> *Aristotle,* Politics, *c. 350 B.C.*

A man thinking or working is always alone, let him be where he will.

> *Thoreau,* Walden, *1854*

In solitude especially do we begin to appreciate the advantage of living with someone who knows how to think.

> *Rousseau,* Confessions

The person who tries to live alone will not succeed as a human being. His heart withers if it does not answer another heart. His mind shrinks away if he hears only the echoes of his own thoughts and finds no other inspiration.

> *Pearl S. Buck,* To My Daughter, with Love, *1967*

If from society we learn to live,
'Tis solitude should teach us how to die;
It hath no flatterers.

> *Lord Byron,* Childe Harold's Pilgrimage, *1818*

They are never alone that are accompanied with noble thoughts.

> *Sir Philip Sidney,* Arcadia, *1580*

There are days when solitude is a heady wine that intoxicates you with freedom, others when it is a bitter tonic, and still others when it is a poison that makes you beat your head against the wall.

> *Colette,* Earthly Paradise, *1966*

A man can be himself only so long as he is alone; . . . if he does not love solitude, he will not love freedom; for it is only when he is alone that he is really free.

> *Schopenhauer,* The World as Will and Idea, *1818*

To dare to live alone is the rarest courage; since there are many who had rather meet their bitterest enemy in the field, than their own hearts in their closet.

> *C.C. Colton,* Lacon, *1825*

Solitude gives birth to the original in us, to beauty unfamiliar and perilous—to poetry. But also it gives birth to the opposite: to the perverse, the illicit, the absurd.

Thomas Mann, Death in Venice, *1913*

What a commentary on our civilization, when being alone is considered suspect; when one has to apologize for it, make excuses, hide the fact that one practices it—like a secret vice.

Anne Morrow Lindbergh, Gift from the Sea, *1955*

One can acquire everything in solitude—except character.

Stendhal, De l'Amour, *1822*

We are fools to depend on the society of our fellowmen. Wretched as we are, powerless as we are, they will not help us; we shall die alone.

Pascal Pensées, *1670*

We are rarely proud when we are alone.

Voltaire, Philosophical Dictionary, *1764*

Isolation breeds conceit.

Charles Dudley Warner, Backlog Studies, *1873*

We're all sentenced to solitary confinement inside our own skins, for life.

Tennessee Williams, Orpheus Descending, *1957*

(*See also* **LONELINESS, PRIVACY**)

SONS

The Mosaic religion had been a Father religion; Christianity became a Son religion. The old God, the Father, took second place; Christ, the Son, stood in His stead, just as, in those dark times, every son had longed to do.

Freud, New Introductory Lectures on Psychoanalysis, *1932*

Walt Whitman, a kosmos, of Manhattan the son. . . .

Whitman, "Song of Myself," *1892*

As for me, I would rather
Be a worm in a wild apple than a son of man.

Robinson Jeffers, "Original Sin," *1948*

SORROW: *See* SAD/MELANCHOLY.

SOUL/SPIRIT

What is a man profited if he shall gain the whole world, and lose his own soul? Or what shall a man give in exchange for his soul?

Matthew 16:26

Out of the night that covers me,
Black as the Pit from pole to pole,
I thank whatever gods may be
For my unconquerable soul.

William Ernest Henley, Echoes, *1888*

Three are the gates to . . . death of the soul:
    The gate of lust,
    The gate of wrath,
    The gate of greed.

Bhagavad-Gita, *250 B.C.*

The world stands out on either side
No wider than the heart is wide;
Above the world is stretched the sky,—
No higher than the soul is high.

Edna St. Vincent Millay, "Renascence," 1912

There is one spectacle grander than the sea, that is the sky; there is one spectacle grander than the sky, that is the interior of the soul.

Victor Hugo, Les Misérables, *1862*

The end of man is to let the spirit in him permeate his whole being, his soul, flesh, and affections. He attains his deepest self by losing his selfish ego.

Robert Musil, The Man without Qualities, *1930*

He who longs to strengthen his spirit
must go beyond obedience and respect.
He will continue to honor some laws
but he will mostly violate both law and custom.

Constantine Peter Cavafy, Strengthening the Spirit, *1903*

The word soul with us seems to be synonymous with *stomach*. We plead and speak not as from the soul but from the stomach. We plead not for God's justice, [but] for our own interests, our rents and profits.

Thomas Carlyle, Past and Present, *1843*

The self is the modern substitute for the soul.
>*Allan Bloom,* The Closing of the American Mind, *1987*

SPACE

The eternal silence of those infinite spaces frightens me.
>*Pascal* Pensées, *1670*

Space . . . is big. Really big. You just won't believe how vastly hugely mind-bogglingly big it is. I mean, you may think it's a long way down the road to the chemist's [druggist's], but that's just peanuts to space.
>*Douglas Adams,* The Hitch-hiker's Guide to the Galaxy, *1979*

Walking in space, man has never looked more puny or more significant.
>*Alexander Chase,* Perspectives, *1966*

Space flights are merely an escape, a fleeing away from one-self, because it is easier to go to Mars or to the moon than it is to penetrate one's being.
>*C.G. Jung, quoted in M. Serrano,* C.G. Jung and Hermann Hesse, *1966*

Space isn't remote at all. It's only an hour's drive away if your car could go straight upwards.
>*Sir Fred Hoyle, London* Observer, *1979*

Peace in space will help us naught once peace on earth is gone.
>*John F. Kennedy, State of the Union message, 1962*

We believe that when men reach beyond this planet [the moon] they should leave their national differences behind them.
>*Kennedy, News conference, February 21, 1962*

(*See also* **MOON-LANDING**)

SPACE, PERSONAL

Some thirty inches from my nose
The frontier of my person goes,
And all the untilled air between
Is private *pagus* or demesne.
>*W.H. Auden, "About the House," 1965*

Personal space refers to an area with invisible boundaries surrounding a person's body into which intruders may not come.

> *Robert Sommer*, Personal Space, *1969*

SPEECH

The great questions of the time are not decided by speeches and majority decisions—that was the error of 1848 and 1849—but by blood and iron.

> *Otto von Bismarck, speech, Prussian Diet, September 30, 1862*

Lecturer, n. One with his hand in your pocket, his tongue in your ear, and his faith in your patience.

> *Ambrose Bierce*, The Devil's Dictionary, *1911*

The tongue is more to be feared than the sword.

> *Japanese proverb*

Speech is civilization itself. The word, even the most contradictory word, preserves content—it is silence which isolates.

> *Thomas Mann*, The Magic Mountain, *1924*

Men [have] feared witches and burned women. It is the function of speech to free men from the bondage of irrational fears.

> *Louis D. Brandeis, Whitney vs. California, 1927*

From listening comes wisdom, and from speaking repentance.

> *Italian proverb*

What orators lack in depth they make up in length.

> *Montesquieu*, Lettres persanes, *1721*

(*See also* **COMMUNICATION, LANGUAGE, TALKING**)

SPEED: *See* AUTOMOBILITY.

SPORTS: COMMENTARIES

In America it is sport that is the opiate of the masses.

> *Russell Baker*, New York Times, *October 3, 1967*

A golf course is the epitome of all that is transitory in the universe, a space not to dwell in, but to get over as quickly as possible.

> *Jean Giraudoux*, The Enchanted, *1933*

Serious sport has nothing to do with fair play. It is bound up with hatred, jealousy, boastfulness, disregard of all rules, and sadistic pleasure in witnessing violence.

George Orwell, Shooting an Elephant, *1950*

If all the year were playing holidays,
To sport would be as tedious as to work.

Shakespeare, Henry IV, Part I

I hate all sports as rabidly as a person who likes sports hates common sense.

H.L. Mencken, Heathen Days

SPORTS: BASEBALL

Didn't come up here to read. Came up here to hit.

Hank Aaron, to Casey Stengel, who told him to hold the bat so he could read the label, quoted in Ueker and Herskowitz, Catcher in the Wry, *1982*

I was pitching on all adrenaline . . . and challenging them. I was throwing the ball right down the heart of the plate.

Roger Clemens, Boston Red Socks pitcher, on his record-breaking 20 strike-outs in 9-inning game, New York Times, *May 1, 1986*

Pitching is . . . the art of instilling fear.

Sandy Kofax, Dodgers pitcher, quoted in Hood, The Gashouse Gang, *1976*

Described variously as the knockdown pitch, the beanball, the duster and the purpose pitch—the Pentagon would call it the peacekeeper—this delightful strategem has graced the scene for most of the 109 years the major leagues have existed. It starts fights. It creates lingering grudges. It sends people to the hospital.

Melvin Durslag, TV Guide, *June 8, 1985*

A player's got to be kept hungry to become a big leaguer. That's why no boy from a rich family ever made the big leagues.

Joe DiMaggio, New York Times, *April 30, 1961*

SPORTS: FOOTBALL

I was a dirt-bag. Now I'm All-Pro.

Jim Burt, NY Giants, quoted in Eric Pooley, "True Blue," New York, *January 26, 1987*

Pro football is like nuclear warfare. There are no winners, only survivors.

Frank Gifford, Giants halfback, quoted in Sports Illustrated, *July 4, 1960*

He's fair. He treats us all the same—like dogs.

Henry Jordan, Green Bay Packers, recalled on Vince Lombardi's death, September 3, 1970

Till I was 13, I thought my name was "Shut Up."

Joe Namath, NY Jets, I Can't Wait until Tomorrow, *1969*

If a man watches three football games in a row, he should be declared legally dead.

Emma Bombeck, quoted by Phil Donahue, NBC-TV, May 22, 1986

Being a sports fan is a complex matter, in part irrational . . . but not unworthy . . . a relief from the seriousness of the real world, with its unending pressures and often grave obligations.

Richard Gilman, New York Times, *January 25, 1987*

SPORTS: BOXING

It's just a job. Grass grows, birds fly, waves pound the sand. I beat people up.

Muhammad Ali, New York Times, *April 6, 1977*

I am not an animal in my personal life. But in the ring there is an animal inside me. Sometimes it roars when the first bell rings. Sometimes it springs out later in a fight. But I can always feel it there, driving me forward. It is what makes me win. It makes me enjoy fighting.

Roberto Duran, welterweight champion, quoted in Newsweek, *June 23, 1980*

I know a lot of people think I'm dumb. Well, at least I ain't no educated fool.

Leon Spinks, Los Angeles Times, *June 28, 1978*

SPORTS: OLYMPIC

My mother was watching on television and she doesn't want me to hurt anyone.

George Foreman, boxing gold medalist, explaining why he didn't knock out his opponent, News Summaries, December 31, 1968

My head was exploding, my stomach ripping, and even the tips of my fingers ached. The only think I could think was, "If I live, I will never run again."

Tom Courtney, gold medalist, quoted in Life, *Summer 1984*

I was nervous, so I read the New Testament. I read the verse about have no fear, and I felt relaxed. Then I jumped farther than I ever jumped before in my life.

Willye White, silver medalist, women's long jump, quoted in Life, *Summer 1984*

SPORTS: TENNIS, GOLF, OTHER

This [defeat] has taught me a lesson, but I'm not sure what it is.

John McEnroe, New York Times, *February 9, 1987*

I just try to concentrate on concentrating.

Martina Navratilova, winner U.S. Open, quoted in US, *October 20, 1986*

People don't seem to understand that it's a damn war out there.

Jimmy Connors, quoted in Tutko and Bruns, Winning Is Everything and Other American Myths, *1976*

If you can react the same way to winning and losing, that . . . quality is important because it stays with you the rest of your life.

Chris Evert Lloyd, quoted in Saffire and Safir, Good Advice, *1982*

Tennis is a perfect combination of violent action taking place in an atmosphere of total tranquillity.

Billie Jean [King], 1974

You drive for show but putt for dough.

Bobby Locke, recalled on his death, March 9, 1987

[Playing golf] is like chasing a quinine pill around a cow pasture.

Winston Churchill, quoted in William Manchester, The Last Lion, *1983*

The game is my wife. It demands loyalty and responsibility, and it gives me back fulfillment and peace.

> *Michael Jordan, basketball player, quoted in* Newsweek,
> *January 5, 1987*

This fastest of all games [hockey] has become almost as much of a national symbol as the maple leaf.

> *Lester B. Pearson, Prime Minister of Canada, 1968*

[Spend a Buck] is good enough for me, [but] I won't say he's a superhorse because you're never a superhorse until you're retired.

> *Angel Cordero, Jr., on winning Kentucky Derby,* New York Times,
> *May 5, 1985*

The centre forward said, "It was an open goal—but I put it straight over the crossbar! I could kick myself!" And the manager said, "I wouldn't bother, you'd probably miss!"

> *Davis Frost, TVam, 1984*

Bravery is believing in yourself; . . . that nobody can teach you.

> *El Cordobés, Spanish matador, quoted in* Newsweek,
> *March 22, 1971*

I like the moment when I break a man's ego.

> *Bobby Fischer, chess champion,* Newsweek, *July 31, 1972*

In the America's Cup, you can't go to your backup quarterback. You can't juggle your batting order. . . . You can't fire the manager either, although Iain Murray might not be safe if George Steinbrenner were the principal owner of the *Kookaburra III.*

> *Dave Anderson, on the victory of the US yacht* Stars and Stripes,
> New York Times, *May 20, 1986*

STATE, HEADS OF

De Gaulle, President of France:
Treaties are like roses and girls: they last while they last.

> Time, *July 12, 1963*

When I want to know what France thinks, I ask myself.

> Ibid., *December 17, 1966*

You have to be sure that the Americans will commit all the stupidities they can think of, plus some that are beyond imagination.

> Ibid., *December 8, 1967*

Deng Xiaoping, Chinese Premier:
It doesn't matter if the cat is black or white, so long as it catches mice.

June 6, 1986

François ("Papa Doc") Duvalier, President of Haiti:
I know the Haitian people because I *am* the Haitian people.

In conversation

Dwight D. Eisenhower, U.S. President:
No one should ever sit in this office over 70 years old, and that I know.

Quoted in Newsweek, *March 2, 1987*

Mikhail S. Gorbachev, Soviet Premier:
Without glasnost there is not, and there cannot be, democratism, the political creativity of the masses and their participation in management.

Address to Party Congress, 1986, Time, *November 9, 1986*

Benjamin Harrison, U.S. President:
We Americans have no commission from God to police the world.

Address to Congress, 1888

Herbert Hoover, U.S. President:
When there is a lack of honor in government, the morals of the whole people are poisoned.

New York Times, *August 9, 1964*

Lyndon B. Johnson, U.S. President:
We have the opportunity to move not only toward the rich society and the powerful society, but upward to the Great Society.

Address, University of Michigan, May 22, 1964

Kenneth Kaunda, President of Zambia:
The power which establishes a state is violence; the power which maintains it is violence; the power which eventually overthrows it is violence.

Quoted in C.M. Morris, ed., Kaunda on Violence, *1980*

John F. Kennedy, U.S. President:
I hear it said that West Berlin is militarily untenable—and so was Bastogne, and so, in fact, was Stalingrad. Any danger spot is tenable if men—brave men—will make it so.

Address to the nation, July 25, 1961

If anyone is crazy enough to want to kill a president of the United States, he can do it. All he must be prepared to do is give his life for the president's.

Quoted in Pierre Salinger, With Kennedy, *1966*

Ayatollah Khomeini, spiritual leader of Iran:

One thing I congratulate everyone on is the great explosion which has occurred in Washington's Black House and the very important [Iran-Contra] scandal which has gripped leaders of America.

New York Times, *November 21, 1986*

Nikita S. Khrushchev, Soviet Premier:

I once said, "We will bury you," and I got into trouble with it. Of course, we will not bury you with a shovel. Your own working class will bury you.

Speech to Westerners, Split, Yugoslavia, August 24, 1963

Golda Meir, Prime Minister of Israel:

It is no accident that many accuse me of conducting public affairs with my heart instead of my head. Well, what if I do? . . . Those who don't know how to weep with their whole heart don't know how to laugh either.

Ms, *April 1973*

François Mitterand, President of France:

A man loses contact with reality if he is not surrounded by his books.

London Times, *May 10, 1982*

Richard M. Nixon, U.S. President:

Under the doctrine of separation of powers, the manner in which the president personally exercises his assigned executive powers is not subject to questioning by another branch of government.

Statement by the White House, May 12, 1973

Mohammed Reza Pahlavi, Shah of Iran:

My main mistake was to have made an ancient people advance by forced marches toward independence, health, culture, affluence, comfort.

Quoted on the occasion of his death, July 27, 1980

Muammar Qaddafi, Libyan head of state:

If Abu Nidal is a terrorist, then so is George Washington.

Newsweek, *January 20, 1986*

Ronald Reagan, U.S. President:

The freedom fighters of Nicaragua ... are the moral equivalent of
our Founding Fathers and the brave men and women of the French
Resistance.

*Speech, National Conservative Political Action Conference,
March 1, 1985*

I've often wondered how some people in positions of this kind ...
manage without having had any acting experience.

Interview with Barbara Walters, ABC-TV, March 24, 1986

Margaret Thatcher, Prime Minister of Great Britain:

What is success? I think it is a mixture of having a flair for the thing
you are doing; knowing that it is not enough, that you have got to
have hard work and a certain sense of purpose.

Parade, *July 13, 1986*

Harry S. Truman, U.S. President:

Any man who has had the job I've had and didn't have a sense of
humor wouldn't still be here.

New Summaries, April 19, 1955

STINGINESS: *See* BENEVOLENCE, GIVING.

STOICS AND EPICUREANS

O miserable minds of men! O blinded hearts! in what darkness of
living and in what dangers you pass this term of existence.... O not
to see that Nature for herself craves after nothing, save that pain
hold off from the body and that the mind experience pleasure free
from care and fear?

Lucretius, On the Nature of Things, *c. 300 B.C.*

To accept whatever comes regardless of the consequences is ... to
be full of that love which comes from a sense of at-one-ness with
whatever.

John Cage, Silence, *1961*

Wipe out imagination, check desire, extinguish appetite, keep the
ruling faculty uppermost.... Regarding death, be neither careless
nor impatient nor contemptuous, but wait for it as one of Nature's
procedures.

Marcus Aurelius, Meditations, *c. 150 A.D.*

The stoical scheme of supplying our wants by lopping off our desires
is like cutting off our feet when we want shoes.

Jonathan Swift, Thoughts on Various Subjects, *1711*

STORIES

I am always at a loss to know how much to believe of my own stories.

Washington Irving, Tales of a Traveler, *1824*

A touch of science, even bogus science, gives an edge to the super-
stitious tale.

V.S. Pritchett, The Living Novel, *1964*

The are several kinds of stories, but only one difficult kind—the
humorous.

Mark Twain, "How to tell a Story," 1895

And were an epitaph to be my story
I'd have a short one ready for my own.
I would have written for me on my stone:
I had a lover's quarrel with the world.

Robert Frost, The Lesson for Today, *1942*

STRANGERS/FOREIGNERS

Admiration for ourselves and our institutions is too often measured
by our contempt and dislike for foreigners.

William Ralph Inge, Outspoken Essays, *1919*

Ants and savages put strangers to death.

Bertrand Russell, Unpopular Essays, *1950*

America shudders at anything alien, and when it wants to shut its
mind against any man's ideas it calls him a foreigner.

Max Lerner, Actions and Passions, *1949*

Whoever live at a different end of the town from me, I look upon as
persons out of the world, and only myself and the scene about me
to be in it.

Jonathan Swift, Thoughts on Various Subjects, *1711*

When one is a stranger to oneself then one is estranged from others
too.

Anne Morrow Lindbergh, Gift from the Sea, *1955*

STRENGTH

If we are strong, our character will speak for itself. If we are weak, words will be of no help.

> *John F. Kennedy, undelivered address, Dallas, November 22, 1963*

What is strength without a double share of wisdom?

> *Milton,* Samson Agonistes, *1671*

Strong men can always afford to be gentle. Only the weak are intent on "giving as good as they get."

> *Elbert Hubbard,* The Note-Book, *1927*

So long as some are strong and some are weak, the weak will be driven to the wall.

> *Nietzsche,* Will to Power, *1888*

We confide in our strength, without boasting of it; we respect that of others, without fearing it.

> *Jefferson to William Carmichael and William Short, 1793*

For my people lending their strength to the years, the gone years and the now years and the maybe years.

> *Margaret Walker,* For My People, *1942*

(*See also* **COURAGE, WEAKNESS**)

STRIVING

To strive, to seek, to find, and not to yield.

> *Alfred, Lord Tennyson,* Ulysses, *1842*

To strive, to seek, *not* to find and not to yield.

> *Georges Duhamel,* Récits du temps de guerre, *1949*

[The sage] himself never strives for the great, and thereby the great is achieved.

> *Lao-tzu,* Tao te Ching, *c. 550 B.C.*

(*See also* **EFFORT, ZEAL**)

STRUGGLE

The struggle to reach the top is itself enough to fulfill the heart of man. We have to believe that Sisyphus was happy.

> *Albert Camus,* The Myth of Sisyphus, *1942*

If there is no struggle, there is no progress. Those who profess to favor freedom, and yet deprecate agitation, are men who want crops without plowing . . . [and] rain without thunder and lightning.

Frederick Douglass, in Blassingame, The Clarion Voice, *1976*

Need and struggle are what excite and inspire us; our hour of triumph is what brings the void. Not the Jews of the captivity, but those of the days of Solomon's glory are those from whom the pessimistic utterances in our Bible come.

William James, The Will to Believe, *1897*

Man was formed by his struggle with exterior forces, so only those things outside of himself can he readily discern.

Ortega y Gasset, The Modern Theme, *1923*

STRUGGLE FOR SURVIVAL

[The] state of universal warfare . . . is at bottom a most merciful provision. . . . Destruction of the . . . sickly, malformed, and least fleet [makes] room for a younger [vigorous] generation.

Herbert Spencer, Social Statics, *1850*

As more individuals are produced than can possibly survive, there must . . . be a struggle for existence, either one individual with another of the same species, or with the individuals of distinct species, or with the physical conditions of life.

Charles Darwin, Origin of Species, *1859*

Without the help of selfishness, the human animal would never have developed. Egoism is the vine by which man hoisted himself out of the swamp and escaped from the jungle.

Blaise Cendrars (d. 1961), Hors la Loi!

Social progress means a checking of the [evolutionary] process at every step and substituting for it . . . the ethical process, which is not the survival of those who happen to be the fittest . . . but of those who are ethically the best.

T.H. Huxley, Evolution and Ethics, *1893*

We are convinced that in the struggle for existence chance serves the weak as well as the strong [and] that cunning often prevails over strength. . . .

Nietzsche, Will to Power, *1888*

Mutual aid is as much the law of animal life as mutual struggle.
Peter Kropotkin, Mutual Aid, *1902*

(*See also* **EVOLUTION**)

STUDY

You have to study a great deal to know a little.
Montesquieu (d. 1755), Pensées et fragments inédits

You [wish] to know my views regarding liberal studies. . . . I deem no study good which results in money-making.
Seneca, Epistolae morales, *c. 50* A.D.

Study without a liking for it spoils the memory [which] retains nothing it takes in.
Leonardo da Vinci, Notebooks, *c. 1500*

As turning the logs will make a dull fire burn, so change of studies a dull brain.
Longfellow, Driftwood, *1857*

To be fond of learning is to be near to knowledge.
Tze-sze, The Doctrine of the Mean, *fifth century* B.C.

The thirst to know and understand,
A large and liberal discontent;
These are the goods in life's rich hand,
The things that are more excellent.
Sir William Watson, "Things That Are More Excellent," 1905

(*See also* **BOOKS, EDUCATION, LEARNING**)

STUPIDITY

Idiot, n. A member of a large and powerful tribe whose influence in human affairs has always been dominant and controlling.
Ambrose Bierce, The Devil's Dictionary, *1911*

There must always be some who're brighter and some who're stupider. The latter make up for it by being better workers.
Bertolt Brecht, Baal, *1926*

The hardest thing to cope with is not selfishness or vanity or deceit-fulness, but sheer stupidity.

> *Eric Hoffer,* The Passionate State of Mind, *1954*

Stupidity often saves a man from going mad.

> *Oliver Wendell Holmes,* The Autocrat of the Breakfast Table, *1858*

Whenever a man does a thoroughly stupid thing it is always from the noblest motive.

> *Oscar Wilde,* The Picture of Dorian Gray, *1891*

(*See also* **FOLLY, IGNORANCE, INTELLIGENCE**)

STYLE

. . . A simple way of saying complicated things.

> *Jean Cocteau,* Plain-chant, *1923*

. . . A peculiar recasting and heightening, under a certain condition of spiritual excitement, of what a man has to say, in such a manner as to add dignity and distinction to it.

> *Matthew Arnold,* On the Study of Celtic Literature, *1867*

A good style should show no signs of effort. What is written should seem a happy accident.

> *W. Somerset Maugham,* Summing Up, *1938*

The great writer finds style as the mystic finds Gods, in his own soul.

> *Havelock Ellis,* The Dance of Life, *1923*

If any man wish to write in a clear style, let him first be clear in his thoughts, and if any would write in a noble style, let him first possess a noble soul.

> *Goethe, in Eckermann's* Conversations, *April 14, 1824*

As to the adjective, when in doubt, strike it out.

> *Mark Twain,* Pudd'nhead Wilson, *1894*

In matters of grave importance, style, not sincerity, is the vital thing.

> *Oscar Wilde,* The Importance of Being Earnest, *1895*

A simple style is like white light. Although complex, it does not appear so.

> *Anatole France,* The Garden of Epicurus, *1894*

Read over your compositions, and wherever you meet with a passage which you think is particularly fine, strike it out.

Samuel Johnson, in Boswell's Life, *April 30, 1773*

A man's style is intrinsic and private with him like his voice or his gesture, partly a matter of inheritance, partly of cultivation. . . . More than a pattern of expression, it is the pattern of the soul.

Maurice Valency, Introduction to Jean Giraudoux: Four Plays, *1958*

Manner is all in all, whate'er is writ,
The substitute for genius, sense, and wit.

William Cowper, Table Talk, *1782*

Style is the perfection of a point of view.

Richard Eberhart, "Meditation Two," Selected Poems 1930–1965

The style is the man himself.

Buffon, Discourse on his reception into the French Academy, 1750

(*See also* **ELOQUENCE, LANGUAGE, WRITING**)

SUBURBS

Slums may well be breeding-grounds of crime, but middle-class suburbs are incubators of apathy and delirium.

Cyril Connolly, The Unquiet Grave, *1945*

Conformity may not always reign in the prosperous bourgeois suburb, but it ultimately always governs.

Louis Kronenberger, Company Manners, *1954*

Commuter—one who spends his life
In riding to and from his wife;
A man who shaves and takes a train
And then rides back to shave again.

E.B. White, "Commuter," 1929

(*See also* **AUTOMOBILITY**)

SUCCESS/FAILURE

To burn always with a hard gem-like flame, to maintain this ecstasy, is success in life.

Walter Pater, The Renaissance, *1873*

There is much to be said for failure. It is more interesting than success.

> *Max Beerbohm,* Mainly on the Air, *1946*

There is but one success—to be able to spend your life in your own way.

> *Christopher Morley,* Where the Blue Begins, *1922*

I think success has no rules, but you can learn a lot from failure.

> *Jean Kerr,* Mary, Mary, *1960*

The moral flabbiness born of the bitch-goddess SUCCESS. That— with the squalid interpretation put on the word success—is our national disease.

> *William James to H.G. Wells, September 11, 1906*

Success, which touches nothing that it does not vulgarize, should be its own reward . . . the ignominy of success is hard enough to bear without the added ignominy of popular applause.

> *Robert B. Cunninghame-Graham,* Success, *1902*

We are neurotically haunted today by the imminence, and by the ignominy, of failure. We know at how frightening a cost one *succeeds:* to fail is something too awful to think about.

> *Louis Kronenberger,* The Cart and the Horse, *1964*

Good people are good because they've come to wisdom through failure We get very little wisdom from success.

> *William Saroyan,* New York Journal-American, *August 23, 1961*

Failure makes people bitter and cruel. Success improves the character of the man.

> *W. Somerset Maugham,* The Summing Up, *1938*

Nothing is more humiliating than to see idiots succeed in enterprises we have failed in.

> *Flaubert,* Sentimental Education, *1869*

Success has ruined many a man.

> *Benjamin Franklin,* Poor Richard's Almanack

I attribute such success as I have had to the use of the periodic sentence.

> *Edmund Wilson, interview, 1962*

(*See also* **AMBITION**)

SUFFERING

He who fears he shall suffer, already suffers what he fears.

> *Montaigne*, Essays, *1588*

Pain and death are a part of life. To reject them is to reject life itself.

> *Havelock Ellis*, On Life and Sex, *1937*

What distinguishes man from his innocent brothers, the animals, . . . is not language, nor reason, nor even civilization, . . . it is man's enormous appetite for suffering.

> *Georges Duhamel (d. 1963)*, Biographie de mes fantômes

What really raises one's indignation against suffering is not suffering intrinsically, but the senselessness of suffering.

> *Nietzsche*, The Geneology of Morals, *1887*

No fear can stand up to hunger, no patience can wear it out, disgust simply does not exist where hunger is; and as to superstition, beliefs, and what you may call principles, they are less than chaff in a breeze.

> *Joseph Conrad*, Heart of Darkness, *1920*

We are healed from suffering only by experiencing it to the full.

> *Proust*, Albertine disparue, *1925*

Man has to suffer. When he has no real afflictions, he invents some.

> *José Marti*, Adulterous Thoughts, *1883*

Blessed art Thou, Lord, who giveth suffering
As a divine remedy for our impurities.

> *Baudelaire*, Les Fleurs du mal, *1861*

Out of my great woe
I make my little song.

> *Heinrich Heine (d. 1856)*, "Aus meinen grossen Schmerzen"

Oh, lift me as a wave, a leaf, a cloud!
I fall upon the thorns of life! I bleed!

> *Shelley*, "Ode to the West Wind," *1819*

We cannot live, suffer or die for somebody else, for suffering is too precious to be shared.

> *Edward Dahlberg*, Because I Was Flesh, *1963*

There is no greater error of Romanticism than the supposed usefulness of suffering.

> *Robert Brasillach (d. 1945),* Le Marchand d'oiseaux

Forget your personal tragedy. We are all bitched from the start and you especially have to be hurt like hell before you can write seriously. But when you get the damned hurt use it—don't cheat with it.

> *Hemingway, quoted in A. Turnbull's* Scott Fitzgerald, *1962*

All the reasoning in the world, all the proof-texts in old manuscripts, cannot reconcile this supposition of a world of sleepless and endless torment with the declaration that "God is love."

> *Oliver Wendell Holmes,* Over the Teacups, *1885*

Although the world is full of suffering, it is full also of the overcoming of it.

> *Helen Keller,* Optimism, *1903*

To be good we must needs have suffered; but perhaps it is necessary to have caused suffering before we can become better.

> *Maurice Maeterlinck, "The Invisible Goodness," 1896*

This is Daddy's little secret for today: Man is born broken. He lives by mending. The grace of God is glue.

> *Eugene O'Neill,* The Great God Brown, *1926*

Most people get a fair amount of fun out of their lives, but on balance life is suffering, and only the very young or the very foolish imagine otherwise.

> *George Orwell,* Shooting an Elephant, *1950*

Man's grandeur stems from his knowledge of his own misery. A tree does not know itself to be miserable.

> *Pascal* Pensées, *1670*

Clergymen and people who use phrases without wisdom sometimes talk of suffering as a mystery. It is really a revelation.

> *Oscar Wilde,* De Profundis, *1905*

Survivor—The cruelest of all afflictions.

> *Chateaubriand,* La Vie de Rancé, *1844*

(*See also* **ADVERSITY, FORTUNE, PLEASURE/PAIN**)

SUICIDE

Despair is not an idea, it's a thing, a thing that tortures, squeezes, and breaks a man's heart, . . . until he goes crazy and throws himself into the arms of death like the arms of a mother.

Alfred de Vigny, Chatterton, *1835*

A wholly psychological and almost incurable disease . . . attacks young, ardent, naive souls in love with the true and the beautiful, . . . who discover the evil and ugliness of society. . . . The disease is willful suicide.

Ibid.

There comes a time in the life of every young person when dying is just as normal and exciting as living.

Colette, Mes Apprentissages, *1936*

Suicide is . . . the sincerest form of criticism life gets.

Wilfred Sheed, The Good Word, *1978*

The moral constitution of any society determines the number of voluntary deaths. In each nation . . . there is a collective force, a certain amount of energy driving people to kill themselves.

Emile Durkheim, Le Suicide, *1897*

Killing time or killing yourself amounts to the same thing, strictly speaking.

Elsa Triolet (d. 1970), Mille regrets

The thought of suicide is a powerful comfort: it helps one through many a dreadful night.

Nietzsche, Beyond Good and Evil, *1886*

The man who, in a fit of melancholy, kills himself today, would have wished to live if he'd waited a week.

Voltaire, Philosophical Dictionary, *1764*

Cliffy the Clown says: You can help solve the OVERPOPULATION PROBLEM this quick, easy way! THIS YEAR, WHY NOT COMMIT SUICIDE? . . . Just leave a note telling your loved ones that you did it to help stave off worldwide famine and they will respect and admire you for your courage.

Robert Crumb, Zap: The Original Zap Comix, No. 6, *1973*

(See also **WORLD-WEARY***)*

SUITABILITY

Send not for a hatchet to break open an egg.

Thomas Fuller, Gnomologia, *1732*

Every beauty, when out of its place, is a beauty no longer.

Voltaire, Philosophical Dictionary, *1764*

Servants and ornaments are to be used only in their proper function.

Panchatantra, fifth century A.D.

SUPERFICIALITY

Anyone who has looked deeply into the world may guess how much wisdom lies in the superficiality of men. The instinct that preserves them teaches them to be flighty, light, and false.

Nietzsche, Beyond Good and Evil, *1886*

Only the shallow know themselves.

Oscar Wilde, "Phrases and Philosophies for the Use of the Young," 1891

(*See also* **ARTIFICIALITY, PROFOUNDITY**)

SUPERMAN/SUPERWOMAN

It is not in giving life but in risking it that man is raised above the animal; that is why superiority has been accorded in humanity not to the sex that brings forth but to that which kills.

Simone de Beauvoir, The Second Sex, *1950*

What do you suppose will satisfy the soul, except to walk free and own no superior?

Walt Whitman, "Laws for Creations," Leaves of Grass, *1892*

The superior man . . . does not set his mind either for or against anything; he will pursue whatever is right. . . . The superior man thinks of virtue, the common man of comfort.

Confucius (d. 479 B.C.), Analects

The mind of the superior man is like Heaven. When it is resentful or angry, it thunders forth its indignation. But once having loosed its feelings, it is like a sunny day with a clear sky. . . . Such is the beauty of true manliness.

Yoshida Shoin Zenshu, Sources of Japanese Tradition, *1960*

Sages are superior to other people only in their cleverness. The fact is that they were all imposters. Among them the least blameworthy was Confucius.

Motoori Noriaga, "Arrowroot," Sources of Japanese Tradition, 1960
in ibid

We are wrong to fear superiority of mind and soul; this superiority is very moral, for understanding everything makes one tolerant and the ability to feel deeply inspires great goodness.

Mme. de Stael, Corinne, 1807

There is nothing noble about being superior to some other person. The true nobility is in being superior to your previous self.

Hindustani proverb

The superior man is ... eyes for the blind, strength for the weak, and a shield for the defenseless. He stands erect by bending above the fallen. He rises by lifting others.

Robert Ingersoll, speech, Republican Convention, 1876

Man has become a superman ... he not only disposes of innate, physical forces, but he commands ... latent forces in nature, which he can put to his service. We are becoming inhuman.

Arthur Schopenhauer, speech, Nobel prize, 1954

I teach you the Overman *[Ubermensch]*. Man is something to be surpassed. What have you done to surpass him?

Nietzsche, Thus Spake Zarathustra, 1883

We're all asked to be Superwoman. I'm not asking it, our society does that. All I can tell you is that I believe it's a lot easier to write books while bringing up kids than to bring up kids while working nine to five plus housekeeping. But that is what our society, while sentimentalizing over Mom and the Family, demands of most women—unless it refuses them any work at all and dumps them onto welfare and says, Bring up your kids on food stamps, Mom, we might need them for the Army.

Ursula K. Le Guin, "The Hand That Rocks the Cradle
..." New York Times, Book Review, January 22, 1989

In our society ... those who are in reality superior in intelligence can be accepted by their fellows only if they pretend they are not.

Marya Mannes, More in Anger, 1958

(*See also* **EXCELLENCE, RANK**)

SUPERSTITION: *See* BELIEF.

SURVIVAL

Self-preservation is the first principle of our nature.

> *Alexander Hamilton,* A Full Vindication . . . , *1774*

Nature is indifferent to the survival of the human species, including Americans.

> *Adlai Stevenson, television speech, September 29, 1952*

Whether science—and indeed civilization in general—can long survive depends upon psychology, that is to say, it depends upon what human beings desire.

> *Bertrand Russell,* New York Times, *March 19, 1950*

(*See also* **DEFENSE, ENDURANCE**)

SWEARING

Swearing was invented as a compromise between running away and fighting.

> *Peter Finley Dunne,* Mr. Dooley's Opinions, *1900*

Madame Bovary is the sexiest book imaginable. The woman's virtually a nymphomaniac but you won't find a vulgar word in the entire thing.

> *Noel Coward,* Private Lives, *1930*

Heck on Earth. Heck is a place where God sends people when they say things like "Aw shoot!" instead of "shit." Visionaries see it as a warm cloakroom, or perhaps a bus terminal at 3:00 a.m. in August.

> *M. McCormick, P.J. O'Rourke, M. Civitello, "Sin Sundries,"* National Lampoon, *1981*

(*See also* **ANGER**)

SYMBOLS

An idea, in the highest sense of that word, cannot be conveyed but by a symbol.

> *Coleridge,* Biographia Literaria, *1817*

In a symbol there is concealment and yet revelation: here therefore, by Silence and by Speech acting together, comes a double significance.

> *Thomas Carlyle,* Sartor Resartus, *1834*

O to be a dragon,
a symbol of the power of Heaven—of silkworm
size or immense; at times invisible.
Felicitous phenomenon!

Marianne Moore, "O To Be a Dragon," 1959

SYMPATHY

When you live next to the cemetery, you can't weep for everyone.

Russian proverb

There is nothing sweeter than to be sympathized with.

George Santayana, The Life of Reason, *1905*

The comforter's head never aches.

Italian proverb

No one is so accursed by fate,
No one so utterly desolate,
But some heart, though unknown,
Responds unto his own.

Longfellow, "Endymion," 1842

When you are in trouble, people who call to sympathize are really looking for the particulars.

Edgar Watson Howe, Country Town Sayings, *1911*

Pity may represent little more than the impersonal concern which prompts the mailing of a check, but true sympathy is the personal concern which demands the giving of one's soul.

Martin Luther King, Jr., Strength to Love, *1963*

True love's the gift which God has given
To man alone beneath the heaven:

.   .   .   .

It is the secret sympathy,
The silver link, the silken tie,
Which heart to heart and mind to mind
In body and soul can bind.

Sir Walter Scott, "The Lay of the Last Minstrel," 1805

(*See also* **PITY, UNDERSTANDING**)

SYSTEMS

A system is nothing more than the subordination of all aspects of the universe to any one of such aspects.

Jorge Luis Borges, "Tlon, Uqbar, Orbis Tertius," Labyrinths, *1962*

I must create a system or be enslaved by another man's.

William Blake, Jerusalem, *1804*

I distrust all systematizers, and avoid them. The will to a system shows a lack of honesty.

Nietzsche, Twilight of the Idols, *1888*

The most ingenious method of becoming foolish is by a system.

Lord Shaftesbury, attributed

(*See also* **PHILOSOPHY, SCIENCE, THEORY**)

TACT

Silence is not always tact and it is tact that is golden, not silence.

Samuel Butler, Note-Books, *1912*

Talk to every woman as if you loved her, and to every man as if he bored you, and . . . you will have the reputation of possessing the most perfect social tact.

Oscar Wilde, A Woman of No Importance, *1893*

Some people mistake weakness for tact. If they are silent when they ought to speak and so feign an agreement they do not feel, they call it being tactful. Cowardice would be a much better name.

Frank Medlicott, Reader's Digest, *July 1958*

(*See also* **DIPLOMAT**)

TALENT

It takes little talent to see what is under one's nose, a good deal of it to know in what direction to point that organ.

W.H. Auden, The Dyer's Hand, *1962*

There is hardly anybody good for everything, and there is scarcely anybody who is absolutely good for nothing.

Lord Chesterfield, Letters to His Son, *January 2, 1748*

Talent is like a faucet; while it is open, you have to write. Inspiration?—a hoax fabricated by poets for their self-importance.

Jean Anouilh, New York Times *October 2, 1960*

Nothing is so frequent as to mistake an ordinary human gift for a special and extraordinary endowment.

Oliver Wendell Holmes, The Poet at the Breakfast Table, *1858*

Talent is a question of quantity. Talent does not write one page: it writes three hundred.

Jules Renard, Journal, *1887*

It is a very rare thing for a man of talent to succeed by his talent.

Joseph Roux, Meditations of a Parish Priest, *1886*

Mediocrity knows nothing higher than itself, but talent instantly recognizes genius.

Sir Arthur Conan Doyle, The Valley of Fear, *1915*

(*See also* **GENIUS**)

TALKING

Though I speak with the tongues of men and of angels, and have not love, I am become as sounding brass, or a tinkling cymbal.

Paul to the Corinthians I, 13:1

Talking is like playing on the harp; there is as much in laying the hand on the strings to stop their vibrations as in twanging them to bring out their music.

Oliver Wendell Holmes, The Autocrat of the Breakfast Table

Is there any place where there is no traffic in empty talk? Is there on this earth one who does not worship himself talking.

Kahlil Gibran, Thoughts and Meditations, *1960*

Talk doesn't cook rice.

Chinese proverb

A dog is not considered good because of his barking, and a man is not considered clever because of his ability to talk.

Chuang Tzu, Works, *fourth century* B.C.

One never repents of having spoken too little but often of having spoken too much.

> *Philippe de Commynes*, Mémoires, *1524*

Loquacity, n. A disorder which renders the sufferer unable to curb his tongue when you wish to talk.

> *Ambrose Bierce*, The Devil's Dictionary, *1911*

A great talker—he has the knack of telling you nothing in a big way.

> *Molière*, Le Misanthrope, *1666*

Talking and eloquence are not the same: to speak, and to speak well, are two things. A fool may talk, but a wise man speaks.

> *Ben Jonson*, Timber, *1640*

The eloquent man is he who is no beautiful speaker, but who is inwardly and desperately drunk with a certain belief.

> *Emerson*, Journals, *1845*

Tell it like it is! . . . That doesn't happen even twice a day in any big city. And is the listener any the less to blame than the speaker? No. Hence, not more than twice on any single day in any city is anyone fully understood.

> *Diderot*, Jack the Fatalist, *1770*

Blessed is the man who, having nothing to say, abstains from giving evidence of the fact.

> *George Eliot*, Impressions of Theophrastus Such, *1879*

(*See also* **SILENCE, SPEECH**)

TASTE

One man's poison ivy is another man's spinach.

> *George Ade*, Ready-Made Fables, *1920*

People care more about being thought to have good taste than about being thought good, clever, or amiable.

> *Samuel Butler (d. 1902)*, Note-Books

"Good taste"—a virtue of museum-keepers. If we scorn bad taste, we shall have neither painting nor dancing, neither palaces nor gardens.

> *Saint-Exupéry*, The Wisdom of the Sands, *1948*

One of the surest signs of the Philistine is his reverence for the superior taste of those who put him down.

> *Pauline Kael,* I Lost It at the Movies, *1965*

Taste is the fundamental quality which sums up all other qualities. It is the ne plus ultra of the intelligence.

> *Le Comte de Lautréamont,* Poésies, *1870*

Taste has no system and no proofs.

> *Susan Sontag,* "Notes on Camp," Against Interpretation, *1961*

Your right to wear a mint-green polyester leisure suit ends where it meets my eyes.

> *Fran Lebowitz,* Metropolitan Life, *1978*

Taste is the intermediate faculty which connects the active with the passive powers of our nature, the intellect with the senses; and its appointed function is to elevate the *images* of the latter, while it realizes the *ideas* of the former.

> *Coleridge,* On the Principles of Genial Criticism, *1814*

(*See also* **IDENTITY, INDIVIDUALISM, INTELLECT**)

TAXES

When everybody has got money they cut taxes, and when they're broke they raise 'em. That's statesmanship of the highest order.

> *Will Rogers,* Autobiography, *1949*

The Income Tax has made more Liars out of the American people than golf has.

> *Rogers,* The Illiterate Digest, *1924*

Taxes, after all, are the dues we pay for the privileges of membership in an organized society.

> *Franklin D. Roosevelt, speech, Wooster, Mass., October 21, 1936*

The point to remember is that what the government gives it must first take away.

> *John S. Coleman, Address, Detroit Chamber of Commerce, 1956*

Compared with other industrialized countries, the United States is undertaxed.

> *George F. Will, "This Week with David Brinkley," ABC-TV, November 1987*

The United States may become the first great power to falter because it lost its ability to collect taxes.

American Bar Association, Wall Street Journal, *April 10, 1984*

(*See also* **ECONOMY, GOVERNMENT**)

TEACHING

For every person wishing to teach there are thirty not wanting to be taught.

W.C. Sellar and R.J. Yeatman, And Now All This, *1932*

The true teacher defends his pupils against his own personal influence. . . . He guides their eyes from himself to the spirit that quickens him.

Amos Bronson Alcott, "Orphic Sayings," The Dial, *1840*

Teachers, who educate children, deserve more honor than parents, who merely gave them birth; for the latter provided mere life, while the former ensure a good life.

Aristotle, quoted in Diogenes Laertius's Lives

The whole art of teaching is simply the art of awakening the natural curiosity of young minds for the purpose of satisfying it afterwards.

Anatole France, The Crime of Sylvestre Bonnard, *1881*

A teacher, like a playwright, has an obligation to be interesting or, at least, brief. A play closes when it ceases to interest audiences.

Haim G. Ginott, Teacher and Child, *1972*

To teach is to learn twice.

Joseph Joubert, Pensées, *1842*

A man who knows a subject thoroughly, a man so soaked in it that he eats it, sleeps it, dreams it—this man can always teach it with success, no matter how little he knows of technical pedagogy.

H.L. Mencken, Prejudices: Third Series, *1922*

Too much rigidity on the part of teachers should be followed by a brisk spirit of insubordination on the part of the taught.

Agnes Repplier, Points of View, *1891*

A teacher who arouses a feeling in us for one good action, one good poem, accomplishes more than the teacher who fills our heads with interminable lists of natural objects.

Goethe, Elective Affinities, *1808*

More than half of all high school students in a national survey could not define basic economic terms like profit and inflation. . . . In a multiple-choice test given to more than 8,000 high school students last spring, only 25 percent gave the correct definition for inflation and [only] 45 percent could identify the term "government budget deficit."

Deirdre Carmody, New York Times, *December 30, 1988*

The new kind of teaching espoused by Rousseau and Dewey . . . encourages the natural development of the child on analogy with the development of an acorn into an oak. . . . [But] a child is not . . . an acorn. Left to itself, a child will not grow into a thriving creature. . . . A child needs to learn the traditions of the particular human society and culture it is born into.

E.D. Hirsch, Jr., Cultural Literacy, *1987*

(*See also* **EDUCATION, LEARNING**)

TECHNOLOGY

Sattinger's Law: It works better if you plug it in.
Arthur Bloch, Murphy's Law and Other Reasons Why Things Go Wrong, *1977*

When a machine begins to run without human aid, it is time to scrap it—whether it be a factory or a government.

Alexander Chase, Perspectives, *1966*

Man is still the most extraordinary computer of all.

John F. Kennedy, speech, May 21, 1963

By his very success in inventing labor-saving devices, modern man has manufactured an abyss of boredom that only the privileged class in earlier civilizations have ever fathomed.

Lewis Mumford, The Conduct of Life, *1951*

If the human race wants to go to hell in a basket, technology can help it get there by jet. It won't change the desire or the direction, but it can greatly speed the passage.

Charles M. Allen, speech, Wake Forest University, April 25, 1967

One has to look out for engineers—they begin with sewing machines and end up with the atomic bomb.

Marcel Pagnol, Critique des critiques, *1949*

Man must be at once more humble and more confident—more humble in the face of the destructive potentials of what he can achieve, more confident of his own humanity as against computers and robots. . . .

Max Lerner, "Manipulating Life," New York Post, *January 24, 1968*

The machine does not isolate man from the great problems of nature but plunges him more deeply into them.

Saint-Exupéry, Wind, Sand, and Stars, *1939*

Only science can hope to keep technology in some sort of moral order.

Edgar Z. Friedenberg, The Vanishing Adolescent, *1959*

If there is technological advance without social advance, there is, almost automatically, an increase in human misery.

Michael Harrington, The Other America, *1962*

Where there is the necessary technical skill to move mountains, there is no need for the faith that moves mountains.

Eric Hoffer, The Passionate State of Mind, *1954*

(*See also* **MACHINE AGE, SCIENCE**)

TEENAGERS: *See* CHILDREN, YOUTH

TELEVISION

. . . A medium—so called because it is neither rare nor well done.

Ernie Kovacs, in conversation

The new electronic interdependence recreates the world in the image of a global village.

Marshall McLuhan, The Medium is the Message, *1967*

Television is the first truly democratic culture—the first culture available to everyone and entirely governed by what the people want. The most terrifying thing is what people do want.

Clive Barnes, New York Times, *December 30, 1969*

Thanks to television, for the first time the young are seeing history made before it is censored by their leaders.

Margaret Mead (d. 1978), in conversation

There is no medical proof that television causes brain damage—at least from over five feet away. In fact, TV is probably the least physically harmful of all the narcotics known to man.
Christopher Lehmann-Haupt, New York Times, *September 24, 1969*

We can put it in its proper perspective by supposing that Gutenberg's great invention had been directed at printing only comic books.
Robert M. Hutchins, News Summaries, *December 31, 1977*

If the Barons of Bad Taste known as network executives believe in chastity as an anti-AIDS measure, it doesn't show on the soaps, night or day.
Martin F. Nolan, Boston Globe, *February 9, 1987*

Mental reflection is so much more interesting than TV, it's a shame more people don't switch over to it.
Robert M. Pirsig, Zen and the Art of Motorcycle Maintenance, *1974*

The hand that rules the press, the radio, the screen and the far-spread magazine, rules the country.
Learned Hand, Address, December 21, 1942

Each day a few more lies eat into the seed with which we are born, little institutional lies from the print of newspapers, the shock waves of television, and the sentimental cheats of the movie screen.
Norman Mailer, Advertisements for Myself, *1959*

(*See also* **CENSORSHIP, PRESS/MEDIA, TASTE**)

TEMPERAMENT

The tranquility or agitation of our temper does not depend so much on the big things which happen to us in life, as on the pleasant or unpleasant arrangements of the little things which happen daily.
La Rochefoucauld, Maxims, *1665*

Certainly there are good and bad times, but our mood changes more often than our fortune.
Jules Renard, Journal, *January 1905*

If health and a fair day smile upon me, I am a very good fellow; if a corn trouble my toe, I am sullen, out of humor, and inaccessible.
Montaigne, Essays, *1588*

(*See also* **CHARACTER, EMOTIONS, PERSONALITY**)

TEMPTATION

There are several good protections against temptations, but the surest is cowardice.

> *Mark Twain,* Following the Equator, *1897*

Why comes temptation but for man to meet
And master and make crouch beneath his foot,
And so be pedestaled in triumph?

> *Robert Browning,* The Ring and the Book, *1869*

When temptations march monotonously in regiments, one waits for them to pass.

> *Frank Moore Colby,* The Colby Essays, *1926*

Who will not judge him worthy to be robbed
That sets his doors wide open to a thief,
And shows the felon where his treasure lies?

> *Ben Jonson,* Every Man in His Humour, *1598*

(*See also* **CORRUPTION, SEDUCTION, SIN**)

TERROR

If the basis of popular government in peacetime is virtue, its basis in a time of revolution is virtue *and terror*—virtue, without which terror would be barbaric; and terror, without which virtue would be impotent.

> *Robespierre, speech, French National Convention, 1794*

Let a man once overcome his selfish terror at his own finitude, and his finitude is, in one sense, overcome.

> *Santayana,* The Ethics of Spinoza, *1910*

Science frees us in many ways . . . from the bodily terror which the savage feels. But she replaces that, in the minds of many, by a moral terror which is far more overwhelming.

> *Charles Kingsley, "The Meteor Shower," sermon, November 26, 1866*

Great men, great nations, have not been boasters and buffoons, but perceivers of the terror of life, and have manned themselves to meet it.

> *Emerson,* The Conduct of Life, *1860*

If peace and survival are to be achieved, the search must almost certainly go beyond the effort to find a balance in thermonuclear terror.

J.K. Galbraith, The Affluent Society, *1958*

THEATER/STAGE

A play should give you something to think about. When I see a play and understand it the first time, then I know it can't be much good.

T.S. Eliot, New York Post, *September 22, 1963*

Drama is action, sir, and not confounded philosophy.

Luigi Pirandello, Six Characters in Search of an Author, *1921*

Plays, gentlemen, are to their authors what children are to woman: they cost more pain than they give pleasure.

Beaumarchais, The Barber of Seville, *1775*

You need three things in the theatre—the play, the actors, and the audience, and each must give something.

Kenneth Haigh, Theatre Arts, *July 1958*

The theater . . . is not life in miniature, but life enormously magnified, life hideously exaggerated.

H.L. Mencken, Prejudices: First Series, *1919*

The structure of a play is always the story of how the birds came home to roost.

Arthur Miller, Harpers, *August 1958*

Every now and then, when you're on stage, you hear the best sound a player can hear. It's a sound you can't get in movies or in television. It is the sound of a wonderful, deep silence that means you've hit them where they live.

Shelley Winters, Theatre Arts, *June 1956*

There is as much difference between the stage and the film as between a piano and a violin. Normally you can't become a virtuoso in both.

Ethel Barrymore, New York Post, *June 7, 1856*

I see the playwright as a lay preacher peddling the ideas of his time in popular forms.

August Strindberg, Miss Julie, *1888*

On the stage it is always *now*, the personages are standing on that razor–edge between the past and the future, which is the essential character of conscious being.

Thornton Wilder, interview, Writers at Work, *1958*

The Happening operates by creating an asymmetrical network of surprises, without climax or consummation; this is the logic of dreams rather than the logic of most art.

Susan Sontag, Against Interpretation, *1961*

(*See also* **TRAGEDY/COMEDY**)

THEOLOGY

. . . an attempt to explain a subject by men who do not understand it. The intent is not to tell the truth but to satisfy the questioner.

Elbert Hubbard, The Philistine, *1915*

Theology moves back and forth between two poles, the eternal truth of its foundations and the temporal situation in which the eternal truth must be received.

Paul Tillich, Systematic Theology, *1951*

The theologian who has no joy in his work is not a theologian at all. Sulky faces, morose thoughts, and boring ways of speaking are intolerable in this science.

Karl Barth, New York Times, *December 11, 1968*

The most tedious of all discourses are on the subject of the Supreme Being.

Emerson, Journals, *1836*

Theological religion is the source of all imaginable follies and disturbances; it is the parent of fanaticism and civil discord; it is the enemy of mankind.

Voltaire, Philosophical Dictionary, *1764*

(*See also* **GOD, RELIGION**)

THEORY

Theory helps us bear our ignorance of facts.

Santayana, The Sense of Beauty, *1896*

It is so much easier to talk of poverty than to think of the poor, to argue the rights of capital than to see its results. Pretty soon we come to think of the theories and abstract ideas as things in themselves.

Walter Lippmann, A Preface to Politics, *1914*

The intention of a theory . . . is to summarize existing knowledge, to provide an explanation for observed events . . . and to predict the occurrences of [future] events. . . .

Claire Selltiz, et al., Research Methods in Social Relations, *1959*

The astonishment of life is the absence of any appearance of reconciliation between the theory and the practice of life.

Emerson, Journals, *1844*

No theory is good except on condition that one use it to go beyond.

André Gide, Journals, *August 5, 1931*

Hypotheses are only the pieces of scaffolding during the course of construction, and which are taken away as soon as the edifice is finished.

Goethe (d. 1832), in M. Ludovici, Nietzsche, The Will to Power

It is better to emit a scream in the shape of a theory than to be entirely insensible to the jars and incongruities of life and take everything as it comes in a forlorn stupidity.

Robert Louis Stevenson, "Crabbed Age and Youth," Virginibus Puerisque, *1881*

(*See also* **FACTS, SCIENCE, SYSTEMS**)

THERAPY

The patient must learn to live with his [neurosis], his conflict, his ambivalence, which no therapy can take away, for if it did it would take with it the actual wellspring of life.

Otto Rank, Austrian psychoanalyst, d. 1939

[Psychoanalysis] is not the only way to resolve inner conflicts. Life itself still remains a very effective therapist.

Karen Horney, Our Inner Conflicts, *1945*

Show me a sane man and I will cure him for you.

C.G. Jung, London Observer, *July 19, 1975*

(*See also* **PSYCHOANALYSIS, PSYCHIATRY**)

THINKING

Deliberation, n. The act of examining one's bread to determine which side it is buttered on.

> *Ambrose Bierce*, The Devil's Dictionary, *1911*

Two kinds of people: . . . those who think and those who don't; the difference comes almost entirely from education.

> *Rousseau*, Emile, *1762*

What is the hardest task in the world? To think.

> *Emerson*, Journals, *1836*

The real problem is not whether machines think but whether men do.

> *B.F. Skinner*, Contingencies of Reinforcement, *1969*

Sometimes I think and other times I am.

> *Paul Valéry*, Variété: Cantiques spirituels, *1924*

What was once thought can never be unthought.

> *Friedrich Dürrenmatt*, The Physicist, *1962*

If a man sits down to think, he is immediately asked if he has a headache.

> *Emerson*, Journals, *1833*

The shrewd guess, the fertile hypothesis, the courageous leap to a tentative conclusion—these are the most valuable coin of the thinker at work.

> *Jerome D. Bruner*, The Process of Education, *1960*

Thinking in its lower grades is comparable to paper money, and in its higher forms it is a kind of poetry.

> *Havelock Ellis*, The Dance of Life, *1923*

To see clearly is poetry, prophecy, and religion— all in one.

> *John Ruskin*, Modern Painters, *1843*

We do not live to think, but, on the contrary, we think in order that we may succeed in surviving.

> *Ortega y Gasset, "In Search of Goethe from Within,"* Partisan Review, *December 1949*

To meditate is to labor; to think is to act.

> *Victor Hugo*, Les Misérables, *1862*

The average man never really thinks from end to end of his life. The mental activity of such people is only a mouthing of clichés.

> *H.L. Mencken*, Prejudices, *1925*

Thinking is the most unhealthy thing in the world and people die of it just as they die of any other disease.

> *Oscar Wilde, "The Decay of Lying,"* Intentions, *1891*

The secret isolated joy of the thinker, who knows that, a hundred years after he is dead and forgotten, men who never heard of him will be moving to the measure of his thought. . . .

> *Oliver Wendell Holmes, Jr.,* The Professor of the Law, *1886*

(*See also* **IDEAS, INTELLECTUAL, PHILOSOPHY**)

THOUGHT(S)

The secret thoughts of a man run over all things, holy, profane, clean, obscene, grave, and light, without shame or blame.

> *Thomas Hobbes,* Leviathan, *1651*

Every real thought on every real subject knocks the wind out of somebody or other.

> *Oliver Wendell Holmes,* The Autocrat of the Breakfast Table, *1858*

Thoughts, like fleas, jump from man to man. But they don't bite everybody.

> *Stanislaw Lec,* Unkempt Thoughts, *1962*

The thoughts that come often unsought, and, as it were, drop into the mind, are commonly the most valuable of any we have.

> *John Locke to Samuel Bold, May 16, 1699*

All the mind's activity is easy if it is not subjected to reality.

> *Proust,* Remembrance of Things Past: Cities of the Plain

Profundity of thought belongs to youth, clarity of thought to old age.

> *Nietzsche,* Miscellaneous Maxims and Opinions, *1878*

My thoughts are my trollops.

> *Diderot,* Le Neveu de Rameau, *1760*

Security, for me, took a tumble not when I read that there were Communists in Hollywood but when I read your editorial in praise of loyalty testing and thought control. If a man is in health, he doesn't need to take anybody else's temperature to know where he is going.

E.B. White to the New York Herald Tribune, November 29, 1947

(*See also* **INTELLIGENCE, MIND, REVERIE**)

THRIFT

A penny saved is a penny to squander.

Ambrose Bierce, The Devil's Dictionary, 1911

Let us all be happy and live within our means, even if we have to borrow money to do it with.

Artemus Ward, "Science and Natural History," 1872

Men do not realize how great an income thrift is.

Cicero, Paradoxa stoicorum, 46 B.C.

Economy, in the estimation of common minds, often means the absence of all taste and comfort.

Sydney Smith, in Lady S. Holland's Memoir, 1855

Anyone who lives within his means suffers from a lack of imagination.

Lionel Stander, quoted in Playboy, December 1967

(*See also* **ECONOMY**)

TIME

Gather ye rosebuds while ye may,
Old time is still a-flying,
And that same flower that smiles today
Tomorrow will be dying.

Robert Herrick, "To the Virgins to Make Much of Time," 1648

To everything there is a season, and a time to every purpose under the heaven. A time to be born, and a time to die; a time to plant and a time to pluck up that which is planted.

Ecclesiastes 3:1–2

Killing time is the chief end of our society.

Ugo Betti, The Fugitive, 1953

Time lost is time when we have not lived a full human life, time un-enriched by experience, creative endeavor, enjoyment, and suffering.

> *Dietrich Bonhoffer*, Letters and Papers from Prison, *1953*

Time is the only true purgatory.

> *Samuel Butler*, Note-Books, *1912*

What is a thousand years? Time is short for one who thinks, endless for one who yearns.

> *Alain (d. 1951)*, Histoire de mes pensées

One's prime is elusive. You little girls, when you grow up, must be on the alert to recognize your prime at whatever time of your life it may occur.

> *Muriel Spark*, The Prime of Miss Jean Brodie, *1962*

The time, the people, and the individual converge only once.

> *Hélène Cixous*, Dedans, *1969*

You cannot step into the same river twice.

> *Heraclitus (fl. 450 B.C.), in Diogenes Laertius*, Lives

I need so much time for doing nothing that I have no time for work.

> *Pierre Reverdy*, Le Livre de mon bord, *1948*

Seize the day! Put no trust in the morrow.

> *Horace*, Odes, *23 B.C.*

Happy the man, and happy he alone,
He who can call today his own;
He who, secure within, can say,
Tomorrow, do thy worst, for I have lived today.

> *John Dryden*, Imitation of Horace, *1685*

Time! The Corrector where our judgments err,
The test of Truth, Love—sole philosopher,
For all beside are sophists.

> *Byron*, Childe Harold's Pilgrimage, *1818*

It is familiarity with life that makes time speed quickly. When every day is a step in the unknown, as for children, the days are long with gathering of experience.

> *George Gissing*, "Winter," The Private Papers of Henry Ryecroft,
> *1903*

There is one kind of robber whom the law does not strike at, and who steals what is most precious to men: time.

> *Napoleon I*, Maxims, *1815*

Time heals griefs and quarrels, for we change and are no longer the same person.

> *Pascal*, Pensées, *1670*

It seems no more than right that men should seize time by the forelock, for the rude old fellow, sooner or later, pulls all their hair out.

> *George Dennison Prentice*, Prenticeana, *1860*

In theory one is aware that the earth revolves, but in practice one does not perceive it, the ground upon which one treads seems not to move, and one can live undisturbed. So it is with Time in one's life.

> *Proust*, The Past Recaptured, *1927*

Half our life is spent trying to find something to do with the time we have rushed through life trying to save.

> *Will Rogers*, Autobiography, *1949*

Both in thought and feeling, even though time is real, to realize the unimportance of time is the gate of wisdom.

> *Bertrand Russell*, Mysticism and Logic, *1917*

Time is the longest distance between two places.

> *Tennessee Williams*, The Glass Menagerie, *1945*

. . . Nothing can bring back the hour
Of splendor in the grass, of glory in the flower.

> *Wordsworth, "Intimations of Immortality," 1807*

Time, which strengthens friendship, weakens love.

> *La Bruyère*, Characters, *1688*

Time, whose tooth gnaws away everything else, is powerless against truth.

> *T.H. Huxley*, Administrative Nihilism, *1871*

Radicals who would take us back to the roots of things often fail because they disregard the fruit Time has produced and preserved. Conservatives fail because they would preserve even what Time has decomposed.

> *Louis D. Brandeis*. Works, *ed. Solomon Goldman, 1954*

(*See also* **ENDURANCE, FUTURE, PAST, PRESENT**)

TIMIDITY

Happiness hates the timid. So does science!

Eugene O'Neill, Strange Interlude, *1928*

If you are reluctant to ask the way, you will be lost.

Malay proverb

Do not be too timid and squeamish about your actions. All life is an experiment.

Emerson, Journals, *1842*

He who is afraid of every nettle should not piss in the grass.

Thomas Fuller, Gnomologia, *1732*

He will never have true friends who is afraid of making enemies.

William Hazlitt, Characteristics, *1823*

(*See also* **COURAGE, FEAR**)

TODAY: *See* **PRESENT, TWENTIETH CENTURY**

TOLERANCE/INTOLERANCE

Be born anywhere, . . . little novelist, but not under the shadow of a great creed, not under the burden of original sin, not under the doom of Salvation.

Pearl Buck (d. 1973), Advice to Unborn Novelists

The equal toleration of all religions . . . is the same thing as atheism.

Pope Leo XIII, Immortale Dei, *1885*

Give tidings, O Mohammed, of agonizing death to disbelievers. . . . Slay the idolaters wherever you find them. . . . Fight them until all persecution has ended and all religions are Allah's.

The Koran, A.D. *651*

The peak of tolerance is most readily achieved by those who are not burdened with convictions.

Alexander Chase, Perspectives, *1966*

Persecution was at least a sign of personal interest. Tolerance is composed of nine parts of apathy to one of brotherly love.

Frank Moore Colby, The Colby Essays, *1926*

(*See also* **CHARITY, HATRED, SYMPATHY**)

TOTALITARIANISM: *See* DESPOTISM, FASCISM

TRADITION

A love for tradition has never weakened a nation, indeed it has strengthened nations in their hour of peril.

Winston Churchill, speech, House of Commons, 1944

The antiquity and general acceptance of an opinion is no assurance of its truth.

Pierre Bayle, Thoughts on the Comet, *1682*

Tradition grows ever more venerable—the more remote its origin the more confused the origin is. The reverence due to it increases from generation to generation, until it becomes holy and inspires awe.

Nietzsche, Human All Too Human, *1878*

A tradition without intelligence is not worth having.

T.S. Eliot, "After Strange Gods," 1934

Remove not the ancient landmark, which the fathers have set.

Proverbs 22:28

It is pure illusion to think that an opinion which passes down from century to century, from generation to generation, may not be entirely false.

Pierre Bayle, Thoughts on the Comet, *1682*

The dead govern the living.

Auguste Comte, Catéchisme positiviste, *1852*

Hardened round us, encasing wholly every notion we form, is a wrappage of traditions, hearsays, mere words.

Thomas Carlyle, Heroes and Hero Worship, *1841*

Few people have ever seriously wished to be exclusively rational. The good life which most desire is a life warmed by passions and touched with that ceremonial grace which is impossible without some affectionate loyalty to traditional forms and ceremonies.

Joseph Wood Krutch, The Measure of Man, *1954*

(*See also* CUSTOMS, HISTORY, PAST)

TRAGEDY/COMEDY

Comedy, the intuition of the absurd, seems to me more heart-rending than tragedy.

Eugène Ionesco, Notes and Contrenotes, *1963*

In tragedy every moment is eternity; in comedy, eternity is a moment.

Christopher Fry, Time, *November 20, 1950*

Tragedy and comedy are simply questions of value; a little misfit in life makes us laugh; a great one is tragedy and cause for expressions of grief.

Elbert Hubbard, The Note-Book, *1927*

If tragedy is an experience of hyperinvolvement, comedy is an experience of underinvolvement, of detachment.

Susan Sontag, "Notes on Camp," Against Interpretation, *1961*

It is very difficult to be wholly joyous or wholly sad on this earth. The comic, when it is human, soon takes upon itself the face of pain.

Joseph Conrad, A Personal Record, *1912*

A tragedy means always a man's struggle with that which is greater than man.

G.K. Chesterton, Outline of Sanity, *1926*

Only a great mind overthrown yields tragedy.

Jacques Barzun, The House of Intellect, *1959*

Writers of comedy have outlook, whereas writers of tragedy have, according to them, insight.

James Thurber, Lanterns and Lances, *1961*

All tragedies are finished by a death,
All comedies are ended by a marriage.

Byron, Don Juan, *1824*

Tragedy is restful: and the reason is that hope, that foul, deceitful thing, has no part in it.

Jean Anouilh, Antigone, *1942*

Why is it that man desires to be made sad, beholding doleful and tragical things, which yet himself would by no means suffer?

St. Augustine, Confessions, *c. A.D. 420*

A tragic situation exists precisely when virtue does *not* triumph but when it is still felt that man is nobler than the forces which destroy him.

George Orwell, Shooting an Elephant, *1950*

Killing time is perhaps the essence of comedy, just as the essence of tragedy is killing eternity.

Miguel de Unamuno (d. 1936), San Manuel Bueno

Definition of tragedy: A hero destroyed by the excess of his virtues. . . . It is the business of the tragic poet to give audiences the pleasure which arises from pity and terror. . . .

Aristotle, Poetics, *c. 330 B.C.*

(*See also* **THEATER/STAGE**)

TRAINING

Train up a child in the way he should go; and when he is old he will not depart from it.

Proverbs, 22:6

Train up a fig tree in the way it should go, and when you are old sit under the shade of it.

Charles Dickens, Dombey and Son, *1848*

It is not difficult to beget children; but after they are born begins the trouble, the worry, and the care to properly train them.

Montaigne, "Education of Children," Essays, *1588*

Man is the only creature that knows nothing and can learn nothing without being taught. He cannot speak nor walk nor eat; in short, he can do nothing at the prompting of nature—but yell.

Pliny the Elder, Natural History, *first century*

'Tis education forms the common mind,
Just as the twig is bent the tree's inclined.

Alexander Pope, Moral Essays, *1735*

(*See also* **DISCIPLINE, EDUCATION, GROWTH AND DEVELOPMENT**)

TRANQUILITY

There's naught, no doubt, so much the spirit calms
As rum and true religion.

Lord Byron, Don Juan, *1824*

When we are unable to find tranquility within ourselves, it is useless to seek it elsewhere.

La Rochefoucauld, Maxims, *1665*

Back of tranquility lies always conquered unhappiness.

David Grayson, Adventures in Contentment, *1907*

If you want inner peace find it in solitude, . . . and if you would find yourself, look to the land from which you came and to which you go.

Stuart L. Udall, The Quiet Crisis, *1963*

(*See also* **MODERATION, PEACE, REST**)

TRANSIENCE

As for man, his days are as grass: as a flower of the field, so he flourisheth.

Psalms 103:15

Loveliest of lovely things are they,
On earth, that soonest pass away.

William Cullen Bryan, "A scene on the Bank of the Hudson," 1827

What a day may bring a day may take away.

Thomas Fuller, Gnomologia, *1732*

A permanent state of transition is man's most noble condition.

Juan Ramón Jiménez, "Heroic Reason," 1957

The world is fleeting; all things pass away;
Or is it we that pass and they that stay?

Lucian, c. A.D. 200

(*See also* **CHANGE, MORTALITY, TIME**)

TRANSLATING

The art of translation lies less in knowing the other language than in knowing your own.

Ned Rorem, Music from Inside Out, *1967*

What is most difficult to render from one language to another is the tempo of its style.

Nietzsche, Beyond Good and Evil, *1886*

It were as wise to cast a violet into a crucible that you might discover the formal principle of its colour and odour, as seek to transfuse from one language into another the creation of a poet.

Shelley, A Defence of Poetry, *1821*

A translation from one language to another should read as if it had been originally written in the second language.

Jacques Barzun, in conversation

(*See also* **LANGUAGE**)

TRAVEL

If an ass goes traveling he will not come home a horse.

Thomas Fuller, Gnomologia, *1732*

In traveling, a man must carry knowledge with him if he would bring home knowledge.

Samuel Johnson, in Boswell's Life, *April 17, 1778*

Traveling is not just seeing the new; it is also leaving behind. Not just opening doors; also closing them behind you, never to return. But the place you have left forever is always there for you to see whenever you shut your eyes.

Jan Myrdal, The Silk Road, *1980*

Travel is the most private of pleasures. There is no greater bore than the travel bore. We do not in the least want to hear what he has seen in Hong Kong.

Vita Sackville-West (d. 1962), Passage to Teheran

No man should travel until he has learned the language of the country he visits. Otherwise he voluntarily makes himself a great baby,—so helpless and so ridiculous.

Emerson, Journals, *1833*

As a member of an escorted tour you don't even have to know the Matterhorn isn't a tuba.

Temple Fielding, Fielding's Guide to Europe, *1963*

You define a good flight by negatives: you didn't get hijacked, you didn't crash, you didn't throw up, you weren't late, you weren't nauseated by the food. So you're grateful.

Paul Théroux, The Old Patagonian Express, *1979*

(*See also* **AUTOMOBILITY, CULTURE, CUSTOMS**)

TREES

No town can fail of beauty, though its walks were gutters and its houses hovels, if venerable trees make magnificent colonnades along it streets.

> *Henry Ward Beecher,* Proverbs, *1887*

Why are there trees I never walk under
But large and melodious thoughts descend upon me?

> *Walt Whitman,* Leaves of Grass, *1892*

The forest is the poor man's overcoat.

> *New England proverb*

One could do worse than be a swinger of birches.

> *Robert Frost, "Birches," 1916*

The planting of trees is the least self-centered of all that we do. It is a purer act of faith than the procreation of children.

> *Thornton Wilder,* The Eighth Day, *1967*

Any fine morning a power saw can fell a tree that took a thousand years to grow.

> *Edwin Way Teale,* Autumn Across America, *1956*

(*See also* **MAN, NATURE**)

TROUBLE

there is bound to be a certain amount of
trouble running any country
if you are president the trouble happens to you
but if you are a tyrant you can arrange things so
that most of the trouble happens to other people

> *Don Marquis,* archy does his part, *1935*

I am most willing to answer all questions about myself. . . . But I am not willing, now or in the future, to bring bad trouble to people who, in my past association with them, were completely innocent of any talk or any action that was disloyal or subversive.

> *Lillian Hellman, letter to the House Committee on*
> *Un-American Activities, May 19, 1952*

(*See also* **ADVERSITY**)

TRUST

She knew how to trust people, . . . a rare quality, revealing a character far above average.
> *Cardinal de Retz,* Mémoires, *1718*

Trust ivrybody—but cut th' ca-ards.
> *Finley Peter Dunne,* Mr. Dooley's Philosophy, *1900*

Confidence is the only bond of friendship.
> *Publius Syrus,* Moral Sayings, *c. 50 B.C.*

A man who doesn't trust himself can never trust anyone else.
> *Cardinal de Retz,* Mémoires, *1718*

Trust yourself only, and another shall not betray thee.
> *Thomas Fuller,* Gnomologia, *1732*

The blessings-of-civilization trust, wisely and cautiously administered, is a daisy. There is more money in it, more territory, more sovereignty, and other kinds of emolument, than there is in any other game that is played. But Christendom . . . has been so eager to get every stake that appeared on the green cloth, that the people who sit in darkness have noticed it . . . and have become suspicious of the blessings of civilization.
> *Mark Twain,* To the Person Sitting in Darkness, *1901*

(*See also* **DISTRUST**)

TRUTH

Artistic growth is, more than it is anything else, a refining of the sense of truthfulness. The stupid believe that to be truthful is easy; only the artist, the great artist, knows how difficult it is.
> *Willa Cather,* The Song of the Lark, *1915*

Truth exists, only lies have to be invented.
> *George Braque (d. 1963),* Pensées sur l'art

Respect for the truth is an acquired taste.
> *Mark Van Doren,* Liberal Education, *1943*

The truth is rarely pure and never simple. Modern life would be very tedious if it were either, and modern literature a complete impossibility.
> *Oscar Wilde,* The Importance of Being Earnest, *1895*

If you do not tell the truth about yourself you cannot tell it about other people.

> *Virginia Woolf*, The Moment and Other Essays, *1948*

There is no such thing as absolute truth. . . . People are less deceived by failing to see the truth than by failing to see its limits.

> *Sénac de Meilhan (d. 1803)*, Histoire de la Vicomtesse de Vassy

I speak the truth, not quite my fill of it, but as much as I dare, and I dare a little more as I grow older.

> *Montaigne*, Essays, *1580*

When truth is buried, it grows, it chokes, it gathers such explosive force that on the day it breaks out, it blows everything up with it.

> *Emile Zola, "J'accuse!"* L'Aurore, *January 13, 1898*

All great truths begin as blasphemies.

> *G.B. Shaw*, Annajanska, *1919*

The great enemy of the truth is very often not the lie—deliberate, contrived, and dishonest—but the myth—persistent, persuasive, and unrealistic.

> *John F. Kennedy, Address, Yale University, 1962*

Pushing any truth out very far, you are met by a counter-truth.

> *Henry Ward Beecher*, Proverbs, *1887*

The truth shall make you free.

> *John 8:32*

We say that the truth will make us free. Yes, but that truth is a thousand truths which grow and change.

> *Walter Lippmann*, A Preface to Politics, *1914*

Some men love truth so much that they seem to be in continual fear lest she should catch cold from overexposure.

> *Samuel Butler*, Note-Books, *1912*

As time goes on, new and remoter aspects of truth are discovered which can seldom be fitted into creeds that are changeless.

> *Clarence Day*, This Simian World, *1926*

Truth is what most contradicts itself.

> *Lawrence Durrell*, Balthazar, *1958*

Ethical axioms are found and tested not very differently from the axioms of science. Truth is what stands the test of experience.

Einstein, Out of My Later Years, *1950*

Truth may sometimes come out of the Devil's mouth.

Thomas Fuller, Gnomologia, *1732*

Say not, "I have found the truth," but rather, "I have found *a* truth."

Kahlil Gibran, The Prophet, *1923*

One truth discovered, one pang of regret at not being able to express it, is better than all the fluency and flippancy in the world.

William Hazlitt, The Plain Speaker, *1826*

Add a few drops of venom to a half truth and you have an absolute truth.

Eric Hoffer, The Passionate State of Mind, *1954*

Truth is tough. It will not break, like a bubble, at a touch, nay, you may kick it about all day like a football, and it will be round and full at evening.

Oliver Wendell Holmes, The Professor at the Breakfast Table

It is the customary fate of new truths to begin as heresies and end as superstitions.

T.H. Huxley, "The Coming of Age of The Origin of Species," *1880*

To me the truth is something that cannot be told in a few words, and those who simplify the universe only reduce the expansion of its meaning.

Anaïs Nin, Diary, *winter 1931–32*

They all want the truth—*a* truth, that is: Something specific, something concrete! They don't care what it is. All they want is something categorical, something that speaks plainly!

Luigi Pirandello, It Is So! (If You Think So), *1917*

Truth often suffers more by the heat of its defenders than from the arguments of its opposers.

William Penn, Some Fruits of Solitude, *1693*

The truths of the past are the clichés of the present.

Ned Rorem, Music from Inside Out, *1967*

You will find that the truth is often unpopular. . . . For, in the vernacular, we Americans are suckers for good news.

> *Adlai Stevenson,* New York Times, *June 9, 1958*

Nowadays flattery wins friends, truth hatred.

> *Terence,* The Woman of Andros, *166 B.C.*

Truth is mighty and will prevail. There is nothing the matter with this, except that it ain't so.

> *Mark Twain,* Notebook, *1935*

Truth is more of a stranger than fiction.

> *Ibid.*

Heaven knows what seeming nonsense may not tomorrow be demonstrated truth.

> *Alfred North Whitehead,* Science and the Modern World, *1925*

Truth is naked—too naked—she doesn't turn men on.

> *Jean Cocteau (d. 1963),* Le Coq et l'Arlequin

(*See also* **ERROR, MYTH**)

TRUTH VS. FALSEHOOD

There are no whole truths: all truths are half-truths. It is trying to treat them as whole truths that plays the devil.

> *Alfred North Whitehead,* Dialogues, *1954*

Let [Truth] and Falsehood grapple; who ever knew Truth put to the worse, in a free and open encounter.

> *John Milton,* Areopagitica, *1644*

When war is declared, truth is the first casualty.

> *Arthur Ponsonby,* Falsehood in Wartime, *1928*

Sometimes it is easier to see clearly into a liar than into a person telling the truth. Truth, like light, is blinding. Falsehood, on the other hand, is a beautiful twilight that enhances every object.

> *Albert Camus,* The Fall, *1957*

A peace-mingling falsehood is preferable to a mischief-stirring truth.

> *Sa'di,* Gulistan, *1258*

The crude commercialism of America, . . . its indifference to the poetical side of things, and its lack of imagination . . . are entirely due to that country having adopted for its national hero a man who, according to his own confession, was incapable of telling a lie.

Oscar Wilde, "The Decay of Lying," 1889

George Washington and the cherry tree has done more harm . . . than any other moral tale in the whole of literature. . . . And the amusing part of the whole thing is that the story of the cherry tree is an absolute myth.

Ibid.

(*See also* **ERROR**)

TRUTH, TEST OF

The ultimate test of what a truth means is the conduct which it dictates or inspires.

William James, Pragmatism, *1907*

There is no permanent absolute unchangeable truth; what we should pursue is the most convenient arrangement of our ideas.

Samuel Butler (d. 1902), Note Books, *1912*

Rational man . . . has a deeply rooted distrust of eternal verities; while he will never deny that they are indispensable, he is convinced that people who take them literally are mad.

Robert Musil, The Man without Qualities, *1930*

To attain the truth in all things, we ought always to believe that what seems white is black if the Hierarchical Church so defines it.

Ignatius Loyola, Spiritual Exercises, *1548*

(*See also* **DOUBT/CERTAINTY, SKEPTICISM**)

TWENTIETH CENTURY

The twentieth century seems afflicted by a gigantic . . . power failure. Powerlessness and the sense of powerlessness may be the environmental disease of the age.

Russell Baker, New York Times, *May 1, 1969*

It is easy enough to praise men for the courage of their convictions. I wish I could teach the sad young of this mealy generation the courage of their confusions.

John Ciardi, Saturday Review, *June 2, 1962*

The trouble with our age is that it is all signpost and no destination.

Louis Kronenberg, Company Manners, *1954*

If civilization has risen from the Stone Age, it can rise again from the Wastepaper Age.

Jacques Barzun, The House of Intellect, *1959*

The three great evils of the twentieth century: . . . misogyny, anti-semitism, and anti-intellectualism.

Julia Kristeva, Citations francaises, *1984*

The atom bombs are piling up in the factories, the police are prowling through the cities, the lies are streaming from the loudspeakers, but the earth is still going round the sun.

George Orwell, Shooting an Elephant, *1950*

Time and space—time to be alone, space to move about—these may well become the great scarcities of tomorrow.

Edwin Way Teale, Autumn Across America, *1956*

In the twentieth century what astonished many of us is not so much that human nature is fundamentally corrupt; we are astonished rather that it does not behave more wickedly than it obviously does.

Morton Irving Seiden, The Paradox of Hate, *1967*

In these times you have to be an optimist to open your eyes when you awake in the morning.

Carl Sandburg, New York Post, *September 9, 1960*

(*See also* **PRESENT**)

TYRANNY

Death is a softer thing by far than tyranny.

Aeschylus, Agamemnon, *458 B.C.*

Somehow this is tyranny's disease, to trust no friends.

Aeschylus, Prometheus Bound

The laws can't be enforced against the man who is the laws' master.

Benvenuto Cellini, Autobiography, *1566*

He who despises his own life is soon master of another's.

English proverb

The benevolent despot who sees himself as a shepherd of the people still demands from others the submissiveness of sheep.

Eric Hoffer, The Passionate State of Mind, *1954*

Of all the tyrannies on human kind
The worst is that which persecutes the mind.

John Dryden, The Hind and the Panther, *1687*

The most tyrannical governments are those which make crimes of opinion, for everyone has an inalienable right to his thoughts.

Spinoza, Religious and Political Philosophy, *1670*

So long as men worship the Caesars and Napoleons, Caesars and Napoleons will duly rise and make them miserable.

Aldous Huxley, Ends and Means, *1937*

The face of tyranny
Is always mild at first.

Racine, Britannicus, *1669*

UNDERSTANDING

We never understand how little we need in this world until we know the loss of it.

James M. Barrie, Margaret Olgivy, *1896*

We don't understand life any better at forty than at twenty, but by then we realize it and admit it.

Jules Renard (d. 1910), Journal

We should not pretend to understand the world only by the intellect; we apprehend it just as much by feeling. Therefore the judgment of the intellect is, at best, only the half of truth, and must, if it be honest, also come to an understanding of its inadequacy.

C.G. Jung, Psychological Types, *1923*

Folks never understand the folks they hate.

James Russell Lowell, The Bigelow Papers: Series II, *1886*

I want, by understanding myself, to understand others. I want to be all that I am capable of becoming. . . . This all sounds very strenuous and very serious. But now that I have wrestled with it, it's no longer so. I feel happy—deep down. *All is well.*

Katherine Mansfield, Journal, *1922, last entry*

No human being can really understand another, and no one can arrange another's happiness.

Graham Greene, The Heart of the Matter, *1948*

Until you understand a writer's ignorance, presume yourself ignorant of his understanding.

Coleridge, Biographia Literaria, *1817*

Since I first gained the use of reason my inclination towards learning has been so violent and strong that neither the scoldings of other people . . . nor my own reflections have been able to stop me from following this natural impulse that God has given me. He alone must know why; and He knows too that I have begged Him to take away the light of my understanding, leaving only enough for me to keep His law, since anything else is excessive in a woman, some say even harmful.

Juana Inés de la Cruz to the bishop of Puebla, in reply to his letter attacking her scholarly work

(*See also* **INTELLIGENCE, PERCEPTION, WISDOM**)

UNHAPPINESS: *See* HAPPINESS, SAD/MELANCHOLY.

UNIVERSE

A man said to the universe:
"Sir, I exist!"
"However," replied the universe,
"The fact has not created in me
A sense of obligation."

Stephen Crane, "War Is Kind," 1899

The universe is not hostile, nor yet is it friendly. It is simply indifferent.

John Haynes Holmes, The Sensible Man's View of Religion, *1933*

Had I been present at the creation, I would have given some useful hints for the better ordering of the universe.

Alfonso X of Castile & Leon (d. 1284), attributed

We cannot in any better manner glorify the Lord and Creator of the universe than that in all things . . . we contemplate the display of his omnificence and perfections with the utmost admiration.

Anton van Leeuwenhoek (d. 1723), Selected Works

All are but parts of one stupendous whole,
Whose body Nature is, and God the soul.

> *Alexander Pope,* An Essay on Man, *1734*

He knows the universe, but himself he does not know.

> *La Fontaine,* Fables, *1668*

The whole visible world is only an imperceptible atom in the ample bosom of nature. No idea approaches it.

> *Pascal,* Pensées, *1670*

This truth within my mind rehearse,
That in a boundless universe
Is boundless better, boundless worse.

> *Tennyson, "The Two Voices," 1832*

The cosmos is a gigantic flywheel making 10,000 revolutions a minute. Man is a sick fly taking a dizzy ride on it. Religion is the theory that the wheel was designed and set spinning to give him a ride.

> *H.L. Mencken,* Prejudices: Third Series, *1922*

Now my suspicion is that the universe is not only queerer than we suppose, but queerer than we *can* suppose. . . . I suspect that there are more things in heaven and earth than are dreamed of in any philosophy.

> *J.B.S. Haldane,* Possible Worlds, *1927*

Nothing troubles me more than time and space, and yet nothing troubles me less.

> *Charles Lamb to Thomas Manning, January 2, 1810*

(*See also* **NATURE, SPACE, WORLD**)

UNIVERSITY

The true university of these days is a collection of books.

> *Carlyle,* Heroes and Hero Worship, *1840*

The university has become the multiversity and the nature of the presidency has followed this change. . . . The president of the multiversity is a leader, educator, wielder of power, pump, he is also officeholder, caretaker, inheritor, consensus seeker, persuader, bottleneck. But he is mostly a mediator.

> *Clark Kerr, "The Uses of the University," Harvard, 1963*

Diversity of opinion within the framework of loyalty to our free society is not only basic to a university but to the entire nation.

James B. Conant, Education in a Divided World, *1948*

Rouse up, O young men of the new age! Set your foreheads against the ignorant hirelings! For we have hirelings in the camp, the court, and the university who would, if they could, forever repress mental and prolong corporeal war.

William Blake, Milton, *c. 1810*

(*See also* **EDUCATION, LEARNING**)

UNKINDNESS: *See* **KINDNESS, SADISM.**

THE UNKNOWN

Penetrating so many secrets, we cease to believe in the unknowable. But there it sits nevertheless, calmly licking its chops.

H.L. Mencken, Minority Report, *1956*

The fairest thing we can experience is the mysterious. It is the fundamental emotion which stands at the cradle of true art and true science.

Einstein, The World As I See It, *1934*

Once men are caught up in an event, they cease to be afraid. Only the unknown frightens them.

Saint-Exupéry, Wind, Sand, and Stars, *1939*

Behind the dim unknown,
Standeth God within the shadow, keeping watch.

James Russell Lowell, "The Present Crisis," *1844*

'Tis very puzzling on the brink
Of what is called Eternity to stare,
And know no more of what is *here,* than *there.*

Lord Byron, Don Juan, *1824*

(*See also* **KNOWLEDGE, UNDERSTANDING**)

UNLEARNING

Only by unlearning [comes] Wisdom.

James Russell Lowell, The Parting of the Ways, *1849*

Education consists mainly in what we have unlearned.

> *Mark Twain,* Notebook, *1935*

That which any one has been long learning unwillingly, he unlearns with proportionable eagerness and haste.

> *William Hazlitt,* The Plain Speaker, *1826*

We can prevent people from learning, but we can't make them unlearn.

> *Ludwig Boerne,* Aphorismen und Fragmente, *1840*

(*See also* **EDUCATION**)

UNSELFISHNESS: *See* BENEVOLENCE, SELFISHNESS.

USEFUL/USELESS

A man cannot sleep in his cradle: whatever is useful must in the nature of life become useless.

> *Walter Lippmann* A Preface to Politics, *1914*

Utility is the great idol of the age, to which all powers must do service and all talents swear allegiance.

> *Schiller,* On the Aesthetic Education of Man, *1795*

A good edge is good for nothing, if it has nothing to cut.

> *Thomas Fuller,* Gnomologia, *1732*

It is a great misfortune to be of use to nobody; scarcely less to be of use to everybody.

> *Baltasar Gracian,* The Art of Worldly Wisdom, *1647*

If you want a golden rule that will fit everybody, this is it: Have nothing in your houses that you do not know to be useful, or believe to be beautiful.

> *William Morris,* The Beauty of Life, *1880*

All art is quite useless.

> *Oscar Wilde,* The Picture of Dorian Gray, *1891*

Nothing can have value without being an object of utility. If it be useless, the labor contained in it is useless, cannot be reckoned as labor, and cannot therefore create value.

> *Karl Marx,* Capital, *1867*

To a poet nothing can be useless.

Samuel Johnson, Rasselas, *1759*

'Tis better to know useless things than to know nothing at all.

Seneca, Epistles, *c. A.D. 50*

Nothing is so useless as a general maxim.

Thomas B. Macaulay, On Machiavelli, *1827*

No man is useless while he has a friend.

Robert Louis Stevenson, Across the Plains, *1892*

As unto the bow the cord is,
So unto the man is woman,
Though she bends him, she obeys him,
Though she draws him, yet she follows,
Useless each without the other!

Longfellow, "The Song of Hiawatha," 1855

UTOPIA: *See* IDEALISM, REFORMERS.

VALUE

What we must decide is perhaps how we are valuable rather than
how valuable we are.

        Edgar Z. Friedenberg, The Vanishing Adolescent, *1959*

To live is in itself a value judgment. To breathe is to judge.

        Albert Camus, The Rebel, *1951*

We never know the worth of water till the well is dry.

        Thomas Fuller, Gnomologia, *1732*

Nothing is intrinsically valuable; the value of everything is attributed
to it, assigned to it from outside the thing itself, by people.

        John Barth, The Floating Opera, *1956*

Everything is worth what its purchaser will pay for it.

        Publius Syrus (fl. 50 B.C.), Moral Sayings

Nothing worth doing is completed in our lifetime; therefore, we
must be saved by hope. Nothing true or beautiful or good makes
complete sense in any immediate context of history; therefore, we
must be saved by faith. Nothing we do, however virtuous, can be
accomplished alone; therefore, we are saved by love.

        Reinhold Niebuhr, The Irony of American History, *1952*

The value of a man can be measured only with regard to other men.

Nietzsche, The Will to Power, *1888*

(*See also* **JUDGING**)

VANITY

Vanity's the very spice of life.

William Cowper, The Task, *1785*

A vain man may become proud and imagine himself pleasing to all when he is in reality a universal nuisance.

Spinoza, Ethics, *1677*

Vanity is truly the motive-power that moves humanity, and it is flattery that greases the wheels.

Jerome K. Jerome, Idle Thoughts of an Idle Fellow, *1889*

What renders other people's vanity insufferable is that it wounds our own.

La Rochefoucauld, Maxims, *1665*

One will rarely err if extreme actions be ascribed to vanity, ordinary actions to habit, and mean actions to fear.

Nietzsche, Human, All Too Human, *1878*

There are no grades of vanity, there are only grades of ability in concealing it.

Mark Twain, Notebook, *1935*

The king grew vain;
Fought all his battles o'er again;
And thrice he routed all his foes,
And thrice he slew the slain.

John Dryden, Alexander's Feast, *1697*

(*See also* **CONCEIT, PRETENSION, SELF-LOVE**)

VARIETY

The joy of life is variety; the tenderest love requires to be renewed by intervals of absence.

Samuel Johnson, The Idler, *1758*

They are the weakest-minded and the hardest-hearted men, that most love variety and change.

John Ruskin, Modern Painters, *1843*

(*See also* **CHANGE, DIFFERENCES, INFIDELITY**)

VICE/VIRTUE

The excess of a virtue is a vice.

Greek proverb

Private Vices, Publick Benefits.

Bernard Mandeville, The Fable of the Bees, *1714*

Man is neither good nor bad; he is born with certain instincts and aptitudes; society, far from degrading him as Rousseau claims, perfects him, . . . but self-interest develops his bad inclinations also.

Balzac, La Comédie humaine, *1841*

It is the function of vice to keep virtue within reasonable bounds.

Samuel Butler (d. 1902), Note-Books, *1912*

Half the vices which the world condemns most loudly have seeds of good in them and require moderate use rather than total abstinence.

Samuel Butler, The Way of All Flesh, *1903*

Vice is seductive and must be painted seductively; but it carries with it sickness and unique moral troubles, which must be described.

Baudelaire, "Honest Dramas and Novels," *1867*

Vices are active and able ministers of depopulation.

Malthus, Essay on Population, *1798*

Men are more easily governed through their vices than through their virtues.

Napoleon I, Maxims, *1815*

Every vice is only an exaggeration of a necessary and virtuous function.

Emerson, Journals, *1836*

To think ill of mankind, and not to wish ill to them, is perhaps the highest wisdom and virtue.

William Hazlitt, Characteristics, *1823*

If you are rich and have everything you want, what reason do you have for being honest or virtuous.

> *Diderot (d. 1784)*, Entretien d'un philosophe avec la maréchale de ***

What is virtue but the trade unionism of the married?

> *G.B. Shaw*, Man and Superman, *1903*

Astronomy was born of superstition; eloquence of ambition, hatred, falsehood, and flattery; geometry of avarice; physics of an idle curiosity; and even moral philosophy of human pride. Thus the arts and sciences owe their birth to our vices.

> *Rousseau*, A Discourse on the Moral Effects of the Arts and Sciences, *1750*

If I have wasted my days in voluptuousness, ah! ye gods, give them back to me so I can waste them again.

> *La Mettrie (d. 1757)*, L'Art de jouir

(*See also* **VIRTUE**)

VICTIM

Power ... marks its victim, denounces it; and excites the public odium and the public hatred, to conceal its own abuses and encroachments.

> *Henry Clay, speech, U.S. Senate, March 14, 1834*

As some day it may happen that a victim must be found,
I've got a little list—I've got a little list,
Of society offenders who might well be underground,
And who never would be missed, who never would be missed.

> *W.S. Gilbert*, The Mikado, *1885*

When the crowd hurls itself in blind fury upon its victim . . . this collective murder does not seem so frightful to them because they share a feeling of unity and purposefulness.

> *Eugene Sue*, The Wandering Jew, *1845*

(*See also* **CRIME, LOSERS, POWER**)

VICTORY: *See* DEFEAT/VICTORY, WAR.

VIOLENCE

Violence is as American as cherry pie.

> *H. Rap Brown, Comment, 1966*

You know what I think about violence. For me it is profoundly moral, more moral than compromise and negotiation.

Benito Mussolini, speech, August, 1925

Be peaceful, be courteous, obey the law, respect everyone; but if someone puts a hand on you, send him to the cemetery.

Malcolm X, Malcolm X Speaks, *1965*

Most Americans would say that they disapproved of violence. But what they really mean is that they believe it should be the monopoly of the state.

Edgar Z. Friedenberg, New York Review of Books, *October 20, 1966*

It is organized violence on top which creates individual violence at the bottom. It is the accumulated indignation against organized wrong, organized crime, organized injustice, which drives the political offender to act.

Emma Goldman, Address to the jury, June 15, 1917

The liberal philosophy . . . holds that unless there is a method . . . by which the governed can make their views effective in some proportion to their weight, the nation is at the mercy of violence in the form of terrorism, assassination, conspiracy, mass compulsion, and civil war.

Walter Lippmann, Vanity Fair, *November 1934*

It is better to be violent, if there is violence in our hearts, than to put on the cloak of non-violence to cover impotence.

Gandhi, Non-violence in Peace and War, *1948*

Wherever a people has grown savage in arms so that human laws have no longer any place among it, the only powerful means of reducing it is religion.

Gambattista Vico, The New Science, *1744*

(*See also* **FORCE, KILLING**)

VIOLENCE, COLONIAL

At the individual level, violence detoxifies. It eliminates the colonial's inferiority complex, his meditative or hopeless attitudes. It makes him courageous [and] rehabilitates him in his own eyes.

Franz Fanon, Les Damnés de la terre, *1961*

[Black Hawk] has done nothing for which an Indian ought to be ashamed. He has fought for his countrymen, the squaws, and papooses, against white men who came . . . to cheat them and take away their lands.

Black Hawk, speech upon surrender, August 27, 1832

Liberty and democracy become unholy when their hands are dyed red with innocent blood.

Gandhi, Non-violence in Peace and War, *1948*

(*See also* **BARBARISM, RACISM**)

VIRTUE

Virtue can be afforded only by the poor, who have nothing to lose.

Alexander Chase, Perspectives, *1966*

When men grow virtuous in their old age, they only make a sacrifice to God of the devil's leavings.

Jonathan Swift, Thoughts on Various Subjects, *1711*

Virtue is an angel, but she is a blind one, and must ask Knowledge to show her the pathway that leads to her goal.

Horace Mann, "Thoughts for a Young Man," 1859

The chief cause of our misery is less the violence of our passions than the feebleness of our virtues.

Joseph Roux, Meditations of a Parish Priest, *1886*

Virtues are virtues only to those who can appreciate them.

Panchatantra, fifth century

The highest virtue is always against the law.

Emerson, The Conduct of Life, *1860*

Virtue is praised, but hated. People run from it, for it is ice-cold and in this world you have to keep your feet warm.

Diderot, Rameau's Nephew, *1762*

It would be useless and almost unjust to insist upon a man's being virtuous if he cannot be so without being unhappy. So long as vice makes him happy, he should love vice.

Baron d'Holbach, Le Système de la nature, *1770*

[Lord,] forgive us for bypassing political duties; for condemning civil disobedience when we will not obey You; for reducing Your holy law to average virtues, by trying to be no better nor worse than most men.

> *United Presbyterian Church,* Litany for Holy Communion, *1968*

(*See also* **VICE/VIRTUE**)

VISION(S)

. . . The art of seeing things invisible.

> *Jonathan Swift,* Thoughts on Various Subjects, *1711*

I have grown to believe
A stone is a better pillow than many visions.

> *Robinson Jeffers, "Clouds of Evening," 1930*

A pile of rocks ceases to be a rock pile when somebody contemplates it with the idea of a cathedral in mind.

> *Saint-Exupéry,* Flight to Arras, *1942*

I mistrust the so-called visionaries: they pursue their pleasurable visions the way a man pursues his loves.

> *Patrice de La Tour du Pin,* La Vie recluse en poésie, *1938*

No man sees far; the most see no farther than their noses.

> *Thomas Carlyle, "Count Cagliostro," 1833*

A great mind is one that can forget or look beyond itself.

> *William Hazlitt,* The Round Table, *1817*

The fellow that can only see a week ahead is always the popular fellow, for he is looking with the crowd. But the one that can see years ahead, he has a telescope but he can't make anybody believe he has it.

> *Mark Twain,* Autobiography, *1949*

(*See also* **IMAGINATION, MIND, PERCEPTION**)

VOCATIONS

Every calling is great when greatly pursued.

> *Oliver Wendell Holmes, speech, Suffolk Bar Association,*
> *February 5, 1885*

The artisan or scientist or the follower of whatever discipline who has the habit of comparing himself not with other followers but with the discipline itself will have a lower opinion of himself, the more excellent he is.

Giacomo Leopardi, Pensieri, *1827*

The price one pays for pursuing any profession, or calling, is an intimate knowledge of its ugly side.

James Baldwin, "The Black Boy Looks at the White Boy," Nobody Knows My Name, *1961*

When men are rightly occupied, their amusement grows out of their work, as the colour-petals out of a fruitful flower.

John Ruskin, Sesame and Lilies, *1865*

The test of a vocation is the love of the drudgery it involves.

Logan Pearsall Smith, Afterthoughts, *1931*

All professions are conspiracies against the laity.

G.B. Shaw, The Doctor's Dilemma, *1913*

(*See also* **EXCELLENCE, TRAINING, WORK**)

VOTING

Vote for the man who promises least; he'll be the least disappointing.

Bernard Baruch, in M. Berger's New York, *1960*

Elections are won by men and women chiefly because most people vote against somebody, rather than for somebody.

Franklin P. Adams, Nods and Becks, *1944*

Those who stay away from the election think that one vote will do no good. 'Tis but one step more to think that one vote will do no harm.

Emerson, Journals, *1854*

No voter in the world ever voted for nothing; in some way he has been convinced that he is to get something for the vote. His vote is all that our Constitution gives him, and it goes to the highest bidder.

Will Rogers, Autobiography, *1949*

Let us never forget that government is *ourselves* and not an alien power over us. The ultimate rulers of our democracy are not a President and senators and congressmen and government officials, but the voters of this country.

Franklin D. Roosevelt, speech, Marietta, Ohio, July 8, 1938

The idea that you can merchandise candidates for high office like breakfast cereal—that you can gather votes like box tops—is . . . the ultimate indignity to the democratic process.

> *Adlai Stevenson, speech, Democratic National Convention,*
> *August 18, 1956*

An election is a moral horror, as bad as a battle except for the blood: a mud bath for every soul concerned in it.

> *G.B. Shaw,* Back to Methuselah, *1921*

(*See also* **CITIZENSHIP, DEMOCRACY, POLITICS**)

WANTS/DESIRES

Our wants serve us almost as well as our possessions.

Jean Guéhenno (d. 1978), Changer la vie

Modern man lives under the illusion that he knows what he wants, while he actually wants what he is supposed to want.

Erich Fromm, Escape from Freedom, *1941*

May your every wish be granted.

Ancient Chinese curse

How few are our real wants! and how easy it is to satisfy them! Our imaginary ones are boundless and insatiable.

Julius Charles Hare and Augustus William Hare, Guesses at Truth, *1827*

Some desire is necessary to keep life in motion, and he whose real wants are supplied must admit those of fancy.

Samuel Johnson, Rasselas, *1759*

We do not succeed in changing things according to our desire, but gradually our desire changes.

Proust, Albertine disparue, *1925*

I look at what I have and think myself unhappy; others look at what I have and think me happy.

> *Joseph Roux,* Meditations of a Parish Priest, *1886*

WAR

War is a continuation of policy by other means. It is not merely a political act but a real political instrument.

> *Karl von Clausewitz (d. 1831),* War, Peace, and Power

A war regarded as inevitable or even probable, and therefore much prepared for, has a very good chance of eventually being fought.

> *George F. Kennan,* The Cloud of Danger, *1977*

War makes rattling good history; but peace is boring.

> *Thomas Hardy,* The Dynasts, *1904*

A good war makes sacred any cause.

> *Nietzsche,* Will to Power, *1888*

War alone brings to its highest tension all human energy and puts the stamp of nobility upon the people who have the courage to face it.

> *Mussolini,* The Italian Encyclopedia, *1932*

Men love war because it allows them to look serious. Because it is the one thing that stops women laughing at them.

> *John Fowles,* The Magus, *1965*

[So] that was war. Just about all he could find in its favor was that it paid well and liberated children from the pernicious influence of their parents.

> *Joseph Heller,* Catch-22, *1961*

War may make a fool of man, but it by no means degrades him; on the contrary, it tends to exalt him, and its net effects are much like those of motherhood on women.

> *H.L. Mencken,* Minority Report, *1956*

War is an unmitigated evil. But it certainly does one good thing: It drives away fear and brings bravery to the surface.

> *Gandhi,* Non-Violence in Peace and War, *1948*

If you want war, nourish a doctrine. Doctrines are the most frightful tyrants to which men ever are subject, because doctrines get inside of a man's reason and betray him against himself.

> *William Graham Sumner,* War, *1903*

No soldier wants a war—they only give their lives to it. Wars are started by you and me, by bankers and politicians, excitable women, newspaper editors, clergymen who are expacifists, and Congressmen with vertebrae of putty. The youngsters in the streets, poor kids, . . . pay the price.

Father Francis P. Duffy (d. 1932), Sermon, New York

No nations are more warlike than those professing Christianity.

Pierre Bayle, Pensées sur la comète, *1682*

We . . . imagined [the war] was being fought by aging men like ourselves. We had forgotten that wars were fought by babies. When I saw those freshly shaved faces, it was a shock. "My God," I said to myself, "it's the Children's Crusade."

Kurt Vonnegut, Jr., Slaughterhouse Five, *1969*

We have grasped the mystery of the atom and rejected the Sermon on the Mount.

General Omar Bradley, Address, Armistice Day, 1948

And when the war is done and youth stone dead
I'd toddle safely home and die—in bed.

Sigfried Sassoon, Base Details, *1918*

Everyone, when there's war in the air, learns to live in a new element: falsehood.

Jean Giraudoux, Tiger at the Gates, *1935*

The quickest way to end a war is to lose it.

George Orwell, Shooting an Elephant, *1950*

War is at best barbarism. . . . Its glory is all moonshine. It is only those who have neither fired a shot nor heard the shrieks and groans of the wounded who cry aloud for blood, more vengeance, more desolation. War is hell.

General William Tecumseh Sherman, speech, Michigan Military Academy, October 19, 1879

War involves in its progress such a train of unforeseen and unsupposed circumstances that no human wisdom can calculate the end. It has but one thing certain, and that is to increase taxes.

Thomas Paine, Prospects on the Rubicon, *1787*

Once we thought a few hundred corpses would suffice
then we saw thousands were still too few

and today we can't even count all the dead
everywhere you look.

> *Peter Weiss,* The Persecution and Assassination of Jean Paul
> Marat as Performed by the Inmates of the Asylum of
> Charenton under the Direction of the Marquis de Sade, *1965*

War is not an adventure, it's a disease. Like typhus.

> *Saint-Exupéry,* Flight to Arras, *1942*

As long as war is regarded as wicked, it will always have its fascination. When it is looked upon as vulgar it will cease to be popular.

> *Oscar Wilde, "The Critic as Artist," 1890*

(*See also* **ATOMIC AGE, KILLING, PEACE**)

WAR, ABOLITION OF

We are advocates of the abolition of war, we do not want war; but
war can only be abolished through war, and in order to get rid of
the gun it is necessary to take up the gun.

> Quotations from Chairman Mao *(d. 1976)*

Diplomats are just as essential to starting a war as Soldiers are for
finishing it. You take Diplomacy out of war and the thing would fall
in a week.

> *Will Rogers,* Autobiography, *1949*

War can be abolished forever by providing clothing, food, and hous-
ing, instead of bombers, destroyers, and rockets.

> *Trygve Lie,* Labor, *September 6, 1947*

What we now need to discover in the social realm is the moral equivalent of war; something heroic that will speak to man as universally
as war does, and yet will be as compatible with their spiritual selves
as war has proved to be incompatible.

> *William James,* The Will to Believe, *1897*

The way to prevent war is to bend every energy toward preventing
it, not to proceed by the dubious indirection of preparing for it.

> *Max Lerner,* Actions and Passions, *1949*

How different the new order would be if we could consult the
veteran instead of the politician.

> *Henry Miller,* The Wisdom of the Heart, *1941*

Vice foments war; it is virtue which actually fights. If there were no virtue, we would live in peace forever.

Vauvenargues, Reflections and Maxims, *1746*

(*See also* **PEACE**)

WAR AND GRANDEUR

In Italy for thirty years under the Borgias they had warfare, terror, murder, bloodshed—they produced Michelangelo, Leonardo da Vinci, and the Renaissance. In Switzerland they had brotherly love, five hundred years of democracy and peace, and what did they produce?—the cuckoo clock.

Graham Greene and Orson Wells, The Third Man, *movie*

Life and fame and wealth—all these must, I say, be defended by fighting. Death in battle is the most glorious for men. Who lives under the sway of his foe—it is he that is dead.

Panchatantra, *fifth century*

Brave people alone have an existence, an evolution, a future. . . . The grandeur of history lies in the perpetual conflict of nations.

Heinrich von Treitschke, Politik, *1897*

War is to men what maternity is to women.

Mussolini, Autobiography

My, how beautiful is war! its songs, its leisure!

Guillaume Apollinaire, L'Adieu du cavalier. *[Apollinaire died in World War I, aged 38.]*

Boys and girls,
And women, that would groan to see a child
Pull off an insect's leg, all read of war,
The best amusement for our morning meal.

Samuel Taylor Coleridge, Fears in Solitude, *1798*

Can we say that in today's [wars] man is pitting his strength, skill, courage, or endurance against man? Certainly not! War has become a contest between machines, industrial enterprise, and financial organizations.

Bronislaw Malinowski, Address, Harvard, September 1936

(*See also* **HEROES, PATRIOTISM**)

WAR AND MEN'S MINDS

We must rouse in the people a unanimous wish for power plus a determination to sacrifice, on the altar of patriotism, life and property, personal opinions and preferences.

> *Friedrich von Bernhardi*, Germany and the Next War, *1912*

People who are vigorous and brutal often find war enjoyable, provided that it is a victorious war and that there is not too much interference with rape and plunder. This is a great help in persuading people that wars are righteous.

> *Bertrand Russell*, Unpopular Essays, *1950*

Since wars begin in the minds of men, it is in the minds of men that the defense of peace must be constructed.

> *UNESCO*, Constitution, *1945*

I wonder if wars don't occur just so adults can play at being children again, regressing contentedly to the age of toy soldiers and crusading knights.

> *Michel Tournier*, Le Roi des aulnes, *1970*

Perhaps the most important single factor in the outbreak of war is misperception: a leader's image of himself; [his] view of his adversary's character; his view of his adversary's intentions, and of his adversary's capabilities.

> *John Stoessinger*, Why Nations Go to War, *1978*

If war is horrible, isn't patriotism the dominant idea that supports it?

> *Guy de Maupassant (d. 1893)*, Les Dimanches

He that is the author of a war lets loose the whole contagion of hell and opens a vein that bleeds a nation to death.

> *Thomas Paine*, The American Crisis, *1776*

We kill because we are afraid of our own shadow, afraid that if we used a little common sense we'd have to admit that our glorious principles were wrong.

> *Henry Miller*, The Wisdom of the Heart, *1941*

All wars are boyish and are fought by boys.

> *Herman Melville*, Battlepieces and Aspects of the War, *1866*

Frankly, I'd like to see the government get out of war altogether and leave the whole field to private individuals.

Joseph Heller, Catch-22, *1955*

(*See also* **ENEMIES, ILLUSION, JESUS**)

WAR: VICTORS, VICTIMS, AND VITAL INTERESTS

What a country calls its vital . . . interests are not things that help its people live, but things that help it make war. Petroleum is a more likely cause of international conflict than wheat.

Simone Weil, Ecrits historiques et politiques, *1960*

The desire of one power for absolute security means absolute insecurity for all the others.

Henry Kissinger, A World Restored, *1957*

After each war there is a little less democracy to save.

Brooks Atkinson, Once Around the Sun, *1951*

Youth is the first victim of war; the first fruit of peace. It takes twenty years or more of peace to make a man; it takes only twenty seconds of war to destroy him.

Baudouin of Belgium, Address, Joint Session of the [U.S.] Congress, May 12, 1959

What are the triumphs of war, planned by ambition, executed by violence, and comsummated by devastation? The means are the sacrifice of many, the end the bloated aggrandizement of the few.

Charles Caleb Colton, Lacon, *1825*

I have come to hate war not only because it kills off the flower of every nation, but because it destroys spiritual values as well as material values.

Ilya Ehrenburg, Saturday Review, *September 30, 1967*

The most shocking fact about war is that its victims and its instruments are human beings, and that these individual beings are condemned by the monstrous conventions of politics to murder or be murdered in quarrels not their own.

Aldous Huxley, The Olive Tree, *1937*

It became necessary to destroy the town in order to save it.

American officer at Ben Tre, Vietnam, February 8, 1968 (attributed)

I think this is the first war in history that on the morrow the victors sued for peace and the vanquished called for unconditional surrender.

Abba Eban, Foreign Minister of Israel, New York Times, *July 9, 1967*

War. There is no solution for it. There is never a conqueror. The winner generates such hatred that he is ultimately defeated.

Michel Simon, New York Times, *March 17, 1968*

War . . . makes the victor stupid and the vanquished revengeful.

Nietzsche, Human, All Too Human, *1878*

Victory at all costs, victory in spite of all terror, . . . for without victory there is no survival.

Winston Churchill, speech, House of Commons, May 13, 1940

The butter to be sacrificed because of the war always turns out to be the margarine of the poor.

James Tobin, speech, Social Sciences Association, December 27, 1967

Nothing except a battle lost can be half so melancholy as a battle won.

The Duke of Wellington, dispatch from Waterloo, 1815

(*See also* **YOUTH, AGE**)

THE WAY

Tao [The Way] that can be told of is not the eternal Tao;
The name that can be named is not the eternal name.
The Nameless is the origin of Heaven and Earth;
The Named is the mother of all things.

Lao-tzu, Tao te Ching, *c. 500 B.C.*

Behold, I send an angel before thee, to keep thee in the way.

Exodus 23:20

Strait is the gate, and narrow is the way, which leadeth unto life, and few there be that find it.

Matthew 7:14

I am the way, the truth and the life.

John 4:6

(*See also* **HEAVEN, SAINTS AND SAINTHOOD**)

WEAKNESS

The spirit indeed is willing, but the flesh is weak.

Matthew 26:41

The greatest of all weaknesses is the fear of appearing weak.

J.B. Bossuet, Politics from Holy Writ, *1709*

Men who are weak never give in when they should.

Cardinal de Retz (fl. 1650), Mémoires

The sick are the greatest threat to the healthy. Not from the strongest but from the weakest does harm come to the strong.

Nietzsche, The Geneology of Morals, *1887*

Biological weakness is the condition of human culture.

Erich Fromm, Escape from Freedom, *1941*

Often we are firm from weakness, and audacious from timidity.

La Rochefoucauld, Maxims, *1665*

We cannot win the weak by sharing our wealth with them. They feel our generosity as oppression.

Eric Hoffer, The Ordeal of Change, *1962*

Oh, you weak, beautiful people who give up with such grace. What you need is someone to take hold of you—gently, with love, and hand your life back to you.

Tennessee Williams, Cat on a Hot Tin Roof, *1955*

(*See also* **IMPOTENCE, LIMITS, STRENGTH**)

WEALTH

Wealth and poverty: the one is the parent of luxury and indolence, and the other of meanness and viciousness, and both of discontent.

Plato, The Republic, *fourth century* B.C.

He is rich who hath enough to be charitable.

Sir Thomas Browne, Religio Medici, *1642*

Be not penny-wise: riches have wings, and sometimes they fly away of themselves; sometimes they must be set flying to bring in more.

Francis Bacon, Essays, *1625*

The average man is rich enough when he has a little more than he has got, and not till then.

> *Dean William Ralph Inge,* Outspoken Essays, *1919*

The rich are more envied by those who have a little, than by those who have nothing.

> *Charles Caleb Colton,* Lacon, *1825*

All heiresses are beautiful.

> *John Dryden,* King Arthur, *1691*

It is easier for a camel to go through the eye of a needle than for a rich man to enter the kingdom of God.

> *Matthew 19:24*

'Tis as hard f'r a rich man to enther th' kingdom of Hiven as it is f'r a poor man to get out iv Purgatory.

> *Finley Peter Dunne,* Mr. Dooley on Making a Will, *1919*

Riches serve a wise man but command a fool.

> *English proverb*

If some appalling disaster befalls, there's
Always a way for the rich.

> *Euripides,* Andromache, *426 B.C.*

All else—valor, a good name, glory, everything in heaven and earth—
is secondary to the charm of riches.

> *Horace,* Satires, *30 B.C.*

The problem of our age is the proper administration of wealth, so that the ties of brotherhood may still bind together the rich and poor in harmonious relationship.

> *Andrew Carnegie,* The Gospel of Wealth, *1889*

The production of wealth is not the work of any one man and the acquisition of great fortunes is not possible without the cooperation of multitudes.

> *Peter Cooper to Samuel Gompers, AFL Convention, 1892*

The wealth of a country is its working people.

> *Theodor Herzl,* Altneuland, *1902*

Ill fares the land, to hastening ills a prey,
Where wealth accumulates and men decay.

> *Oliver Goldsmith,* The Deserted Village, *1770*

Inherited wealth is a big handicap to happiness. It is as certain death to ambition as cocaine is to morality.

William K. Vanderbilt, interview, 1905

Surplus wealth is a sacred trust which its possessor is bound to administer in his lifetime for the good of the community.

Carnegie, Gospel of Wealth

What a miserable thing life is: you're living in clover, only the clover isn't good enough.

Bertolt Brecht, Jungle of Cities, *1924*

Pearls around the neck—stones upon the heart.

Hanan J. Ayalti, Yiddish Proverbs, *1949*

(*See also* **GREED, POVERTY, RICHES**)

WEATHER

We shall never be content until each man makes his own weather and keeps it to himself.

Jerome K. Jerome, The Idle Thoughts of an Idle Fellow, *1889*

Satellite photography in the 1970s gave rise to the long-range weather forecast, a month at a time. This in turn gave rise to the observation that the long-range weather forecast was wrong most of the time. In turn, this gave rise to the dropping of the long-range weather forecast and to the admission that really accurate forecasting could only cover the next day or two, and not always then.

Miles Kington, Nature Made Ridiculously Simple, *1983*

A cloudy day, or a little sunshine, have as great an influence on many constitutions as the most real blessings or misfortunes.

Joseph Addison, The Spectator, *1712*

Who knows wither the clouds have fled?
In the unscarred heaven they leave no wake;
And the eyes forget the tears they have shed,
The heart forgets its sorrow and ache.

James Russell Lowell, "The Vision of Sir Launfal," 1848

For the man sound in body and serene of mind there is no such thing as bad weather; every day has its beauty, and storms which whip the blood do but make it pulse more vigorously.

George Gissing, "Winter," The Private Papers of Henry Ryecroft, 1903

The mist, like love, plays upon the heart of the hills and brings out surprises of beauty.

Rabindranath Tagore, Stray Birds, *1916*

Who has seen the wind? Neither you nor I:
But when the trees bow down their heads
The wind is passing by.

Christina Rossetti, "Sing-Song," *1872*

O wild West Wind, though breath of Autumn's being,
Thou, from whose unseen presence the leaves dead
Are driven, like ghosts from an enchanter fleeing,
Yellow, and black, and pale, and hectic red,
Pestilence-stricken multitudes.

Shelley, "Ode to the West Wind," *1819*

WEDDINGS

Bride, n. A woman with a fine prospect behind her.

Ambrose Bierce, The Devil's Dictionary, *1911*

When two people are under the influence of the most violent, most insane, most delusive, and most transient of passions, they are required to swear that they will remain in that excited, abnormal, and exhausting condition continuously until death do them part.

G.B. Shaw, Getting Married, *1908*

If it were not for the presents, an elopement would be preferable.

George Ade, Forty Modern Fables, *1901*

I guess walking slow getting married is because it gives you time to maybe change your mind.

Virginia Cary Hudson, O Ye Figs and Juleps, *1962*

Nothing so surely introduces a sour note into a wedding ceremony as the abrupt disappearance of the groom in a cloud of dust.

P.G. Wodehouse, A Pelican at Blanding, *1969*

(*See also* **MARRIAGE**)

WIFE

If ever two were one, then surely we.
If ever man were loved by wife, then thee;

If ever wife was happy in a man,
Compare with me ye women if you can.

> *Anne Bradstreet, "To My Dear and Loving Husband," 1678*

The comfortable estate of widowhood, is the only hope that keeps up a wife's spirits.

> *John Gay,* The Beggar's Opera, *1728*

When a woman gets married it's like jumping into a hole in the ice in the middle of winter: you do it once, and you remember it the rest of your days.

> *Maxim Gorky,* The Lower Depths, *1903*

He that hath wife and children hath given hostages to fortune; for they are impediments to great enterprises, either of virtue or mischief.

> *Francis Bacon, "Of Marriage and Single Life," 1625*

In the long run wives are to be paid in a peculiar coin—consideration for their feelings. As it usually turns out this is an enormous, unthinkable inflation few men will remit, or if they will, only with a sense of being overcharged.

> *Elizabeth Hardwick,* Seduction and Betrayal, *1974*

Whilst you are proclaiming peace and good will to men, you insist upon retaining an absolute power over wives. . . . Do not put such unlimited power into the hands of the husbands. Remember, all men would be tyrants if they could.

> *Abigail to John Adams, March 31, 1776*

Nora: Our house has never been anything but a playpen. I have been your doll wife, just as I was Daddy's doll child. . . .
Torwald: First and foremost, you are a wife and mother.
Nora: I no longer believe that. I believe, first and foremost, that I am an individual, every bit as much as you are.

> *Henrik Ibsen,* A Doll's House, *1879*

Faithful women are all alike. They think only of their fidelity and never of their husbands.

> *Jean Giraudoux,* Amphitryon, *1929*

When a man steals your wife, there is no better revenge than to let him keep her.

> *Sacha Guitry,* Elles et toi, *1948*

A lost wife can be replaced, but the loss of character spells ruin.

Malay proverb

If a wife . . . has persisted in going out, has acted the fool, and wasted her house, . . . her husband may divorce her, or he may take another woman to wife and the first shall live as a slave in her husband's house.

Hammurabi's Code, c. 2040 B.C.

(*See also* **WOMAN**)

WILL: *See* DECISION, SELF-DETERMINATION.

WINE

God made the waters, man made the wines.

Victor Hugo, Les Contemplations, *1856*

No longer drink water [exclusively], but use a little wine for the sake of your stomach and your frequent ailments.

Paul to Timothy 1, 5:23

It's a Naive Domestic Burgundy Without Any Breeding, But I think you'll be Amused by its Presumption.

James Thurber, Men, Women, and Dogs, *1943*

[Wine] unlocks secrets, bids hopes be certainties, thrusts cowards into the fray, takes loads off anxious hearts, teaches new accomplishments. The life-giving wine cup, . . . whom has it not made free even in the pinch of poverty!

Horace (d. 8 B.C.), Epistles

And Noah he often said to his wife when he sat down to dine, "I don't care where the water goes if it doesn't get into the wine."

G.K. Chesterton (d. 1936), "Wine and Water"

Excellent wine generates enthusiasm. And whatever you do with enthusiasm is generally successful.

Philippe de Rothschild, in conversation, May 9, 1980

To take wine into our mouths is to savor a droplet of the river of human history.

Clifton Fadiman, New York Times, *March 8, 1967*

The vine bears three kinds of grapes: the first of pleasure, the next of intoxication, and the third of disgust.

> *Anacharsis (fl. 600 B.C.)*, quoted in Diogenes Laertius Lives,
> *c. A.D. 200*

Only the first bottle is expensive.

> *French proverb*

(*See also* **DRINK, TASTE**)

WINTER/SUMMER

The trumpet of a prophecy! O Wind!
If winter comes, can spring be far behind?

> *Percy Bysshe Shelley*, "Ode to the West Wind," *1819*

Summer is icumen in,
Lhude sing cucu!
Groweth seed, and bloweth med,
And springth the wude nu—
Sing cucu!

> *Anonymous*, "Cuckoo Song," *c. 1250*

Winter is icumen in,
Lhude sing Goddamm,
Raineth drop and staineth slop,
And how the wind doth ramm!
Sing: Goddamm!

> *Ezra Pound*, "Ancient Music," *1916*

Honest winter, snow-clad and with frosted beard, I can welcome not uncordially; but that long deferment of the calendar's promise, that weeping gloom of March and April, that bitter blast outraging the honour of May—how often has it robbed me of heart and hope.

> *George Gissing*, The Private Papers of Henry Ryecroft, *1903*

I should like to enjoy this summer flower by flower, as if it were to be the last one for me.

> *André Gide*, Journals, *May 18, 1930*

Winter changes into stone the water of heaven and the heart of man.

> *Victor Hugo*, Les Misérables, *1862*

What is so rare as a day in June?
Then, if ever, come perfect days;

Then heaven tries the earth if it be in tune,
And over it softly her warm ear lays.

James Russell Lowell, "The Vision of Sir Launfal," *1848*

Youth's the season made for joys,
Love is then our duty.

John Gay, The Beggar's Opera, *1728*

Winter is cold-hearted,
Spring is yea and nay,
Autumn is a weather-cock
Blown every way.
Summer days for me
When every leaf is on its tree.

Christina Rossetti, "Summer," *1862*

Summer set lip to earth's bosom bare,
And left the flushed print in a poppy there.

Francis Thompson, "The Poppy," *1891*

The first day of spring was once the time for taking the young virgins into the fields, there in dalliance to set an example in fertility for nature to follow. Now we just set the clock an hour ahead and change the oil in the crankcase.

E.B. White, "Hot Weather," *One Man's Meat,* *1944*

A little season of love and laughter,
Of light and life, and pleasure and pain,
And a horror of outer darkness after,
And dust returneth to dust again.

Adam L. Gordon (d. 1870), "The Swimmer"

WISDOM

The price of wisdom is above rubies.

Job 28:18

The beginning of wisdom is to call things by their right names.

Chinese proverb

Four be the things I am wiser to know:
Idleness, sorrow, a friend, and a foe.

Dorothy Parker, "Enough Rope," *1927*

Knowledge is proud that he has learned so much;
Wisdom is humble that he does not know more.

William Cowper, The Task, *1785*

Knowing what is right does not make a sagacious man.

Aristotle, Nichomachean Ethics, *c. 350 B.C.*

Wisdom consists not so much in knowing what to do in the ultimate as in knowing what to do next.

Herbert Hoover, Reader's Digest, *July 1958*

There is this difference between happiness and wisdom: he that thinks himself the happiest man, really is so; but he that thinks himself the wisest, is generally the greatest fool.

Charles Caleb Colton, Lacon, *1825*

The road to wisdom?
—Well, it's plain
and simple to express:
Err
and err
and err again
but less
and less
and less.

Piet Hein, "The Road to Wisdom," Grooks, *1966*

Knowledge can be communicated, but not wisdom. One can find it, live it, be fortified by it, but one cannot communicate and teach it.

Hermann Hesse, Siddhartha: Govinda, *1923*

Wisdom lies not in reason, but in love.

André Gide (d. 1951), Nouvelles Nourritures

We do not receive wisdom, we have to discover it for ourselves by a voyage that no one can take for use, . . . a voyage that no one can spare us.

Marcel Proust, Remembrance of Things Past: Within a Budding Grove, *1918*

Such is the nature of men, that howsoever they may acknowledge many others to be more witty, or more eloquent, or more learned, yet they will hardly believe there be many so wise as themselves.

Thomas Hobbes, Leviathan, *1651*

(*See also* **KNOWLEDGE, MIND, UNDERSTANDING**)

WISE PERSON

I said, "I will be wise," but it was far from me.

Ecclesiastes 7:23

A wise man has no extensive knowledge;
He who has extensive knowledge is not a wise man.

Lao-tzu, Tao te Ching, *c. 550 B.C.*

The heart of a fool is in his mouth, but the mouth of a wise man is in his heart.

Benjamin Franklin, Poor Richard's Almanack, *1757*

Wise men are not wise at all times.

Emerson, The Conduct of Life, *1860*

He is no wise man that cannot play the fool on occasion.

Thomas Fuller, Gnomologia, *1732*

The art of being wise is the art of knowing what to overlook.

William James, Principles of Psychology, *1890*

Ever since Socrates, playing the sage among fools has been a dangerous business.

Diderot, Jack the Fatalist, *1770*

The growth of wisdom may be gauged exactly by the diminution of ill-temper.

Nietzsche, The Wanderer and His Shadow, *1880*

Of the demonstrably wise there are but two: those who commit suicide, and those who keep their reasoning faculties atrophied by drink.

Mark Twain, Note-Book, *1935*

Not by constraint or severity shall you have access to true wisdom, but by abandonment, and childlike mirthfulness. If you would know aught be gay before it.

Thoreau, Journal, *June 23, 1840*

WIT

The well of true wit is truth itself.

George Meredith, Diana of the Crossways, *1885*

A witty saying proves nothing.
>> *Voltaire (d. 1778),* Diner du Comte de Boulainvilliers

Impropriety is the soul of wit.
>> *Somerset Maugham,* The Moon and Sixpence, *1919*

It is not enough to possess wit. One must have enough of it to avoid having too much.
>> *André Maurois,* De la Conversation, *1921*

Many get a reputation for being witty and lose thereby the credit of being sensible.
>> *Baltasar Gracián,* The Art of Worldly Wisdom, *1647*

Wit is so shining a quality that everybody admires it: most people aim at it, all people fear it, and few love it unless in themselves.
>> *Lord Chesterfield to his godson, December 18, 1765*

Wit has a deadly aim and it is possible to prick a large pretense with a small pin.
>> *Marya Mannes,* But Will It Sell? *1964*

What is perfectly true is imperfectly witty.
>> *Walter Savage Landor,* Imaginary Conversations, *1853*

Wit is the salt of conversation, not the food.
>> *William Hazlitt,* Lectures on the English Comic Writers, 1819

The greatest fault of a penetrating wit is to go beyond the mark.
>> *La Rochefoucauld,* Maxims, *1665*

(*See also* **CLEVERNESS, PUNS, SARCASM, SATIRE**)

WOMAN

A woman is a foreign land,
Of which, though there he settle young,
A man will ne'er quite understand
The customs, politics, and tongue.
>> *Coventry Patmore,* The Angel in the House, *1856*

Learning is nothing without cultivated manners, but when the two are combined in a woman, you have one of the most exquisite products of civilization.
>> *André Maurois,* Ariel, *1924*

The [female] sex was made to be subjugated, and I predict that the nations of Europe will have no morals and no peace until they have put her in her place.

> *Restif de la Bretonne,* Le Paysan perverti, *1775*

The program of our National Socialist Women's Movement has but a single point, and that point is the Child—that tiny creature which must be born and grow strong, for in the child alone the whole life-struggle has its meaning.

> *Adolf Hitler, speech to the women of Nuremberg, 1934*

A man . . . must always think about women as Orientals do: he must conceive of woman as a possession, as property that can be locked away, as something predestined for service and achieving her perfection in that.

> *Nietzsche,* Beyond Good and Evil, *1886*

The prejudice against color is no stronger than that against sex. . . . The Negro's skin and the woman's sex are both prima facie evidence that they were intended to be in subjection to the white [Anglo-Saxon] man.

> *Elizabeth Cady Stanton, speech, New York Legislature,*
> *February 18, 1860*

Women have served all these centuries as looking-glasses providing the magic and delicious power of reflecting the figure of man as twice its natural size.

> *Virginia Woolf,* A Room of One's Own, *1929*

When she stopped conforming to the conventional picture of femininity she finally began to enjoy being a woman.

> *Betty Friedan,* The Feminine Mystique, *1963*

One is not born a woman, one becomes one.

> *Simone de Beauvoir,* The Second Sex, *1949*

The light that lies
In woman's eyes
Has been my heart's undoing.

> *Thomas Moore, "The Time I've Lost in Wooing," c. 1810*

The gate of the subtle and profound female
Is the root of Heaven and Earth.
It is continuous, and seems to be always existing.
Use it and you will never wear it out.

> *Lao-tzu,* Tao te Ching, *c. 550 B.C.*

A woman without a man cannot meet a man, any man, . . . without thinking, even if it's for a half-second, Perhaps this is *the* man.

> *Doris Lessing,* The Golden Notebook, *1962*

If women had wives to keep house for them, to stay home with vomiting children, to get the car fixed, fight with the painters, run to the supermarket, . . . listen to everyone's problems, . . . just imagine the number of books that would be written, companies started, professorships filled, public offices that would be held, by women.

> *Gail Sheehy,* Passages, *1976*

To be a woman and a writer
is double mischief, for
the world will slight her
who slights "the servile house,"
and who would rather
make odes than beds.

> *Dilys Laing, "Sonnet to a Sister in Error," 1957*

Women are never stronger than when they arm themselves with their weaknesses.

> *Mme. du Deffand to Voltaire,* Letters, *1759–1775*

Forgetting is woman's first and greatest art.

> *Richard Aldington,* The Colonel's Daughter, *1931*

A woman can be anything that the man who loves her would have her be.

> *James M. Barrie,* Tommy and Grizel, *1900*

There is no other purgatory but a woman.

> *Beaumont and Fletcher,* The Scornful Lady, *1614*

Here's to woman! Would that we could fall into her arms without falling into her hands.

> *Ambrose Bierce, in C.H. Grattan,* Bitter Bierce, *1929*

Intimacies between women often go backwards, beginning in revelations and ending up in small talk without loss of esteem.

> *Elizabeth Bowen,* The Death of the Heart, *1936*

Alas! the love of women! it is known
To be a lovely and a fearful thing.

> *Byron,* Don Juan, *1824*

Now what I love in women is, they won't
Or can't do otherwise than lie, but do it
So well, the very truth seems false.

Ibid.

Variability is one of the virtues of a woman. It avoids the crude requirement of polygamy. So long as you have one good wife you are sure to have a spiritual harem.

G.K. Chesterton, Alarms and Discursions, *1910*

There is no fury like a woman searching for a new lover.

Cyril Connolly, The Unquiet Grave, *1945*

A woman never sees what we do for her, only what we don't do.

Georges Courteline, La Paix chez soi, *1903*

What is woman?—only one of Nature's agreeable blunders.

Mrs. Hannah Cowley, Who's the Dupe? *1779*

The entire being of a woman is a secret which should be kept.

Isak Dinesen, Last Tales, *1957*

Women are most fascinating between the ages of thirty-five and forty, after they have won a few races and know how to pace themselves. Since few women ever pass forty, maximum fascination can continue indefinitely.

Christian Dior, Collier's, *June 10, 1955*

I have been a woman for fifty years, and I've never yet been able to discover precisely what I am.

Jean Giraudoux, Tiger at the Gates, *1935*

If men knew how women pass the time when they are alone, they'd never marry.

O. Henry, The Four Million, *1906*

A woman never forgets her sex. She would rather talk with a man than an angel any day.

Oliver Wendell Holmes, The Poet at the Breakfast Table, *1858*

A woman does not spend all of her time in buying things; she spends part of it in taking them back.

Edgar Watson Howe, Country Town Sayings, *1911*

At first a woman doesn't want anything but a husband, but just as soon as she gets one, she wants everything else in the world.

Ibid.

American women: How they mortify the flesh in order to make it appetizing! Their beauty is a vast industry, their enduring allure a discipline which nuns or athletes might find excessive.

Muggeridge, The Most of Malcolm Muggeridge, *1966*

Women are a decorative sex. They never have anything to say, but they say it charmingly.

Oscar Wilde, The Picture of Dorian Gray, *1891*

If woman had no existence save in the fiction written by men, one would imagine her a person of the utmost importance; very various: heroic and mean; splendid and sordid; infinitely beautiful and hideous in the extreme; as great as a man, some think even greater.

Virginia Woolf, A Room of One's Own, *1929*

An intelligent woman is a woman with whom one can be as stupid as one wants.

Paul Valéry, Mauvaises pensées et autres, *1941*

A woman is only a woman, but a good cigar is a smoke.

Walt Kelly, Pogo, *1971*

(*See also* **WIFE, MEN VS. WOMEN**)

WOMEN'S MOVEMENT

Don't ask f'r rights. Take them. An' don't let anny wan give thim to ye. A right that is handed to ye f'r nawthin' has somethin' th' matter with it.

Finley Peter Dunne ("Mr. Dooley"), American Magazine, *1906*

We are here to claim our rights as women, not only to be free, but to fight for freedom. It is our privilege, as well as our pride and our joy, to take some part in this militant movement, which . . . means the regeneration of all humanity.

Christabel Pankhurst, speech, London, March 23, 1911

The Bible and the Church have been the greatest stumbling blocks in the way of women's emancipation.

Elizabeth Cady Stanton, Free Thought Magazine, *1896*

What has the women's movement learned from [Geraldine Ferraro's] candidacy for vice president?—Never get married.

> *Gloria Steinem*, Boston Globe, *May 14, 1987*

The people I'm furious with are the women's liberationists. They keep getting up on soapboxes and proclaiming women are brighter than men. That's true, but it should be kept quiet or it ruins the whole racket.

> *Anita Loos*, New York Times, *February 10, 1974*

The major achievement of the women's movement in the 1970s was the Dutch treat.

> *Nora Ephron*, Heartburn, *1983*

We have lived through the era when happiness was a warm puppy, and the era when happiness was a dry martini, and now we have come to the era when happiness is "knowing what your uterus looks like."

> *Ephron*, Crazy Salad, *1975*

It's hard to fight an enemy who has outposts in your head.

> *Sally Kempton*, Esquire, *1970*

It is naive in the extreme for women to be regarded as equals by men . . . so long as they persist in . . . animal-like behavior during sexual intercourse. I am referring . . . to the outlandish PANTING, GASPING, MOANING, SOBBING, WRITHING, SCRATCHING, BITING, SCREAMING conniptions . . . integral to the pre-, post-, AND orgasmic stages of intercourse.

> *Terry Southern, "Letter to the Editor of Ms.,"* National Lampoon
> Encyclopedia of Humor, *1972*

The women's movement hasn't changed *my* sex life at all.

> *Zsa Zsa Gabor*, Playboy, *1979*

Anyone can have the key to the executive washroom, but once a woman gets inside, what is there? A lavatory.

> *Germaine Greer*, Time, *1984*

Is it too much to ask that women be spared the daily struggle for superhuman beauty in order to offer it to the caresses of a subhumanly ugly mate?

> *Greer*, The Female Eunuch, *1970*

Emeralds! Aren't they divine? Jack gave them to me to shut up about Women's Lib.

William Hamilton's Anti-Social Register, *1974*

During the feminist revolution, the battle lines were again simple. It was easy to tell the enemy, he was the one with the penis. This is no longer strictly true. Some men are okay now. We're allowed to like them again. We still have to keep them in line, of course, but we no longer have to shoot them on sight.

Cynthia Heimel, Sex Tips for Girls, *1983*

Feminism is far from dead, but . . . the movement has lost some of its zip. . . . Women are scared and don't know where to look for guidance, since it seems as if all the leaders of the feminist movement have retreated into their individual lairs, emerging only at infrequent intervals to snarl. Very upsetting, but we mustn't blame our erstwhile leaders. They're tired. They've been slogging away for years and are sick of being called strident bull-dykes. Who can blame them for being out of sorts?

Ibid.

How much fame, money, and power does a woman have to achieve on her own before you can punch her in the face?

P.J. O'Rourke, Modern Manners, *1983*

Whatever women do, they must do twice as well as men to be thought half as good. Luckily, this is not difficult.

Charlotte Whitton, former mayor of Ottawa.

(*See also* **MARRIAGE, MEN, RIGHTS**)

WOMEN'S WAYS

Women are traditionally trained to place others' needs first . . . their satisfaction to be in making it possible for others to use their abilities.

Tillie Olsen, Silences, *1978*

I know women's ways: They won't when you will, and when you won't they're dying for it.

Terence (d. 159 B.C.), Eunuchus

When women kiss it always reminds one of prizefighters shaking hands.

Mencken, A Book of Burlesques, *1920*

The great question, . . . which I have not been able to answer, despite my thirty years of research into the feminine soul, is "What does a woman want?"

> *Sigmund Freud, in Rolo,* Psychiatry in American Life, *1963*

(*See also* **CHILDHOOD, DAUGHTERS, SOCIETY**)

WORDS

Thought itself needs words. It runs on them like a long wire. And if it loses the habit of words, little by little it becomes shapeless, somber.

> *Ugo Betti,* Goat Island, *1946*

Words have weight, sound and appearance; it is only by considering these that you can write a sentence that is good to look at and good to listen to.

> *W. Somerset Maugham,* The Summing Up, *1938*

Words . . . are the great foes of reality.

> *Joseph Conrad,* Under Western Eyes, *1911*

"When I use a word," said Humpty Dumpty, in rather a scornful tone, "it means just what I choose it to mean—neither more nor less."

> *Lewis Carroll,* Through the Looking-Glass, *1872*

Words are really a mask. They rarely express the true meaning; in fact, they tend to hide it.

> *Hermann Hesse, in M. Serrano,* C.G.Jung and H. Hesse, *1966*

You can stroke people with words.

> *F. Scott Fitzgerald,* The Crack-Up, *1945*

Words not only affect us temporarily; they change us, they socialize or unsocialize us.

> *David Riesman,* The Lonely Crowd, *1950*

Words, like Nature, half reveal
And half conceal the Soul within.

> *Alfred, Lord Tennyson, "Im memoriam A.H.H.," 1850*

Without knowing the force of words, it is impossible to know human beings.

> *Confucius,* Analects, *c. 500 B.C.*

A word is dead
When it is said,
Some say.
I say it just
Begins to live.

Emily Dickinson, poem, c. 1872

Slogans are both exciting and comforting [but] some of mankind's most terrible misdeeds have been committed under the spell of certain magic words [and] phrases.

James Bryant Conant, Address, Harvard, 1934

Written words . . . have the power to bring out the best and the worst of human nature. . . . Those who vowed to kill [Salman Rushdie, author of **Satanic Verses,**] actually wish to kill our entire civilization.

Amos Oz, New York Times Book Review, *March 12, 1989*

(*See also* **LANGUAGE, MEANING, SPEECH, WRITING**)

WORK

. . . expands so as to fill the time available for its completion.

C. Northcote Parkinson, Parkinson's Law, *1962*

Work keeps us from three great evils: boredom, vice, and want.

Voltaire, Candide, *1759*

No fine work can be done without concentration and self-sacrifice and toil and doubt.

Max Beerbohm, And Even Now, *1920*

We have to work, if not from inclination, then from desperation since . . . work is less boring than amusing oneself.

Baudelaire, Mon Coeur mis a nu, *1862*

No race can prosper till it learns there is as much dignity in tilling a field as in writing a poem.

Booker T. Washington, Address, Atlanta, September 1895

Relax yourself from one job by doing a different one.

Ernest Renan, Inaugural Lecture, Collège de France, 1857

We continue to overlook the fact that work has become a leisure activity.

Mark Abrams, London Observer, *June 3, 1962*

There's no point in living if you have to work.

André Breton, Nadja, *1928*

I don't like work . . . but I like what is in work—the chance to find yourself. Your own reality—for yourself, not for others—which no other man can ever know.

Joseph Conrad, Heart of Darkness, *1902*

The ant is knowing and wise; but he doesn't know enough to take a vacation.

Clarence Day, This Simian World, *1920*

What is work? and what is not work? are questions that perplex the wisest of men.

Bhagavad-Gita

Every man's task is his life-preserver.

Emerson, The Conduct of Life, *1860*

A man is not idle because he is absorbed in thought. There is a visible labor and an invisible labor.

Victor Hugo, Les Misérables, *1862*

I like work: it fascinates me. I can sit and look at it for hours. I love to keep it by me: the idea of getting rid of it nearly breaks my heart.

Jerome K. Jerome, Three Men in a Boat, *1889*

Love labor: for if thou dost not want it for food, thou mayest for physic. It is wholesome for the body and good for thy mind.

William Penn, Some Fruits of Solitude, *1693*

My nature is subdued
To what it works in, like the dyer's hand.

Shakespeare, Sonnets, *1609*

Let us be grateful to Adam our benefactor. He cut us out of the "blessing" of idleness and won for us the "curse" of labor.

Mark Twain, "Pudd'nhead Wilson's New Calendar," 1897

(*See also* **EFFORT, LEISURE, REST**)

WORKERS

When white-collar people get jobs, they sell not only their time and energy, but their personalities as well. They sell by the week, or

month, their smiles and their kindly gestures, and they must practice
that prompt repression of resentment and aggression.

C. Wright Mills, White Collar, *1956*

I tell you, sir, the only safeguard of order and discipline in the modern
world is a standardized worker with interchangeable parts. That
would solve the entire problem of management.

Jean Giraudoux, The Madwoman of Chaillot, *1945*

During the whole period of written history, it is not the workers but
the robbers who have been in control of the world.

Scott Nearing, From Capitalism to Communism, *1945*

In a pinch the liberals can always be counted on to back up the principles of the established order—private property in the implements of
production, special privileges, and the more moderate and lucrative
phases of imperialism.

Nearing, Modern Monthly, *1950*

What Egyptian bondage do you suppose . . . was ever so cruel as
a modern English forge, with its steel hammers? What Egyptian
worship of garlic or crocodile ever so damnable as modern English
worship of money?

John Ruskin to Fors Clavigera, 1871

[Freedom:] emancipation from compulsory toil by which mankind
satisfies its economic wants, together with emancipation from degrading poverty, long hours of labor, and economic insecurity.

Mortimer J. Adler, The Idea of Freedom, *1958*

Workingmen we all are in so far as we have the desire to make
ourselves useful to human society in any way whatsoever.

Ferdinand Lassalle, Arbeiter-Programm, *1862*

The trouble with us in the past has been that we were too often drawn
into an alliance with the wrong side. Selfish employers of labor have
flattered the Church by calling it the great conservative force, and
then called upon it to act as a police force while they paid but a
pittance of wages to those who worked for it.

George William (Cardinal) Mundelein, Address, Holy Name Society,
Chicago, January 2, 1938

When more and more people are thrown out of work, unemployment
results.

Calvin Coolidge, New York Herald Tribune, *September 29, 1954*

(*See also* **MACHINE AGE, TECHNOLOGY, VALUE**)

WORLD

The world is a comedy to those that think, a tragedy to those that feel.

> *Horace Walpole to Horace Mann, December 31, 1769*

The world is a gambling-table so arranged that all who enter the casino must play and all must lose more or less heavily in the long run, though they win occasionally by the way.

> *Samuel Butler, "Lord, What Is Man?"* Note-Books, *1912*

Every man takes the limits of his own field of vision for the limits of the world.

> *Schopenhauer,* Pessimism, *1851*

The world is too much with us; late and soon,
Getting and spending we lay waste our powers:
Little we see in Nature that is ours. . . .

> *William Wordsworth, "The World Is Too Much with Us," 1807*

"The world is my idea"—this is a truth which holds good for everything that lives and knows, though man alone can bring it into reflective and abstract thought.

> *Schopenhauer,* The World as Will and Idea, *1818*

The most beautiful thing in the world is, of course, the world itself.

> *Wallace Stevens, F. Doggett and R., Buttel, eds., 1980*

Ah, love, let us be true
To one another! for the world which seems
To lie before us like a land of dreams,
So various, so beautiful, so new,
Hath neither joy, nor love, nor light,
Nor certitude, nor peace, nor help for pain.

> *Matthew Arnold, "Dover Beach," 1867*

. . . Wandering between two worlds, one dead,
The other powerless to be born.

> *Arnold,* From the Grande Chartreuse, *1855*

The most incomprehensible thing about the world is that it is incomprehensible.

> *Einstein, quoted in his obituary, April 19, 1955*

I have loved not the world, nor the world me;
I have not flattered its rank breath, nor bowed
To its idolatries a patient knee,
Nor coined my cheek to smiles, nor cried aloud
In worship of an echo.

Byron, Childe Harold's Pilgrimage, *1818*

For the world, I count it not an inn, but an hospital; and a place not to live in, but to die in.

Sir Thomas Browne, Religio Medici, *1642*

What's wrong with this world is, it's not finished yet. It is not completed to that point where man can put his final signature to the job and say, "It is finished. We made it and it works."

William Faulkner, Address, Wellesley, Mass., June 8, 1952

The unrest which keeps the never-stopping clock of metaphysics going is the thought that the non-existence of this world is just as possible as its existence.

Faulkner, "The Problem of Being," 1911

This world, after all our sciences, is still a miracle: wonderful, inscrutable, magical and more, to whoever will think of it.

Thomas Carlyle, Heroes and Hero Worship, *1841*

The world is hard to love, though we must love it because we have no other, and to fail to love it is not to exist at all.

Mark Van Doren, Autobiography, *1958*

"To what end was this world formed?" said Candide.
"To infuriate us," replied Martin.

Voltaire, Candide, *1759*

The world is so full of a number of things,
I'm sure we should all be as happy as kings.

Robert Louis Stevenson, A Child's Garden of Verses, *1885*

(*See also* **LIFE, TWENTIETH CENTURY, UNIVERSE**)

WORLD-WEARY

Death is losing its terror. It is the emergency exit for a world that is becoming more frightening than death ever was.

Julian Green, Diary, *December 28, 1958*

The more I saw of the world, the less I was able to adjust to its ways.
Rousseau, Confessions, *1765*

There is an inevitable divergence, attributed to the imperfections of the human mind, between the world as it is and the world as men perceive it.
James W. Fulbright, speech, U.S. Senate, March 27, 1964

(*See also* **ANXIETY, SAD/MELANCHOLY, SUICIDE**)

WORLD'S END

This is the way the world ends
Not with a bang but a whimper.
T.S. Eliot, The Hollow Men, *1925*

The world began without man and it will end without him.
Claude Lévi-Strauss, Tristes Tropiques, *1955*

The human race has today the means for annihilating itself—either in a fit of complete lunacy, in a big war, by a brief fit of destruction, or by careless handling of atomic technology, through a slow process of poisoning and of deterioration in its genetic structure.
Max Born, Bulletin of the Atomic Scientists, *1957*

WORSHIP

Man is a venerating animal. He venerates as easily as he purges himself. When they take away from him the gods of his fathers, he looks for others ahead.
Max Jacob, "Hamlet-ism," Art poétique, *1922*

God waits to win back his own flowers as gifts from man's hands.
Rabindranath Tagore, Stray Birds, *1916*

The worship of God is not a rule of safety—it is an adventure of the spirit, a flight after the unattainable.
Alfred North Whitehead, Science and the Modern World

God prefers bad verses recited with a pure heart to the finest verses possible chanted by the wicked.
Voltaire, Philosophical Dictionary, *1764*

Does not every true man feel that he is himself made higher by doing reverence to what is really above him?
Thomas Carlyle, Heroes and Hero Worship, *1841*

The various modes of worship, which prevailed in the Roman world, were all considered by the people, as equally true; by the philosopher, as equally false; and by the magistrate, as equally useful.

> *Edward Gibbon*, Decline and Fall of the Roman Empire, *1776*

(*See also* **PRAYER, RELIGION**)

WORTH: *See* VALUE.

WRITER

The law of the writer, what makes him tick, and . . . makes him the equal, if not the superior, of the statesman, is [his] judgment about things human, his absolute devotion to principle.

> *Balzac,* La Comédie humaine, *1841*

The nobility of our calling will always be rooted in two commitments difficult to observe: refusal to lie about what we know, and resistance to oppression.

> *Albert Camus, speech accepting the Nobel Prize, 1957*

Thoughts fly and words go on foot. Therein lies all the drama of a writer.

> *Julien Green,* Diary, *May 4, 1943*

All good books are alike in that they are truer than if they had really happened and after you are finished reading one you will feel that that all happened to you.

> *Ernest Hemingway,* Esquire, *December 1934*

For me two things are equally intolerable: to know that children are dying of hunger is one, and the other: that a writer may be prevented from writing.

> *Yves Berger (b. 1931),* Que peut la littérature?

The writer's only responsibility is to his art. He will be completely ruthless if he is a good one. He has no peace until then. Everything goes by the board: honor, pride, decency, security, happiness, all, to get the book written.

> *William Faulkner, interview, New York, 1956*

If a writer has to rob his mother, he will not hesitate: The "Ode on a Grecian Urn" is worth any number of old ladies.

> *Faulkner, quoted in M. Cowley,* Writers at Work, *1958*

No man can write who is not first a humanitarian.

Faulkner, Time, *February 25, 1957*

Great authors are admirable in this respect: in every generation they make for disagreement. Through them we become aware of our differences.

André Gide, Pretexts, *1903*

The writer is the Faust of modern society, the only surviving individualist in a mass age. To his orthodox contemporaries he seems a semi-madman.

Boris Pasternak, London Observer, *December 20, 1959*

There are two classes of authors: the one writes the history of their times, the other their biography.

Thoreau, Journal, *April 22, 1841*

A writer is congenitally unable to tell the truth and that is why we call what he writes fiction.

William Faulkner, interview, New York, 1956

Life can't ever really defeat a writer who is in love with writing, for life itself is a writer's lover until death—fascinating, cruel, lavish, warm, cold, treacherous, constant.

Edna Ferber, A Kind of Magic, *1963*

There is no way that a writer can be tamed and rendered civilized or even cured. . . . The only solution known to science is to provide the patient with an isolation room, where he can endure the acute stages in private and where the food can be poked in to him with a stick.

Robert Heinlein, The Cat Who Walks through Walls, *1985*

A writer is somebody for whom writing is more difficult than it is for other people.

Thomas Mann, Essays of Three Decades, *1947*

Russia, France, Germany and China. They revere their writers. America is still a frontier country that almost shudders at the idea of creative expression.

James A. Michener, Modern Maturity, *August 1985*

In America, only the successful writer is important, in France all writers are important, in England no writer is important, and in Australia you have to explain what a writer is.

Geoffrey Cottrell, New York Journal-American, *September 22, 1961*

Every author, however modest, keeps a most outrageous vanity chained like a madman in the padded cell of his breast.

Logan Pearsall Smith, Afterthoughts, *1931*

When a writer becomes the center of his [own] attention, he has become a nudnick, and a nudnick who believes he is profound is even worse than just a plain nudnick.

Isaac Bashevis Singer, New York Times, *November 26, 1978*

For the modern consciousness, the artist (replacing the saint) is the exemplary sufferer. And among artists, the writer, the man of words, is the person to whom we look to be able best to express his suffering.

Susan Sontag, Against Interpretation, *1961*

(*See also* **AUTOBIOGRAPHY, NOVEL/NOVELIST, POET**)

WRITING, ART OF

My method is to take the utmost trouble to find the right thing to say, and then to say it with the utmost levity.

G.B. Shaw, Answers to Nine Questions

To the man with an ear for verbal delicacies—the man who searches painfully for the perfect word, and puts the way of saying a thing above the thing said—there is in writing the constant joy of sudden discovery, of happy accident.

H.L. Mencken, A Book of Prefaces, *1917*

Against the disease of writing one must take special precautions, since it is a dangerous and contagious disease.

Peter Abelard (d. 1142), Abelard to Héloise, *Letter 8*

Achilles exists only through Homer. Take away the art of writing from this world, and you will probably take away its glory.

Chateaubriand, Les Natchez, *1826*

You must write for yourself, above all. That is [your] only hope of creating something beautiful.

Gustave Flaubert to Mlle. Leroyer de Chantepie, 1858

Writing well is at one and the same time good thinking, good feeling, and good expression; it is having wit, soul, and taste, all together.

Buffon, Address on his nomination to the French Academy, 1753

Vigorous writing is concise. A sentence should contain no unnecessary words, a paragraph no unnecessary sentences, for the same reason that a drawing should have no unnecessary lines and a machine no unnecessary parts.

William Strunk, Jr., The Elements of Style, *1918*

Writing, I think, is not apart from living. Writing is a kind of double living. The writer experiences everything twice. Once in reality and once in that mirror which waits always before or behind.

Catherine Drinker Bowen, Atlantic, *December 1957*

To me, the greatest pleasure of writing is not what it's about, but the inner music the words make.

Truman Capote, McCall's, *November 1967*

Sit down and put down everything that comes into your head and then you're a writer. But an author is one who can judge his own stuff's worth, without pity, and destroy most of it.

Colette, Casual Chance, *1964*

Literature is the art of writing something that will be read twice.

Cyril Connolly, Quote, *September 12, 1965*

Whom the gods wish to destroy they first call promising.

Connolly, quoted in Newsweek, *March 19, 1984*

Writing is an exploration. You start from nothing and learn as you go.

E.L. Doctorow, New York Times, *October 20, 1985*

Writing is the manual labor of the mind: a job, like laying pipe.

John Gregory Dunne, Esquire, *October 1986*

A book is like a quarrel: one word leads to another, and may erupt in blood or print, irrevocably.

Will and Ariel Durant, A Dual Autobiography, *1977*

Writing is a difficult trade which must be learned slowly by reading great authors; by trying at the outset to imitate them; by daring then to be original; and by destroying one's first productions.

André Maurois, New York Journal-American, *July 31, 1963*

Writing is a way of talking without being interrupted.

Jules Renard, Journal, *April 10, 1895*

A mediocre mind thinks it writes "divinely"; a good mind thinks it writes "fairly well."

La Bruyère, Characters, *1688*

Take eloquence and wring its neck.

Paul Verlaine, "L'Art poétique"

This letter is long because I didn't have time to write a short one.

Pascal, Lettres provinciales, *1656*

Having imagination, it takes you an hour to write a paragraph that, if you were unimaginative, would take you only a minute. Or you might not write the paragraph at all.

Franklin P. Adams, Half a Loaf, *1927*

Among all types of writing, there is none in which authors are more apt to miscarry than in works of humour, as there is none in which they are more ambitious to excel.

Joseph Addison, The Spectator, *1712*

When a man can observe himself suffering, and is able, later, to describe what he's gone through, that means he was born for literature.

Edouard Bourdet, Vient de paraitre, *1927*

To write is to become disinterested. There is a certain renunciation in art.

Albert Camus, Notebooks 1935–1942, *1962*

Writing has laws of perspective, of light and shade, just as painting does, or music. If you are born knowing them, fine. If not, learn them. Then rearrange the rules to suit yourself.

Truman Capote, interview, Writers at Work, *1958*

A writer needs three things, experience, observation, and imagination, any two of which, at times any one of which, can supply the lack of the others.

William Faulkner, interview, New York, *1956*

The most beautiful things are those that madness prompts and reason writes.

André Gide, Journals, *1894*

A writer and nothing else: a man alone in a room with the English language, trying to get human feelings right.

John K. Hutchens, New York Herald Tribune, *September 10, 1961*

The fact that many people should be shocked by what he writes practically imposes it as a duty upon the writer to go on shocking them.

> *Aldous Huxley, "Vulgarity in Literature,"* Music at Night, *1931*

No man but a blockhead ever wrote for anything except money.

> *Samuel Johnson, in Boswell's* Life, *April 5, 1776*

The writer writes in order to teach himself, to understand himself, to satisfy himself; the publishing of his ideas, though it brings gratification, is a curious anticlimax.

> *Alfred Kazin,* Think, *February 1963*

To make a book is as much a trade as to make a clock: something more than intelligence is required to become an author.

> *La Bruyère,* Characters, *1688*

Every great writer is a writer of history, let him treat on almost what subject he may. He carries with him for thousands of years a portion of his times.

> *Walter Savage Landor,* Imaginary Conversations, *1853*

It is one test of a fully developed writer that he reminds us of no one but himself.

> *Melvin Maddocks,* Christian Science Monitor, *May 2, 1963*

i never think at all when i write
nobody can do two things at the same time
and do them both well.

> *Don Marquis,* Archy's Life of Mehitabel, *1933*

Sin is the writer's element.

> *Francois Mauriac,* Second Thoughts, *1961*

I always do the first line well, but I have trouble with the others.

> *Molière,* The Ridiculous Précieuses, *1659*

True ease in writing comes from art, not chance,
As those move easiest who have learned to dance.

> *Alexander Pope,* An Essay on Criticism, *1711*

Our passions shape our books; repose writes them in the intervals.

> *Proust,* The Past Recaptured, *1927*

What another person would have done as well as you, don't do it. What another would have said as well as you, don't say it; what another would have written as well, don't write it. Be faithful to what exists inside yourself and nowhere else, thus making yourself indispensable.

André Gide (d. 1968), Journal

In literature, there are only oxen. The biggest ones are the geniuses— the ones who work eighteen hours a day without tiring.

Jules Renard, Journal, *1887*

A writer lives, at best, in a state of astonishment. Beneath any feeling he has of the good or evil of the world lies a deeper one of wonder at it all. To transmit that feeling, he writes.

William Sansom, Blue Skies, Brown Studies, *1961*

The good writing of any age has always been the product of *someone's* neurosis, and we'd have a mighty dull literature if all the writers that came along were a bunch of happy chuckleheads.

William Styron, interview, Writers at Work, *1958*

There is no royal path to good writing; and such paths as do exist do not lead through neat critical gardens, various as they are, but through the jungles of self, the world, and of craft.

Jessamyn West, Saturday Review, *September 21, 1957*

Literature is strewn with the wreckage of men who have minded beyond reason the opinion of others.

Virginia Woolf, A Room of One's Own, *1929*

Every great and original writer, in proportion as he is great and original, must himself create the taste by which he is relished.

Wordsworth, Lyrical Ballads, *preface, 1800*

All good writing is *swimming under water* and holding your breath.

F. Scott to Frances Scott Fitzgerald, n.d.

One does not write a love story while making love.

Colette (d. 1954), Lettre au petit Corsaire

The one thing a writer has to have is not balls. Nor is it even . . . a room of her own, though that is an amazing help. . . . The one thing a writer has to have is a pencil and some paper. That's enough, so long as she knows that she and she alone is in charge of that pencil, and responsible, she and she alone, for what it writes on that paper. In other words, that she's free. Never wholly free. Maybe very partially. . . . But in this, responsible; in this, autonomous, in this, free.

Ursula K. Le Guin, "The Hand That Rocks the Cradle Writes the Book," New York Times Book Review, January 22, 1989

(*See also* **CREATIVITY, LITERATURE, POETRY**)

WRONGDOING

A good man can be stupid and still be good. But a bad man must have brains—absolutely.

Maxim Gorky, The Lower Depths, 1903

If once a man indulges himself in murder, very soon he comes to think little of robbing, and from robbing he comes next to drinking and Sabbath-breaking, and from that to incivility and procrastination.

Thomas De Quincey, "On Murder Considered as One of the Fine Arts," 1854

How oft the sight of means to do ill deeds
Make deeds ill done!

Shakespeare, King John, 1597

Men whose wit has been mother of villany once
Have learned from it to be evil in all things.

Sophocles, Philoctetes, 409 B.C.

Most vices may be committed very genteelly: a man may debauch his friend's wife genteelly; he may cheat at cards genteelly.

Samuel Johnson, in Boswell's Life, April 6, 1775

Those who are once found to be bad are presumed to be so forever.

Latin proverb

(*See also* **CRIME, PUNISHMENT, SIN**)

YANKEE

A tough but nervous, tenacious but restless race; materially ambitious, yet prone to introspection, and subject to waves of religious emotion. . . . A race whose typical member is eternally torn between a passion for righteousness and a desire to get on in the world.

Samuel Eliot Morison, Maritime History of Massachusetts, *1921*

The Yankee is one who, if he once gets his teeth set on a thing, all creation can't make him let go.

James T. Farrell, introduction to Mencken's Prejudices:
A Selection, *1958*

YOUTH

Youth is like spring, an overpraised season.

Samuel Butler, The Way of All Flesh, *1903*

There is nothing more poetic in the freshness of its passions than a 16-year-old heart. The morning of life is like the dawn of a day, full of purity, visions, and harmony.

Chateaubriand, René, *1802*

Give me those days with heart in riot,
The depths of bliss that touched on pain,
The force of hate, and love's disquiet—
Ah, give me back my youth again.

Goethe, Faust, Part I, *1808*

Crabbed age and youth cannot live together;
Youth is full of Pleasaunce, age is full of care;

. . . .

Youth is hot and bold, age is weak and cold;
Youth is wild, age is tame.
Age, I do abhor thee; youth I do adore thee.

Shakespeare, The Passionate Pilgrim, *attributed*

Adolescents tend to be passionate people, and passion is no less real because it is directed toward a hot-rod, a commercialized popular singer, or the leader of a black-jacketed gang.

Edgar Z. Friedenberg, The Vanishing Adolescent, *1959*

Young girls like the excess of any quality. Without knowing, they want to suffer, to suffer they must exaggerate; they like to have loud chords struck on them.

Elizabeth Bowen, The House in Paris, *1935*

What have you done, you there,
Weeping incessantly,
Tell me, what have you done
With your youth?

Paul Verlaine, Sagesse, *1881*

Wasting one's youth is better than doing nothing at all with it.

Georges Courteline, Philosophie, *1917*

As for me, I had to wait until I was thirty-two before my father gave me the last kick in the behind. That is what the family was like in my day.

Marcel Pagnol, Marius, *1929*

While we are young the idea of death or failure is intolerable to us; even the possibility of ridicule we cannot bear.

Isak Dinesen, "The Deluge at Norderney," Seven Gothic Tales, *1934*

It is an illusion that youth is happy, an illusion of those who have lost it.

Somerset Maugham, Of Human Bondage, *1915*

The "teen-ager" seems to have replaced the Communist as the appropriate target for public controversey and foreboding.

Edgar Z. Friedenberg, The Vanishing Adolescent, *1959*

I go to school to youth to learn the future.

Robert Frost, West Running Brook, *1928*

Youth, even in its sorrow, always has a brilliancy of its own.

Victor Hugo, Les Misérables, *1862*

Youth is perpetual intoxication; it is a fever of the mind.

La Rochefoucauld, Maxims, *1665*

It is, indeed, one of the capital tragedies of youth—and youth is the time of real tragedy—that the young are thrown mainly with adults they do not quite respect.

H.L. Mencken, Baltimore Evening Sun, *October 8, 1928*

As a result of all his education, from everything he hears and sees around him, the child absorbs such a lot of lies and foolish nonsense, mixed in with essential truths, that the first duty of the adolescent who wants to be a healthy adult is to disgorge it all.

Romain Rolland, Jean Christophe, *1904*

Adolescence—the only time we ever learned anything.

Marcel Proust, Within a Budding Grove, *1919*

Don't laugh at a youth for his affections; he is only trying on one face after another to find a face of his own.

Logan Pearsall Smith, Afterthoughts, *1931*

What is youth except a man or woman before it is ready or fit to be seen?

Evelyn Waugh, in D. Gallagher, ed., A Little Order, *1981*

The young men of this land are often called a "lost" race—they are a race that has never yet been discovered. And the whole secret, power, and knowledge of their own discovery is locked within them—they know it, feel it, have the whole thing in them—and they cannot utter it.

Thomas Wolfe, The Web and the Rock, *1939*

(*See also* **ADOLESCENCE, BOYS, DAUGHTERS**)

"Z"

ZEAL

Zeal's a dreadful termagant,
That teaches saints to tear and rant.

Samuel Butler (d. 1680), Hudibras

Zeal without knowledge is fire without light.

Thomas Fuller, Gnomologia, *1732*

Too much zeal offends
where indirection works.

Euripides, Orestes, *408 B.C.*

There is a wholly mistaken zeal in politics as well as in religion. By persuading others, we convince ourselves.

Junius, pseudonymous correspondent, Public Advertiser, *London, No. 35, 1769–1771*

Violent zeal for truth hath an hundred-to-one shot to be either petulancy, ambition, or pride.

Jonathan Swift (d. 1745), Thoughts on Religion

Zeal and curiosity are the twin scourges of the soul: the latter prompts us to poke our noses into everything; the former prevents our leaving anything in doubt or undecided.

Montaigne, Essays, *1580*

(*See also* **ENTHUSIASM, FANATICISM**)

ZEN BUDDHISM

When I eat, I eat.
When I sleep, I sleep.

Zen Buddhist formula

Zen is a way of liberation, concerned not with discovering what is good or bad or advantageous, but what is.

Alan Watts, Life, *April 21, 1961*

(*See also* **PHILOSOPHY, RELIGION, WISDOM**)

ZEST

What hunger is in relation to food, zest is in relation to life.

Bertrand Russell, The Conquest of Happiness, *1930*

Exuberance is beauty.

William Blake, The Marriage of Heaven and Hell, *1790*

My candle burns at both ends;
It will not last the night;
But ah, my foes, and oh, my friends—
It gives a lovely light!

Edna St. Vincent Millay, A Few Figs from Thistles, *1922*

(*See also* **ENTHUSIASM, PASSION, PLEASURE**)